Legal Aspects of International Business: A Canadian Perspective

SECOND EDITION

Mary Jo Nicholson

2007
Emond Montgomery Publications Ltd.
Toronto, Canada

Emond Montgomery Publications Limited
60 Shaftesbury Avenue
Toronto ON M4T 1A3
http://www.emp.ca

Printed in Canada.

We acknowledge the financial support of the Government of Canada through the Book Publishing Industry Development Program (BPIDP) for our publishing activities.

The events and characters depicted in this book are fictitious. Any similarity to actual persons, living or dead, is purely coincidental.

Acquisitions editor: Peggy Buchan

Marketing director: Dave Stokaluk

Copy editor and indexer: Paula Pike, WordsWorth Communications

Production editor: Nancy Ennis, WordsWorth Communications

Proofreader: David Handelsman, WordsWorth Communications

Text and cover designer: Tara Wells, WordsWorth Communications

Library and Archives Canada Cataloguing in Publication

Nicholson, Mary Jo
    Legal aspects of international business : a Canadian perspective / Mary Jo Nicholson. — 2nd ed.

Includes index.
ISBN-13: 978-1-55239-216-4
ISBN-10: 1-55239-216-3

    1. Commercial law—Textbooks.   2. Foreign trade regulation—Textbooks.   3. Commercial law—Canada—Textbooks.   I. Title.

KE1940.N52 2007   343'.087   C2006-906501-2

Contents

3 Current and Emerging Challenges in the Global Regulatory Environment

4 The European Union and Other Regional Trade Arrangements

5 The North American Free Trade Agreement (NAFTA)

6 Canada's Response to Global Rules: Domestic Rules on Imports and Exports

7 Negotiating the International Sale of Goods

8 Ancillary Contracts for the International Transaction: Financing, Transportation, and Insurance

9 Intellectual Property and International Business

10 Legal Aspects of Different Foreign Market Entry Strategies

11   Settlement of International Business Disputes

Preface

Why This Book Was Written

Although this book is a second edition, the first having been published in 1997, many parts of it have been completely rewritten due to the dynamic nature of the subject matter and also the increased sophistication and enhanced general knowledge of the reader. I began the preface of the first edition with the oft-quoted statement that Canada has been described as "a trading nation but not a nation of traders." I believe that this has changed somewhat. Canadians are now much more aware that the world is their market. Advanced technology, the Internet, concerns about privacy and terrorism, and the threat of global pandemics have all contributed to a heightened sense of living in a global village.

The material that formed the basis for the first edition of this book was originally developed and written for fourth-year students enrolled in a course entitled Legal Aspects of International Trade in the Faculty of Business at Ryerson University in Toronto. This course was, as far as I am aware, the first such course offered by a Canadian university to business students. This predated the programs offered by the Forum for International Trade Training, which recognized the importance of legal content in equipping Canadians for international business transactions. As a lawyer advising clients in the area of international transactions, I had observed the frequency with which legal considerations permeated almost every aspect of international business strategy. For this reason, I developed the conviction that a course in the legal aspects of international business made a great deal of sense for business students, especially in a university that prides itself on being pragmatic and innovative. At the time that the material was first developed, materials in this area were relatively inaccessible as the Internet had not yet provided us with the overwhelming mass of information that we have today. When I first prepared this course for Canadian students, primary sources were not nearly as accessible as they are now and had to be supplemented by textbooks from the United Kingdom and from the United States, which provided excellent material, but always from the perspective of another country. Because I felt it was important that Canadians view this subject from their own perspective, and not from that of another country's policy and legislation, I began to assemble materials for Canadians.

Readership

This book is intended primarily for students of international business, which should now include all business students. The content can be approached at different levels and, for this reason, should be suitable for students in undergraduate programs at colleges and universities, but can also be used for students in graduate business programs. Although the book was originally written for a course specifically addressing the legal aspects of international trade, it is not intended to be limited to such courses. Much of the material is relevant to other courses in international business, such as an introduction to international business, or international business strategy, and also for students in international relations, economics, and politics and public administration programs. The reader need not have an understanding of the law to comprehend the material. The text is written so that a reader who does not have this knowledge base will comprehend the discussion. Such readers would, however, benefit from referring to one of the excellent introductory business law textbooks available in Canada to provide the desirable knowledge base in Canadian law.

I expect that this volume will also be useful to lawyers who are in general practice and have not had the advantage of specific courses relating to international transactions or law. For such practitioners, this book should prove to be a valuable first resource, providing immediate basic information and indicating where to look for more detailed information. Law students will find the book useful for similar reasons.

Approach

My approach is to present the materials from the Canadian point of view. We are a nation that has supported international cooperation: in peacekeeping operations, protection of the environment, membership in multinational organizations, and the development of common rules for international trade. We are a nation influenced by our European roots, with a tradition of common law and civil law, but we are also a nation with strong ties to the United States, Asia, and Latin America.

This book may be divided into two main parts. Chapters 1 through 5 deal with the macro-environment of international business—that is, the multilateral agreements between sovereign states that set the stage for the transaction of global business. These chapters are devoted to trading rules made by governments that affect individuals involved in international business. International organizations play an increasingly significant role in regulating international business. The World Trade Organization, the North American Free Trade Agreement, the European Union, and emerging regional trading groups have become an important part of the regime in which international business operates, and are examined in detail.

Chapters 6 through 11 of the book deal with the micro-environment of international business—that is, the laws that have a more direct impact on international business transactions. For this reason, users of this book may choose to use only those chapters relating to the subject matter of their particular course—for example, an international business transactions course, or a course on import and export. A more general course on, say, the global environment of business might choose to use only the first five chapters. Chapter 9, "Intellectual Property and International Business," is included in the "micro" part of the book because it is an essential part of so many international business transactions, but could also be included in the "macro" part because it reflects the global rules that have been established for intellectual property. Those readers who are familiar with the first edition of the book will note that the content from the previous chapter 13, "Developing Issues Relevant to International Business," has been moved to chapter 3 of the present volume and renamed "Current and Emerging Challenges in the Global Regulatory Environment." This is a reflection of the fact that these issues can no longer be described as "developing." Note also that the material appropriately follows the discussion of the WTO in chapter 2. Although the book is a relatively slim volume, there is a great deal of material, more than enough for two courses, particularly if the instructor requires students to enrich their study with current and practical examples of international business transactions.

This material is not intended as a law school textbook. It is designed for readers who require accessible information to assist them in understanding global business. It is not a casebook. Indeed, there are very few substantial readings from reported cases. Because this book is intended to provide a practical tool for readers, I have provided short excerpts from cases or practical examples for the purpose of providing some background to assist them in comprehending current events, or as cautionary tales in the hope that readers will learn from the costly experiences of others.

Special Features

The list of learning objectives at the beginning of each chapter helps the reader focus on the major themes in the chapter by providing a simple "road map" at the outset. Examples are clearly set out in boxes to illustrate the issues discussed in the text. Review questions are included to help the reader test his or her own knowledge of the chapter contents. An attempt has been made to avoid legalese, while at the same time introducing the reader to the specialized vocabulary used in the field of international business. A glossary is included to assist the reader with this specialized vocabulary.

A Caution

The purpose of this book is to help readers become confident, knowledge-able, and successful Canadian business persons. Although the material is meant to help readers identify potential risk management issues and avoid common mistakes, it is not intended as a substitute for legal advice and should not be relied on as such. This is particularly true because the subject matter is dynamic; rules are changed and modified continually. The analysis presented here represents the views and opinions of the author. If legal advice or other professional advice is required, the services of a qualified professional adviser should be sought.

Acknowledgments

This book would never have been completed without the unfailing support of my family: Catherine, Alex, Shane, Mary, and Joan, who were always gracious and supportive, and accepting of the time that completion of this project involved. The project would never have been undertaken in the first place without the inspiration of the students in the School of Business Management at Ryerson University, whose enthusiasm for learning was the catalyst to begin. I would also like to thank Samantha Majic for her help with the early stages of the manuscript, editors Paula Pike and David Handelsman for their excellent assistance, and Peggy Buchan of Emond Montgomery for her calm support throughout the project.

Mary Jo Nicholson
Toronto
November 2006

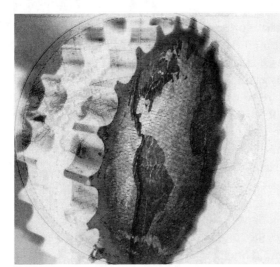

CHAPTER 1

International Organizations and International Law

INTRODUCTION

Effective management in today's global business environment requires decision makers to have a comprehensive and current knowledge base that extends well beyond our own borders or even North America. We can no longer separate business into discrete categories of "domestic" and "international or multinational." Today's businesses, even if located entirely within Canada, face competition from the rest of the world, and will quite likely deal with suppliers or services that are located outside this country.

The growing complexity, interconnectedness, and diversity of the global business environment, coupled with a borderless workforce, advances in information technology, and the increasing importance of trade agreements, have transformed the

LEARNING OBJECTIVES

After reading this chapter you will understand:

- why it is necessary for all businesses, even those perceived as local or "domestic," to possess a current knowledge of the global business environment
- how international agreements and treaties are created
- why international treaties affect the laws and regulations of businesses that are based only in Canada
- what is meant by the term "sovereignty" and why it is significant
- the history, characteristics, and purpose of some well-known international organizations and agreements, and their limitations
- what international law is—and is not
- the two major branches of international law and how they differ

business environment. **Globalization** has removed the barriers that segmented national from international markets, and separated small and large firms' competitive space. It is now increasingly difficult for small and medium-sized businesses to thrive by taking refuge in their traditionally protected domestic markets. If they are to compete effectively, businesses must be supported by a knowledge of the geography, politics, and economics of the world at large. Because the global business environment is in a state of constant flux, today's business person must be a keen observer of international organizations and events that may directly or indirectly affect the success of any business venture.

This chapter describes some of the organizations and agreements that are significant for business today, and discusses their history, purpose, and limitations. It also introduces the concept of international law and describes the two traditionally recognized branches of this discipline—that is, public international law and private international law.

HOW INTERNATIONAL AGREEMENTS ARE MADE

In domestic business, we are familiar with the concept of contract between individuals or businesses. This is similar to the domestic principle of **privity of contract**, the concept that only those who are parties to the contract can enforce the rights and obligations it contains. We also know that nations do not enter into "contracts" with each other; instead, they negotiate **treaties** or **conventions**, or **multilateral** or **bilateral agreements**. A treaty is simply a binding agreement between two or more **states**, whereas a convention is a binding agreement among states that has been sponsored by an international organization. There are many other names used to describe treaties such as international agreements, accords, protocols, covenants, even an exchange of letters or notes.

It is important to be familiar with the process of treaty creation. The first step is negotiation of the terms of the treaty by representatives of national governments. This negotiation will result in a draft text for the proposed treaty, which may be signed by representatives of the national governments. The signature of a treaty, unlike the signature of a domestic contract, does not result in a legally binding obligation. It simply represents a preliminary and general endorsement of the treaty provisions and indicates that the signatory country intends to undertake a careful examination of the treaty before it confirms its position. At a minimum, signing the treaty indicates that a country commits not to undermine the principles of the treaty, and, at the maximum, it indicates that it is government policy to commit fully to the treaty as it is currently written. A treaty will not usually come into force until it has been **ratified** by a specified number of the governments of the participating countries. Ratification must be done by the appropriate organ of the state, and this organ will vary from one country to another—for example, its Parliament, Senate, or Crown. A treaty, like a domestic contract, regulates relations only among countries (the parties) that have ratified the treaty.

The question then arises: what is the effect of a treaty on the rights and obligations of the citizens of a signatory country? The effect of treaties on a signatory's domestic law depends on whether a treaty is a **self-executing** or a **non-self-executing treaty**. If a treaty is self-executing, it becomes part of the signatory's domestic law without further implementing legislation in that country, and provides substantive rights and obligations within the country. A non-self-executing treaty imposes requirements upon the government of the signatory country but does not impose any requirements or privileges on the citizens or subnational governments (for example, provinces) of the country. Although this area of law is complex, and is often debated extensively by legal scholars, it is safe to say that most treaties and agreements are non-self-executing. Sometimes the negotiators of a treaty will clarify this point by including a term in the treaty stating that the provisions of the treaty will become directly effective within a signatory state upon the treaty's ratification. The division between self-executing and non-self-executing treaties is not always clear and this lack of clarity can lead to domestic political problems, particularly if government policy in a country has changed since the treaty's negotiation, perhaps due to the election of a new government. Technically, if a treaty requires implementing legislation, a state may be in default of its treaty obligations if it fails to pass the necessary domestic laws. The significance of non-self-executing treaties and conventions for the individual business is that they oblige national governments to change domestic laws to conform to the obligations. One very good example of this requirement is the North American Free Trade Agreement (NAFTA), which required Canada, the United States, and Mexico to pass enabling legislation. Another interesting example of this obligation is the Kyoto Protocol (see box 1.1).

Canada ratified the Kyoto Protocol in December 2002, but has not yet passed implementing legislation. While there have been some accusations that the federal government has acted improperly in ratifying the treaty without first consulting with the provinces, the weight of legal opinion seems to suggest that the federal government has acted within its treaty-making powers. While the legality of the ratification is probably not in doubt,

---

BOX 1.1   THE KYOTO PROTOCOL

The Kyoto Protocol (or treaty) is actually a follow-up to the 1992 UN Framework Convention on Climate Change (UNFCCC). The UNFCCC is a broadly worded document that binds 174 nations to address the problems of climate change and sustainable development. The final draft of the Kyoto Protocol was negotiated in December 1997, and by 1998 35 nations, including Japan, Canada, and members of the European Union (EU), had signed the treaty. The treaty requires participating countries to cut emissions of carbon dioxide and other greenhouse gases by 5.2 percent by 2012, and includes a clause providing that the treaty will come into effect when countries that account for 55 percent of greenhouse gas emissions have ratified it. Kyoto supporters were seriously concerned that the treaty would not come into effect due to the absence of support from the United States, the world's top polluter. With Russia's ratification, however, the crucial target of 55 percent of emitters was met, and the treaty came into effect in February 2005.

---

there have certainly been political problems because many businesses and some provinces, such as Alberta, are concerned about the business costs of implementing this treaty. Canada did not negotiate a federal state clause that would have limited the application of the treaty to those provinces that had agreed to implement it. It can be argued that, under the Canadian Constitution, the subject matter of the Kyoto Protocol falls under federal *and* provincial jurisdiction. Without conceding this, the federal government has tried to achieve consensus on Canada's approach to honouring the agreement and has issued what is essentially a discussion document, entitled *Moving Forward on Climate Change: A Plan for Honouring Our Kyoto Commitment.* Because the Kyoto Protocol deals with climate change and the quality of the air we breathe, it can certainly be argued that jurisdiction over this subject is inherently extra-provincial as well as international, comparable to interprovincial transportation or communication. This is an issue that may ultimately have to be determined by the Supreme Court of Canada if the federal government and some provinces continue to disagree on the framework for implementing Canada's obligations under the Kyoto Protocol. If the policy of the federal government changes and implementation of the Kyoto Protocol is no longer a political priority, the discussion above may become less urgent, at least as it applies to Kyoto. In any event, the situation remains a good example of the impact of treaties on the domestic law of participating countries, and the vulnerability of treaty goals, in the face of changing domestic priorities and governments.

THE CONCEPT OF SOVEREIGNTY

In order to understand the powers as well as the limitations of any global organization or agreement, it is necessary to be familiar with the concept of **sovereignty**. Sovereignty is the supreme and independent power and authority claimed by a nation state over its own territory. International treaty arrangements commit national governments to certain actions and policies that will affect their domestic policies, and these commitments also limit a national government's ability to implement domestic policies that conflict with the international obligations undertaken. Treaty commitments represent a limitation on the sovereignty or freedom of action for the signatory government. The situation may be compared with entering into a contract whereby a business agrees to perform or not perform a certain action. By agreeing to this legal obligation, the future choices of the business may be curtailed. This give and take is the usual contractual exchange—something is relinquished and something is gained as a result of entering into a contract. If the net result is beneficial, the contract is a wise choice.

There are obvious distinctions between a country signing a treaty and a business entering into a contract. First, a contract often has a definite term, after which both parties are free from any obligations under it. Treaties are usually indefinite and have no termination date; a country may only withdraw and such withdrawal is often complicated. Second, a company exists for the profit of its shareholders and whether or not shares are held is a choice investors make. Theoretically, shares can be sold if the investor is unhappy with a contract the company has made. In a democratic country, governments and policies change in response to the opinions of the voting public and the idea of constraining future government policy does not always sit well with the voting public.

In international decision making, just as in business decision making, the pros and cons of entering into an agreement must be weighed. Often it is necessary in order to achieve the desired result—whether that is an improvement in international behaviour or the establishment of a joint venture in a foreign country—to limit future choices by entering into a contract or, at the international level, a treaty. Thus, a dominant issue that will continue to preoccupy national policy makers is the extent to which sovereignty should be protected by individual nations and the extent to which it should be relinquished in order to gain the advantages of participation in a larger community. A necessary corollary to the rise of supra-national organizations is some weakening of the power of national governments. A tension is thus created between a nation's need to relinquish some control of its domestic policy and its natural desire to preserve its sovereignty. This tension is often evident in the United States where there is a prevalent fear of international bodies imposing rules and burdens on American citizens that are not approved by the US Congress. Added to these fears is the perception that many international bodies are under the influence of **non-governmental organizations** (**NGOs**) that are not politically accountable to anyone. While these concerns are also frequently expressed in Canada, there are vast attitudinal differences between Canada and the United States when it comes to the acceptance of multilateral negotiations (see box 1.2).

BOX 1.2   HOW CANADA AND THE UNITED STATES DIFFER IN THEIR APPROACHES TO TRADE AGREEMENTS

In Canada there is a difference between treaty-making powers and treaty-implementing powers. Treaty-making authority rests exclusively with the federal executive branch of government—that is, the prime minister and members of Cabinet. No legislative concurrence either by Parliament or the provincial legislatures has ever been legally required prior to ratification of treaties by the federal government. Integration of treaty obligations into Canadian law is, however, generally considered to require legislative action. If the subject matter of a treaty is within federal legislative jurisdiction as set out in s. 91 of the *Constitution Act, 1867*, it is the federal Parliament that enacts the necessary legislation. If the subject matter of the treaty is within provincial legislative jurisdiction under s. 92, then the provincial legislatures must enact the necessary legislation. This jurisdictional distinction can create significant difficulties for the federal government when it negotiates international treaties. If issues are clearly within provincial legislative jurisdiction—for example, labour standards, child custody, or education—the federal government will consult with the provinces. The federal government may negotiate a clause with the provinces agreeing that the treaty applies only to provinces that have committed themselves to implementing the treaty.

The US approach to treaties may be described as cautious or even reluctant. This reluctance is based on its history as a North American nation that broke away from colonial rule by way of a violent revolution. The US Constitution grants power to the president to make treaties with the "advice and consent" of two-thirds of the Senate. This is different from other US legislation, which requires approval by a simple majority in both the Senate and the House of Representatives. The United States also takes a different view from many other nations concerning the relationship between international and domestic law. Many nations view international agreements as superseding domestic law; but the view in the United States is that international agreements become a part of the body of US federal law and, as a result, Congress can modify or repeal treaties by subsequent legislative action, even if this modification amounts to a violation of the treaty. In addition, an international agreement that is inconsistent with the US Constitution is void under US domestic law, just as any other federal law that is in conflict with the US Constitution is void. Technically, the US Supreme Court could rule a treaty provision to be unconstitutional and void under domestic law, although this has never occurred. When negotiating a treaty, the United States usually requires that a **reservation** be included, stating that it will assume no obligations that are in violation of the US Constitution.

SIGNIFICANT INTERNATIONAL ORGANIZATIONS AND AGREEMENTS

With this information about treaties and their effect on national sovereignty in mind, we will briefly examine some of the more important international organizations created by treaties and agreements. Although the organizations described here do not have an immediate effect on businesses in the sense of directly imposing specific rules, they have a tremendous impact on the global business environment. It is necessary to know about the characteristics and activities of these organizations in order to make the best possible strategic business decisions.

The United Nations

The United Nations is the first international organization that comes to the minds of most people. Founded after World War II by 51 countries, its mandate is

- to maintain international peace and security;
- to develop friendly relations among nations;
- to cooperate to solve problems of an economic, social, cultural, or humanitarian nature; and
- to promote and encourage human rights and fundamental freedoms.

Although the United Nations has no direct role in the legal or regulatory aspects of international business, the impact of its action or inaction on the conduct of international business should not be underestimated.

Currently, the United Nations has 191 members and is organized as follows:

1. *The General Assembly.* Each member state or country sends a delegate to the UN General Assembly and each state has one equal vote, regardless

of its size, population, or political influence. The General Assembly is a quasi-legislative body, because its function is to discuss matters within the scope of the UN Charter. It may recommend action, but what power there is to enforce the Charter rests with the Security Council.

2. *The Security Council.* The Security Council has 15 members—5 of which are permanent members. The 5 permanent members are China, France, the United Kingdom, the United States, and the former USSR whose seat is now occupied by Russia. The 10 non-permanent members are elected by the General Assembly every two years. The permanent members have a veto over non-procedural issues in the Security Council. Thus, just one of these countries can block any action proposed by the Security Council. The Security Council is responsible for maintaining international peace and security, and it is the only UN organization with the authority to use armed force.

3. *The Secretary General.* The secretary general is the UN's chief administrative officer and is responsible for running the Secretariat, which is the UN's "civil service." Nominations for the secretary general are initiated in the Security Council, and elections are held in the General Assembly.

Reform of the UN and its institutions has been the subject of debate for many years because the organization is increasingly seen to be nearing a state of atrophy. Its sorry state became most obvious with its failure to stop the invasion of Iraq in 2003 as well as such humanitarian disasters as the war in Sudan and the threat of Iran and North Korea in their pursuit of nuclear weapons.[1] In autumn 2004, Secretary General Kofi Annan told the General Assembly that the UN had "come to a fork in the road" and appointed a 16-member blue-ribbon panel designated the High Level Panel on Threats, Challenges and Change. The task faced by the Panel was a daunting one because the UN at present is "riven with divisions between rich countries and poor, between the Security Council and the General Assembly, between the nuclear powers and others, between the Arabs and Israelis and the Indians and Pakistanis, and most significant, between a unilateralist US administration and a multilateralist UN membership."[2]

The Panel issued its report in December 2004[3] and wisely concluded that reforming what the UN does is more important than achieving organizational changes, given that any change to the organization would require an amendment to the UN Charter, which would require 127 votes in the General Assembly and the approval of all 5 existing permanent members of the Security Council. The Panel addressed three main areas: existing global conflicts, use of force, and the makeup of the Security Council.

The Panel first addressed and described the problems faced by the UN today: interstate conflict; internal violence, including state collapse and genocide; social and economic threats to peace; the proliferation of weapons of mass destruction; terrorism; and organized crime and corruption.

The second area the Panel addressed is the use of force. The UN Charter sanctions the use of force in self-defence (Article 51) or when authorized by the Security Council to prevent a breach of the peace or an act of aggression (chapter VII). The Charter forbids intervention "in matters which are essentially within the domestic jurisdiction of any state." This has been one cause of the UN's inaction in conflicts such as those in Rwanda and Darfur. The panel endorsed the emerging norm of the "responsibility to protect"—the idea that when a state cannot or will not protect its citizens, the responsibility to do so falls temporarily on the international community, embodied in the Security Council. The Panel proposed five basic guidelines that all states and the Security Council should bear in mind when deciding whether to use force:

- *Seriousness of the threat:* is the threat serious enough to justify **prima facie** the use of force?
- *Proper purpose:* is the primary purpose of the proposed use of force to halt or avert the threat in question?
- *Last resort:* has every non-military option been explored and exhausted?
- *Proportional means:* is the proposed force the minimum necessary to meet the threat?
- *Balance of consequences:* is it clear that the consequences of action will not be worse than the consequences of inaction?

Lastly, the Panel addressed the anachronistic makeup of the Security Council and proposed two possible solutions, each of which would expand the membership to 24 and allow for much greater regional representation without creating any new members with veto powers.

In September 2005, a world summit was convened to consider both the reform of the UN and the progress of the Millennium Development Goals (see box 1.3). The results of this summit were somewhat disappointing due partly to differences between the United States and a number of middle-income developing nations.[4] The document finally agreed to was significantly weaker than reformers had hoped, but it did

- authorize the creation of a peace-building commission to supervise reconstruction of countries after wars;
- recommend replacing the discredited UN Commission on Human Rights with a "tougher" Human Rights Council;
- recognize the Security Council's "responsibility to protect"; and
- recommend an "early" reform of the Security Council.

> ### BOX 1.3   MILLENNIUM DEVELOPMENT GOALS
>
> The Millennium Development Goals were adopted by the world's coun-
> tries in 2000 as a blueprint for building a better world in the 21st century.
> These goals represent an ambitious agenda for international develop-
> ment, security, and human rights, and a target of 2015 has been set for
> achieving these goals. The goals represent a commitment to
>
> - eradicate extreme poverty and hunger;
> - achieve universal primary education;
> - promote gender equality, empower women, and reduce child
>   mortality;
> - improve maternal health;
> - combat HIV/AIDS, malaria, and other diseases;
> - ensure environmental sustainability; and
> - develop a global partnership for development.[1]

1   See www.unmilleniumproject.org/goals/index.htm.

Areas that were omitted from the final document altogether, as too contentious, included sections on disarmament and non-proliferation, and the
International Criminal Court.

The UN is indeed at a crossroads. Although it is much criticized for what
it does not achieve, it nevertheless continues to be the only multilateral
organization with truly global membership and at the very least serves as an
important catalyst for multilateral action on many world problems. Any list
of UN-affiliated organizations and UN-sponsored conventions provides an
immediate overview of the organization's impact on many areas of concern
in the world.

Organizations Affiliated with the United Nations
Among the many organizations affiliated with the United Nations are the
following:

- United Nations Conference on Trade and Development (UNCTAD)
- United Nations Commission on International Trade Law (UNCITRAL)
- United Nations Relief and Works Agency (UNRWA)
- United Nations Children's Fund (UNICEF)
- United Nations Development Programme (UNDP)
- United Nations Environment Programme (UNEP)
- International Labour Organization (ILO)
- Food and Agriculture Organization of the UN (FAO)
- World Health Organization (WHO)
- World Intellectual Property Organization (WIPO).

UNCTAD and UNCITRAL are of particular importance to international business. **UNCTAD** is the UN's arm to promote the integrated treatment of trade and development and the related issues of investment, finance, technology, enterprise development, and sustainable development. UNCTAD promotes the integration of developing countries into the world economy. It is a knowledge-based organization that aims to inform current policy debates and thinking on development, based on the premise that domestic policies and international action should be mutually supportive in bringing about sustainable development. It carries out the following three key functions:

- it serves as a forum for intergovernmental deliberations;
- it undertakes research, policy analysis, and data collection for governments and experts; and
- it provides technical assistance and cooperates with other organizations and donor countries engaged in helping developing countries and economies in transition.

UNCITRAL was established by the General Assembly in 1966 to address the disparities in national laws governing international trade, because these disparities were perceived as creating obstacles to the flow of trade. UNCITRAL's mandate is to bring about the progressive harmonization and unification of the law of international trade, and it has become the core legal body of the UN system in the field of international trade law. Significant recent initiatives include a new draft Convention on the Use of Electronic Communications in International Contracting and a *Legislative Guide on Insolvency Law* to help create a unified international standard for insolvency.

The Bretton Woods System

Before the end of World War II, the **Allies** held meetings at Bretton Woods, New Hampshire in the United States for the purpose of creating a system to prevent further economic and military catastrophes. This is the origin of the reference to **Bretton Woods Institutions**. Discussions at these meetings concentrated on the financial problems faced by nations in the post-war era. There was a consensus among the Allies that freer trade and the creation of a trans-national bank would help in reconstruction after the war. Two major organizations and one "agreement that became an organization" resulted from the Bretton Woods conferences: the **International Monetary Fund**, the **World Bank**, and the **General Agreement on Tariffs and Trade**.

The International Monetary Fund

The International Monetary Fund (IMF) was established to promote international monetary cooperation, exchange stability, and orderly exchange arrangements; to foster economic growth and high levels of employment;

and to provide temporary financial assistance to countries to help ease balance of payments adjustment. The IMF is the central institution of the international monetary system, which is the system of international payments and exchange rates among national currencies that enables business to take place between countries. In 1945, when the IMF was first established, its purpose was essentially to promote financial and monetary stability by promoting fixed exchange rates. While nominally this purpose has remained unchanged, IMF operations have developed to meet the changing needs of the evolving world economy. At present, the IMF

- monitors economic and financial developments and policies in member countries;
- provides loans to member countries with balance of payments problems; and
- provides technical assistance and training to countries in financial difficulty.

The IMF provides financing not for particular economic sectors or projects but for the general support of a country's balance of payments and international reserves while the country takes policy actions to address its difficulties. The IMF's performance, mission, and relevance have been the subject of a great deal of criticism recently. For this reason, the IMF has undertaken a sweeping strategic review of its operations. At the heart of the ongoing criticism is the question of the IMF's primary purpose: is it a bank of last resort; a global financial enforcer; a crisis manager; an economic think tank; a club; or some combination of these?

The World Bank

The World Bank and the IMF complement each other's work. While the IMF's focus is chiefly on macroeconomic performance, and on macroeconomic and financial sector policies, the World Bank is concerned mainly with longer-term development and poverty reduction issues. Its mission is to fight poverty and improve the living standards of people in the developing world. Its activities include providing loans to developing countries and countries in transition to finance infrastructure projects, the reform of particular sectors of the economy, and broader structural reforms. The World Bank consists of five closely associated institutions, each of which plays a distinct role in the mission to fight poverty and improve living standards for people in the developing world. These institutions are:

- *The International Bank for Reconstruction and Development (IBRD).* The IBRD provides loans, and guarantees analytical and adviser services to middle-income and creditworthy poorer countries.

- *The International Development Association (IDA).* The IDA provides interest-free credits and grants to the world's poorest countries—that is, countries that have little or no capacity to borrow on market terms. IDA resources help support country-led poverty reduction strategies for the purpose of raising productivity, providing accountable governance, and improving private investment climate and access to education and health services.
- *The International Finance Corporation (IFC).* The IFC promotes economic development through the private sector. Working with business partners, it invests in sustainable private enterprises in developing countries. It provides equity, low-interest loans, structured finance and risk management products, and advisory services for its clients. It also finances markets that are deemed too risky by commercial investors in the absence of IFC participation.
- *The Multilateral Investment Guarantee Agency (MIGA).* The MIGA helps promote foreign direct investment in developing countries by providing guarantees to investors against non-commercial risks, such as expropriation, currency inconvertibility and transfer restriction, war and civil disturbances, and breach of contract. It also provides technical assistance and advisory services to help countries attract and retain foreign investment.
- *The International Centre for Settlement of Investment Disputes (ICSID).* The ICSID supports foreign investment by providing international facilities for the settlement of investment disputes.

The World Bank is run like a cooperative, with its member countries as shareholders. The number of shares that a country has is based roughly on the size of its economy. The United States is the largest shareholder, holding approximately 16 percent of the total votes. The other four largest shareholders are France, Germany, Japan, and the United Kingdom. The World Bank's president is, by tradition, a national of the largest shareholder. Appointed for a five-year renewable term, the president is responsible for the overall management of the World Bank.

The General Agreement on Tariffs and Trade

Although the characteristics of the General Agreement on Tariffs and Trade (GATT) are discussed in more detail in chapter 2, it is appropriate to mention the GATT here because it has its origins in the Bretton Woods conferences. Delegates at those meetings had hoped to establish an **International Trade Association (ITO)**, in addition to the IMF and the World Bank. The mandate for the ITO was to promote and stabilize world trade. After several years of discussion, a charter was proposed in 1947 in Havana, Cuba. Sufficient support for ratification of this charter was not achieved because the US Congress failed to approve US participation in the ITO. The result was that the ITO was never formally established. The remnant of these discussions was the GATT, the surviving document that the parties had agreed upon. This agreement became, by default over time, the international agency for trade.

The International Chamber of Commerce

The International Chamber of Commerce (ICC) was founded in 1919 with the mission of serving world business by promoting trade and investment, open markets for goods and services, and the free flow of capital. The organization serves as an advocate for world business and makes representations to governments and intergovernmental organizations, promoting choices favourable to the world business community. The ICC has the highest level of consultative status with the UN and its specialized agencies. Since 1946, the ICC has taken part in a broad range of activities with the UN and its specialized agencies, including the Conference on Financing for Development, the World Summit on Sustainable Development, and the World Summit on the Information Society.

Working with national governments all over the world through its national committees, the ICC's activities cover a broad spectrum, from providing arbitration and dispute resolution, to making the case for open trade and the market economy system, to advocating business self-regulation, to fighting corruption, to combating commercial crime. Significant contributions of the ICC include:

- the ICC Court of Arbitration—the longest established ICC institution and the world's leading body for international commercial arbitration;
- the Uniform Customs and Practice for Documentary Credits (UCP)—the common rules that enable international banks to finance billions of dollars worth of world trade each year;
- Incoterms—the standard international trade definitions commonly used in international contracts; and
- business self-regulation of e-commerce—the codes developed by business to establish international norms in this relatively new business area.

Organisation for Economic Co-operation and Development

The Organisation for Economic Co-operation and Development (OECD) is an intergovernmental organization comprising 30 countries that work together to address the economic, social, and environmental challenges of the globalizing world economy. The OECD has played a prominent role in fostering good governance in the public service and in corporate activity and is well known for its individual country surveys and reviews. Its membership is limited to countries having a commitment to a market economy and a pluralistic democracy. It began in 1948 as the Organisation for European Economic Co-operation (OEEC), which was established by Western European nations to implement the provisions of the Marshall Plan that was established to aid in the recovery of Europe after World War II. Membership was expanded to include the United States, Canada, and Japan and, in 1961, it became the OECD. As the world economy changed and expanded, so too did the work of the OECD. At present, its work encompasses the following areas:

- economics;
- statistics;
- the environment;
- international law;
- development;
- public governance;
- trade;
- financial affairs;
- taxation;
- science, technology, and industry;
- employment and social cohesion;
- education; and
- agriculture.

The OECD's original focus has also broadened to include extensive contacts with non-member countries and it now maintains cooperative relations with at least 100 such countries.

Present members of the OECD are:

Australia	Hungary	Norway
Austria	Iceland	Poland
Belgium	Ireland	Portugal
Canada	Italy	Slovak Republic
Czech Republic	Japan	Spain
Denmark	Korea	Sweden
Finland	Luxembourg	Switzerland
France	Mexico	Turkey
Germany	Netherlands	United Kingdom
Greece	New Zealand	United States

G7, G8, and G20

Although the G7, G8, and G20 organizations are not supported by a trans-national administration, as are all the other organizations we have examined, they are nevertheless important and influential in the current global business environment.

G7 and G8

This organization began as the G6 and has its roots in the 1973 oil crisis and the subsequent global recession. Under the leadership of the United States, France, West Germany, Italy, Japan, and the United Kingdom agreed to an annual meeting to be organized under a rotating presidency. Canada joined in 1976, and in 1991, following the end of the **Cold War**, Russia began meeting with the G7. The G7 became the G8 at the instigation of then US President Clinton as a gesture of appreciation for Russia's pursuit of economic reform and for its neutrality with respect to the eastward expansion of NATO.

The country holding the presidency of the G8 hosts a series of ministerial-level meetings and a three-day summit each year at which topics of current concern such as global warming, poverty in developing countries, and world health problems are discussed. Because these topics are controversial, there is much criticism of the G8, described by some as an unofficial "world government." The annual summits are often the focus of anti-globalization protests.

G20

The G20 is an informal forum that seeks to promote an open and constructive dialogue between industrial nations and emerging-market countries on issues that relate to the international monetary and financial system. It also provides a platform for discussion of current international economic questions. G20 members develop a common position on issues that relate to international currency and financial systems and foster the establishment of internationally recognized standards and practices to promote transparency of fiscal policy, as well as policies to combat money laundering and the financing of terrorism.

The genesis of the G20 occurred in Berlin in 1999. The G20 now brings together industrial and emerging-market countries from all regions of the world. Together, the member countries represent nearly 90 percent of global gross national product, 80 percent of world trade, and two-thirds of the world's population.[5] The G20, like the G8, has no permanent staff of its own. Like the G8, the current chairing country coordinates the group's work and organizes its meetings. Current members of the G20 are:

Argentina	Germany	Russia
Australia	Iceland	Saudi Arabia
Brazil	Indonesia	South Africa
Canada	Italy	Turkey
China	Japan	United Kingdom
European Union	Korea	United States
France	Mexico	

To ensure that the G20's activities are closely aligned with those of the Bretton Woods Institutions, the managing director of the IMF, the president of the World Bank, as well as the chairpersons of the International Monetary and Financial Committee and Development Committee of the IMF and World Bank, participate in its deliberations, as well as experts from private sector institutions.

INTERNATIONAL LAW

In the international environment, legal scholars distinguish between public and private international law. **Public international law** has been traditionally defined as the law regulating relations among nations, and **private international law**, sometimes referred to as conflict of laws, is law regulating the affairs of private persons (including corporations) located in different countries. In recent years the line between public and private international law has become somewhat blurred because of the proliferation of conventions and bilateral and multilateral trade agreements, which have the effect of directly making rules for businesses or requiring signatory countries to pass legislation that affects the rights of private persons and businesses in signatory countries.

Is International Law Really Law?

There has always been some controversy over the definition of law. Most people agree that laws are rules, but of course not all rules are laws. How do we differentiate between rules and laws? Blackstone, one of the definitive jurists of the English common law, defined the law as "a rule of civil conduct, prescribed by the supreme power in a state, commanding what is right and prohibiting what is wrong."[6] A second definition is that a law is a rule that can be enforced by the courts.[7] Another accepted definition is that the law is a body of enacted or customary rules recognized by a community as binding.[8] The debate as to whether international law is law is centred on the fact that there is no one global law-making or law-enforcing body with authority to act on behalf of the global community. There is also debate among scholars as to how customary international law is defined or established, but this debate is beyond the scope of our examination. What can be said with certainty is that international law such as it is, is constantly developing and evolving, and its influence on the conduct of business is undeniable.

Public International Law

As previously stated, public international law involves the relationships among states and is reflected in treaties, conventions, and the charters of international organizations. It is generally confined to rules and principles of general application that deal with the conduct of states and of international organizations and with their relations among themselves.

The International Court of Justice

At present, some public international law disputes are heard by the **International Court of Justice (ICJ)**, also known as the World Court, in The Hague in the Netherlands. Two factors limit the Court's effectiveness and power. The first is the rule that decisions are binding only upon the parties to the dispute, and the second is the fact that a state may not be brought before the Court unless that state has accepted the Court's jurisdiction, either generally or for the purpose of the dispute in question. The ICJ does not hear commercial disputes involving private litigants because only countries may be parties before the Court. For this reason, the ICJ is of little practical significance for private businesses.

What Are the Sources of International Law?

Article 38(1) of the Statute of the International Court of Justice lists the sources of law that the Court is permitted to use. This provides us with a useful summary of the sources of international law. These are:

- *conventions* establishing rules between or among contracting states;
- *international custom*, as evidence of a general practice accepted as law;
- *general principles* recognized by civilized nations; and
- *judicial decisions and teachings* of various nations, as subsidiary means for determining the rules of law.

It is important to note that these principles are stated in order of their importance, with conventions carrying the most weight. Only where the first-named source is not available or determinative of the dispute will the Court proceed down the list.

Private International Law

As mentioned above, private international law involves private parties in international transactions. It is also described as **conflict of laws**—the question of whose country's laws will govern a transaction. This area will be dealt with further when we discuss international business dispute settlement in chapter 11. Treaties, such as the Convention on the International Sale of Goods (CISG), that govern relationships between private parties in different countries are being used more often as a means of predetermining applicable laws and eliminating "conflict of law" questions because these can be expensive and time consuming for the parties. We will consider the CISG in chapter 7, "Negotiating the International Sale of Goods." Remember that conventions are binding only on those states and businesses located in the signatory countries.

NOTES

1   "Towards a More Relevant United Nations," *The Economist*, December 1, 2004.

2   See Paul Heinbecker, "101 Ways to Change the United Nations," *Globe and Mail*, December 3, 2004, A23.

3   See "A More Secure World: Our Shared Responsibility," online: www.un.org/secureworld.

4   Including Pakistan, Cuba, Iran, Egypt, Syria, and Venezuela.

5   See G-20 Archival website, online: http://www.bundesbank.de/g20.

6   Sir William Blackstone, *Commentaries on the Laws of England*. 4 vols. (Oxford: Oxford at the Clarendon Press, 1778).

7   See McInnes, Kerr, VanDuzer, and Carmody, *Managing the Law: The Legal Aspects of Doing Business* (Toronto: Prentice Hall, 2003).

8   See *The Canadian Oxford Dictionary*, 2nd ed. (Don Mills, ON: Oxford University Press).

REVIEW QUESTIONS

1. What is the difference between a treaty and a convention?
2. What is the significance of a country signing a treaty or convention?
3. What is the significance of a country ratifying a treaty or convention?
4. What is the difference between a self-executing and a non-self-executing treaty?
5. Is the Kyoto Protocol now in effect? What is Canada's position with respect to this treaty? What is the position of the United States? What is the significance of the two countries' positions for business?

6. What is meant by sovereignty and what is the significance of this concept in the context of treaties and other international agreements?
7. Describe the different requirements in Canada and the United States with respect to ratification of a treaty. How does this reflect the differing attitudes of the two countries toward international obligations?
8. Describe the mandate and the present organizational set up of the UN.
9. Describe some of the problems that currently affect the UN's ability to fulfill its mandate.
10. Describe the work of UNCTAD and UNCITRAL.
11. What are the Bretton Woods Institutions and what is the role of each of these?
12. Is the International Chamber of Commerce an intergovernmental organization? Why was it founded and what are some of its achievements?
13. Describe the history and purpose of the OECD. What is it best known for?
14. What is the G7 and what is its relationship to the G8? How is it structured and how does it achieve its mandate?
15. Describe the origin and purpose of the G20.
16. Why is there some debate as to whether international law is really law?
17. What is the difference between public international law and private international law?
18. Why is the International Court of Justice of little practical significance for private businesses?
19. What are the acknowledged sources of public international law?
20. Why is private international law sometimes described as the conflict of laws?

CLASS ACTIVITIES

Have students, individually or in teams, search reputable media sources and identify and present stories that relate to the following:

- The Kyoto Protocol.
- The UN—its reform or current issues being debated in the Security Council or the General Assembly.
- Has the World Bank or the IMF been in the news lately? If yes, describe the issue.
- What is the story of the IMF's intervention in the Argentine Financial Crisis of 1997-1999?
- How would an individual Canadian business or industry association achieve a voice in or hope to influence the International Chamber of Commerce?

- Has the OECD been in the news lately? If yes, what is the story?
- Has the G8 or the G20 had meetings in the last six months? If yes, what were the issues discussed and what was the impact of their meetings on business or the general public?
- Provide an example of a public or private international law story that has been in the news lately.

FURTHER READING

Aust, Anthony. (2000). *Modern Treaty Law and Practice.* Cambridge: Cambridge University Press (see foreword by Sir Arthur Watts).

Trebilcock, M.J., and Howse, R. (2001). *The Regulation of International Trade.* New York: Routledge.

WEBSITES

United Nations:
   www.un.org

United Nations Commission on International Trade Law:
   www.uncitral.org

United Nations Conference on Trade and Development:
   www.unctad.org

United Nations Environment Programme:
   www.unep.org

United Nations Development Programme:
   www.undp.org

International Monetary Fund:
   www.imf.org

World Bank:
   www.worldbank.org

International Chamber of Commerce:
   www.iccwbo.org

Organisation for Economic Co-operation and Development:
   www.oecd.org

Canada's G8 Website:
   www.g8.gc.ca

Group of 20 (G-20):
www.g20.org/Public/index.jsp

International Court of Justice:
www.icj-cij.org

International Law:
www.un.org/law

International Law Association:
www.ila-hq.org
(an excellent website leading to sources and information about international law)

CHAPTER 2

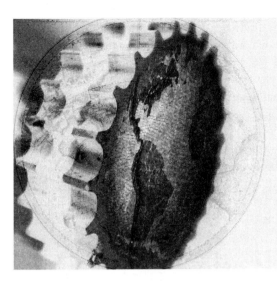

The World Trade Organization

THE WORLD TRADE ORGANIZATION'S PREDECESSOR: THE GENERAL AGREEMENT ON TARIFFS AND TRADE

A familiarity with the philosophy and provisions of the General Agreement on Tariffs and Trade (GATT) and the World Trade Organization (WTO) is fundamental to an understanding of the regulation of modern international trade. The GATT was described almost 20 years ago as the "cornerstone of the world trading system and of Canadian international trade." This statement would be as apt today as when it was made with the proviso that the GATT has now been replaced by the WTO. It is important to realize, however, that the GATT and the WTO do not *mandate* free trade. They are simply international agreements that provide for freeing trade and for preventing trade discrimination. They establish rules that enable

LEARNING OBJECTIVES

After reading this chapter you will understand:

- the purpose of the WTO, its historical relationship to the GATT, and the fundamental rules of the WTO
- why the WTO can be described as a "bundle of agreements" and what agreements make up the bundle
- dumping and anti-dumping duties; subsidies and countervailing duties; and safeguard protection and when countries may use it
- tariffs and non-tariff barriers
- the unique aspects of trade in agricultural products and in textiles, and how trade in services differs from trade in goods
- intellectual property protection provided by the WTO
- the WTO dispute settlement system

member countries to expand trade by making voluntary trade concessions among themselves on a relatively transparent, multilateral basis, and discourage member countries from practising trade discrimination against other trading partners that are members.

At the time of the original negotiation and drafting of GATT just after World War II, nations were preoccupied with the goal of reducing tariffs, as these were seen to be the primary obstacles to freer trade. The trading environment has changed dramatically since then, but the fundamental rules developed in the late 1940s remain the foundation for regulation in today's trading environment. As mentioned in chapter 1, the GATT is the agreement that survived the failure to establish the International Trade Organization (ITO) in 1947. The GATT was not an international organization in the true sense, but an international agreement signed originally by only 23 countries. These countries believed that the peace negotiated after World War II would not survive if nations returned to the protectionist trade policies that proliferated in the 1930s. At that time, a number of dominant trading blocs had developed: the British Empire, the French Union, the Japanese Co-Prosperity Sphere, Germany and Eastern Europe, and the United States and Latin America. Each bloc sought to restrict and even eliminate trade with the rest of the world. The early supporters of the GATT believed that a trading system based on open markets and full competition secured through multilaterally agreed rules was the best insurance against further hostilities on the scale of the two world wars. The GATT that survived the failure of the ITO was not really an organization but a "collection of agreements" that became an organization.

There were two major roles anticipated for the GATT at that time—the first, simply to develop a code of rules governing trade relations among different countries, and the second, to provide a forum where countries could discuss trade problems and address trade-related issues. There was no overriding supra-national enforcement mechanism in the GATT and no international superstructure to punish rule breakers. The only enforcement mechanism was the members' desire to make the agreement work and the economic leverage they had to retaliate against another member that violated the rules.

The Fundamental Rules Developed by the GATT

At the time that the GATT was negotiated, the parties agreed upon three basic rules that became the foundation of the trading rules in the GATT and continue in the WTO today. These are the **binding concessions rule**, the most-favoured-nation (MFN) rule, and the national treatment rule.

Tariffs and the Binding Concessions Rule

When the GATT was negotiated, the major barriers to trade were tariffs. A **tariff** is simply a charge imposed by a government on a good being imported into a country. The initial goal of the GATT was to oversee the progressive lowering of tariffs in successive rounds of reciprocal bargaining among GATT members. Countries were encouraged, but not required, to lower particular tariffs. Today, once a country lowers a tariff, it becomes "bound" and the country is obligated not to increase the tariff above the bound level. The tariff commitments of each member country are set out in the various protocols to the GATT.

The Most-Favoured-Nation Rule

The **most-favoured-nation rule** requires that tariffs be applied equally to all member countries—that is, tariffs negotiated between any two GATT countries should be available to all other member countries. This rule embodies the principles of non-discrimination and reciprocity, which are at the very foundation of the GATT. This rule has had a significant effect on world trade and is legitimately credited with the substantial progress in lowering tariffs worldwide. It is, however, subject to a number of exceptions incorporated in the GATT. Two of the most important exceptions are the special tariff rate accorded to developing countries, referred to as the **generalized system of preference (GSP)**, and the acceptance of free trade areas and customs unions.

SPECIAL TREATMENT FOR DEVELOPING COUNTRIES

As the GATT rules became more familiar with use, it became apparent that it was a handicap for the developing countries to be subject to the full discipline of all the rules. Over the years, the rules were changed to alleviate some of the hardships for these countries. Greater latitude was permitted with respect to subsidies to promote economic development, and also for currency exchange restrictions to address balance of payment difficulties. In 1965, it was agreed that developed countries could make commitments to developing countries to reduce or remove tariffs without creating the same obligation of most-favoured-nation treatment to other countries. This philosophy was reinforced by the adoption in 1971 of the GSP. Under this system, developed countries agreed to grant preferential treatment on a wide range of exports from developing countries.

FREE TRADE AREAS AND CUSTOMS UNIONS

A **free trade area** is an arrangement among two or more countries that agree to remove substantially all duties and restrictions of commerce among them, but retain independent schedules for tariffs and other barriers applicable to other countries. A **customs union** is similar in that substantially all duties and restrictions on commerce among the participating countries are removed, but, in addition, members agree to adopt a common tariff that applies to all goods imported from other countries (a common external tariff). Thus, each of these arrangements derogates from the MFN principle because their very essence is preferential treatment among members. The GATT (and subsequently the WTO) adopt the approach that such agreements are acceptable provided they are entirely trade creating—that is, they facilitate trade among members and do not raise any new barriers for trade with non-members.

The National Treatment Rule

The **national treatment rule** requires that once a good or service is legally present in a country, it must receive the same treatment as a domestic good or service. There must be exactly the same tax and regulatory treatment as is extended to local goods. The case in box 2.1 is an example of the GATT's policy on national treatment.

Additional Rules

In addition to the three basic rules, the GATT contained rules providing for

- the prohibition of quantitative restrictions (quotas) except in certain circumstances;
- freedom of transit of goods;
- anti-dumping and countervailing duties;
- the administration of customs duties;
- a relationship with the International Monetary Fund with respect to exchange rates and controls;
- subsidies;
- the activities of state trading enterprises; and
- trade and economic development.

The Importance of "Rounds" in the Multilateral Trading Environment

Major negotiating sessions of the GATT, and later the WTO, are referred to as rounds. Due to the complexity, detail, and importance of the issues discussed, these rounds may extend over several years. Significant rounds in GATT history included the Kennedy Round from 1964 to 1967; the Tokyo Round from 1973 to 1979, and most important, the Uruguay Round from 1987 to 1993. The most recent round is the Doha Round, which began in 2001 and was still in progress at the time of writing.

BOX 2.1   BEER AND ALCOHOLIC BEVERAGES FROM THE UNITED STATES: CANADA VIOLATES NATIONAL TREATMENT RULE

In 1988, a GATT panel upheld a complaint made by the United States that Canadian provincial liquor boards were discriminating against US products with respect to listings, markups, and point of sale. The rules for US products were less favourable than those applied to Canadian alcoholic beverages. Canada was advised to bring its practices into conformity with Article 3 of GATT, and offer national treatment to these US products in the Canadian market.

In 1992, a similar complaint was made by the United States against Canada, this time relating to the treatment of US beer in Canadian provincial markets. The panel found that several discriminatory practices existed in individual Canadian provinces. These included taxes that were levied on beer containers for imported beer, but not for domestic beer; a requirement that imported beer be sold only in six-packs; and differential markups that favoured Canadian domestic beer. Once again, Canada was found to be in violation of the principle of national treatment and ordered to change its discriminatory practices.

The goals for the Uruguay Round were ambitious and were developed at a time when the multilateral trading system established by the GATT was in serious jeopardy. Although enormous progress on reducing tariff barriers had been made, the world trading system was threatened by the growing use of protectionist measures, the proliferation of bilateral and multilateral trade agreements, and the increasing use of unilateral measures by members. As world trade had expanded, business in all countries was exposed to greater competition, and trade policy had an increasingly direct effect on voters, companies, and their employees. Because democratically elected governments tend to pursue domestic policies that are popular with voters, legislation is often adopted that is inconsistent with long-term international trade policy obligations. This presents difficulties for a global institution trying to establish a rational trading system.

At the outset of the Uruguay Round negotiations, it was apparent that member countries were increasingly resorting to protective measures and practices that didn't exist at the time the GATT was drafted. Hopes for a successful outcome of the Uruguay Round were not high. It was not uncommon during the Uruguay Round to see articles in the media with the headline or the conclusion that "The GATT Is Dead." Detailed negotiations in the Uruguay Round continued for seven years, and the deadline for negotiations was extended numerous times after the scheduled end in December 1991.

THE ESTABLISHMENT OF THE WORLD TRADE ORGANIZATION

The Marrakesh Agreement, 1994

Just when the world had all but abandoned any hope for a successful outcome of the Uruguay Round, in December 1993 an agreement to create the World Trade Organization (WTO) was reached. The agreement to create the WTO was formally signed by more than 100 countries in Marrakesh, Morocco on April 15, 1994, and it came into effect on January 1, 1995. At the time of the WTO's creation, more than half of the signatories had ratified the Uruguay Round agreements, and by mid-2005 the WTO had 148 countries as full members. The agreements represented a significant advance over the GATT for a number of reasons, most notably that they included rules on trade in services and rules governing intellectual property, as well as providing for a greatly improved dispute settlement process.

BOX 2.2   CURRENT WTO MEMBERSHIP

Albania	September 8, 2000	Colombia	April 30, 1995
Angola	November 23, 1996	Congo	March 27, 1997
Antigua and Barbuda	January 1, 1995	Costa Rica	January 1, 1995
Argentina	January 1, 1995	Côte d'Ivoire	January 1, 1995
Armenia	February 5, 2003	Croatia	November 30, 2000
Australia	January 1, 1995	Cuba	April 20, 1995
Austria	January 1, 1995	Cyprus	July 30, 1995
Bahrain, Kingdom of	January 1, 1995	Czech Republic	January 1, 1995
Bangladesh	January 1, 1995	Democratic Republic of	
Barbados	January 1, 1995	the Congo	January 1, 1997
Belgium	January 1, 1995	Denmark	January 1, 1995
Belize	January 1, 1995	Djibouti	May 31, 1995
Benin	February 22, 1996	Dominica	January 1, 1995
Bolivia	September 12, 1995	Dominican Republic	March 9, 1995
Botswana	May 31, 1995	Ecuador	January 21, 1996
Brazil	January 1, 1995	Egypt	June 30, 1995
Brunei Darussalam	January 1, 1995	El Salvador	May 7, 1995
Bulgaria	December 1, 1996	Estonia	November 13, 1999
Burkina Faso	June 3, 1995	European Communities	January 1, 1995
Burundi	July 23, 1995	Fiji	January 14, 1996
Cambodia	October 13, 2004	Finland	January 1, 1995
Cameroon	December 13, 1995	Former Yugoslav Republic	
Canada	January 1, 1995	of Macedonia (FYROM)	April 4, 2003
Central African Republic	May 31, 1995	France	January 1, 1995
Chad	October 19, 1996	Gabon	January 1, 1995
Chile	January 1, 1995	The Gambia	October 23, 1996
China	December 11, 2001	Georgia	June 14, 2000

Germany	January 1, 1995	New Zealand	January 1, 1995
Ghana	January 1, 1995	Nicaragua	September 3, 1995
Greece	January 1, 1995	Niger	December 13, 1996
Grenada	February 22, 1996	Nigeria	January 1, 1995
Guatemala	July 21, 1995	Norway	January 1, 1995
Guinea	October 25, 1995	Oman	November 9, 2000
Guinea Bissau	May 31, 1995	Pakistan	January 1, 1995
Guyana	January 1, 1995	Panama	September 6, 1997
Haiti	January 30, 1996	Papua New Guinea	June 9, 1996
Honduras	January 1, 1995	Paraguay	January 1, 1995
Hong Kong, China	January 1, 1995	Peru	January 1, 1995
Hungary	January 1, 1995	Philippines	January 1, 1995
Iceland	January 1, 1995	Poland	July 1, 1995
India	January 1, 1995	Portugal	January 1, 1995
Indonesia	January 1, 1995	Qatar	January 13, 1996
Ireland	January 1, 1995	Romania	January 1, 1995
Israel	April 21, 1995	Rwanda	May 22, 1996
Italy	January 1, 1995	Saint Kitts and Nevis	February 21, 1996
Jamaica	March 9, 1995	Saint Lucia	January 1, 1995
Japan	January 1, 1995	Saint Vincent & the Grenadines	January 1, 1995
Jordan	April 11, 2000	Saudi Arabia	December 11, 2005
Kenya	January 1, 1995	Senegal	January 1, 1995
Korea, Republic of	January 1, 1995	Sierra Leone	July 23, 1995
Kuwait	January 1, 1995	Singapore	January 1, 1995
Kyrgyz Republic	December 20, 1998	Slovak Republic	January 1, 1995
Latvia	February 10, 1999	Slovenia	July 30, 1995
Lesotho	May 31, 1995	Solomon Islands	July 26, 1996
Liechtenstein	September 1, 1995	South Africa	January 1, 1995
Lithuania	May 31, 2001	Spain	January 1, 1995
Luxembourg	January 1, 1995	Sri Lanka	January 1, 1995
Macao, China	January 1, 1995	Suriname	January 1, 1995
Madagascar	November 17, 1995	Swaziland	January 1, 1995
Malawi	May 31, 1995	Sweden	January 1, 1995
Malaysia	January 1, 1995	Switzerland	July 1, 1995
Maldives	May 31, 1995	Chinese Taipei	January 1, 2002
Mali	May 31, 1995	Tanzania	January 1, 1995
Malta	January 1, 1995	Thailand	January 1, 1995
Mauritania	May 31, 1995	Togo	May 31, 1995
Mauritius	January 1, 1995	Trinidad and Tobago	March 1, 1995
Mexico	January 1, 1995	Tunisia	March 29, 1995
Moldova	July 26, 2001	Turkey	March 26, 1995
Mongolia	January 29, 1997	Uganda	January 1, 1995
Morocco	January 1, 1995	United Arab Emirates	April 10, 1996
Mozambique	August 26, 1995	United Kingdom	January 1, 1995
Myanmar	January 1, 1995	United States of America	January 1, 1995
Namibia	January 1, 1995	Uruguay	January 1, 1995
Nepal	April 23, 2004	Venezuela (Bolivarian Republic of)	January 1, 1995
Netherlands—For the Kingdom in Europe and for the Netherlands Antilles	January 1, 1995	Zambia	January 1, 1995
		Zimbabwe	March 5, 1995

BOX 2.3   WTO OBSERVER GOVERNMENTS (COUNTRIES THAT ARE NOT YET MEMBERS, BUT MAY QUALIFY IN THE FUTURE)

Afghanistan	Holy See (Vatican)	Sao Tomé and Principe
Algeria	Iran	Serbia
Andorra	Iraq	Seychelles
Azerbaijan	Kazakhstan	Sudan
Bahamas	Lao People's Democratic	Tajikistan
Belarus	Republic	Tonga
Bhutan	Lebanese Republic	Ukraine
Bosnia and Herzegovina	Libya	Uzbekistan
Cape Verde	Montenegro	Vanuatu
Equatorial Guinea	Russian Federation	Vietnam
Ethiopia	Samoa	Yemen

Domestic Approval of Membership

As we know from chapter 1, treaties must be not only signed, but also ratified. Most countries wishing to ratify an international treaty must first pass domestic legislation providing for ratification of the treaty and providing for the adoption of the treaty into their own domestic law. This was certainly the case with respect to the WTO agreements, which contained obligations that required domestic provisions to enable countries to honour the terms. In Canada, for example, we took the provisions of the anti-dumping and subsidies and countervailing measures agreements and incorporated them into our own legislation, the *Special Import Measures Act* **(SIMA)**, an Act of the Parliament of Canada. Canada was one of the first countries to ratify the WTO agreements on anti-dumping, and it did so without reservation.

By way of contrast, let us examine the approach of the United States. The United States has a long history of adopting a very cautious approach to multilateral commitments that limit its absolute freedom to act independently in its own interests. Fully cognizant that reaping the benefits of expanded orderly trading arrangements under the WTO requires a government to relinquish some of its flexibility to pass measures to protect its own market, the US Congress was not prepared to wholeheartedly endorse US accession to the WTO. The implementing legislation in the United States provides for a review of the US participation in the WTO every five years. Under this provision, the president must submit a special report to Congress and a procedure is provided for a motion of Congress to consider withdrawal from the WTO, although such a resolution does not actually require the president to begin withdrawal action. So far, two such reviews by Congress have taken place, in 2000 and in 2005, and each time a large majority of legislators have voted against withdrawal. The legislation nevertheless represents a clear indication on the part of US lawmakers that they are not prepared to cede too much sovereignty to an international organization without retaining a right to withdraw if conditions change, or US interests are perceived to be unduly threatened.

The Accession Process for New Members

Any country wishing to join the WTO must go through the accession process, first applying for membership and describing in detail the country's institutional structure, trade and economic policies, investment and privatization policies, intellectual property regimes, and other issues affecting international trade. The next stage in the process is fact finding by a working party and, usually, parallel bilateral talks with major trading partners. Negotiations between the applicant country and individual countries will cover such matters as tariff rates and specific market access commitments as well as policies on trade in goods and services. The applicant will commit to a set of "bound" tariffs that cannot be raised, but can be lowered after accession. Although the negotiations are bilateral, the applicant country's commitment will apply equally to all WTO members under the normal MFN rules. Once the working party and bilateral access negotiations are complete, the terms of accession are drafted and, if approved by a two-thirds majority of WTO members, the applicant country may formally join the WTO.

BOX 2.4   CHINA JOINS THE WTO AT LAST

After 15 years of diplomatic struggle and negotiations in which China had to satisfy its trading partners, notably the United States and the European Union, that it was doing enough to open its economy to international competition, China formally became a member of the WTO in 2001. As a result, China, at that time the world's ninth largest exporter, gained non-discriminatory access to world markets, having agreed to open its domestic markets to foreign products and services, especially in the areas of telecommunications and financial services. Observers predicted that China's accession to the WTO might result in a tipping of the balance of negotiations in the WTO to less developed countries as well as an increase in China's political leverage in the organization. Some predicted an increase of volume of disputes for the WTO due to the sheer volume of trade from China, and worried that China would be reluctant to honour some of the commitments made under WTO agreements. So far, these fears have not materialized. It is apparent that other countries are losing some share of world markets due to increased competition from Chinese exports. Domestically, sectors of the Chinese economy that had enjoyed high protection through tariff and non-tariff barriers in the past now face greater competition from imports.

The WTO Is a "Bundle of Agreements"

Countries acceding to the WTO must adopt all the agreements reached in the Uruguay Round. This is a somewhat daunting list of approximately 60 agreements, annexes, decisions, and understandings. Dealing with the agreements is easier if they are viewed as one umbrella agreement establishing the WTO with five major aspects of agreement relating to

1. trade in goods,
2. trade in services,
3. intellectual property protection,
4. dispute settlement, and
5. the review of members' trade policies.

The principle of a single undertaking was adopted with respect to membership in the WTO, which means that each member must adopt the entire "bundle of agreements" and does not have the option of acceding to some and rejecting others that it finds less acceptable. It is also important to realize that these agreements are not static—they are renegotiated from time to time and new agreements may be added. It is expected that the Doha Round of negotiations, still in progress, will result in a number of changes and additions to the current agreements.

BOX 2.5   UMBRELLA AGREEMENT ESTABLISHING THE WTO

Goods (GATT)	Services (GATS)	Intellectual property (TRIPS)
Dispute settlement		
Trade policy reviews		

WTO Provisions Relating to Trade in Goods

Tariffs

While there is no legally binding agreement that sets out the targets for tariff reductions, there was agreement to substantially cut tariffs as a result of the Uruguay Round. These commitments are found in the schedules annexed to the Marrakesh Protocol to the General Agreement on Tariffs and Trade, 1994.

These annexed schedules comprise more than 22,500 pages listing individual countries' commitments to cut and bind customs duty on specific categories of imported goods. These market access schedules are not simply announcements of tariff rates; they represent commitments not to increase tariffs above the listed rates. In other words, they are **bound tariffs**—countries can break this commitment only with difficulty. They must negotiate with countries most affected by the change to the bound tariff, and may possibly have to pay compensation for any trading partners' consequent loss of trade.

Rules on Dumping, Subsidies, and Contingencies

Although the principle of binding tariffs and applying them equally to all trading partners by virtue of the MFN rule is central to the operation of the WTO, there are also agreements that allow exceptions to these rules in some circumstances. These exceptions allow countries to act in a way that would normally break the WTO principles of bound tariffs and non-discrimination. The three principal areas of exception are

- actions to protect domestic industry from dumping (selling at a price lower than that in the home market);
- actions to counteract subsidies (government help given to producers, manufacturers, or exporters); and
- actions, called safeguards, to temporarily limit imports so as to protect domestic industry from a surge in imports.

DUMPING AND ANTI-DUMPING ACTIONS

Dumping occurs when a company exports a product at a price lower than the price it usually charges in its home market. The WTO Anti-Dumping Agreement allows governments to act against dumping where there is genuine or material injury to the competing domestic industry. There are three necessary elements that must be present to justify an anti-dumping action:

- a demonstration that dumping is taking place: the fact that the product is being sold at less than the normal price in the home market must be proven.
- a calculation of the extent of the dumping. There are several methods to calculate a product's usual value. The most common and simplest method is based on the price in the exporter's domestic market. A second method is the price charged by the exporter in another country. A third method involves a calculation based on the combination of the exporter's production costs, other expenses, and normal profit margins. The margin of dumping must be more than 2 percent of the export price of the product.
- a demonstration that the dumping is causing or is threatening to cause injury to the domestic industry.

A detailed investigation must be conducted to evaluate all relevant economic factors affecting the state of the industry in question. If there is a connection between the dumping and adverse effects or the threat of adverse effects on the industry, anti-dumping duties may be imposed. Once these three requirements are met, the importing country may impose an extra import duty on the particular product from the specified exporting country in order to bring the price closer to the "normal value" and remove the injury to the domestic industry in the importing country. Member countries must inform the WTO Committee on Anti-dumping Practices about all preliminary and final anti-dumping actions, promptly and in detail. They must also report on all investigations twice a year. Where countries disagree over the imposition of **anti-dumping (AD) duties** in a particular case, they are encouraged to consult with each other and attempt to resolve their differences, but if these consultations fail, they can resort to the WTO dispute settlement procedure.

BOX 2.6 WHAT IS DUMPING IN THE EYES OF THE LAW?

Consider the following simplified scenario:

A Brazilian shoe manufacturer is able to manufacture ladies' sandals in Brazil and sell them to a wholesaler in Brazil for a price equivalent to Cdn$15. This price is sufficient for the manufacturer to cover all costs and recover his usual percentage of profit. The same manufacturer sells the sandals to a wholesaler in Canada. The extra cost of export to Canada (covering packing, shipping, insurance, and customs duties and handling) is Cdn$2.00 per pair.

An equivalent pair of sandals manufactured in Canada and sold to the Canadian wholesaler with the usual allowance for profit to the manufacturer is $22. The "made in Canada" sandals appear in Canadian retail shoe outlets priced from $30 to $35.

Assume that the Brazilian-made sandals appear in Canadian retail shoe outlets at prices between $22 and $25. Are these sandals being dumped into the Canadian market?

SUBSIDIES AND COUNTERVAILING MEASURES

A subsidy is any financial or commercial benefit given to a producer, manufacturer, or grower by any government. The WTO Agreement on Subsidies and Countervailing Measures attempts to discipline the use of subsidies and regulate the actions that countries may take to offset the effects of subsidies accorded to goods that are then exported. Many of the criteria allowing countries to impose countervailing duties to offset the negative effects of subsidies are parallel to those in the Anti-Dumping Agreement. **Counter-vailing duties (CVD)** may be charged only after the importing country has conducted a detailed investigation similar to that required for an anti-dumping action. There are rules for deciding whether a product is being subsidized, criteria for determining whether imports of subsidized products are causing injury to domestic industry, procedures for initiating and conducting investigations, and rules on the implementation and duration (normally five years) of countervailing measures. Because subsidies may play an important role in developing countries and in the transformation of centrally planned economies, least-developed countries and developing countries with less than $1,000 per capita GDP are exempted from disciplines on prohibited export subsidies.

BOX 2.7 BYRD AMENDMENT: UNITED STATES FOUND TO BE IN VIOLATION OF WTO RULES

Usually, moneys collected by countries imposing anti-dumping or countervailing duties are paid into the treasury of the importing country. There is no direct financial incentive or benefit for individual complainants. The Byrd Amendment (the *Continued Dumping and Subsidy Offset Act*), passed by Congress in 2000, directs the US government to pay the anti-dumping and countervailing duties collected to companies that have brought forward the cases in the first place. Eleven members of the WTO including the European Union, China, and Canada brought a complaint to the WTO.

In 2002, a WTO panel found that the provision was incompatible with WTO rules and recommended that the United States repeal it. This decision was confirmed by the WTO Appellate Body in 2003. The United States was then given 11 months by a WTO arbitrator to bring its legislation into compliance. This period expired on December 27, 2003. At the end of 2005, finally responding to pressure from WTO member countries and concerns within the United States about the legality of the provision, the United States passed a law providing that after October 2007, anti-dumping and countervailing duties would no longer be subject to disbursements under the Byrd Amendment. Thus, the United States has somewhat reluctantly, and very belatedly, responded to the WTO ruling.

SAFEGUARDS

Under WTO rules, a member country may restrict imports of a product temporarily if its domestic industry is injured or threatened with injury caused by a surge in imports. An import surge may be an absolute increase in imports, or it may be a relative increase—that is, an increase in the imports' share of a shrinking market. As is the case with anti-dumping and subsidy actions, industries or companies may request that their government take safeguard action. The agreement sets out requirements for transparency in safeguard investigations by national authorities and provides that such investigations must be open to the public and include a consideration as to whether a safeguard measure would be in the public interest.

The criteria for determining serious injury are established, as is the principle that safeguard measures should be applied only to the extent necessary to prevent or remedy serious injury. While, in principle, safeguard measures should not be targeted at imports from a particular country, the agreement provides for quotas to be allocated among supplying countries. Safeguard measures should not be imposed for more than four years, although this period can be extended up to eight years in some circumstances.

There is also provision for the exporting country to seek compensation through consultations with the importing country; and the importing country may, in some circumstances, be entitled to take equivalent retaliatory action. Developing countries have some protection because the agreement provides that an importing country can apply a safeguard measure to developing country exports only if the developing country is supplying more than 3 percent of the imports of that product, or if developing countries with less than 3 percent collectively account for more than 9 percent of total imports of the product. Governments are required to report each phase of their safeguard investigation and decision making to the WTO Safeguards Committee. When China became a member of the WTO in 2001, it did so under special terms that allow importing countries to impose short-term safeguards on Chinese goods until 2013 if they can show those goods to be causing "material injury" to domestic producers. See box 2.11 relating to the agreements that China has made with the European Union and the United States. These arrangements are made under the "umbrella" of the WTO safeguard provision.

Non-Tariff Barriers

Philosophically, the WTO's only acceptable form of import control is a tariff. Countries, however, often resort to a number of other measures that they may impose that adversely affect trade. These include import licensing; rules for the valuation of goods at customs; pre-shipment inspection requirements; rules of origin requirements; and certain investment measures.

IMPORT LICENSING

The Agreement on Import Licensing Procedures provides that import licensing must be simple, transparent, and predictable. There are guidelines on how governments should assess applications for licences and time limits for handling licensing applications. Governments must publish sufficient information for businesses to know how and why licences are granted. The agreement requires that countries notify the WTO when new import licensing procedures are changed.

VALUATION OF GOODS AT CUSTOMS

This agreement (Agreement on Implementation of Article VII of the GATT, 1994) has as its goal the development of a fair, uniform, and neutral system for the valuation of goods for customs purposes. The system is intended to conform to commercial realities and prohibits the use of arbitrary or fictitious customs values. Detailed valuation rules are prescribed and all member countries are expected to follow them.

PRE-SHIPMENT INSPECTIONS

The Pre-shipment Inspection Agreement places obligations on governments using pre-shipment inspection to implement practices of non-discrimination, transparency, and protection of confidentiality. It further obliges governments to develop specific guidelines for price verification and for avoiding unreasonable delay and conflicts of interest by inspection agencies. The agreement also establishes an independent review procedure to resolve disputes between an exporter and an inspection agency. The practice of employing specialized independent entities to check shipment details such as price, quantity, and quality of goods ordered from overseas is a common one, particularly in developing countries. Used by governments of countries concerned with matters such as capital flight, commercial fraud, and customs duty evasion, they are often necessary to compensate for inadequacies in local customs administration.

RULES OF ORIGIN

The rules of origin are the criteria used to define where a product was made. The Rules of Origin Agreement requires that WTO members ensure that their rules of origin are transparent; that they are administered in a consistent, uniform, impartial, and reasonable manner; and that they do not restrict, distort, or disrupt international trade. The agreement aims for common or harmonized rules of origin among all WTO members.

INVESTMENT MEASURES

The **Agreement on Trade-Related Investment Measures (TRIMS Agreement)** applies to domestic rules for investment measures that discriminate against foreigners and foreign goods. The TRIMS Agreement prohibits investment measures that lead to restrictions in trade quantities—rules that limit a company's imports or set export targets for companies, known as "trade-balancing requirements."

Trade in Agricultural Products: A Unique Challenge

Tariffs on all agricultural products are now bound. Under GATT rules, agricultural products were subject to quotas and import restrictions and as much as 30 percent of world agricultural products were subject to such trade-limiting restrictions. The new WTO rules require that all trade barriers in agriculture be made more transparent by converting quotas and import restrictions to tariffs, which will gradually be reduced. This is often referred to as **tariffication**. The new rules are intended to limit the distortions that characterize world trade in agricultural products. Trade is considered to be

BOX 2.8   TRADE LIBERALIZATION AND THE CANADIAN DAIRY INDUSTRY

Canada protected its dairy industry for many years by using a supply management system—the systematic use of production and border controls to maintain national supplies at a level just sufficient to satisfy projected domestic demand at a target price. The goal of such a system is to stabilize and enhance dairy farm incomes. Milk boards are responsible for allocating production quotas, licensing producers, and establishing producer prices. Fluid-milk production and imports are limited to maintain provincial fluid-milk prices. To maintain the predetermined price, the level of industrial milk production and imports of industrial milk products are restricted, and this was accomplished prior to the WTO, by way of restrictive import quotas.

Because the new WTO rules for agricultural products require tariffs only, these quotas that Canada had imposed on imports of dairy products had to be converted to tariffs (tariffication). These tariff rate quotas are two-tiered tariffs, with a minimum access quantity at a low tariff, and any volume of imports above the minimum access quantity at a high tariff. The high-tariff rates that Canada imposed for imported products such as milk, cheese, butter, ice cream, and skim milk powder ranged from 237 to 351 percent and remain close to these levels. As expected, these new published rates generated considerable press coverage and controversy as it became apparent to the general public that the supply management system achieves its goals by limiting competition in the domestic market. Milk boards continue to exist in Canada and present a difficult political issue because they are important to the dairy industry but inconsistent with the philosophy of free trade in agricultural products.

distorted when prices are higher or lower than usual, and when quantities produced, bought, and sold are also higher or lower than usual—that is, higher or lower than the levels that would usually exist in a competitive market.

Historically, countries' reasons for supporting and protecting their farmers included the desire to ensure that enough food was produced to meet the country's needs; to shield farmers from the effects of weather and wide variations in world prices; and to preserve rural society. Such policies have proved expensive for national governments and have created surpluses leading to export-subsidy wars. Developing countries with less money for agricultural subsidies have suffered disproportionately. While the Agreement on Agriculture in the Uruguay Round represented substantial progress, it was merely a first step toward fair competition and a less-distorted economic sector. Governments are still permitted to support their rural economies, but preferably through policies that cause less distortion to trade. Developing countries do not have to cut their subsidies or lower their tariffs as much as developed countries, and they are given extra time to complete their obligations. Least-developed countries are not required to conform to the new rules. Member countries have agreed to continue negotiations toward reform of this area with policies that are more market oriented but this has been a difficult issue in the Doha Round of negotiations and one on which little real progress has been made.

BOX 2.9   WTO DISPUTE SETTLEMENT BODY RULES AGAINST CANADA IN DAIRY EXPORT CASE

After acceding to the WTO and agreeing to the new rules on agriculture, Canada developed a two-tier pricing policy with the intention of conforming to WTO rules but at the same time protecting Canada's supply management system for the dairy sector. Under this program, farmers accepted a lower price for milk used to make products destined for export markets than for milk sold domestically within Canada. Although under this system, there was no direct subsidy paid to the farmers and Canada did not capture a larger share of the international market, the United States and New Zealand brought a complaint to the WTO Dispute Settlement Body alleging that Canada was unfairly pricing its milk destined for export markets. The WTO panel first ruled against Canada in 1999, stating that the milk pricing program constituted an export subsidy. As a result, Canada changed its milk export pricing program in 2000, bringing it into compliance with WTO rules. In 2002, a subsequent WTO panel ruled that Canada's dairy export practices continue to violate the WTO rules prohibiting export subsidies.

Continued heavy farm subsidization by many wealthy countries, as much as hundreds of billions of dollars per year, has created a glut of worldwide production that undermines global food prices. Some countries have cut farm subsidies only to find that their farmers need emergency support after domestic and global prices decline.

EXPORT SUBSIDIES AND AGRICULTURE

The Agreement on Agriculture also prohibits export subsidies on agricultural products unless the subsidies are specified in a member's list of commitments. An export subsidy is simply a subsidy provided to goods produced in one country and exported to another country.

International Product Standards

Under Article 20 of the GATT, governments may make trade-related rules in order to protect human, animal, or plant life or health provided that such rules are neither discriminatory to imported goods nor disguised protectionist measures. This provision has been preserved in the WTO and there are, in addition, two specific WTO agreements that deal with food safety and animal and plant health and safety and product standards.

THE SANITARY AND PHYTOSANITARY MEASURES AGREEMENT

The Sanitary and Phytosanitary Measures Agreement (SPS Agreement) allows members to take scientifically based measures to protect public health, provided that such measures are based on internationally established guidelines and risk-establishment procedures. Such rules may be applied only to the extent necessary to protect human, animal, or plant life or health and must not arbitrarily or unjustifiably discriminate against imports.

Theoretically, countries may use measures that result in higher standards domestically than internationally, if there is scientific justification, and they can to some extent apply the **precautionary principle**. The precautionary principle is the concept of taking protective action before there is complete scientific proof of risk. This is founded on the idea that protective action should not be delayed simply because full scientific information is not available. In the fields of food safety and plant and animal health protection, the need for taking precautionary actions in the face of scientific uncertainty has long been widely accepted. There may be instances when a sudden outbreak of an animal disease, for example, is suspected of being linked to imports, and trade restrictions must be immediately imposed while further information about the source of the outbreak and its extent are gathered. The discipline of risk assessment, one of the basic obligations of the SPS Agreement, was developed to guide action in the face of incomplete knowledge about risks to health. It focuses on probabilities of hazards occurring, and their probable consequences, because complete knowledge is very rare. Furthermore, it is virtually impossible to scientifically prove the safety of a food or product; rather, scientists seek evidence of any harm. Article 3.3 of the SPS Agreement mandates a precautionary approach that explicitly permits members to adopt SPS measures, which are more stringent than measures based on the relevant international standards. Article 5.7 of the agreement allows members to take provisional measures when sufficient scientific evidence does not exist to permit a final decision on the safety of a product or process. The provisional measure must take into consideration available pertinent information. The member adopting the measure must seek to obtain a more objective assessment of risk, and must review the SPS measure within a reasonable period of time.

The agreement also includes provisions on control, inspection, and approval procedures.

BOX 2.10   THE EUROPEAN UNION'S ATTEMPT TO LIMIT IMPORTS OF HORMONE-TREATED BEEF: AN ONGOING DISPUTE

In response to concerns of EU citizens about the risks presented by beef injected with natural and synthetic growth hormones, the European Union imposed a ban on the import of such beef. The United States challenged the restriction under the SPS Agreement and in 1998 the ban was found by a WTO panel and the Appellate body not to be based on a risk assessment that followed scientific principles and procedures. The case raised difficult issues and required a consideration of the uncertainty presented by divisions of scientific opinion. A further difficulty in the case was the fact that much of the European concern related to situations where hormones were used in contravention of sound veterinary practice, but the risk assessment did not deal specifically enough with those risks and hence was found not to conform to the SPS Agreement. Significantly, the European Union did not invoke Article 5.7 in its defence, because the import ban was not a provisional measure. The European Union has been unwilling to remove its restrictions on the import of the hormone-treated beef, with the result that the WTO in 1999 authorized the United States and Canada to collect penalties of more than $100 million per year in extra duties on European exports. The European Union brought the issue back to the WTO where unprecedented open hearings were held in 2005. The EU argued that fresh scientific evidence showed that the European Union has complied with the 1998 WTO judgment. In January 2006, the panel hearing the case advised that due to the complexities of the issue, it would not be able to complete its work within the usual time frame. To date, there has been no report from the panel.

TECHNICAL REGULATIONS AND STANDARDS

The Technical Barriers to Trade (TBT) Agreement was negotiated in the Uruguay Round to ensure that domestic technical regulations and product standards did not interfere substantially with international trade. The agreement sets out a code of good practice for the preparation, adoption, and application of standards by governments and government bodies. Procedures used to decide whether a product conforms with national standards must be fair and equitable, and methods that give domestically produced goods an unfair advantage are not acceptable.

Countries must establish inquiry points and national notification authorities to answer questions about product regulation rules.

Trade in Textiles

Trade in textiles was a difficult issue for the GATT and also for the WTO. The Multifibre Arrangement (MFA) was negotiated in 1974 under GATT auspices at a time when the developed countries were confronted with a rapid increase in exports of textile products from low-wage and developing countries. Ostensibly established to expand and liberalize trade in textiles and provide for orderly growth patterns in the industry, the arrangement was actually for the purpose of protecting the textile industries and consequently jobs in the textile industries of the developed countries. The MFA provided a framework whereby textile-importing countries negotiated bilaterally with textile-exporting countries to establish quotas on a product-by-product basis. This arrangement conflicted with two important GATT principles— the MFN principle and the principle of preference for tariffs over quantitative restrictions (quotas). As well, it went against the articulated intention of giving preferential treatment to help developing countries participate fully in international trade opportunities. At the end of the Uruguay Round, the MFA was replaced with the WTO's Agreement on Textiles and Clothing (ATC). This agreement replicated much of the philosophy and trading restrictions of the MFA but expired on January 1, 2005, at which time quotas were supposed to end and textiles were to be fully subject to usual WTO rules.

WTO Rules Relating to Trade in Services

The General Agreement on Trade in Services (GATS) was negotiated at the Uruguay Round in response to the exponential growth of the service economy in the years after the establishment of the GATT. The communications and technology revolution necessitated a set of multilateral rules to govern this rapidly expanding sector of the global economy. There were and still are daunting challenges in developing rules to govern this area, because

BOX 2.11   THE EUROPEAN UNION AND THE UNITED STATES FIND IT DIFFICULT TO ADAPT TO NEW TEXTILE TRADE RULES

With the expiration of the textile quotas at the beginning of 2005, powerful textile lobbies in Europe and the United States have been frantically lobbying for legislative action to stop the flood of cheap Chinese apparel from swamping their businesses. The low-tech, low-skill textile industry has been losing jobs to the developing world for some time. For example, it is estimated that France has lost about one-third of its jobs in the textile sector between 1993 and 2003. Both the European Union and the United States have negotiated agreements under which China agreed to new quotas on a number of categories of textile goods. These agreements run until 2007 and are said to be for the purpose of giving domestic manufacturers in the European Union and the United States time to adjust to a world of unfettered competition. The reason China has had to agree to these quotas in spite of the expiration of the ATC is that when it joined the WTO, it agreed on separate measures for textiles and allowed safeguards to be imposed whenever imports threaten "market disruptions." It is notable that this was the reason given for the original MFA in 1974.

In 2005, the retailers of Europe and the United States had placed a significant volume of orders for textile goods from China only to watch helplessly as these goods were tied up for months in warehouses and customs checkpoints. The resulting shortages of these goods produced anger among consumers and merchants, and increased awareness on the part of the general public as to the impact of trade agreements on daily life. Textile imports to the United States from China were said to have increased by 97 percent in the first half of 2005.

Source: *The Economist*, September 1, 2005.

trade in services is much more complicated and varied than is trade in goods. For example, the border, so significant in the trade in goods, plays very little part in the trade in services. A major challenge has been to understand how services are traded, what services can be regulated, and how best to regulate them. There were few precedents to build on. The GATT itself was of limited help. For this reason, the resulting GATS is merely a first step and *simply begins a process of negotiations*. Negotiators began by agreeing that the GATS would cover all internationally traded services, including, for example, banking, telecommunications, tourism, and professional services. It is Canada's policy to provide open access to its markets in exchange for greater access to foreign markets for its services. Canada has proposed improved market access in the following service sectors:

- accounting, engineering, and legal services;
- financial services;
- courier services;
- tourism;
- transport; and
- the temporary movement of business people.

BOX 2.12 MAY 2005—CANADA PARTICIPATES IN WTO SERVICES NEGOTIATIONS

As was stated above, the GATS really just began a process of negotiations on trade in services. As a growing exporter of services, particularly in the financial, professional, environmental, and energy sectors, Canada sees an opportunity to bring better-paying jobs to Canada while providing greater choice and lower costs to consumers. In addition, its trade officials see opportunities for Canadian businesses in the emerging economic powerhouses of China, India, and Brazil. For these reasons, Canada has proposed to liberalize its trade rules to

- facilitate the temporary entry of intra-corporate transferees;
- remove limits on the number of senior computer specialists permitted to enter Canada to work on specific projects;
- modify requirements for professional qualifications and provide for more liberal residency requirements;
- remove some restrictions on cross-border transportation providers;
- remove residency requirements for trading in securities and commodities futures;
- remove the requirement that certain insurance services be provided by public monopoly;
- modify the rules that require only one form of establishment for foreign suppliers of banking services;
- modify the rules pertaining to direct ownership and the control requirements for foreign-owned subsidiaries;
- remove some exemptions favouring the United Kingdom, Ireland, and the United States; and
- improve the ability of businesses to establish a commercial presence in Canada by removing the requirement of residency for corporate boards, and allowing foreign service suppliers to acquire land in certain provinces.

The Canadian proposals do not include commitments on health, public education, social, or cultural services, and the offer is considered legally binding only if the Canadian government is satisfied with the overall level of trade liberalization achieved at the end of negotiations.

Different Types or "Modes" of Trade in Services

Four ways of trading services are recognized by the WTO negotiators:

- cross-border supply of services—for example, international telephone calls;
- consumption abroad—for example, tourism;
- commercial presence—for example, a foreign company setting up subsidiaries or branches to provide services in another country; and
- presence of natural persons to supply services in another country— for example, consultants.

Most-Favoured-Nation Rule Applies to Services

Once a country allows foreign competition in a sector, equal opportunities in that sector are given to service providers from all other WTO members. At the time that the GATS was negotiated, a number of countries that already had preferential agreements in services with specific trading partners, either bilaterally or in regional groups, were allowed to extend that more favourable treatment by listing them as most-favoured-nation exemptions.

National Treatment Rule Applies to Services

The right of market access to provide services is not automatically extended by all countries to all other member countries. Market access to individual countries is available only after negotiations. As a result of these negotiations, a country's commitment appears in schedules that list the sectors being opened and the extent of market access being given in each sector. Governments may limit the extent of market access by, for example, imposing restrictions on foreign ownership in certain sectors. Once these commitments of market are made, however, the country is bound by them, just as it is bound by the tariff concessions it has agreed to make with respect to trade in goods.

Government Services and GATS Commitments

Government services are explicitly excluded from the GATS agreement and there is no clear intention to force a government to privatize its service industries. Government services are defined in the GATS as "those that are not supplied commercially and do not compete with other suppliers." Such services are not subject to any GATS discipline and are not meant to be covered by the negotiations and commitments on market access and national treatment. While the GATS does not require any service to be deregulated, once there is deregulation and foreign suppliers are present, they are entitled to function under the same regulations as those that apply to nationals.

Governments retain their right to set qualification requirements for professionals and to set standards to ensure consumer health and safety. Consistent with WTO philosophy, these qualifications and standards must not be discriminatory, and once foreign qualifications are recognized from one country, other member countries must also be given a chance to negotiate comparable agreements.

BOX 2.13   GATS AND HEALTH AND EDUCATION SERVICES IN CANADA

There is under the GATS a "standstill rule" that stipulates that once a country has made a commitment to the GATS, it cannot introduce new restrictions on foreign service providers without giving some form of compensation to the countries affected by such protectionist measures.

Thus, there is nothing in the GATS rules that requires that health and education services be privatized or liberalized, but once a domestic government makes a decision to privatize these lucrative services, subsequent governments are likely to be bound by that decision to the extent that it may be difficult to reverse the policy of the previous government without significant difficulty and expense.

Requirement for Transparency

Governments are required to publish all relevant laws and regulations for services and set up inquiry points within their bureaucracies for foreign companies and governments. This requirement includes the obligation to notify the WTO of any changes in regulations that apply to services that fall under specific commitments. It is important to note that the GATS does not require any service to be deregulated, and governments maintain their right to set levels of quality, safety, and price and to pursue their own policy objectives, provided that the overall rules are adhered to.

Protection of Intellectual Property

Intellectual property has been defined by the World Intellectual Property Organization as "creations of the mind" and can be divided into two categories: industrial property, which includes patents, trademarks, industrial designs, and geographic indications of source; and copyright, which includes literary and artistic works, including artists' performances, phonogram recordings, and radio and television content. Intellectual property was brought into the realm of WTO rules for the first time with the negotiation of the **Agreement on Trade-Related Aspects of Intellectual Property Rights (TRIPS Agreement)**. As part of the Uruguay Round negotiations, this agreement represents a significant step in international protection of intellectual property rights. The extent of intellectual property protection and enforcement of intellectual property rights had varied significantly from country to country. As this form of property gained in significance, there was considerable uncertainty as to its protection, which was a deterrent to trade in a number of areas, in a number of countries. The TRIPS Agreement attempts to bring protection of intellectual property under common international rules. It was negotiated because of pressure primarily from developed countries—notably the United States and those of the European Union, and these new rules are not without controversy, as will be discussed in chapter 9. The agreement establishes member countries' obligations to provide minimum levels of protection for copyright, trademarks, geographical indications, industrial designs, patents, integrated circuit topographies (computer chips), and trade secrets.

The Basic Principles of Intellectual Property Protection

Two WTO non-discrimination rules apply to intellectual property (IP) protection: national treatment and most-favoured-nation treatment. WTO members agreed that IP protection should ensure that producers and users benefit from technological innovation and technology transfer for the betterment of economic and social welfare. Signatory countries agreed that the starting point for IP protection would be the existing main international agreements established by the **World Intellectual Property Organization (WIPO)**:

- the Paris Convention for the Protection of Industrial Property (patents, industrial designs, etc.); and
- the Berne Convention for the Protection of Literary and Artistic Works (copyright).

The various forms of intellectual property and their protection will be discussed in chapter 9. The TRIPS Agreement adds a significant number of new or higher standards to these pre-existing agreements.

Plurilateral Agreements

Two agreements have a smaller number of signatories than the other WTO agreements but are still significant to international trade. These are the Agreement on Trade in Civil Aircraft and the Agreement on Government Procurement.

The Agreement on Trade in Civil Aircraft
This agreement has about 30 signatories and came into force in 1980. The agreement eliminates import duties on all civil aircraft, their engines, parts, and components, and flight simulators and their parts and components, and imposes rules on purchases of civil aircraft, inducements to purchase, and government financial support for the civil aircraft sector. The agreement does not apply to military aircraft.

The Agreement on Government Procurement
This agreement has about 30 signatories and came into force in 1981. Recognizing the fact that political pressure on governments to favour domestic suppliers over their foreign competitors is very strong, it is designed to open up as much business as possible to international competition. The agreement reinforces rules guaranteeing fair and non-discriminatory conditions of international competition and provides for transparency in laws, regulations, procedures, and practices regarding government procurement and prescribes rules against discrimination against foreign products or suppliers. As of 1996, the agreement also applies to procurement of services and procurement at the sub-central level (states, provinces, departments, and prefectures). The agreement applies only to contracts over specified threshold values.

ENSURING TRANSPARENCY: TRADE POLICY REVIEWS

To ensure that trade regulations and policies are transparent, WTO member governments have to inform the WTO of specific measures, policies, or laws through regular notifications, and the WTO, through the Trade Policy Review Body, conducts regular reviews of each country's trade policies. These reviews cover trade in goods, services, and intellectual property. The Trade Policy Review Body is actually the WTO General Council performing a trade policy monitoring function. The reviews, called "peer reviews" because they are carried out by other WTO members, take into account member countries' wider economic and developmental needs, their policies and objectives, and the external economic environment. All WTO members come under scrutiny, but the frequency of reviews depends on the country's size. The four biggest traders at present—the European Union, the United States, Japan, and Canada (referred to as "the Quad")—are examined approximately once every two years; the next 16 countries in terms of their share of world trade are reviewed every four years; and the remaining countries are reviewed every six years, with the possibility of less frequent reviews for the least-developed countries. The reports, including the policy statement by the government under review and the report written by the WTO Secretariat, are published on the WTO website.

DISPUTE SETTLEMENT IN THE WTO

It is the dispute settlement aspect of the WTO's functions that is most in the public eye and is most criticized in the media. Many observers allege that WTO decisions are narrow and not in the best interests of the world at large. However, these crticisms are not merited, because the WTO dispute settlement system is simply a system for settling disputes about existing rules. It is not a rule-making body; it is not empowered to make any new rules; it may simply apply the existing rules to a given set of facts. The WTO lacks any open, transparent process for making rules, with the result that an expectation has developed that the dispute settlement system will serve this function. This is no more appropriate than expecting our domestic courts to make new law governing the many aspects of a complex society. This is the mandate of our elected representatives. The dispute settlement system has as its primary goal the positive resolution of the dispute at hand; it cannot be a substitute for an effective system for making new rules that the WTO presently lacks.

Principles and Priorities

Although there existed a procedure for settling disputes under the GATT, there was no fixed settlement timetable, and rulings were easy to block. As a result, many cases dragged on for a number of years and produced no conclusive results. After the Uruguay Round, a more structured dispute settlement process was adopted with clearly defined stages. With the addition of much stricter timelines, it is now impossible for the country losing a case to block the adoption of the ruling, because the old rule for adoption by consensus was eliminated. Instead, the rule is now the reverse. Rulings are now automatically adopted unless there is a consensus to reject a ruling, known as a "reverse consensus." This means that decisions will be adopted unless every member of the dispute settlement body, including the nation that has won the dispute, votes against its adoption.

The stated priority of the WTO dispute settlement system is to settle disputes, not to pass judgment. The only direction that comes from the WTO as a result of a dispute is a direction that the losing member take action to bring its laws or policies into conformity with WTO agreements. The preferred solution is that the countries concerned discuss their problems and settle the dispute by consultation. Thus, the first stage in any dispute is consultation between the governments concerned, and even when a case progresses to later stages, consultation and mediation remain available to the parties.

The Dispute Settlement Body

Disputes usually arise when one country adopts a trade policy measure or takes some other action that is considered by one or more of its fellow member countries to be a breach of WTO obligations. The settlement of these disputes is the responsibility of the **Dispute Settlement Body (DSB)**, which is really the General Council of the WTO (all WTO members) sitting in a different capacity. The DSB has significant authority, which includes:

- establishing panels of experts to hear a case;
- accepting or rejecting panel or appeal decisions;
- monitoring the implementation of rulings and recommendations of panels and appeal bodies; and
- authorizing retaliation if a country does not comply with a ruling.

Box 2.14 illustrates the key stages in the resolution of a WTO dispute.

The Panels

Panels are made up of three and possibly five experts from different member countries. A panel's function is to apply the evidence presented by the affected countries to the appropriate WTO rules and to decide whether there has been a breach of a WTO obligation. The panelists are usually chosen in consultation with the disputing countries from a permanent list of well-qualified candidates from various countries. If the disputing countries cannot agree on the composition of the panel, the WTO director general will appoint the panelists. The panelists serve independently in their individual capacities and cannot receive instructions from any government. The panel's report is passed to the DSB, which may only reject the report if there is a consensus among all members to do so.

The Appellate Body

Either side may appeal a panel's ruling. Appeals are heard by three members of the permanent seven-member Appellate Body. These individuals must have recognized standing in the field of law and international trade and may not be affiliated with any government. They represent the range of WTO membership and are appointed for a four-year term. The Appellate Body review is limited to issues of law covered in the panel report and to legal interpretations developed by the panel. The Appellate Body may not re-examine existing evidence or examine new issues. The appeal can uphold, modify, or reverse a panel's legal findings and conclusions. Decisions

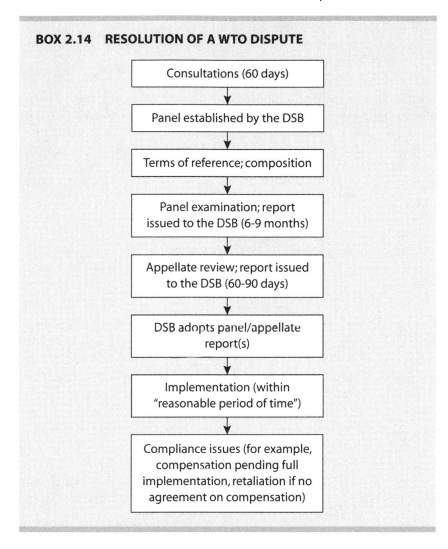

BOX 2.14   RESOLUTION OF A WTO DISPUTE

Consultations (60 days)

↓

Panel established by the DSB

↓

Terms of reference; composition

↓

Panel examination; report issued to the DSB (6-9 months)

↓

Appellate review; report issued to the DSB (60-90 days)

↓

DSB adopts panel/appellate report(s)

↓

Implementation (within "reasonable period of time")

↓

Compliance issues (for example, compensation pending full implementation, retaliation if no agreement on compensation)

are to be made within 90 days. The DSB then has 30 days to accept or reject the appeal decision, and, as with a panel decision, rejection is possible only by consensus, as described above.

Compliance with Rulings and Sanctions

The compliance phase of WTO dispute settlement does not always produce a timely and effective implementation of adopted rulings. There are two main reasons for this. The first reason is that the deadlines for implementation or imposition of sanctions are often extended well beyond the strict timetable that governs the earlier stages of WTO disputes. The second and more important reason is that disputing governments are free to reach settlements that are contrary to WTO rules, even after a legally binding Appellate Body report has been adopted.

There are additional factors that contribute to delay and uncertainty. The procedural details of compliance reviews are not well articulated in the dispute settlement rules, and panel and Appellate Body decisions are not specific about how compliance should be achieved. Theoretically, if a country has been found to be in violation of a WTO agreement, it should remedy the default as soon as possible, and that should bring its policy into conformity with the ruling or recommendation. In practice, matters are not so simple. Compliance involves not only law, but also international politics. Because of the delicate balance between individual country sovereignty on one hand, and the supra-national legal obligations under a multilateral agreement on the other, considerable leeway is allowed. We have already seen that this is the case, as illustrated in the Byrd Amendment case, above in box 2.7.

If the country is not able to bring its policy into compliance in the short term, it may be given a "reasonable period of time" to do so. If it fails to act, it must enter into negotiations with the complaining country or countries in order to determine mutually acceptable compensation. If no satisfactory compensation is agreed on, the complaining countries may ask the DSB for permission to impose limited trade sanctions against the offending country. Sanctions are supposed to be imposed in the same sector as the dispute. This is not always practical or effective. This compliance phase of dispute settlement may be lengthy and is also largely beyond the control of the WTO. Losing defendants have often exceeded the prescribed "reasonable" period of time to comply with rulings. Although governments have largely tended to comply with adopted rulings, agreements are often made by disputing governments that do not comply with the Appellate Body's ruling or honour the time limits. This prevalence of such bargaining between "litigants" after apparently "binding" rulings highlights the fact that the dispute settlement system is not a complete legal system such as one would find in the domestic courts of individual countries yet it is an important source of flexibility in the WTO system and may lead to satisfactory settlements for both parties.

It has been said that the United States and the European Union are the "twin titans" of international trade. Each has a large stake in the success of the WTO. Thus, the success of the dispute settlement system depends at least in part on their support. Some observers believe that the Appellate Body has altered the reasoning of a number of panels, often interpreting WTO rules in a manner that is deferential to powerful defendants, but always using legal principles rather than openly bowing to political pressures. It is possible that, at present, a cooperative equilibrium has been reached between the European Union, the United States, and the Dispute Settlement Body. Two particularly difficult cases (each with a long history beginning in the GATT) illustrate the behaviour of the two trading giants (see boxes 2.15 and 2.16).

BOX 2.15   THE EU BANANAS CASE

The United States and several Latin American countries challenged the EU's banana import regime, which favoured bananas from former European colonies and from developing countries with special access to the EU market under the Lome Convention. As early as 1994, a GATT panel issued a ruling that the European Union was in violation of multilateral trade rules, but, as was then possible, the European Union blocked adoption of the ruling.

A US-based corporation, Chiquita, whose Latin American operations were adversely affected, lobbied the Clinton administration and Congress to pursue the case with the result that the United States, Ecuador, Guatemala, Honduras, and Mexico requested a WTO panel in 1996. They alleged that the European Union had engaged in multiple violations of WTO obligations, but principally the MFN rule. Both the panel and the Appellate Body found in favour of the complainants. The aftermath of these decisions was acrimonious, with the United States and Ecuador moving aggressively to impose sanctions on the European Union and rejecting repeated alterations of the EU banana regime as inadequate. There were arguments about the proper sequencing of WTO compliance reviews and sanctions. Finally in April 2001, the United States reached a settlement with the European Union whereby a tariff-only regime would be gradually adopted by the European Union by 2006, more than eight years after the original rulings of WTO violations were made.

BOX 2.16   THE US FOREIGN SALES CORPORATIONS CASE

This controversy arose partly because the United States taxes its corporations on their worldwide income, whereas many European countries tax only corporate income earned within their borders. As compensation, the United States has passed various legislative measures over the years providing for a lower tax rate on export income earned by qualifying offshore corporations, known as **foreign sales corporations (FSCs)**. FSCs are essentially shell companies established in tax havens such as the Bahamas and the Cayman Islands through which export transactions are routed to obtain sizable tax breaks. The WTO first ruled against such US legislation in early 2000, stating that the FSCs constituted an illegal trading subsidy. The WTO also ruled against the US replacement legislation, the *Extraterritorial Income Exclusion Act*, in 2002. The European Union then prepared a list of US products on which it proposed to apply sanctions in the form of countervailing duties and obtained the WTO's permission to implement these in early 2004. In late 2004, the United States passed the *American Jobs Creation Act of 2004*. Although the European Union was not entirely satisfied with the US legislative response, and had asked the WTO to examine the grandfather clauses of the newly signed bill, the European Union lifted its retaliatory tariffs affecting about $4 billion worth of American exports on January 1, 2005.

REVIEW QUESTIONS

1. Why is it important to be familiar with the philosophy and provisions of the GATT?
2. Do the GATT and WTO require countries to engage in freer trade? Explain your answer.
3. Describe the three fundamental rules developed by the GATT and incorporated into the WTO.
4. What was the significance of the Uruguay Round? The Marrakesh Agreement?
5. Why is it necessary for countries to pass domestic legislation before they can ratify WTO agreements?
6. What is the significance of China's entry into the WTO for China itself, for other trading nations, and for the WTO?
7. What is meant by a "bound tariff"?
8. What is dumping? Is it illegal per se under the WTO? What may member countries do if products are dumped into their domestic market?
9. What is a subsidy? Is it illegal per se under the WTO? What may member countries entitled to do if products that are subsidized enter their domestic markets?
10. How do the WTO provisions on safeguards differ from those on dumping and subsidies?
11. What are some of the factors that make governing trade in agricultural services so difficult for developed and lesser-developed countries?
12. What is the Sanitary and Phytosanitary Measures Agreement (SPS Agreement)? What is its significance for global business persons?
13. What is the Technical Barriers to Trade (TBT) Agreement and what is its significance for global business persons?
14. Do we have global free trade in textile products? Explain.

15. Why is agreement in trade in services so difficult? How are the rules different from the rules governing trade in goods?

16. What are some of the issues with respect to government services? What is the rule with respect to services now provided by governments?

17. Describe the major areas of intellectual property protected by the TRIPS Agreement.

CLASS ACTIVITIES

There are many decided WTO cases that raise interesting examples of the principles discussed in this chapter. These cases may be accessed through the WTO website (see below). Choose one or more of these cases. Identify what the legal issue is in the case. Do you agree with the decision of the WTO in the case? Have a debate in class, with several students presenting the arguments for each side.

FURTHER READING

Jones, Kent. (2005). *Who's Afraid of the WTO?* Oxford: Oxford University Press.

Gallagher, Peter, Low, Patrick, and Stoler, Andrew L. (Eds.). (2005). *Managing the Challenges of WTO Participation: 45 Case Studies.* Cambridge, UK: Cambridge University Press.

WEBSITES

General websites with current international law information:

British Broadcasting Corporation (BBC):
http://news.bbc.co.uk

Canadian Broadcasting Corporation (CBC):
www.cbc.ca

The Economist:
www.economist.com

Canadian Council on International Law:
www.ccil-ccdi.ca

Foreign Affairs and International Trade Canada:
www.dfait-maeci.gc.ca

International Chamber of Commerce:
www.iccwbo.org

G8 and G20:

>   The best way to find up-to-date information on these organizations is to do an Internet search, because the responsibility to host the website is passed to a different host country each year

International Monetary Fund:

>   www.imf.org

Legal Information Institute:

>   The Institute is a global organization for the dissemination of international law information. Many countries have individual websites for this. The three best for Canadians are:
>   www.canlii.org
>   www.law.cornell.edu
>   www.worldlii.org

Organisation for Economic Co-operation and Development (OECD):

>   www.oecd.org

United Nations:

>   www.un.org

United Nations Millennium Project:

>   www.unmilleniumproject.org

United Nations Commission on International Trade Law (UNCITRAL):

>   www.uncitral.org

United Nations Conference on Trade and Development (UNCTAD):

>   www.unctad.org

World Bank:

>   www.worldbank.org

World Intellectual Property Organization (WIPO):

>   www.wipo.org

World Trade Organization:

>   www.wto.org

Estey Centre Journal of International Law and Trade Policy:

>   www.esteyjournal.com
>   (recommended for peer-reviewed articles on international law and trade policy)

CHAPTER 3

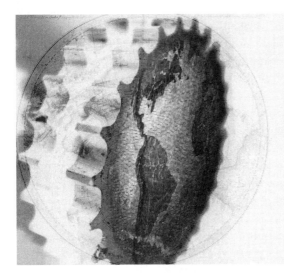

Current and Emerging Challenges in the Global Regulatory Environment

INTRODUCTION

This chapter examines several seemingly unconnected topics. What these topics do have in common is that each of them represents an area of significant challenge to business in today's globalized economy.

It is no accident that this chapter follows the chapters in which we examined the role, and to some extent the rules, of international organizations such as the United Nations (UN), the World Bank, the International Monetary Fund (IMF), and the World Trade Organization (WTO). We are now in a position to understand the limitations of the power and authority of these organizations and to assess some of the realities of the global business environment in that light.

LEARNING OBJECTIVES

After reading this chapter you will understand:

- the ways in which the global community acts collectively

- the increasing role of NGOs and businesses in international negotiations and processes

- the role of the UN in protecting the natural environment; the history and characteristics of the Kyoto Protocol; other multilateral agreements to protect the environment; and the role of the WTO and its impact on the environment

- the difference between product standards and process standards under WTO rules

- the interface between international trade and the protection of workers

- the issue of bribery and corruption in international business and measures taken to minimize it

There is a growing awareness of ethical and moral issues in business and a growing realization that these issues have the potential to affect not only society at large, but also the corporation's bottom line. We have witnessed the rise of the so-called **global civil society**—manifested by public demonstrations, by the increasing awareness of consumers of their ability to shape the world, and by the ever-increasing numbers of **non-governmental organizations** (NGOs) and their success in influencing multilateral negotiations.

The business sector is also increasingly influential in shaping global governance, and its potential role in international law making should not be underestimated. Some commentators have suggested replacing the common reference to NGO with the term "civil society," which would include NGOs and the business sector. As we review some of the topics in this chapter, it will become apparent how much both NGOs and the business sector have contributed to the creation of international norms and to multilateral regulation.

Corporate social responsibility at the national level as well as the supra-national level is much discussed in the media. Although the term may mean different things to different constituencies, it is generally accepted to include such values as environmental stewardship; **triple bottom-line reporting**; community involvement; contribution to the community; transparency; and accountability. An important question is: who regulates these matters—that is, who participates in the rule making and who enforces these rules? The answer varies depending on what area of shared responsibility or concern is being addressed.

Traditionally, the international law system regulated the relations between sovereign states. Non-state actors were simply not recognized as participants. With the rise of globalization and consequent transborder issues, this system has become outdated and inadequate. Although non-governmental actors cannot replace states with respect to many functions, they have an important role in providing ideas, information, pressure for results, and the necessary support for the development of regulations and codes of accepted conduct in the emerging areas of concern to international business. Governments acting alone may lack sufficient legitimacy in the global arena, because legitimacy is based on public trust, and public trust requires some consensus across borders as to how the costs and benefits of globalization should be managed. The idea of the nation state acting solely in its own domestic interests as the sole determinant of the global order is no longer appropriate to address today's issues.

The Growth and Significance of NGOs

Non-governmental organizations have become increasingly influential in international negotiations and processes. NGOs are often instrumental in initiating international action, influencing the negotiation of treaties and other legal instruments, and helping to monitor state compliance with international norms. Although they seldom have official status and the level of their participation may be controlled by states or international organizations on a case-by-case basis, NGOs can have a significant influence on the norm-creating process by providing specific expertise and by exercising their political power. They are able to make their knowledge and resources available to government officials and intergovernmental organizations, advocating, promoting, and even initiating multilateral conventions. They may also help to correct mistakes by pointing out errors or inconsistencies in proposals for new agreements. NGOs employ various methods of lobbying, from issuing communiqués, to participating in corridor conversations directly with international decision makers, as well as raising awareness in the general public. The media play an important role in disseminating the views of NGOs and, of course, the Internet has proved a boon to NGOs as we witnessed in the events surrounding the collapse of the Multilateral Investment Talks in 1998 (discussed in chapter 10).

NGO involvement in the regulatory system does not necessarily cease once a treaty or convention is agreed on and signed. The NGO may continue its work by lobbying home governments to ratify the treaty and may be involved in the monitoring and enforcing of state obligations, whether by "shaming" parties into compliance, acting as watchdogs, or acting as intervenors in national courts. While it has been suggested that the input of NGOs on the international scene is comparable to public participation in domestic democracies, this analogy is flawed, because NGOs are not necessarily representative of the population at large—even in one state, much less for the global public at large; and, as critics are eager to point out, they are not democratic organizations themselves.

This uncertainty as to the role of NGOs is underscored by the fact that there is not even an agreed-upon definition of an NGO. There is no definition of NGO in the UN Charter, although the UN Economic and Social Council stated in 1996 that an NGO is an organization that is not established by a governmental entity or an intergovernmental agreement. The idea that an NGO must be a non-profit entity is widely accepted, but the requirement is notably absent from the Economic and Social Council's statement and from other multilateral organizations' definitions, such as that of the Organization for American States (OAS).

The International Chamber of Commerce
There are many examples of NGOs that are active in areas of concern to international business. One of the foremost of these NGOs is the International Chamber of Commerce (ICC)—a global business organization that

advocates on behalf of international business. The ICC's activities cover a wide range of issues that include providing arbitration and dispute resolution; advocating for open trade and the market economy system; promoting business self-regulation; and fighting corruption and commercial crime. Its notable achievements include the development of uniform international rules and standards that companies adopt voluntarily and incorporate into their dealings and contracts. Important examples include:

- the ICC Arbitration Rules and the establishment of the ICC International Court of Arbitration;
- the Uniform Customs and Practice for Documentary Credits (UCP 500) —the rules that banks use to finance international trade transactions;
- the incoterms—the standard international trade definitions widely adopted for international sales contracts;
- codes on the self-regulation of e-commerce, advertising and marketing, sponsoring and advertising practice, sales promotion, marketing and social research, direct sales practice, and marketing on the Internet; and
- the ICC Business Charter for Sustainable Development.

Regulation of Transnational Corporations

A series of major environmental disasters in the 1980s, including the toxic chemical leak in Bhopal, India in 1984 and the oil spill from the Exxon Valdez in 1989, generated interest in the need for international codes of conduct to monitor the working activities of **transnational corporations (TNCs)**. What emerged in practice was essentially industry self-regulation. In the 1990s, in keeping with the popularity of the "free market" philosophy, voluntary initiatives and corporate self-regulation gathered momentum and a number of voluntary codes of conduct were agreed upon by organizations representing TNCs. In the early 1990s, most guidelines focused on providing benchmarks and advice on improving corporate environmental conduct and establishing sustainable business practices and frameworks. Later, the concern of civil society turned to sweatshop abuses and labour violations. By the turn of the 21st century, there were increased calls for "corporate accountability" and stronger regulation of TNCs. Some of the more notable initiatives of this period and their dates are given below:

- 1989—the formation of the Coalition for Environmentally Responsible Economies (CERES), which provides a 10-point code of corporate environmental conduct (the Ceres Principles).
- 1991—the creation of the ICC Business Charter for Sustainable Development, which sets out 16 principles for environmental management.

- 1992—the formation of the US Business Council for Sustainable Development (BCSD), which declared a voluntary plan of action that emphasizes sustainable development objectives consistent with economic growth.
- 2000—the passage of the World Diamond Council Resolution on "conflict diamonds," which outlines a system to track trade in diamonds for illicit purposes such as war and inhumane acts.

INTERNATIONAL TRADE AND THE ENVIRONMENT

The Natural Environment: Who Protects and Regulates It?

Achieving the protection and regulation of the natural environment is difficult because what must be protected is not only the environment in individual countries or states, but also the **global commons**—that is, the environment outside the territory of individual countries, such as the oceans and the atmosphere. Pollutants, storms, and climate change do not respect international boundaries, so the traditional concept of sovereign states making rules that affect their own territory does not serve today's world. When the global environment is threatened, distinctions between domestic, foreign, and international rule making are counterproductive, because all countries have an interest in ensuring that the global commons, and indeed the environment of every country, is preserved and protected. In the absence of an established, international law-making body, and an effective enforcement system, and in light of the surviving and tenaciously retained sovereignty of individual countries, it is difficult to protect the global commons within the confines of an international system that is based on state sovereignty and individual country regulation.

The question of which international institution should take the lead on environmental issues is a difficult one to answer. The UN has no direct mandate to do this, although many of its agencies have exercised leadership in the area and have sponsored many international conventions. The WTO is sometimes looked to because it has widespread membership and it has the most effective dispute settlement mechanism of any multilateral organization. There is however, the legitimate objection that when environmental concerns come before the WTO, they are interpreted through the trade-oriented rules of that organization, and environmental concerns are therefore subordinated to the economic and trade interests that the WTO is designed to serve. For this reason, many environmentalists advocate that environmental rules be dealt with by a forum other than the WTO. In addition to the question as to which international organization should be responsible for the environment is the question that haunts international regulators in any area: is it possible to create legally binding international rules?

The United Nations Framework Convention on Climate Change

The **United Nations Framework Convention on Climate Change** (**UNFCCC** or "Climate Change Convention") was opened for signature at the groundbreaking UN Conference on the Environment and Development held in Rio de Janeiro in 1992, and was entered into force with the requisite number of signatures in March 1994. The UNFCCC established a process for responding to climate change and set up a system whereby governments report information on their national greenhouse gas emissions and their strategies to mitigate climate change. Developed countries agreed to promote the transfer of funding and technology to help developing countries respond to climate change. It is interesting to note that NGOs and various business entities had a significant influence on these negotiations and on the process that led to the Kyoto Protocol.

The Kyoto Protocol

The Kyoto Protocol—an addendum to the Climate Change Convention—was agreed to in Japan in 1997. The Protocol commits rich countries to cuts in emissions of greenhouse gases by 2012, using 1990 as a baseline. The Protocol was intended to make a start in achieving the goals set out in the UNFCCC and to serve as a precedent for later agreements that would impose deeper cuts and bring in developing countries. Significantly, the United States signed and ratified the Climate Change Convention, but not the subsequent Kyoto Protocol, which requires that signatories take action to prevent climate change as opposed to simply agreeing that climate change is a problem. As we learned in chapter 1, because of the absence of US support, there was considerable doubt for some time as to whether the Kyoto Protocol would come into force. However, when Russia agreed to become a party to it in 2004, the agreement was saved. (The agreement had to be signed by not less than 55 parties to the UNFCCC, including parties that accounted, in total, for at least 55 percent of global carbon dioxide emissions for 1990. Unfortunately, large emitters such as the United States, China, and India are not participating at this time.)

The Kyoto Protocol was never intended to solve the problem of climate change by the end of the first commitment period in 2012. Rather, it envisaged a long-term process comprising five-year commitment periods.

There are five main features to the Kyoto Protocol: legally binding commitments by developed countries; market-based mechanisms to help states meet their commitments; special consideration for developing countries; monitoring procedures; and compliance and dispute resolution.

LEGALLY BINDING COMMITMENTS BY DEVELOPED COUNTRIES
Developed countries have agreed to instigate domestic policies and measures to cut their greenhouse gas emissions. The Protocol does not oblige governments to implement any particular policy before 2012, but lists various measures that may help mitigate climate change and promote sustainable development. The list includes:

- enhancing energy efficiency;
- protecting and enhancing greenhouse gas sinks;
- promoting sustainable agriculture;
- promoting renewable energy, carbon sequestration, and environmentally friendly technologies;
- removing subsidies for environmentally damaging activities;
- promoting emissions reductions;
- addressing transport sector emissions; and
- controlling methane emissions through recovery and use in waste management.

Land use and change of land use in the forestry sector are seen as providing relatively low-cost opportunities to combat climate change, either by increasing the removal of greenhouse gases from the atmosphere through carbon sinks (one example is by planting trees), or by reducing emissions from this resource sector by curbing deforestation.

MARKET-BASED MECHANISMS: EMISSIONS TRADING
The Protocol allows states to use market-based measures for meeting their commitments. These mechanisms permit signatories to the Protocol to alter their assigned amounts of greenhouse gases by cross-border trading of emission allowances and credits (carbon sinks and clean development mechanisms, or investment projects that yield emission credits arising from emission reductions). The Protocol contemplates significant participation of the private sector operating at the international level. The success of the Protocol is heavily dependent on the business activities of private or non-state actors. Although individual state governments will have a critical influence on the operation and success of this scheme through domestic and international policy, it is private entities that will invest and transfer emission allowances. Their involvement, however, will be governed by the regulations

of their home governments. Through emissions trading, developed countries such as Canada may acquire credits from other countries that find it easier to meet their emissions targets. This will enable developed countries to reduce their overall cost of mitigating climate change.

BOX 3.1 TRANSALTA FIRST CANADIAN COMPANY TO MAKE AN EMISSIONS SWAP DEAL

It has been estimated that the Alberta oil sands deposits have the potential to satisfy the world's demand for petroleum for the next century. However, developing the oil sands produces massive greenhouse gas emissions. (For example, in 2002 it was estimated that 20 percent of Canada's greenhouse gas emissions came from the oil sands.) In spite of the fact that Canada has not yet set its greenhouse gas reduction targets, TransAlta, a power generation company, is preparing for expected carbon restraints and has broken new ground in a recent business-to-business deal between TransAlta Corp. and Agricola Super Ltd., a Chilean hog business. The Calgary company has agreed to pay Agricola US$9 million for credits worth 1.75 million tonnes of greenhouse gas emissions. Agricola has cut down on its own greenhouse gases (methane from hog farming), leaving it with four million credits to sell abroad.

This scheme has been entered into for a period of 10 years and has been approved by both countries' governments. Transalta has been a leader in its commitment to environmental responsibility while many other Canadian companies are waiting for the government to establish an official and obligatory framework under which they must operate.

DEVELOPING COUNTRIES

The Protocol recognizes that developing countries have difficulties cutting back on greenhouse emissions and so they receive special consideration. An adaptation fund is included for their benefit.

MONITORING PROCEDURES

Signatory countries to the Protocol have agreed to an accounting system, regular reporting by member countries, and in-depth review of these reports by expert review teams.

COMPLIANCE AND DISPUTE RESOLUTION

A compliance committee will assess and deal with any cases of non-compliance. With respect to disputes, as in most international agreements, the parties must first try to settle a dispute that arises through negotiation. A second step may be to refer the dispute to the **International Court of Justice (ICJ)**, arbitration, or conciliation. Only the signatories (states) may submit disputes to the ICJ. There are three distinct sets of rules and procedures that apply in cases of non-compliance by states: in-depth expert review, a multilateral consultative process, and a non-compliance procedure. The private sector's role will be limited to influencing the formation of environmental norms and promoting compliance with those norms.

Because the issue of climate change is so wide-ranging, the work of the UNFCCC is interlinked with the work of many other international organizations that also have the objective of sustainable development.

BOX 3.2   FINANCIERS SEE OPPORTUNITIES AS CARBON TRADERS

One significant group of attendees at the UN Kyoto Protocol conference in Montreal in December 2005 was financiers looking for business opportunities created by the Kyoto Protocol. Carbon markets already trade several billion dollars per year in emissions credits. Although this market is small, it is expected to grow exponentially. The European Union set up a credit-trading scheme for carbon funds in 2005 and traded nearly $4 billion in emissions credits in less than one year. Carbon funds operate much like mutual funds with investors purchasing greenhouse gas emissions credits mainly from environmentally friendly wind, solar, or agricultural projects. The World Bank manages eight carbon funds with private and public participants that total about $1 billion. These markets help transfer money from developed-country investors to clean-energy projects in developing countries such as burning of methane from manure from agricultural operations.

Other Multilateral Agreements for the Protection of the Environment

Since the formation of the UN, and the Bretton Woods institutions (see chapter 1), the international environmental community (as opposed to the international trade community) has been working toward common action in a number of areas to preserve the environment. A number of UN specialized agencies have been concerned with environmental issues, among them, the **Food and Agricultural Organization (FAO)**, the **World Health Organization (WHO)**, and the **United Nations Educational, Scientific, and Cultural Organization (UNESCO)**. The **United Nations Environmental Program (UNEP)** was established by the UN in 1972 to coordinate and assist with the negotiation of global environmental treaties. An extensive list of environmental agreements entered since 1933 is shown on its website (http://www.unep.org). Representative of these agreements are the following:

1946	The International Convention for the Regulation of Whaling
1971	Convention on Wetlands of International Importance Especially as Waterfowl Habitat (Ramsar)
1973	Convention on International Trade in Endangered Species of Wild Fauna and Flora (CITES)
1979	Convention on Long-Range Transboundary Air Pollution
1985	Convention for the Protection of the Ozone Layer, and Montreal Protocol 1987
1989	Basel Convention on the Control of Transboundary Movements of Hazardous Wastes and Their Disposal
1999	Basel Protocol on Liability and Compensation for Damage Resulting from Transboundary Movements of Hazardous Wastes and Their Disposal
2000	Framework Agreement for the Conservation of Living Marine Resources on the High Seas of the South Pacific (Galapagos Agreement)
2000	Cartagena Protocol on Biosafety to the Convention on Biological Diversity, Montreal
2001	Stockholm Convention on Persistent Organic Pollutants
2002	ASEAN Agreement on Transboundary Haze Pollution
2002	Convention for Cooperation in the Protection and Sustainable Development of the Marine and Coastal Environment of the Northeast Pacific

The WTO and the Environment

Differing Attitudes Toward the Adoption of Environment Values in Trade Rules

The intersection of international trade law and environmental sustainability has been subject to much scrutiny in the media and in academic circles. The General Agreement on Tariffs and Trade (GATT), a central agreement in the WTO's arsenal of rules, was drafted in 1947, long before the environmental aspects of trade were prominent in the minds of the negotiators. Today there is a great deal of debate over whether the WTO, and indeed international trade generally, is bad for the environment. This is a highly polarized debate with the WTO itself referring to the "mutual supportiveness of trade and the environment" when it launched the Doha Round of multilateral trade talks. Detractors, on the other hand, contend that trade is harmful to the environment and encourages a "race to the bottom," where countries establish or tolerate lax environmental laws to encourage multinational companies to move to these countries to minimize production costs. The discussion would be more meaningful and less emotionally charged if there were a recognition that the debate is really about the effect of economic activity on the environment and that this is a topic that can be debated at the domestic level as well as at the international level. The real issue here is the challenge of achieving sustainable development and economic justice—not a debate that is confined to international trade rules.

Developed and developing countries have different attitudes toward the connection between trade and the environment. Developing countries are suspicious of any formalized link, seeing this as an opportunity for rich countries to hold them to standards that were not applied by developed countries when they were achieving their own present high level of economic development. Developing countries see environmental concerns as a potential excuse for a new form of **protectionism**—enabling restrictions of markets in developed countries for the very products on which developing countries depend. A further factor is the distrust of developing countries of NGOs, which are often at the forefront of campaigns for environmental protection. These organizations are seen in some countries as well-funded arms of developed country governments.

Relevant Rules of the GATT
Pertinent to this discussion is the recognition of the basic tenets of free trade: that goods must not be restricted from crossing borders, and that there must be no discrimination between goods in domestic markets on the basis of country of origin. In this context the following articles of the GATT are relevant:

- Article I: Most-favoured-nation treatment must be extended by each contracting party to the imports and exports of all other contracting parties.
- Article III: National treatment must be extended to the products or services of one member imported into the territory of another—that is, they must be accorded treatment no less favourable than that given to like products or services of domestic origin.
- Article XI: Import and export quotas and licences are prohibited with certain exceptions for critical shortages, grading or marketing standards, and domestic marketing or production programs.

These articles create the expectation on the part of WTO member countries that their exports will be accepted by other WTO member countries;

however, under WTO law established by dispute settlement decisions, it is possible for a member country to act inconsistently with these rules and be excused under the provisions of Article XX.

- Article XX: Individual countries may impose import-restricting measures that are necessary to protect human, animal, or plant life or health, as well as measures relating to the conservation of exhaustible natural resources.

It is this provision that has proven the most effective for providing legitimacy to a country that protects the environment by using trade-related measures. The text of the provision is set out in box 3.3.

BOX 3.3 GATT ARTICLE XX GENERAL EXCEPTIONS

Subject to the requirement that such measures are not applied in a manner which would constitute a means of arbitrary or unjustifiable discrimination between countries where the same conditions prevail, or a disguised restriction on international trade, nothing in this Agreement shall be construed to prevent the adoption or enforcement by any contracting party of measures:

(a) necessary to protect public morals;

(b) necessary to protect human, animal or plant life or health;

(c) relating to the importation or exportation of gold or silver;

(d) necessary to secure compliance with laws or regulations which are not inconsistent with the provisions of this Agreement, including those relating to customs enforcement, the enforcement of monopolies operated under paragraph 4 of Article II and Article XVII, the protection of patents, trade marks and copyrights, and the prevention of deceptive practices;

(e) relating to the products of prison labour;

(f) imposed for the protection of national treasures of artistic, historic or archaeological value;

(g) relating to the conservation of exhaustible natural resources if such measures are made effective in conjunction with restrictions on domestic production or consumption;

(h) undertaken in pursuance of obligations under any intergovernmental commodity agreement which conforms to criteria submitted to the CONTRACTING PARTIES and not disapproved by them or which is itself so submitted and not so disapproved;

(i) involving restrictions on exports of domestic materials necessary to ensure essential quantities of such materials to a domestic processing industry during periods when the domestic price of such materials is held below the world price as part of a governmental stabilization plan; Provided that such restrictions shall not operate to increase the exports of or the protection afforded to such domestic industry, and shall not depart from the provisions of this Agreement relating to non-discrimination;

(j) essential to the acquisition or distribution of products in general or local short supply; Provided that any such measures shall be consistent with the principle that all contracting parties are entitled to an equitable share of the international supply of such products, and that any such measures, which are inconsistent with the other provisions of this Agreement shall be discontinued as soon as the conditions giving rise to them have ceased to exist.

The GATT/WTO Decisions Relating to Trade and the Environment

The attitudes of the WTO panels have changed over time and appear to be evolving toward the recognition of the importance of the environment as a factor in international trade rules. The two cases that graphically illustrate this development are the *Tuna-Dolphin* cases and the *Shrimp-Sea Turtle* cases.

THE TUNA-DOLPHIN CASES

First Tuna-Dolphin Case (1991)

In 1988, the United States passed amendments to the *Marine Mammal Protection Act* that provided that foreign standards should be comparable to those of the United States with respect to the unintentional taking of dolphins by commercial fishers who are fishing for tuna and other fish. An embargo on yellow fin tuna caught by purse-seine nets in the eastern tropical Pacific zone was imposed on certain countries, including Mexico. Fishing with purse-seine nets was alleged to be one of the methods that resulted in an unacceptable number of dolphins being sacrificed in the commercial pursuit of tuna. Mexico referred the question to a GATT panel, which found that the import embargo was a clear violation of the prohibition on quantitative restrictions in Article XI, and also could not be justified under Article XX because the wording of the clause is "sanitary measure to safeguard the life or health of humans, animals or plants *within the jurisdiction of the importing country*" (emphasis added). The Mexican government never sought the necessary approval of the GATT Council for this decision because it feared that to do so would undermine US support for the ongoing NAFTA negotiations at that time. There was, however, a second *Tuna-Dolphin* case.

Second Tuna-Dolphin Case (1994)

In this case, the European Community and the Netherlands acting for the Netherlands Antilles brought the case to the GATT. (Note that hearing two cases involving similar facts and parties is not precluded under the GATT dispute settlement system because there is no formal system of precedent or *stare decisis*.) In this case the panel again found that the US restrictions were not in accordance with GATT provisions, stating that although Article XX *did not restrict a country from applying conservation measures to protect natural resources outside its territory*, the import embargoes imposed by the United States in this case were too restrictive and unduly limited the right of access to US markets.

Although these cases were not adopted by the GATT Council and thus never formally became a part of GATT law, they did provide support for critics of the WTO system, who alleged that environmental issues were seen only through the lens of international trade protagonists. The *Shrimp-Sea Turtle* cases, however, illustrate the flexibility of the dispute settlement system and the increased willingness of panels to acknowledge the importance of the environment, even in the face of the GATT rules developed in 1947.

THE SHRIMP-SEA TURTLE CASES

First Shrimp-Sea Turtle Case (1998)

The facts of this case are very similar to those of the *Tuna-Dolphin* cases. The United States prohibited the importation of shrimp that had been caught by methods that harmed sea turtles and mandated that US-designed Turtle Excluder Devices (TEDs) be used to catch shrimp. It had applied these restrictions to its own industry and was seeking to restrict access to its market as a way of ensuring that other countries would implement the same or similar measures. In fact, the way in which the United States had applied the import restrictions was arbitrary because some countries were excluded where others were not. As well, some countries received information and assistance in conforming with the techniques, while others did not. In the case brought by India, Malaysia, Thailand, and Pakistan, the WTO Appellate Body ruled against the US import restrictions on the grounds that the United States had adopted the measures unilaterally and had not consulted with other countries or taken into account the different conditions that they faced. It was this case that prompted some protesters at the WTO Seattle meeting in 1999 to dress up as sea turtles in protest against the WTO's alleged lack of concern for the environment.

Second Shrimp-Sea Turtle Case (2002)

In response to the first *Shrimp-Sea Turtle* decision, the United States changed its guidelines to provide that countries could apply for certification, even if they did not require the use of the US-designed TEDs, if the harvesting country demonstrated that it had implemented and was enforcing a comparably effective regulatory program to protect sea turtles. The new rules also provided that the United States would negotiate to agree on what measures would be accepted as "comparably effective." Malaysia brought a complaint to the WTO alleging that this measure was not sufficient and that the United States had still failed to comply with the previous ruling. The WTO Appellate Body found in favour of the United States, stating that the new US measure was sufficiently flexible to take into account the specific conditions prevailing in any exporting country and that such a measure was legal under GATT Article XX. This was a significant decision because it marked the first time that an environmental process or production method was declared WTO-compliant, and points to the possibility that the WTO dispute settlement process is adapting to the realities of a world in which the general public does not support expanded trade at the expense of the natural environment.

The WTO and International Product Standards

The acceptance of a process or production method in the *Shrimp-Sea Turtle* case leads us quite naturally to a consideration of WTO rules that relate to product standards. As we see from the cases discussed above, the assumption under traditional GATT rules was that **product-related standards** were acceptable under GATT national treatment provisions because they allow imports and domestic products to be treated in a similar way, based on their particular properties. **Process-related standards**, on the other hand, allow one country to dictate to another country how manufacturing or harvesting will be undertaken in another country's territory, a violation of national sovereignty and not in accordance with the basic philosophy of the GATT. At least two international agreements are in direct conflict with this philosophy: the Montreal Protocol on Substances That Deplete the Ozone Layer, which provides for bans on the import of products produced with, but not containing, controlled substances, and CITES, which provides for a system of export and import controls to restrict trade in endangered species. Both these conventions have as their goal the control of production in other countries.

With respect to the WTO, the safest conclusion is that process and production methods affecting trade are not prohibited outright. If they are contrived to protect domestic producers and workers from import competition, they will not be acceptable. Some supporters of action on climate change advocate a system of border taxes that are based on environmental standards for production processes. Their argument is that, faced with increasingly stringent regulation in Kyoto countries, emission-intensive industries will move to countries that have imposed no such restrictions and will then export the products back to the Kyoto-observant countries. There appears to be little factual evidence of such a trend, but, if it occurs, it is an issue that will have to be addressed. These suggestions are controversial because it is likely that any such restrictions would be imposed by developed countries on imports from developing countries. Such activity is sometimes referred to as "eco-imperialism." The official position of the WTO, published in its guides and on its website, is that process and production method restrictions are a violation of trade rules. The best conclusion at present is that there is a limited acceptance of these controls, provided they can be justified under GATT Article XX, depending on how overwhelming the evidence is of environmental damage and how fairly such rules are applied to all countries.

INTERNATIONAL TRADE AND LABOUR REGULATION

The question of the interface between international trade and domestic labour regulation has not received the same attention, nor is the relationship as highly developed as is the interface between international trade and the environment. Nevertheless, the interaction of labour standards and international trade has emerged as a contentious issue in the relations between developed and developing countries in the WTO. Proponents of the international enforcement of labour standards, particularly organized labour and social activists in developed countries, argue that lax labour practices and substandard working conditions exist in many developing countries and should be offset by appropriate trade policy measures in order to "level the playing field." They believe that workers in developing countries are subject to exploitative and abusive working conditions and that their wages are suppressed.

Their proposed solution to labour exploitation is for the WTO and regional trade agreements to adopt mechanisms to ensure that labour standards can be enforced through international trade rules. On the other hand, opponents of this idea take the position that attaching labour standards to the WTO and trade agreements will not achieve the goal of improving wages and working conditions of workers in poorer countries, and could in fact make things worse for these workers. At present, there is no provision for a linkage of international trade and labour rules in the WTO. The WTO contains only one explicit reference to labour, in Article XX, where a prohibition on imports of goods made with prison labour is authorized.

The essential issues raised by this debate are similar to those of the trade and environment debate because the same three factors exist in each situation. These are:

- a specific, multilateral organization, the International Labour Organization (ILO), exists outside the WTO for the protection of labour;
- norms have been established outside the international trading system and there is no formal mechanism for their adoption or integration by the WTO; and
- there is no consensus on whether one country has the authority to dictate its domestic policy in another country.

Multilateral Labour Rules

Codified labour standards vary greatly from country to country and their range and enforcement depend for their efficacy and enforcement on the per capita income, political and social development, and institutions of the various countries. At present, there are eight fundamental ILO conventions that form the basis of international labour rules. These cover the following areas:

- prohibition of forced labour (Conventions 29 and 105);
- freedom of association and protection of the right to organize and to participate in collective bargaining (Conventions 87 and 98);
- equal remuneration for men and women for work of equal value (Convention 100);
- non-discrimination in employment and occupation (Convention 111); and
- minimum age of employment of children and abolition of the worst forms of child labour (Conventions 138 and 182).

A review of these conventions reveals that these labour standards are based on human rights and reflect the four fundamental standards of (1) freedom of association, (2) elimination of forced labour, (3) abolition of child labour, and (4) elimination of discrimination. Absent from these standards and the conventions listed above is the idea of a fair wage. Wage policy remains controversial because of the obvious problems associated with requiring equalization of wage levels at the international level. The motives behind wage standards are likely to be mixed. Although they may indeed be based on altruism, they may also be based on the desire by developed countries to protect home markets and workers. It can be expected that the discussion about a connection between trade rules and labour standards will intensify in the near future as the consequences of China's exponential export growth are felt in major developed-country markets.

Are International Labour Rules a Legitimate Goal for the WTO?

The issue of trade and labour standards is a highly sensitive one for the WTO. It has been observed that there is no issue that inspires more intense debate among WTO member governments than the issue of trade and core labour standards. Many officials from developing countries believe that the campaign to bring labour issues into the WTO is actually a bid by industrial nations to undermine the comparative advantage of lower-wage countries. This issue is not new and was significant in the 1940s when the GATT was negotiated with respect to low wage rates in Japan. In that case, the GATT negotiators did not include labour standards in the mechanisms for fair trade protection. Their decision was a reflection of the difficulty of imposing such constraints on members with such major differences in economic development. The situation is no easier at present.

There was some effort by the United States to promote this issue at the Seattle meeting in 1999 with the result that a working group was established by the WTO. This move was very unpopular with developing countries, and may well have been motivated by domestic political considerations faced by the US administration at that time. The issue of recognizing core labour standards in the WTO remains contentious, and for this reason there is more lip service than activity relating to the protection of labour standards internationally. The official policy of the WTO is to defer to the ILO in this area.

Developed-Country Consumers and the Issue of International Working Conditions

Advocates of the enforcement of international labour standards through trade agreements believe that such regulation will improve the working conditions and wages of workers in poor countries, and reduce the wage differential between workers in wealthy and poor countries. They argue that regulation will help protect the jobs of workers in developed countries. These advocates contend that goods from low labour standards countries displace products made by workers in high labour standards countries and thus reduce employment because multinational enterprises tend to outsource jobs to countries with lower labour standards to take advantage of lower labour costs. Many economists disagree with these conclusions and argue that empirical evidence does not support them.

Perhaps another approach for concerned people and groups in developed countries is to make greater use of the consumer power within their own countries, and build upon the conscientious consumer who is willing to pay more for a product not produced in exploitative conditions. Many people do not like to think that their sporting equipment or computers were made by a third world worker earning a pittance in appalling conditions.

These people may choose not to buy goods from companies with a reputation for exploiting workers in developing countries (a good example of this is the Nike shoe boycott). Consumer opinion can be used to provide market-based pressure for improvements in labour standards.

Bilateral and Multilateral Trade Agreements and Labour

There are only three sources of bilateral or multilateral agreements that incorporate trade and labour rules: those found in the EU's Social Charter, which contains provisions on employment and remuneration, and health and safety protection in the workplace; NAFTA, with its side agreement on labour (see chapter 5); and recent bilateral and multilateral trade agreements negotiated by the United States. The most advanced model of US regional trade agreements with provisions for the protection of labour is the Dominican Republic-Central America Free Trade Agreement (DR-CAFTA). This agreement reflects the values espoused in the US *Trade Act of 2002*, where the US Congress identified the following four key labour negotiating goals for free trade agreements:

- the promotion of ILO core labour rights;
- provisions ensuring that countries do not weaken or reduce the protections of their domestic labour laws;
- the promotion of ratification of the ILO Convention on Child Labour; and
- **capacity building** to promote respect for core labour standards.

While the importance of these goals is reflected to some extent in the bilateral trade agreements between the United States and Singapore, Chile, and Jordan, respectively, it is the DR-CAFTA that most fully reflects an advance toward these objectives. The agreement protects the human rights–related areas of freedom of association, a ban on forced labour, and a ban on child labour. It also promotes protections that do not have the status of human rights protection such as the establishment of adequate working conditions, including a minimum wage, maximum hours of work, and the promotion of occupational health and safety.

BRIBERY AND CORRUPTION: THE EFFECT ON INTERNATIONAL BUSINESS

Corruption is one of the most serious challenges facing contemporary business. Corrupt practices undermine good government and the rule of law; they distort public policy; they lead to the misallocation of resources; and they disproportionately hurt the poor. IMF research shows that countries with high levels of corruption have lower rates of investment and growth, and spend less on education. In an increasingly wired global economy, information and money can be transferred almost instantaneously across borders, increasing the potential for bribery and money laundering. However, the freer flow of information creates opportunities for greater transparency and accountability. The issue of bribery of foreign public officials is one that has worried international businesses for many years and has received considerable attention in the last several decades, partly for altruistic reasons but also because it is now recognized that there is a strong business case for anti-corruption programs.

The US Foreign Corrupt Practices Act

The United States has taken the lead in this area with the passage of the *Foreign Corrupt Practices Act* (FCPA). This legislation makes it illegal for Americans or US corporations to pay bribes to public officials in other countries. Passed by the US Congress in 1977, in the wake of the Watergate scandal and revelations of large-scale bribery of foreign officials by large American corporations, the Act prohibits a US firm from paying or offering to pay a foreign official for assistance in obtaining or retaining business. It also prohibits payments to a person when the payer knows that a portion of the payment will go to a public official. Violation of these provisions exposes an individual or a corporation to very high fines and possible prison terms.

The OECD Convention

The Organisation for Economic Co-operation and Development's (OECD's) work toward a multinational anti-bribery agreement dates back to 1989, when the United States was the only country to impose criminal sanctions for bribes paid anywhere in the world. Businesses in the United States complained that the FCPA put them at a competitive disadvantage and petitioned for a softening of its provisions. The response of the US government was not to change their own legislation but to call on the OECD to join in the anti-corruption effort. The time was ripe for such an initiative because the Cold War had ended, the Asian financial crisis had occurred, and it was becoming obvious that individual countries could not adequately control international corruption. In 1998, after several years of negotiations, the OECD adopted the Convention on Combating Bribery of Foreign Public Officials in International Business Transactions (the "Anti-Bribery Convention"). The Convention criminalizes acts of offering or giving bribes, but not of soliciting or receiving bribes; and it covers only bribery aimed at public officials, not bribes of private sector representatives or political party officials. The Anti-Bribery Convention came into effect after ratification by 5 of the 10 largest OECD exporters, accounting for at least 60 percent of the group's total exports. The Convention is not self-executing—it requires passage of domestic legislation in each of the signatory countries.

Canada's Response to the OECD Anti-Bribery Convention

Canada passed anti-bribery legislation in 1998 for the purpose of conforming to the OECD Convention. The Canadian *Corruption of Foreign Public Officials Act* creates three new offences:

- bribery of a foreign public official in the course of business or an attempt to do so;
- possession of property or proceeds, knowing it was obtained or derived from the bribery of foreign public officials, or derived from laundering that property or those proceeds; and
- laundering, using, transporting, or altering the property or proceeds obtained or derived from the bribery of foreign public officials.

These offences are all indictable and carry prison terms of 5 to 10 years and a potential fine of up to $50,000. "Business" is defined in this statute to include any business, trade, profession, or undertaking whose object is profit. "Foreign public official" (FPO) includes any person holding a legislative, administrative, or judicial position in a foreign state, or a person who performs public duties or functions for a foreign state, including a person employed by a state agency. If the employees, representatives, or agents of a Canadian business pay a bribe, the officers and directors of the business will be liable. It is thus of utmost importance that company-wide, written anti-bribery policies and education be adopted by Canadian businesses.

BOX 3.4 CALGARY COMPANY FACES PROSECUTION UNDER THE CORRUPTION OF FOREIGN PUBLIC OFFICIALS ACT

In July 2002, a US immigration officer who worked at the Calgary International Airport pleaded guilty to accepting bribes from Hydro Kleen Group Inc., an Alberta-based company. The official who had provided "favours" to Hydro Kleen in the course of his employment was sentenced to six months' imprisonment.

Facilitation Payments

For companies who do business in developing countries, obtaining access to basic services (such as phone lines), building permits, and other documents essential for day-to-day operations can be an issue. The culture of many countries makes "**facilitation payments**" commonplace. This is particularly true in poor countries that pay their officials very little and perhaps sporadically. For this reason, Canadian and US anti-bribery legislation allows for facilitation payments, although the anti-bribery legislation in the United Kingdom and some other countries does not. A facilitation payment is a payment made to a low-level official to obtain or speed up the performance of a routine or non-discretionary duty. The situation is clear where the official has control over the timing of the act, but does not have official power to withhold the service entirely. The philosophy behind facilitation payments is that they are not bribes because the payment is not for special treatment, such as exemption from a rule that would normally apply—for example, a product standard that a shipment does not meet. The line is, however, somewhat blurred in practice, and for this reason, ethicists and many ethically responsible companies recommend against these "legally permissible," but "ethically questionable" payments.

Transparency International: A Formidable Force in Combatting International Corruption

Transparency International (TI), an international NGO, is devoted to combatting corruption at the national and at the international levels. Working with civil society, business, and governments, it raises awareness about the damaging effects of corruption, advocates policy reform, and works toward the implementation of multilateral conventions, and subsequently monitors compliance by governments and corporations. Founded in 1993, TI now has 90 national chapters around the world. Its focus is on the corruption of the public sector by the private sector. TI's philosophy is that without the containment of corruption, the disparity of wealth between rich and poor countries cannot be addressed; private sector development cannot provide the optimal contribution to social economic development; the world's resources will be abused; and sustainable development will be hampered. TI has also identified a consistent correlation between impoverishment and high levels of corruption in countries.

REVIEW QUESTIONS

1. Describe the role of NGOs in helping to shape civil society both nationally and internationally. Provide at least one example of an NGO that operates domestically in Canada and one that operates internationally. Describe the mission, activities, and the accomplishments of each.

2. Why is the single nation state's making laws for its own territory and citizens no longer a viable model for 21st century global issues?

3. Describe the ICC and provide four examples of important initiatives that help international business.

4. Provide four examples of TNCs' ability to monitor their own global activities. Provide two examples not given in your text.

5. What is meant by the term "global commons" and what is the underlying difficulty in developing rules to protect it?

6. What has the UN contributed to the global attempt to limit climate change? How has Canada participated to date in efforts to control climate change? How have our major trading partners dealt with this issue?

7. What are some of the organizations working to protect the environment and what conventions have been adopted to further these goals? Name four.

8. Why is GATT Article XX so significant to a discussion of whether or not the WTO has any role to play in the protection of the environment? What is the major underlying problem with this provision as a foundation for individual countries attempting to protect the global commons? How do the *Tuna-Dolphin* and *Shrimp-Sea Turtle* cases illustrate the changing attitudes of WTO panels in this area?

9. What is the difference between product-related standards and process-related standards? Provide an example of each. What are the WTO rules relating to each?

10. What labour standards are perceived as human rights–based and protected by international conventions? What area of labour protection is noticeably absent from these conventions? What is the attitude and approach of the United States to core labour standards?

11. Why do developed and developing countries have different attitudes toward adoption of global rules for the protection of labour and the environment?

12. Describe the basic rules of the OECD Anti-Bribery Convention, and the Canadian and US legislation prohibiting bribery of foreign officials. Assuming that the purpose of these initiatives is to eliminate

corruption in international business transactions, identify two major weaknesses in the Convention and the legislation of Canada and the United States.

DISCUSSION QUESTIONS

1. The material in this chapter is somewhat controversial and lends itself well to debates. Your instructor will divide the class into debate teams. Each team will present one perspective on the issue. Some suggested debate topics are:

   • Do we have a situation of declining state or individual country authority in the world today?
   • Regulation of international labour standards should be the exclusive domain of the WTO.
   • Regulation of international environmental standards should be the exclusive domain of the WTO.
   • Regulation of climate change is detrimental to the interests of Canadian and international business.
   • The WTO should allow the free use of process standards to ensure fair labour standards throughout the world.
   • The WTO should allow the free use of process standards to ensure a level playing field for developed-country products that must be produced in countries with high labour and environmental standards.
   • The OECD Convention on Combating Bribery of Foreign Public Officials in International Business Transactions, and the Canadian and US anti-corruption legislation (1) go too far in regulating international business, or (2) do not go far enough in regulating international business.

2. There are a number of emerging issues not discussed here that are important to the international business community. Choose one or more of the following topics for student research and presentations:

   a. Does freer international trade contribute to the global fight on poverty?
   b. What is the appropriate response to the need for greater border security in the face of international terrorism? What are the implications for the protection of privacy and freedom of movement?
   c. How can the global business community address the threat of major health pandemics?

FURTHER READING

Condon, Bradly J. (2002). *NAFTA, WTO and Global Business Strategy: How AIDS, Trade and Terrorism Affect Our Economic Future.* West Port, CT: Greenwood Publishing Group.

Sachs, Jeffrey. (2005). *The End of Poverty: Economic Possibilities for Our Time.* New York: Penguin.

Sampson, Gary P. (2005). *The WTO and Sustainable Development.* New York: United Nations University Press.

WEBSITES

Climate Change
Canadian Foundation for Climate & Atmospheric Sciences:
www.cfcas.org

Canadian Centre for Policy Ingenuity:
www.climateforchange.ca

UN Climate Change Conference Montreal, 2005:
www.montreal2005.gc.ca

Global Non-Governmental Anti-Corruption Activity
Transparency International:
www.transparency.org

TRACE (Transparent Agents and Contracting Entities):
www.traceinternational.org
(an international non-profit organization that vets, certifies, and
trains intermediaries for its member companies)

Publish What You Pay:
www.publishwhatyoupay.org
(a campaign that urges all companies, especially extractive companies,
to publish information on all payments made to host country
governments)

International Chamber of Commerce (ICC):
www.iccwbo.org
(first published its rules on extortion and bribery in international
business transactions in 1977 and revised them in 1999. It encourages
business self-regulation and seeks to influence organizations that
have developed international conventions to fight corruption)

Business for Social Responsibility:
www.bsr.org
(a global organization that helps member companies achieve success in ways that respect ethical values, people, communities, and the environment. BSR provides information, tools, training and advisory services to make corporate social responsibility an integral part of business operations and strategies. BSR is a non-profit organization that promotes cross-sector collaboration and contributes to global efforts to advance the field of corporate social responsibility)

CHAPTER 4

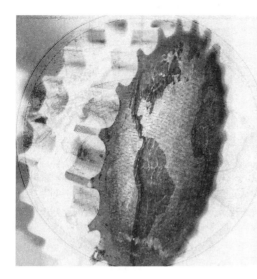

The European Union and Other Regional Trade Arrangements

INTRODUCTION

In an economist's ideal model, the removal of trade barriers between countries leads to greater prosperity. This is certainly the underlying philosophy of the World Trade Organization (WTO). However, certain factors—the WTO's policy of decision making only by consensus, the long duration of its trade rounds, and its efforts to ensure that countries' individual sovereignty will not be overridden—have slowed the pace of progress and contributed to growing impatience on the part of less prosperous member states. The slow pace of global progress toward trade liberalization and economic cooperation is one of the factors that has led to greater activity in the area of bilateral and regional trade agreements. Different levels of integration have emerged and can be described in stages, beginning

LEARNING OBJECTIVES

After reading this chapter you will understand:

- the different levels of integration found in regional trade agreements

- the history, goals, and present membership of the EU, and the major institutions of the EU and what role they play in governing the EU

- the history and present status of the common currency in the EU

- the "four freedoms of the single market"

- important characteristics of EU competition law and policy

- the importance of seeking expert legal advice before negotiating and signing agreements involving business in the EU

- product liability requirements in the EU

with the least integrated form of favourable treatment and progressing through five stages to the most integrated form of cooperation thus far observed. These stages are not necessarily progressive; it cannot be assumed that the formation of any one regional trade grouping will pass through each of these stages in order. These stages are:

- *Preferential tariff.* The countries involved offer each other lower tariffs than are applicable to countries that are not parties to the agreement.
- *Free trade area.* Two or more countries agree to remove substantially all tariff and non-tariff barriers between them while maintaining their own external tariff schedules against other countries.
- *Customs union.* The countries involved eliminate trade barriers among themselves and impose a common external tariff.
- *Common market.* The countries agree to common policies for the internal operation and integration of the combined market that has been created.
- *Economic and monetary union.* The countries agree to create a single central bank, coordinate monetary policy, and adopt a common currency in addition to creating a common market.

A provision for customs unions and free trade areas was included in the General Agreement on Tariffs and Trade (GATT) at the insistence of the prime movers behind the GATT—the United States, Britain, and France. These nations had practical and historical reasons for wishing to continue the strong trading links that were already established through regional hegemony and colonial trading patterns. It was also felt that *any* movement toward economic integration was a step in the right direction.

The formation of an agreement among nations that provides better terms for members than for non-members is a derogation of the most-favoured-nation principle. This was tolerated by the contracting parties to the GATT for a number of reasons. These arrangements were considered beneficial for fostering trade within regions as long as they did not raise barriers to others. There were also historical relationships to be considered, such as Britain's relationship with her colonies and former colonies, and the desire of Middle Eastern and Central American states to form regional agreements. Developing countries also wanted the freedom to work together to achieve better economic conditions. The primary principle behind the GATT provision allowing customs unions and free trade areas is that the arrangement must be trade creating, not trade restricting or diverting—that is, there must be no increase in trade barriers against third-party members of the GATT. The rules further provided that the parties remove duties on substantially all trade among themselves, with the exception of some quantitative and balance of payments restrictions, and that the parties must notify the GATT before the agreement is implemented.

THE HISTORICAL DEVELOPMENT OF THE EUROPEAN UNION

Early Development

A well-known European newspaper recently observed: "guided by treaties that scarcely anybody can understand, towards a destination on which nobody can agree, the European Union has survived, and often thrived, for almost half a century."[1] The European Union (EU) is Canada's second-largest trading partner. It is not only the earliest post–World War II regional trade grouping, it is also the most successful and highly developed, providing an important example of the movement toward economic integration.

After World War II, Europe felt threatened by the potential domination of the two superpowers—the United States and the USSR. In this climate, the idea of a united Europe emerged and had a certain attraction for the formerly fiercely nationalistic states. A forerunner of the EU was the European Coal and Steel Community (ECSC), which was formed in 1952. Its members were France, Belgium, Germany, Italy, Luxembourg, and the Netherlands. Under the treaty establishing this trading community, the members agreed to remove tariff barriers on shipments of coal, iron, and scrap metal. In 1957, the same six countries founded the European Atomic Community and, more importantly, signed the **Treaty of Rome**. It was this treaty that

---

BOX 4.1 WHY DO THE NAMES WE USE FOR THE EUROPEAN UNION CHANGE?

In this book, you will notice that three different abbreviations for the European Union are used. This is a reflection of the change in name that occurred over the years. So, if we are referring to an event at a certain point in time, we refer to the union using its name at that time. These names, their abbreviations, and their date of creation are as follows:

- European Economic Community (EEC): created in 1957 by the Treaty of Rome
- European Community (EC): created in 1986 after the *Single European Act*
- European Union (EU): created in 1993 by the Treaty on European Union (TEU).

established the European Economic Community (EEC). The treaty has had far-reaching effects on Europe's economic history and, indeed, on today's global trading environment. The purpose of the Treaty of Rome was to create a common market in which all countries agreed to gradually eliminate all trade barriers among themselves and form a common tariff on all goods entering the EEC.

Important Treaties in the EU's Development

The Single European Act

After 1957, the next major development for Europe was the adoption of the **Single European Act**, signed by the then 12 members of the EEC, which became the European Community (EC) in 1986. This Act strengthened the ability of the member countries to achieve the objectives of the Treaty of Rome by enabling most of the approximately 300 necessary **directives** to be adopted by majority vote instead of the previously required unanimous consent. Directives prescribe objectives for legislation, but leave the method for achieving those objectives up to individual member countries. The stated objective of the *Single European Act* was to progressively establish a single market by the end of 1992. The single market was envisaged as an area without internal borders to goods, services, capital, and people. This involved the abolition of barriers of all kinds, harmonization of rules, legislation, and tax structures, strengthening of monetary cooperation, and imposition of measures to encourage European firms to work together. As well, the **four freedoms of the single market** were promoted:

- *Unrestricted movement of goods*—ensures that imports move freely within the EC once they enter any member state.
- *Unrestricted movement of capital*—enhances competition and choice in financial services, gives borrowers access to more diverse and cheaper financing, and permits more competitive financing for investment and trade within the EC.
- *Unrestricted movement of services*—frees the movement of services among member states.
- *Unrestricted movement of people*—allows labour to move freely within the EC.

Additional goals included eliminating technical barriers—that is, once a product meets the technical standards of any EC member, it may have unrestricted distribution to all EC countries. A further goal was the removal of all fiscal barriers—that is, reducing the differences in indirect taxes that distort trade among member states. An additional and very important goal was that of opening the public procurement market to competition from firms from other countries.

The Maastricht Treaty

The **Treaty on European Union (TEU)**, also known as the **Maastricht Treaty**, was entered into force in 1993. It was this treaty that changed the name of the European Community to the European Union (EU). This treaty also created the European concept of the **three pillars**, which set out the distribution of responsibilities in the EU.

The Maastricht Treaty is named for the city in the Netherlands where the leaders of the EC met in December 1991. The agreement is one of the major events in the history of the European region because it resulted in significant progress toward greater integration of European monetary, foreign, and social policy. European federalists hoped for a commitment to economic and monetary union at this meeting, while others were reluctant, taking the view that economic and monetary union necessarily entails political union.

The revolutions in Eastern Europe in 1989 added some urgency to the movement to reform the EC. The Eastern European nations were looking to the EC to provide them with aid and to eventually admit them to the European "club"; however, some members of the EC feared that such expansion would weaken the EC. For this reason, they felt increased pressure to strengthen the EC. These were some of the factors that contributed to the remarkable progress toward European unity made at Maastricht. Provisions agreed to

---

BOX 4.2   THE THREE PILLARS SHOWING THE DISTRIBUTION OF RESPONSIBILITIES IN THE EU

The First Pillar	The Second Pillar	The Third Pillar
(areas where member states have relinquished some of their sovereignty to EU institutions)	(matters managed on an intergovernmental basis)	(matters relating to police and judicial cooperation in criminal matters—managed on an intergovernmental basis)
Customs union and the single market (including the four freedoms)	Foreign policy Security policy	Police cooperation
Agriculture policy		Racism
Environmental policy		Crime
Competition and trade policy		Terrorism
Fiscal and monetary issues (common currency)		

at Maastricht were ambitious and more extensive than most observers had predicted.

The Treaty of Amsterdam

The Treaty of Amsterdam, signed in 1997, was negotiated to provide clarification on civil rights, personal mobility and citizenship, common foreign policy, and security, and to set some pre-conditions for further enlargement of the EU community. The treaty incorporated the principles of the Schengen Agreement on the gradual abolition of border checks for people crossing national borders within the EU. A single external frontier was agreed on where checks are carried out in accordance with harmonized rules for a common visa regime and an improved coordination of police, customs, and the judiciary. At present, 13 member states in the EU participate in Schengen along with non-members Norway and Iceland. Except for cooperation between police forces and the judiciary, the United Kingdom and Ireland do not as yet participate in this arrangement.

The Treaty of Nice

The Treaty of Nice, in force since 2003, redefined, clarified, and extended the legislative, administrative, executive, and judicial powers of the EU—increasing opportunities for qualified majority voting.

The Charter of Fundamental Rights

In 2000, the European Commission, the European Council, and the EU Parliament jointly signed and proclaimed the **Charter of Fundamental Rights of the European Union**. The Charter incorporates a sweeping range of civil, political, economic, and social rights and synthesizes the constitutional traditions and international obligations common to the EU member states. The rights described are divided into six categories: dignity, freedoms, equality, solidarity, citizens' rights, and justice. These rights go well beyond the enshrined rights in Canada and the United States, referring to such rights as the reconciliation of one's family and professional life; the right to social security benefits, services, and health care. The legal status of the Charter is not clear because it is so far only a political document, but it is nonetheless influential. The new European constitution would have clarified the legal status of the Charter, but, as discussed below, the constitution was not approved.

The Common Currency

After many years of doubt as to whether the goal of a common currency for Europe would be achieved, the Euro was adopted as the common currency for 11 member states on January 1, 1999. The 11 member states were Belgium, Germany, Spain, France, Ireland, Italy, Luxembourg, the Netherlands, Austria, Portugal, and Finland. Greece adopted the Euro as its currency on January 1, 2001, bringing the present number of member states that have adopted the Euro to 12. Euro notes and coins have replaced the national currencies in all participating member states and the dual circulation period for old and new currencies ended in 2002. The transition was achieved remarkably smoothly, and statistics indicate substantial transaction cost savings due to the adoption of the Euro. The European Central Bank, located in Frankfurt, has responsibility for ensuring that member states conform to the common currency rules.

Growing Membership in the EU

From the original six members, the EU has now expanded to 25, with two further accessions expected by 2008. The population of the EU now exceeds 450 million people.

Applications for Membership

Turkey first applied to join what was then the EC in 1959. Turkey's membership in the EU has long been a difficult issue for the Europeans, whose attitudes toward Turkish membership have been at best ambivalent and at worst openly hostile. Having delayed Turkey's membership for years with various lesser agreements, including a customs union and association agreement, the EU heads of government started formal negotiations with Turkey in late 2005. Turkey has had to take significant steps domestically to be accepted at this negotiating table. These steps include abolishing the death penalty, accepting Kurdish as a language in schools, abolishing state security

---

BOX 4.3   PRESENT MEMBER STATES IN THE EU AND THEIR ACCESSION DATES

1957	Belgium, France, Germany, Italy, Luxembourg, the Netherlands
1973	Denmark, Ireland, United Kingdom
1981	Greece
1986	Portugal, Spain
1995*	Austria, Finland, Sweden
2004	Hungary, Poland, Czech Republic, Slovakia, Slovenia, Lithuania, Estonia, Latvia, Cyprus, Malta

---

* Norway did not join in 1995, its electorate having defeated approval for membership in a national referendum.

courts, revising the penal code, and tightening civilian control over the army. A precondition of Turkey's entry is its recognition of Cyprus's Greek-Cypriot government, one reason why the Cypriots and Greeks have supported entry talks with Turkey.

In the post-9/11 world, the entry of Turkey into the EU has assumed much greater significance, not only for Europeans, but for the West as well. Anticipated by 2015 to have a larger population than any present EU state, Turkey presents major challenges for the EU in two sensitive areas: agriculture and poor regions—two areas that are potentially very expensive. The admission of Turkey into the EU is seen by many as a test of the West's genuine commitment to encourage ties with moderate and democratic Islamic communities, with the result that there is considerable pressure on Europeans to overcome their apprehension and extend their comity eastward.

Two other countries, Bulgaria and Romania, have applied for EU membership and are expected to be accepted as members by 2008.

The Issue of a New Constitution for the EU

Because the institutions and the governance of the EU have been developed by successive treaties over a period of years, it is generally acknowledged that there is a need to consolidate all existing European treaties into a single document that can serve as a constitution for the EU. Successive intergovernmental conferences have been held to address the issues of the delimitation of power between the EU and its member states, the status of the *Charter of Fundamental Rights*, the simplification of the existing treaties, and the role of the national parliaments. The challenges faced by these conferences are daunting. While it is generally agreed that the enlargement of the EU makes a new constitution necessary, the tension between making the enlarged community work, and the domestic pressure to maintain national sovereignty cannot be underestimated. Endless compromises need to be made requiring negotiators and drafters to grapple with issues such as common policies of defence and immigration, migration, agriculture, border security, single currency requirements, labour markets, and, perhaps most insurmountable, the cost of it all. The draft constitution that emerged in 2004 was ambitious; it

- provided for the consolidation of all European treaties into a single document;
- incorporated the *Charter of Fundamental Rights* into EU law;
- provided for EU law to have primacy over national law (a principle previously established by the jurisprudence of the EU Court of Justice);
- committed the EU to the progressive development of a common defence policy;

- committed the EU to creating common rules on asylum and immigration;
- extended majority voting to areas not already covered;
- provided for formal legal personality for the EU, enabling it to sign international agreements;
- retained national vetoes over direct taxation, foreign and defence policy, and financing of the EU budgets;
- provided for a double-majority voting system whereby laws would be passed if 55 percent of countries representing 65 percent of the EU's population approve;
- created a president of the EU Council who would serve for up to five years;
- created a foreign minister for the EU;
- proposed limits for the European Commission, abandoning the principle that all member states must have a commissioner at all times;
- gave new powers to the EU Parliament to amend laws, control the budget, and approve the choice of the president of the EU Commission;
- introduced a subsidiarity provision under which, if a third of the national parliaments object to an EU law, the EU Commission must reconsider it; and
- created an explicit right for countries to withdraw from the EU.

It was agreed that all 25 EU members must ratify the constitution before it could come into force. Hopes for closer political integration suffered a serious setback in May and June of 2005 when voters in France and the Netherlands, two original members and traditionally strong supporters of European unity, defeated the draft constitution in specific referenda held for the purpose of approval of the initiative. Since then, the EU's constitutional talks have entered a "cooling-off" phase. However, the issues addressed in the new constitution must still be dealt with, although it is now likely that this will occur in the time-honoured EU piecemeal fashion.

THE INSTITUTIONS OF THE EU

European Council

The European Council is an unofficial body that is not technically one of the EU institutions. Made up of the presidents and/or prime ministers of all the member countries, it provides the high-level political direction for policy in the EU. As an intergovernmental forum, it does not create law in any sense. It meets up to four times a year with the president of the EU Commission. These meetings are referred to as EU summit meetings.

FIGURE 4.1 INSTITUTIONS OF THE EU

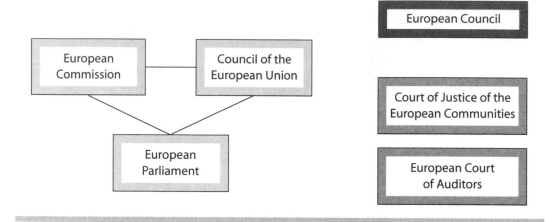

The Council of the European Union

Care must be taken not to confuse the Council of the European Union—an official law-making component of the EU system—with the European Council—the intergovernmental body described above.

Composition and Functions of the Council

The Council of the European Union is referred to simply as "the Council" and is the EU's main decision-making body. Each member state sends one representative to Council meetings. The duty of cabinet or ministerial-level representatives is to represent their member state and each is empowered to commit his or her government. Each minister is answerable to his or her national parliament and to the citizens of his or her own country. Which ministers are chosen to attend the various meetings of the Council will depend upon what subjects are on the agenda. Governments may vary their ministerial representation according to the subject matter to be considered. Although the Council is a single entity, it may be configured into different councils that represent nine areas of interest:

- general affairs and external relations;
- economic and financial affairs;
- justice and home affairs;
- employment, social policy, health, and consumer affairs;
- economic competitiveness;
- transport, telecommunications, and energy;

- agriculture and fisheries;
- environment; and
- education, youth, and culture.

Most of the responsibilities of the Council relate to the community domain, and include passage of EU laws jointly with the EU Parliament, coordination of the broad economic policies of member states, conclusion of international agreements, and approval of the EU budget jointly with the EU Parliament. The responsibility to develop a common foreign and security policy and to coordinate cooperation between the national courts and police forces in criminal matters relates to areas in which member states have not relinquished their national powers but are simply working together (the second and third pillars shown in box 4.2).

How the Council Operates

The presidency of the Council rotates every six months, with an individual from a different EU country assuming the role for each period. Each EU country has a permanent team headed by the country's ambassador to the EU. These permanent representatives meet weekly within the Permanent Representative Committee known as COREPER and prepare the work of the Council. (Up to four times a year the presidents and/or prime ministers of all the member countries come together with the president of the EU Commission and meet as the European Council.) Voting in the Council is based on member countries' populations, at present allocated as follows:

Germany, France, Italy, and the United Kingdom	29 each
Spain and Poland	27 each
Netherlands	13
Belgium, Czech Republic, Greece, Hungary, and Portugal	12 each
Austria and Sweden	10 each
Denmark, Ireland, Lithuania, Slovakia, and Finland	7 each
Cyprus, Estonia, Latvia, Luxembourg, and Slovenia	4 each
Malta	3

In particularly sensitive areas, such as common foreign and security policy, taxation, asylum and immigration policy, Council decisions must be unanimous. On most issues, however, the Council makes its decision by "qualified majority voting"—that is, a majority of member states approve, a minimum of 232 votes is cast in favour, and the votes in favour represent at least 62 percent of the EU population.

The European Commission

The term "European Commission" is used in two ways: (1) to describe its commissioners and (2) to describe its structure.

Commissioners to the European Commission are appointed by their home countries—at present, one per country. A new Commission is appointed every five years with member state governments first agreeing on a designate as the new commission president. Once this individual is approved by the EU Parliament, he or she, in discussion with member governments, chooses the other members of the Commission. The choices must then be approved by the EU Parliament. Although the appointed commissioners have often held political positions in their countries of origin, once they are members of the European Commission they are committed to acting in the interests of the EU as a whole, and do not take instructions from their national governments. This commitment reflects the intention that the Commission be independent of national governments because its mandate is to represent and uphold the interests of the EU as a whole. The Commission has two functions: first, to draft proposals for new European laws, which it presents to the EU Parliament and the Council; and second, to function as the EU's executive arm—that is, to be responsible for implementing the decisions of Parliament and the Council, and to manage the day-to-day business of the EU by implementing policies, running programs, and "paying the bills." The Commission remains politically accountable to the EU Parliament, which has the power to dismiss the whole Commission by adopting a motion of censure. The Commission attends all the sessions of the EU Parliament, where it must clarify and justify its policies and reply to written and oral questions posed by members of the EU Parliament (MEPs).

The term "European Commission" also refers to the institution itself and its staff. The day-to-day running of the Commission is carried out by administrative officials, experts, translators, and secretarial staff that total more than 25,000 people.

The Commission has four main roles: proposing new legislation, implementing EU policies and the budget, enforcing European law, and representing the EU internationally.

Proposing New Legislation

The Commission has the right of initiative—that is, it alone is responsible for drawing up proposals for new European legislation, which it presents to the EU Parliament and the Council. These proposals are in the interests of the European Union itself, not those of specific countries or industries. The Commission consults with various interest groups and with the Economic and Social Committee and the Committee of the Regions; as well, it seeks the opinions of national governments. Once a legislative proposal is in draft form, it is placed on the agenda of the next Commission meeting and, if at least 13 of the present 25 commissioners approve the proposal, it is adopted and sent to Council and the EU Parliament.

Implementing EU Policies and the Budget
As the EU's executive body, the Commission is responsible for managing and implementing the EU budget. While most of the actual spending is done by national and local authorities, it is the Commission that is ultimately responsible for supervising this, together with the Court of Auditors. In addition to its budgetary responsibility, the Commission is charged with managing policies such as the common agricultural policy, the competition policy, and cross-border partnerships such as regional partnerships and Europe-wide student exchanges.

Enforcing European Law
The Commission is responsible for making sure that EU law is properly applied in all the member states. If an EU country is not applying an EU law, the Commission will advise the member government in an official letter stating the details of the infringement and setting a deadline for a response. If the response of the member state is deemed by the Commission to be unsatisfactory, the Commission will refer the matter to the EU Court of Justice.

Representing the EU Internationally
The Commission represents the EU in such international forums as the WTO and has the responsibility of negotiating international agreements on behalf of the EU.

The European Parliament
Since 1979, members of the European Parliament have been elected directly by the more than 450 million citizens of EU member countries. Elections are held every five years for the 732-member chamber. MEPS do not sit in national blocs, but in seven Europe-wide political groups that range in position from strongly pro-federalist pan-Europeans, to reluctant Euroskeptics.

The EU Parliament has three main roles: to pass European laws, to provide democratic supervision, and to approve the budget.

Passing European Laws
By virtue of co-decision (see page 98), the EU Parliament and the Council are on an equal footing with respect to legislation in a number of areas. The EU Parliament is also able to initiate new laws by asking the European Commission to put forward proposals.

Democratic Supervision
Democratic supervision includes approval of nominations for the EU Commission, described above, as well as the regular examination of reports of the Commission. The EU Parliament has the power to censure the Commission

by calling for its mass resignation. Parliament also monitors the work of the Council, by asking questions and having the president of the Council attend the Parliament's plenary sessions. In addition, the Parliament examines petitions from citizens sets up committees of inquiry, and provides input to every EU summit meeting.

Budgetary Responsibility
The EU Parliament shares responsibility for approval of the annual EU budget with the Council. The EU Parliament's Committee on Budgetary Control monitors annual budgetary expenditures, and Parliament must approve the European Commission's activities by granting a discharge on an annual basis.

The Court of Justice
Established in 1952, the European Court of Justice (ECJ) is based in Luxembourg. Its function is to settle legal disputes between EU member states, EU institutions, businesses, and individuals and to ensure that EU legislation is interpreted and applied uniformly in all EU countries. The ECJ comprises one judge per member state although all 25 judges rarely sit as a full court. The ECJ either sits as a Grand Chamber of 13 judges or in smaller chambers of three or five judges. The judges are appointed for a six-year renewable term by joint agreement among the EU member governments. Procedurally, the court functions more like a civil, rather than a common-law, court. It is assisted by eight advocates general whose role is to present reasoned opinions publicly and impartially on the cases brought before the court. At the first stage, all parties involved submit written statements, and at the second stage—the public hearing stage—the parties' lawyers argue their case before the judges and the advocates general. The advocates general then provide an opinion (if the court believes that the case raises a new point of law), after which the judges deliberate and deliver their judgment. Judgments of the ECJ are decided by a majority and pronounced at a public hearing. Unlike in the common-law tradition, dissenting opinions are not expressed.

In 1989, a Court of First Instance was created to assist in handling the ECJ's workload and to provide EU citizens with better legal protection. This court rules on actions brought by private individuals, companies, and organizations and in cases that relate to competition law.

There are four typical types of cases decided by the ECJ.

Preliminary Rulings
National courts in each member country are responsible for ensuring that EU law is properly applied in their jurisdictions. To assist with this, the

national courts may ask the Court of Justice for a preliminary ruling on the interpretation or validity of an EU law.

Failure by a Member Country to Fulfill an Obligation

The European Commission is charged with ensuring the integrity of the EU as a whole and may begin proceedings against any EU country if it reasonably believes that a member state is not complying with its obligations under EU law. If the court finds that the member country has not complied, the country must remedy the situation or the court may impose a fine.

Action for Annulment

If any member state, the Council, the Commission, or the EU Parliament believes that a particular EU law is illegal, it may ask the court to annul it. This action is also available to private individuals if a law directly and adversely affects them as individuals. If the court finds that the law in question was not correctly adopted or is not in accordance with the EU treaties, it may declare the law null and void.

Actions for Failure to Act

The EU treaties oblige the EU Parliament, the Council, and the Commission to make certain decisions under certain circumstances. If they fail to do so, a member state, another community institution, or, in certain circumstances, individuals or companies can bring a complaint to the court and ask that the matter be judicially determined.

The Court of Auditors

The Court of Auditors, established in 1975, is charged with responsibility to ensure that the EU budget is correctly implemented and that sound financial management is practised. The court is completely independent of the other EU institutions. The Court of Auditors provides the EU Parliament and Council with an annual audit report. The court comprises one member from each EU country, appointed by the Council for a renewable term of six years.

HOW DOES THE EU MAKE DECISIONS?

The rules and procedures for EU decision making are established by the various EU treaties. Specific treaty articles determine which legislative procedure must be followed for a particular initiative. Generally, the European Commission proposes new legislation, and it is the Council and Parliament that pass the proposal. The three main procedures are co-decision, consultation, and assent.

Co-decision

Co-decision is the procedure used to enact most new laws in the EU. During this procedure, Parliament shares legislative power equally with the Council. If the two institutions cannot agree to pass a proposed law, the law is placed before a conciliation committee that is composed of an equal number of Council and Parliament representatives. Once this committee has reached agreement, the proposal is resubmitted to Parliament and Council.

Consultation

During the consultation process, Council consults with Parliament as well as the European Economic and Social Committee and the Committee of the Regions as to the merits of a Commission proposal. Parliament may then approve the Commission proposal, reject it, or ask for amendments. If Parliament requests amendments, the Commission will consider them and, if the suggestions for amendment are accepted, the amended proposal is considered by the Council, which either approves it or amends it further. If Council wishes to amend the Commission's amended proposal, it must do so unanimously.

Assent

Assent is similar to consultation except that Parliament cannot amend the proposal; it must either be accepted or rejected. Acceptance requires an absolute majority of parliamentary votes cast. This procedure is reserved for very important decisions.

It is recognized in the EU that these decision-making procedures require simplification. The proposed constitution attempted to clarify and streamline these rules, as well as make the EU more open and democratic by requiring EU ministers to hold their law-making sessions in public, providing citizens the right to submit petitions asking the Commission for specific new laws, and giving national parliaments a greater role in monitoring commission proposals. Whether these proposals will be saved after the 2005 defeat of the constitution remains to be seen.

HARMONIZATION OF LAW IN THE EU

The single market is created by the harmonization of laws of the member countries. This is the process of making the different countries' laws uniform in either form or results. The Treaty of Rome gives the Council and the European Commission power to make regulations, issue directives, take decisions, and make recommendations or deliver opinions. The effect of these actions may be explained as follows:

- A *regulation* is binding in its entirety and is directly applicable in all member states. This is the method commonly used to regulate agriculture and competition—see, for example, the recent Merger Regulation.
- A *directive* prescribes objectives and is binding on each member state to which it is addressed, although the national authorities of the member state are free to determine the form and method that will be used to achieve the mandated result. Countries usually have three years to implement a directive. Examples of directives include EU environmental and product liability rules.
- A *decision* is binding on the member state, firm, or individual to whom it is addressed. An example of this is the recent decision by the European Commission that Microsoft had violated EU competition law by leveraging its near monopoly for PC operating systems.
- A *recommendation* or an *opinion* is of persuasive value but has no binding effect. An example of this action is the recent recommendation on sexual harassment.

EUROPEAN LEGAL PROVISIONS RELEVANT TO CANADIAN BUSINESS

The body of EU law is immense and is growing very rapidly. A general text such as this cannot hope to do more than alert its readers to the potential for issues or situations that are either so common as to be notable, or are unique to the EU and not easily foreseeable by the Canadian business person. The discussion below is not meant to be exhaustive, but is included to help readers anticipate problems and appreciate the importance of obtaining competent, specialized, legal advice before embarking on serious negotiations and legal commitments in, or affecting, Europe.

Competition Law

Competition law has always been of central importance to the EU. It involves such sensitive areas as national regulatory goals, market power, and political strategy. These basic provisions are found in Articles 81 and 82 of the Treaty of Rome and cover anti-competitive agreements between firms, abuse of dominant position, and company mergers. (These same provisions have been incorporated into more recent legislation as Articles 85 and 86.) A number of different and not always mutually compatible objectives lie at the heart of EU competition policy. These objectives include enhancing efficiency, protecting consumers and smaller firms from large aggregations of economic power, and facilitating and protecting the creation of a single European market.

Article 81 (now Article 85)—Concerted Market Behaviour

This provision generally prohibits concerted market practices, "which may affect trade between Member States and which have as their object or effect the prevention, restriction or distortion of competition within the common market." Specifically, the provision enumerates specific market activities of particular concern—namely, price fixing, limitations on production, market-sharing, discrimination among parties, and tie-ins. The article addresses only joint or collusive conduct as opposed to the conduct of a single actor.

BOX 4.4   THE DYESTUFFS CASE
(European Court of Justice, 1972)

In this case, the ECJ considered allegations that there had been concerted practices in the dyestuffs industry. It was proved that 80 percent of the dyestuffs market was supplied by 10 producers; that these firms possessed differing cost structures; that there were a large number of dyes produced by each firm; that while standard dyes could be replaced by other products, this was not the case with specialist dyes; that the market for specialist dyes tended to be **oligopolistic**; and that the European market in dyestuffs consisted of five separate national markets that had different price levels. The court considered price increases in individual country markets in 1964, 1965, and 1967 and found that the increases were factually connected. It concluded that the increases revealed progressive cooperation between the dyestuffs firms, and that the dividing up of the market into five national markets with different price levels and structures made it improbable that a spontaneous and equal price increase would occur in all the national markets. The court, therefore, concluded that the uniform increase in those different markets could only be explained by a common intention on the part of the dyestuffs firms to adjust the level of prices and to avoid the risk of changing the conditions of competition. The firms were found to be in violation of the provisions of Article 81 (now 85) of the Treaty of Rome.

Preservation of the Single European Market

One of the major goals of Article 81 (now 85) is to preserve the single European market and to prevent its fragmentation into single country markets.

BOX 4.5   SINGLE COUNTRY MARKET?

**Consten & Grundig v. European Commission
(European Court of Justice, 1966)**

The German company Grundig appointed the French company Consten as its exclusive dealer for Grundig products in France, the Saar, and Corsica. Consten undertook not to sell products that would compete with Grundig products and not to export the Grundig products directly or indirectly to any other countries. Grundig had appointed dealers in other European countries and had imposed similar restrictions on them. Another French company, UNEF, bought Grundig products from a German dealer and sold them in France at cheaper prices than Consten had set. Consten sued UNEF in France and the case was referred to the European Court of Justice.

The court was asked whether a manufacturer can restrict imports and exports of its products within the common market by imposing territorial prohibitions and limitations in its dealers.

The court held that such restrictions are a violation of Article 81 of the Treaty of Rome and that artificial national divisions of the common market are prohibited. The court concluded that parallel imports are valuable because they reduce national price differences.

Extraterritorial Application of EU Competition Law

Like the United States, the EU asserts a right to enforce its competition policy beyond its own borders. An early and famous example of this assertion of extraterritorial reach is the Canadian Woodpulp Producers decision, which involved the EEC.

BOX 4.6   EEC EXTRATERRITORIAL REACH

Canadian Woodpulp Producers (Decisions of the European Commission and the European Court of Justice, 1985)

Three trade associations located in Canada, the United States, Sweden, Finland, Norway, Portugal, and Spain agreed on prices for the upcoming quarter either through regular exchanges of price proposals by telex or telephone or in meetings. Members of the associations quoted prices for woodpulp in United States dollars. They banned resale by the EEC purchasers within the EEC and banned the export of the woodpulp from the EEC.

The European Commission was asked several questions:

1. Has there been a violation of Article 85(1)? Is there evidence
   a. of an agreement or concerted practice between an association of undertakings?
   b. that competition in the EEC may be prevented, restricted, or distorted as a result?
   c. that trade between the member states of the EEC is affected?
2. Does the EEC have jurisdiction over these associations, which are not domiciled in the EEC?

The Commission had little difficulty in determining that the agreements and concerted practices of the producers and their associations prevented, restricted, or distorted competition in the EEC, and it threatened to levy an immediate fine on each producer totalling 10 percent of the world turnover of the producer or 1,000,000 European currency units (ecus), whichever was greater. Although none of the woodpulp producers was located in the EEC, the threat of such a large fine was sufficient to persuade them to agree that future quotes, sales, and invoices for 50 percent of their woodpulp would be in the local currency of the buyer. The Commission believed that this would make future concerted practices more difficult.

The Commission's decision was appealed to the European Court of Justice where it was upheld.

Article 82 (now Article 86)—Control of Market Power

While Article 81 addresses the concerted behaviour of two or more firms, Article 86 addresses the behaviour of a single, dominant firm that abuses its market power. The provision does not prohibit market power or monopoly in itself; it prohibits the abuse of market power.

The *Continental Can* case is an illustration of the lack of clarity that exists with respect to the application of Article 86. While most legal commentators agree that Article 86 does not condemn dominance in itself, there does seem to be a "special responsibility" imposed on dominant firms. But the boundaries of this special responsibility are not clear from the cases, and this results in uncertainty for a firm that is in a dominant position as to what it is allowed to do. It is also unclear from the cases whether the provision is intended to protect consumers, or competitors, or both. It is interesting to compare the approach of the EU and the United States in competition or antitrust cases: the United States tends to look at mergers from the consumer's perspective, whereas the EU considers not only how the merger will affect the consumer but also how it will affect other companies.

BOX 4.7   ABUSE OF MARKET POWER: CONTINENTAL CAN CASE

(European Court of Justice, 1973)

Continental Can (CC) was a US manufacturer of metal packaging that had a presence in Europe through a German firm, SLW, that it acquired in 1969. In 1970, CC attempted to acquire a controlling interest in a Dutch company, TDV. The European Commission found that CC had a dominant position in Europe for certain types of packaging and that there had been an abuse of that position by the purchase of TDV. CC argued before the European Court of Justice that there had been no abuse.

The issue before the court was whether the structure of the firm itself was enough to create an abuse under Article 82 (now 86). The court held that the acquisition was a violation of Article 82 (86) because it placed the competitive market structure in jeopardy and that there was no need for any real causal link between the dominance and a forbidden action. The fact that the merger was a threat to competitors was enough to bring it within the prohibition of the article.

The EU Merger Regulation

The 1990s saw a remarkable increase in overall merger activity, both in the EU and around the world. There has been an increase in the number of large-scale transactions between global players. These mergers go beyond a simple consolidation of activities in different regions of the world; they can be described as the worldwide integration and consolidation of activities. Sometimes a series of mergers has completely transformed an entire industry on a worldwide basis. One such example is the oil industry where the first merger between BP and Amoco was swiftly followed by mergers between Exxon and Mobil, BP and Arco, and TotalFina and Elf. These mergers were dealt with under the comprehensive Merger Regulation, which came into effect in 1990. This regulation was passed to clarify the application of EU competition policy to mergers. The test for the legality of a transaction under the Merger Regulation is that it must not create or strengthen a dominant position, either in the form of single dominance or in the form of collective dominance. Abuse of dominant position has been defined as a position of economic strength that enables an enterprise to prevent effective competition being maintained in the relevant market by giving it the power to behave independently of its competitors, customers, and ultimately all consumers. It is this provision that forms the basis of the EU Merger Regulation. The central test under the regulation is one of "compatibility" with the common market. According to the test, a concentration that creates or strengthens a dominant position as a result of which effective competition would be significantly impeded in the common market or a substantial part of it *shall be declared incompatible with the common market.*

There are a number of instances where the European Commission has found the creation or strengthening of a single dominance at the level of a world market is incompatible with the common market. This was the case in the merger between Aerospatiale Alenia and de Havilland. In the *Aerospatiale-de Havilland* case, a European consortium, Aerospatiale-Alenia, agreed to buy de Havilland, a Canadian company owned by Boeing, a US firm. Aerospatiale and de Havilland each specialized in producing smaller commuter aircraft. The European Commission ruled that the proposed merger would create a situation in which there could be an abuse of dominant position in the European market for commuter aircraft. As a result, the merger failed and de Havilland was subsequently purchased by the Canadian firm, Bombardier.

Another case in the aircraft sector concerned the high-profile Boeing–McDonnell Douglas merger in 1997. The merger of the two US aircraft production companies was approved by the US antitrust authorities in the US Justice Department, but the European Commission threatened to reject the merger on the grounds that Boeing already controlled more than 60 percent of the global market for commercial aircraft and that its only real rival was the European consortium Airbus Industries, which at that time had an estimated 30 percent of the market. McDonnell Douglas had less than 10 percent. The Commission objected to the contract that Boeing had signed with American Airlines, Delta Air Lines, and Continental Airlines whereby Boeing would be the exclusive supplier of aircraft to those companies. Although the Commission could not technically block the merger, the fines that the Europeans threatened to impose would have made it difficult for Boeing to operate in Europe. As a result, Boeing waived its exclusive supply contracts involving the three major US airlines, and agreed to license some of its patents on commercial aircraft to its rivals.

It is in connection with the Merger Regulation provision that the EU has most often asserted its "right" to extraterritorial jurisdiction over companies not domiciled in the EU.

Two other cases of particular interest to North Americans are the proposed Honeywell–General Electric merger in 2001 and the more recent *Microsoft* case. In the *Honeywell* case, the US Department of Justice had approved the proposed merger, requiring only minimal disposals by General Electric, but the concerns of the EU and its consequent demands for changes in the deal completely exceeded the expectations of the American companies, and, as a result, the parties abandoned the merger, which was estimated to have a value of $45 billion. The concerns of the EU were chiefly related to market dominance. They perceived that competition in regional and jet engines would be reduced and that the combined companies would dominate the aviation and aerospace service market, and the exit of rivals, and lead to monopolization of the market and total dominance of General Electric. The case caused great consternation in the United States, and temporarily soured relations between the US Department of Justice and the European Commission.

BOX 4.8   ABUSE OF MARKET POWER: THE MICROSOFT CASE (European Commission, 2004–6)

The European Commission was asked to investigate whether Microsoft has used its dominant position with Windows OS to limit competition from rival makers of server software used to run printers, password sign-ins, and file access for small work groups. In 2004, the Commission concluded after a five-year investigation that Microsoft had violated Article 82 by leveraging its near monopoly in the market for computer operating systems into the markets for work group server operating systems and for media players. The Commission found that Microsoft had abused its market power by deliberately restricting operability between Windows PCs and non-Microsoft work group servers, and by tying its Windows Media Player to the Windows operating system. This enabled Microsoft to acquire a dominant position in the market for work group server operating systems and threatened competition in that market. The Commission ruled that Microsoft could retain the right to offer a version of its Windows operating system duet with the Windows Media Player, but had to refrain from using any commercial, technological, or contractual terms that would have the effect of rendering the unbundled version of Windows less attractive or less satisfactory in terms of performance. In particular, PC manufacturers were not to be given a discount conditional on their buying Windows together with the Windows Media Player. The Commission ordered Microsoft to disclose to its competitors the interfaces required for the competitors' products to be able to interface with the Microsoft Windows operating system. The Commission stated that "dominant companies have a special responsibility to ensure that the way they do business does not prevent competition on the merits and does not harm consumers and innovation. ... This decision restores the conditions for fair competition in the markets concerned and established clear principles for the future conduct of a company with such a strong dominant position." Microsoft has made some changes but not enough to satisfy the Commission and the case has not been fully resolved at the time of writing.

Control of Vertical Restraint Agreements

One important area of competition policy relates to vertical agreements. A **vertical agreement** is an agreement made between parties that are at different levels of the production process, such as a distribution agreement between a manufacturer and a retailer, or agent. A vertical restraint agreement is one that limits the activities of actors down the "vertical line." There is considerable controversy among competition policy analysts as to whether these agreements are economically harmful. Vertical restraint agreements vary widely in their terms and their effect; however, some of these agreements will be found by the Commission to violate the terms of Article 85. Potential disadvantages to the competitive market include limitation of opportunity for competitors in a market; risk to consumers; the use of such agreements to mask **horizontal agreements**; and division of the market along national or regional lines. Particularly worrying to the Commission is an exclusive distribution agreement where the producer agrees to supply the product only to a particular distributor within a particular territory, often buttressed by attempts to prevent third parties from selling into the contract territory of the designate distributor. The use of export bans that prohibit a distributor from exporting the product outside a designated area will be judged particularly severely, as will any other attempt to establish absolute territorial protection for a distributor. If a firm is contemplating an exclusive distribution agreement, legal advice should be sought because an exemption may be required. Exemptions are available as either qualifying under a **block exemption** or as an individual exemption.

Exemption from the Application of Article 85

Agreements that on their face are violations of Article 85 may seek exemption. Although an individual exemption may be sought from the Commission, this is an expensive undertaking and not to be embarked upon lightly. The philosophy of the Commission is that for an agreement that restricts competition to qualify for exemption, it must contribute to the improvement of production or distribution, or promote technical and economic progress and constitute an improvement on the situation that would otherwise exist. Block exemptions are available for generic types of agreements. Agreements that come within the terms of a block exemption do not need to be notified and approved by the Commission. Block exemptions are available in a number of areas, including specialization agreements, research and development agreements, vertical restraint agreements, technology transfer agreements, and franchising agreements. Expert legal advice is required for a firm contemplating such agreements in the EU.

Product Liability

In 1985, the EU passed a Directive on Product Liability. A system of almost **strict liability** is mandated by this directive, which has been widely perceived by American writers to have brought European law with respect to products closer to that of the United States and exceeds the criteria for liability in Canada, which sets a lower standard for manufacturers and distributors. There is also a Machinery Directive (1989), which expands the system of strict liability in the EU to protect the health and safety of workers against risks of defective machinery.

In addition, there is the Directive on General Product Safety (1992). This directive, which imposes a general duty of safety on producers of consumer products, possibly goes further than the laws of Canada and the United States. It creates labelling and monitoring requirements and imposes an obligation to market only safe products.

EU Technical Standards

Technical standards are one of the most significant barriers to Canadians seeking to do business in the EU. The EU has adopted common technical standards for all countries based on recognition of international standards. Once a product has been accepted into one country of the EU, it can circulate freely within all the EU countries. The EU countries have agreed to mandatory mutual recognition of accepted standards and testing procedures.

One of the best methods that companies can use to ensure that their standards will not be in violation of the stringent EU requirements is to conform to the ISO Standards of Quality Assurance and Quality Management (**ISO 9000**). Developed in Europe, this quality standard has been used in North America since the late 1980s. These standards are published in the *ISO Compendium*, which has four parts:

- 9001, which applies to services and service industries;
- 9002, which applies to manufacturing;
- 9003, which relates to computer hardware and software; and
- 9004, which is the Quality Management Guideline and provides information on the application and implementation of 9001 to 9003.

The ISO 9000 provides a structured process through which companies can improve the quality of the products and services that they provide and maintain the level of quality they achieve. There are several phases to the ISO 9000 process:

- *Pre-audit.* The level of quality delivered by the present structure, processes, and procedures are examined to identify any weak links.

- *Process mapping and detailed documentation.* What is actually done in the company is examined and documented.
- *Training.* To assist in mastery of new processes and procedures, training is provided.
- *Compliance audit.* After the changes have become established practices, a compliance audit is conducted to determine whether the objectives have been met.
- *Registration audit.* A registration audit is conducted by an outside firm with registrar status to confirm that the company conforms to the guidelines and its attestations of quality. A certification is valid for three years.
- *Periodic maintenance audits.* Maintenance audits are conducted to ensure that the company complies with the quality levels for which it is certified.

The ISO 9000 standards enable harmonization of standards on an international scale and provide a business with the opportunity to reduce its exposure to third-party liability. Since the end of 1992, many products entering the EU have had to bear the CE (Conformitée Europeanne) mark as a tangible sign of conformity to community directives and rules. In addition to being mandatory in the EU, these standards provide a valuable marketing advantage in all markets.

OTHER REGIONAL TRADE GROUPINGS

The first years of the 21st century have witnessed an enormous proliferation of bilateral trading arrangements, a reflection of the relative ease of reaching an agreement when there are only two parties, as opposed to the daunting task of achieving consensus among all the members of the WTO, which is the chief reason that progress in the Doha Round of trade talks has been so disappointing. The movement toward bilateral free trade agreements has been much criticized by trade policy analysts as creating a "spaghetti bowl of agreements" with conflicting provisions that may have the effect of delaying multilateral negotiations that would eventually achieve freer trade worldwide. Closely related to the phenomenon of bilateral free trade agreements is the growth of regional free trade agreements. Like Canada, the United States, and Mexico, which were able to sign a trilateral trade agreement in the face of disappointing progress in the Uruguay Round, many nations are taking advantage of the geography, culture, and customs that they share to reach regional free trade agreements. The status of these agreements is continually changing and any list or description of the current state of these agreements is bound to be out of date almost immediately. A representative sample of these important arrangements follows.

Canada

In addition to NAFTA (discussed in the next chapter), Canada has free trade agreements with Israel as of 1996 and Chile as of 1997. Negotiations are presently under way for a free trade agreement between Canada and the group of four Central American countries, which consists of El Salvador, Guatemala, Honduras, and Nicaragua.

The Americas

The list of free trade agreements negotiated by the various countries in Latin America is extensive. The most ambitious of these projects, the **Free Trade Area of the Americas (FTAA)**, remains a dream. If established, the FTAA would be the largest trading bloc in the world—comprising an area with 800 million inhabitants and a combined GDP of $11.4 trillion. Although negotiations among the prospective 34 American countries, including Canada and the United States, began at the First Summit of the Americas in Miami in 1994, they have so far been unsuccessful. The two largest economies, the United States and Brazil, have had serious differences, and, as time has passed, more and more countries have turned to more realistic negotiations with fewer countries involved.

The last 20 years have seen considerable trade liberalization and broader economic policy reform in Latin America. So far, Latin America has approached freer trade through regionalism, characterized by the creation of subregional preferential agreements that remain open to new members and whose members remain free to pursue other agreements. Numerous bilateral agreements have also been reached, resulting in a complex and enlarging matrix of diverse trade and economic treaty arrangements. Thus we presently have, in addition to NAFTA, free trade agreements among Colombia, Mexico, and Venezuela, the bilateral trade agreements signed by Mexico with Bolivia, Chile, Costa Rica, Nicaragua, and the Northern Triangle (El Salvador, Guatemala, and Honduras), as well as the free trade agreement between Canada and Chile. In addition, there is the free trade agreement between the Central American countries and the Dominican Republic, and the Colonia Protocol for Mercosur, the investment agreement between the Caribbean Community and Common Market (CARICOM) and the Dominican Republic, as well as Decision 291 of the Andean Community. One result of such agreements is a substantial drop in average tariff rates in Latin America: from over 40 percent in the mid-1980s to less than 12 percent in 1999.

In 2005 the United States and six Latin American countries (Costa Rica, Nicaragua, the Dominican Republic, El Salvador, Honduras, and Guatemala) signed CAFTA, the Central American Free Trade Agreement. This is part of an ambitious US policy of entering into numerous free trade agreements. The United States now has entered into free trade agreements with more than 15 countries in the last decade and was in the process of negotiating a further 11 at the time of writing.

Canada, in addition to NAFTA, has free trade arrangements with Chile and Costa Rica.

Europe

The EU has been very active in the pursuit of regional free trade agreements and has concluded many agreements with countries as disparate as Egypt, Chile, Mexico, and South Africa. Negotiations are under way with Mercosur, the Gulf Cooperation Council (Bahrain, Kuwait, Oman, Qatar, Saudi Arabia, and UAE), Western Africa, Central Africa, the Caribbean, SADC (Angola, Botswana, Lesotho, Mozambique, Namibia, Swaziland, and Tanzania), and the 14 Asian Pacific countries.

Asia

Association of South East Asian Nations (ASEAN)

The Association of South East Asian Nations (ASEAN) was established in 1967 with the Bangkok Declaration. The original members were Indonesia, Malaysia, the Philippines, Singapore, and Thailand. Brunei Darussalam became the sixth member in 1984, and Vietnam the seventh in 1995. Lao PDR and Myanmar joined in 1997 and Cambodia in 1999. At the time of formation, the members were reluctant to cede strong powers to the association, preferring to maintain a high level of individual sovereignty. For this reason, ASEAN has a flexible and loose structure. Even with subsequent improvements in the structure, ASEAN remains an intergovernmental regional organization with no supra-national law-making powers. This is perhaps a reflection of Eastern decision making with its emphasis on informal and discreet discussions behind the scenes rather than the Western preference for structure and firm rules. The aims and purposes of the Association are (1) to accelerate economic growth, social progress, and cultural development in the region and (2) to promote regional peace and stability through abiding respect for justice and the rule of law in the relationship among countries in the region and adherence to the principles of the United Nations Charter. Economic cooperation in ASEAN has been slow to develop because of the dominance of national interests. Increasingly, however, Asian nations are making arrangements to cooperate to create freer trade within the region.

ASEAN Free Trade Area (AFTA)

In 1992, the leaders of ASEAN agreed to establish an ASEAN Free Trade Area (AFTA) within 15 years beginning January 1, 1993. The primary instrument for implementing the AFTA is the Common Effective Preferential Tariff Scheme (CEPT). It provides that, once all countries accept that a specific good is to be covered under the CEPT, then all member countries must give the preferential tariff. Although unprocessed agricultural products were originally excluded from this scheme, member countries agreed in 1994 to phase such products into the CEPT scheme.

Asian Pacific Economic Community (APEC)

The Asian Pacific Economic Community (APEC), a very loosely confederated group born of the Asia-Pacific Conference in 1993, is more a vision than an organization. Eighteen leaders of nations bordering the Pacific Ocean agreed that, by 2010, the developed countries should offer their developing neighbours free access to their markets and, by 2020, developing nations will offer the same. "Free access" has not been clearly defined, however.

South Asian Association for Regional Cooperation (SAARC)

In May 1985, seven nations of the Indian subcontinent signed a preferential trade agreement. Members of this association are India, Pakistan, Bangladesh, Sri Lanka, Nepal, Bhutan, and the Maldives.

South Asian Free Trade Area (SAFTA)

The South Asian Free Trade Area (SAFTA) was formed during a South Asian Association for Regional Cooperation (SAARC) conference in 2004 and promises to be a major milestone in South Asian trade relations. Regional trade in this area has been dominated by India, which is a major exporter and minor importer in the region. It is hoped that the agreement will encourage more imports from Pakistan to India and encourage the "big two" to overcome their bilateral differences.

Africa

While there are associations of countries in Africa, they have tended to have political, rather than economic, underpinnings. Some of these associations are described here, but this is a volatile region and subject to precipitous change. The future of these associations is uncertain.

Customs and Economic Union of Central Africa

The Customs and Economic Union of Central Africa was established in 1966 and is an association of French-speaking African nations that includes

Cameroon, the Central African Republic, the Republic of the Congo, Equatorial Guinea, and Gabon. Also known by its name in French, Union Douanière et Économique de l'Afrique Centrale (UDEAC), this group formed a customs union among its members. UDEAC signed a treaty for the establishment of the Economic and Monetary Community of Central Africa (CEMAC) to promote the entire process of subregional integration, and agreed to monetary union, with the Central African franc as a common currency. UDEAC was officially superseded by CEMAC in June 1999.

East Africa Customs Union (EAC)
Initiated in 1999, the East Africa Customs Union (EAC) is an association of East African countries: Kenya, Tanzania, Uganda, Ethiopia, Sudan, and Zambia. Progress on the EAC Customs Union Protocol has been slow; however, the union "began operations" in January 2005.

Economic Community of West African States (ECOWAS)
Formed in 1975, the Economic Community of West African States (ECOWAS) is an association of West African countries, including Côte d'Ivoire, Benin, Burkina Faso, Cape Verde, Gambia, Ghana, Guinea, Guinea-Bissau, Liberia, Mali, Mauritania, Niger, Nigeria, Togo, Sierra Leone, and Senegal.

There is currently speculation that a new African association may be formed, partly as a result of the re-emergence of South Africa. The new association, the Indian Ocean Economic Union, would unite South Africa, Mauritius, Mozambique, Madagascar, and India. Promoters of the union point out that the Indian Ocean is a natural and historic trade route. Such a union could cover 1.4 billion consumers and produce regional trade worth as much as US$250 billion.

The Middle East
The Middle East is notable in the context of the present movement toward integration through bilateral and multilateral trade agreements for the absence of activity in this area. Although the United States and the EU are actively seeking bilateral agreements with various Middle Eastern countries, there is little initiative emanating from the region itself.

Council of Arab Unity (CAEU)
The Council of Arab Unity (CAEU) was created in 1964 to implement the Arab Economic Unity Agreement among the states of the Arab League. Its 12 members are Egypt, Iraq, Jordan, Kuwait, Libya, Mauritania, Palestine, Somalia, Sudan, Syria, and the two Yemenis. The ultimate goal of the CAEU is to achieve complete economic unity among the member states.

Australasia

The first trade agreement in this region was the Closer Economic Relations Trade Agreement (CER) between Australia and New Zealand, a WTO-consistent trade agreement that came into force in 1983. As of 2006, Australia has free trade agreements with Singapore, Thailand, and the United States. It is presently negotiating with China, the United Arab Emirates, and Malaysia. In partnership with New Zealand, it is negotiating a regional free trade agreement between CER and ASEAN.

NOTE

1 "Towards an Uncertain Future," *The Economist*, November 22, 2003.

REVIEW QUESTIONS

Note that most of the answers for these questions will be found in the text. Some questions, however, address the current status of issues, and students should ensure that their information is up to date by searching current media sources.

1. What is the difference between a free trade area and a customs union? Why do both appear to derogate from the MFN principle? Why are they tolerated and approved by the WTO?
2. Name the present members of the EU. What countries are at the applicant stage? What are some of the issues that influence the negotiations for accession of these applicant countries?
3. Briefly describe the milestones in the development of the EU from the Treaty of Rome to the present.
4. Describe the three pillars of the EU.
5. What is the connection between the EU *Charter of Fundamental Rights* and the status of a constitution for the EU? What is the present status of a constitution for the EU?
6. Are all countries in the EU members of the European Monetary Union (that is, have they all adopted the common currency)?
7. Name the major institutions of the EU, and briefly describe their composition and function.
8. Briefly describe the three main procedures for decision making in the EU.
9. Describe how the EU achieves harmonization of its laws.
10. What are the three main prohibitions provided by EU competition law and where is the law relating to these found? What types of activities are prohibited by this area of EU law?

11. Describe the *Dyestuffs* case and explain why it is significant.
12. What is the significance of the *Grundig* case and what does it remind us about EU competition law?
13. In what area of competition law is the European Commission most likely to assert extraterritorial jurisdiction and why?
14. Describe two cases in which the findings of the European Commission affected mergers agreed to by firms located outside of Europe.
15. Describe the current status of the *Microsoft* case.
16. What is the difference between an individual exemption and a block exemption under Article 85?
17. Briefly describe any recent bilateral or limited multilateral agreements for freer trade in the Americas, Europe, Asia, Africa, the Middle East, and Australasia.

EXERCISES

1. Find a recent case involving the application of the EU *Charter of Fundamental Rights* and describe it.
2. Find a recent case involving the application of Article 85 of the Treaty of Rome and describe it.
3. Find a recent case involving the application of Article 86 of the Treaty of Rome and describe it.
4. Integration in the EU has proceeded at different speeds in different periods; it has been variously characterized as: growth, renewal, great leaps forward, and, on the other hand, hesitation, stagnation, disagreement, and second thoughts. Which of these descriptions do you think would apply to the EU at present and why?
5. Has there been activity in regional trade groupings recently? Using the Internet, check the status of bilateral and multilateral agreements by reference either to region (that is, the Americas, Europe, the Middle East, Africa, Asia, and Australasia) or to individual countries in which you have an interest.

FURTHER READING

Craig, Paul, and De Burca, Grainne. (2003). *EU Law: Text, Cases and Materials*, 3rd ed. Oxford: Oxford University Press.

Deards, E., and Hargreaves, S. (2004). *European Union Law Textbook.* Oxford: Oxford University Press.

Hartley, T.C. (2003). *The Foundations of European Community Law.* Oxford: Oxford University Press.

Steiner, J., and Woods, L. (2003). *Textbook on EC Law,* 8th ed. Oxford: Oxford University Press.

WEBSITES

Europa—the European Union On-Line:
> http://europa/eu
> (official site of the European Union providing up-to-date coverage of EU affairs and essential information on EU integration as well as access to current EU legislation and links to related institutions and agencies)

Canadian multilateral and bilateral activity:
> Foreign Affairs and International Trade Canada:
> www.dfait-maeci.gc.ca
> www.international.gc.ca/tna%2Dnac
> (Trade Negotiations and Agreements)

US multilateral and bilateral activity:
> US Department of State:
> www.usinfo.state.gov
> www.state.gov

European multilateral and bilateral activity:
> European Commission:
> http://ec.europa.eu/trade/issues/bilateral/index_en.htm

The Americas:
> Free Trade Area of the Americas:
> www.ftaa-alca.org/alca_e.asp

> Organization of the American States:
> www.sice.oas.org
> (source for all trade agreements in the region)

Asia:

ASEAN and ASEAN Free Trade Area:
www.aseansec.org

SAARC/SAFTA:
www.saarc-sec.org/main.php

Central Africa:

UDEAC and CEMAC:
www.africa-union.org

East Africa:

East Africa Customs Union:
www.eac.int

West Africa:

Economic Community of West African States:
www.ecowas.int

Middle East:

Council of Arab Economic Unity:
www.caeu.org.eg/english/intro

Australasia:

Australian Department of Foreign Affairs and Trade:
www.dfat.gov.au

CHAPTER 5

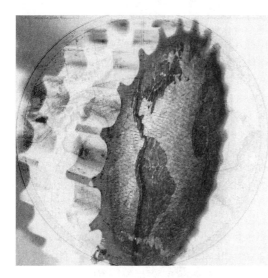

The North American Free Trade Agreement (NAFTA)

INTRODUCTION

Canadians have now lived with the reality of a free trade agreement governing trade with our largest trading partner, the United States, for almost two decades. The Canada–US Free Trade Agreement (CFTA) entered into force on January 1, 1989. It was created, at least partially, as a result of frustration with the apparent lack of progress toward the modernization of the General Agreement on Tariffs and Trade (GATT) rules in the Uruguay Round of trade talks. Because Canada and the United States had similar or complementary commercial regulation in many areas and an enormous shared market, the two countries were able to accelerate the GATT process on a bilateral basis.

Talks with Mexico followed several years later with the result that the North American Free Trade

LEARNING OBJECTIVES

After reading this chapter you will understand:

- the similarity between provisions in NAFTA and the WTO
- NAFTA rules for trade in goods
- NAFTA energy and water provisions
- why Canadian culture might not be protected under NAFTA
- NAFTA rules for trade in services and movement of labour, and how protection for trade and labour developed
- dispute settlement methods and the facts behind the softwood lumber dispute
- the debate about the rights of foreign investors in Canada

Agreement (NAFTA), then described as "CFTA-plus," came into force on January 1, 1994. Although Mexico was not a major trading partner for Canada, it was considered important policy for Canada to participate fully in NAFTA. Canada's participation would prevent the United States from negotiating a separate agreement with Mexico, thus beginning a process of bilateral US free trade agreements that would result in Canada's being relegated to simply one of the "spokes" around a US hub, with Mexico, Chile, and Costa Rica forming the remaining spokes. In this scenario, the United States would benefit from an imbalance in bargaining power in each negotiation. Figure 5.1 illustrates the bilateral hub-and-spoke trading arrangement that might have resulted and the multilateral NAFTA trading arrangement that exists among the United States, Canada, and Mexico.

The CFTA and NAFTA are much easier to understand if they are viewed in the context of the GATT, because the approach and philosophy, the concepts and the language, all come from the GATT. Viewed in this context, the agreements are not as revolutionary or surprising as is often believed, particularly by the general public. For example, both agreements include the national treatment rule, which originated in the GATT. As we know, the essence of this rule is that once goods, services, or investments are imported into a member country, they must be treated in the same way as domestic goods, services, and investment.

FIGURE 5.1   BILATERAL VERSUS MULTILATERAL TRADING ARRANGEMENT

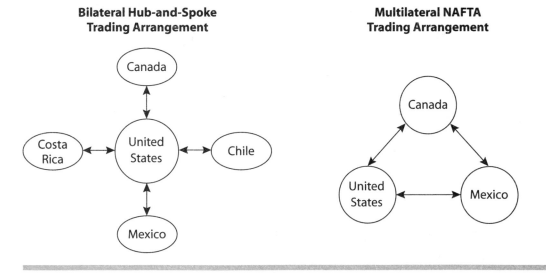

NAFTA's purpose was to create a free trade area characterized by national treatment, most-favoured-nation (MFN) treatment, and transparency. More specifically, the agreement was intended to

- facilitate the cross-border movement of goods and services within the free trade area;
- promote conditions of fair competition within the free trade area;
- protect intellectual property rights;
- create effective procedures for joint administration of the agreement;
- create effective mechanisms to resolve disputes; and
- establish a framework for further cooperation to expand and enhance the benefits of the agreement.

This agreement, like many international trade agreements, invokes passionate debates as to its merits and its shortcomings. This is not surprising, given that trade liberalization creates both winners and losers, viewed over either the short or long term. But analyzing such trade agreements is difficult because the economic activities of the parties are complex, and political and social variables must be considered as well. Analysis of the pros and cons is further complicated by the fact that these agreements generate derivative legal relationships between and among state and non-state entities.

RULES RELATING TO TRADE IN GOODS

Tariffs

Each NAFTA country retains its own external tariffs that are applied to goods from non-member countries, but levies a lower tariff or no tariff on the goods "originating" from the other NAFTA members. NAFTA did not affect the phase-out of tariffs that had been agreed on under the CFTA. This phase-out was completed on January 1, 1998, and since that date virtually all tariffs on Canada–US trade in **originating goods** have been eliminated. Some tariffs remain in place for certain products from Canada's supply-managed sectors (eggs, dairy, and poultry products). In the United States, tariffs remain in place for certain products such as sugar, dairy, peanuts, and cotton.

On January 1, 2003, the final tariff reduction in the Canada–Mexico phase-out schedule was completed. The Mexican administration proceeded with the tariff cuts in the face of significant political opposition from certain sectors. These reductions were substantial and resulted in the average tariff on US goods falling from the pre-NAFTA average of 10 percent to less than one-half of 1 percent. Mexico had previously had high tariffs and strict controls on imports, and the virtual elimination of these trade barriers has contributed to a massive penetration of imports into the Mexican market.

Rules of Origin

The rules of origin are significant for the exporter as well as for the importer because these rules determine which goods will qualify for tariff-free treatment under NAFTA. This favourable treatment is often referred to as **area treatment**—the area being the territories of Canada, the United States, and Mexico. There were some problems with the original rules of origin under the CFTA. Such policies were illustrated by the notorious *Honda* case in 1992, where finished cars with engine blocks manufactured in Ohio and incorporated into Hondas manufactured in Ontario were ruled by US Customs as not meeting North American content regulations. The case resulted in considerable consternation, and was ultimately settled in the context of NAFTA negotiations where negotiators took great care to improve the rules of origin to prevent further incidents. The result is a much more complex system. The rules under the CFTA were 10 pages, and the rules under NAFTA are at least 180 pages. The rules are too complex to be examined in detail here; instead, we will look at four basic rules that may be used to determine whether a good qualifies as an originating good within the NAFTA area and is, therefore, eligible for preferential tariff treatment. Generally speaking, a good qualifies for area treatment if it meets any of the following conditions:

- the good is wholly obtained or produced entirely in North America;
- the good is substantially transformed within a NAFTA country with the result that the tariff classification has changed;
- each of the non-originating goods used in the production of the good has undergone a change in tariff classification as a result of production in North America; or
- the finished good has not achieved a tariff classification change but the good contains sufficient regional value content.

The Harmonized Commodity Description and Coding System

The Harmonized Commodity Description and Coding System (HS) is the basis for tariff classifications under NAFTA and has been adopted by most of the world's major trading countries. Developed by the Customs Cooperation Council, the system comprises 21 sections divided into 99 chapters, which are then subdivided into headings and subheadings. An HS Committee meets at four- or five-year intervals to ensure that the text is current and reflects technological change and the changing patterns of international trade. The third major revision will take effect on January 1, 2007 and will clarify and update the text for the needs of today's international trade.

Because the rules for area treatment under NAFTA are highly dependent upon tariff classification, it is of utmost importance for producers to carry out an accurate origin analysis to ensure that non-originating materials as well as the finished goods are properly classified under the HS. Importers will require an accurate **certificate of origin**. Exporters should be aware of the potential legal liability for certificates that are improperly completed. Importers, on the other hand, must be aware of the importance of the certificate of origin when negotiating a purchase. They may wish to consider including a term in their purchase order or other contractual document that provides that the exporter or manufacturer must provide a suitable certificate of origin and, if the certificate proves to be incorrect, incomplete, or unreliable, the purchaser or importer will be indemnified for any extra costs or duties incurred as a result.

Customs and Border Procedures

Border risk in the form of longer transit times and heightened uncertainty about timely delivery to the US market poses an ongoing threat to Canada's most important trade relationship. Canadians have had to deal with the reality that "security trumps trade" in the minds of US legislators, and that market access is of much more importance to Canada than it is to the United States. For this reason, in December 2001, in the wake of 9/11, the Canada–US Smart Border Declaration was agreed upon to create a border that facilitates security as well as the flow of people and commerce. Canada has created a new Canada Border Services Agency in order to integrate the customs functions from Canada Customs and Revenue Agency, the intelligence functions previously undertaken by Citizenship and Immigration, and the import functions previously carried out by the Canadian Food Inspection Agency.

Importers cannot claim area or preferential treatment unless they possess a valid certificate of origin. The importer must make a written declaration, based on a certificate of origin, that the good qualifies as originating, and they must possess a certificate of origin at the time the declaration is made. These certificates are the responsibility of the exporter, although it may be the producer that actually completes them. The three countries have developed a common certificate of origin that may be issued for any single import exceeding a value of US$1,000 or for multiple imports of identical goods within a 12-month period.

The three NAFTA countries have provided for uniform regulations relating to the interpretation, application, and administration of the rules of origin, which in turn will be adopted by each country into its domestic legislation. The parties have also agreed that

- each country must provide for the speedy issuance of advance rules of origin rulings;

- each country must provide exporters from other NAFTA countries with the same review and appeal rights and advance rulings as are available to exporters within its own territory; and
- they will cooperate in administering the rules of origin and establish a working group to address future amendments to the rules of origin.

Technical Barriers to Trade and Technical Standards

NAFTA establishes clear rules aimed at reducing the potential for using standards as a disguised barrier to trade while, at the same time, reserving the right of each government to impose standards that are more stringent than international standards. The principle of national treatment is confirmed with respect to standards provisions and trade in goods and services. The parties have agreed not to use standards-related measures to create any unnecessary obstacles to trade among the countries. The three countries have also agreed to work jointly to enhance the level of safety and protection of human, animal, and plant life and health, the environment, and consumers.

NAFTA countries are free to adopt, apply, and enforce standards-related measures including measures relating to safety; the protection of human, animal, or plant life or health; the environment; or consumers. Member countries are free to choose the appropriate level of protection based on an assessment of risk, but national treatment and MFN status must be extended to goods from other countries. There is also agreement to make compatible the respective standards-related measures of the three countries. The Committee on Standards-Related Measures has been established with representatives from each country. The Committee's functions include:

- monitoring the implementation and administration of the NAFTA provisions on standards-related measures, including the progress of the working groups and subcommittees;
- facilitating the process of making measures compatible;
- providing a forum for members to consult on standards matters, including the provision of technical advice and recommendations; and
- enhancing cooperation on standards-related measures and considering standards-related measures of other organizations, including the GATT.

Sanitary and Phytosanitary Measures

Sanitary and phytosanitary (SPS) measures are taken by governments for the protection of humans, animals, or plants from pests, diseases, or contaminants. NAFTA does not provide for any specific standard but sets out an approach designed to ensure that these measures are adopted for scientific reasons and not as disguised measures for trade protection. Each country may set SPS measures at a level it considers appropriate, provided there is scientific evidence to support the measure.

SELECTED AREAS OF INTEREST OR CONTROVERSY

Anti-Dumping and Countervailing Duty Provisions

As we know from our study of the World Trade Organization (WTO), dumping and subsidies are frowned upon, but not illegal. Under WTO rules, importing countries are permitted to levy duties on goods that are dumped or subsidized according to the domestic law of the importing country, which is expected to conform to the overall prescription of the WTO. Critics allege that the United States has a history of bowing to pressure from industry lobby groups and using anti-dumping (AD) duties and countervailing duties (CVD) aggressively. This has been a source of uncertainty and concern to Canadian exporters for decades and, with respect to softwood lumber, extending back before Confederation. For this reason, an important goal for Canada in the negotiations for the CFTA was to obtain agreement to adopt common definitions of dumping and subsidies and common AD and CVD law. However, this was not politically saleable to the United States because it knew that these terms would be completely unacceptable to US domestic industries that benefited from the strong protection that the existing situation provided. The compromise that was reached was the agreement that each country would retain its own AD and CVD laws, but a system of **binational panels** would be developed to oversee the **competent investigating authorities** in each country and determine whether they were applying their own law fairly to the situation. Thus, the right of parties to appeal AD and CVD decisions by their own officials was transferred from the previous domestic appeal bodies to binational panels. This was an important compromise on the part of the two parties to the CFTA, and the provisions were incorporated substantially unchanged into Chapter 19 of NAFTA, which will be discussed at greater length later in this chapter.

Energy

Energy was a critical issue in the negotiations for the CFTA and for NAFTA. Energy provisions apply to crude oil, natural gas, refined products, basic petrochemicals, coal, electricity, and nuclear energy. Because Canada is the United States' largest foreign supplier of oil, natural gas, and electricity, the negotiations were of utmost importance to both parties in the CFTA. When the CFTA was negotiated, the Canadian goal was to ensure unimpeded access to the US market, and the American goal was to limit Canada's ability to jeopardize ready access to these energy sources at reasonable prices (remembering the Trudeau government's National Energy Policy and creation of Petro-Canada in 1980, which gave the federal government considerable power to tax energy, and impose energy policies such as a two-tier price system). When negotiations concluded, both Canada and the United States had achieved their goals.

Canada's goals in the NAFTA negotiations were

- to maintain and enhance its US energy export position;
- to avoid a separate US–Mexico trade agreement that could relegate Canada to a "spoke" relationship; and
- to coordinate Canadian and US regulatory policies on Canadian natural gas exports (following an attempt by California to inhibit Canadian natural gas sales).

Because the North American market was largely integrated at the time of the NAFTA negotiations, tariffs were not an issue.

The energy chapter of NAFTA reiterates national treatment requirements, tax, and general quantitative limitation rights, and requires parties to keep market-based objectives in view by ensuring that domestic regulatory bodies "avoid disruption of contractual relationships to the maximum extent practicable, and provide for orderly and equitable implementation of the measures." While Canada has retained the right to have all significant energy contracts reviewed by the **National Energy Board (NEB)**, the Board is required to give effect to the NAFTA provisions. With respect to natural gas exports, the NEB has moved from the more conservative domestically protective surplus test and least-cost-alternative criteria for assessing longer-term export applications, to a market-based approach with a domestic consumer complaints procedure, export impact assessment, and public interest scan. This is a more market-based approach. For example, in 2002, the NEB rejected a request from the province of New Brunswick to implement rules that would require consideration as to whether supplies could meet both domestic and export demand when reviewing applications for short-term export orders for supplies of Scotian shelf natural gas.

All three countries are prohibited from imposing minimum or maximum import or export price requirements, although import and export licensing systems are allowed. In situations of short supply, import and export restrictions on energy trade are allowed within carefully defined limits that include:

- preventing or relieving critical shortages on a temporary basis;
- conserving exhaustible natural resources; and
- ensuring essential supplies for domestic industries.

Any restrictions on exports based on the above must be imposed equally on the domestic market. There are also provisions allowing a party to restrict imports or exports for reasons of national security, but the restrictions may not reduce the proportion of total supply based on the level of the preceding three years. This prohibition originated in the CTA and has been preserved for Canada and the United States in NAFTA. Mexico, for which ownership of energy resources and domestic policy relating to energy are particularly sensitive, negotiated an exemption to this provision.

The energy provisions benefit Canada in several ways. For the energy industry, they ensure stability, provide a marketing benefit for the industry, and benefit producer provinces. They also remove the possibility of federal energy taxes and regulatory policies such as the 1980 National Energy Program. However, the provisions are also controversial. The idea of access by the United States to Canadian natural resources on the same terms as Canadians causes some discord because there is a fear of loss of sovereignty and diminishing domestic policy flexibility. However, it is important not to exaggerate the effect of the article restricting our ability to limit supplies: Canada is required to provide the United States with its pro rata historical share of supply only if restrictions are implemented. There is no obligation to maintain exports to the United States at a constant proportion in ordinary circumstances.

Agriculture

Because the climate conditions and sensitive areas of agricultural trade vary among the three countries, agricultural issues tend to be limited to trade between two parties—for example, the United States and Mexico or the United States and Canada. For this reason, the three countries agreed to a series of bilateral agreements on agriculture in certain areas. US–Canada agricultural tariffs continued to be covered by the CFTA after the negotiation of NAFTA. Each of the three countries agreed to revise its domestic support policies to ensure minimal distortions in trade. Nagging problems in sensitive areas have, however, continued for the three parties. The United States and Mexico have differences over sugar, fruit, and corn, and Canada has had continuing problems protecting its marketing board system for the dairy, poultry, and egg sectors, as well as ongoing problems defending the existence and operation of the Canadian Wheat Board.

The NAFTA Decision on Canadian Butter,
Dairy, Poultry, and Egg Tariffs
After the Uruguay Round in 1994, the World Trade Organization prohibited the practice of imposing quotas on agricultural imports for the purpose of

protecting domestic markets. This new rule required such quotas to be converted to tariffs (tariffication), which would be more transparent and would eventually be lowered through successive WTO negotiating rounds. Canada, having negotiated protection for these quotas in the CFTA and NAFTA, imposed very high tariffs (as high as 300 percent in some cases). Canada believed these tariffs were authorized under the protection it had negotiated and the provision in NAFTA that states in Article 103:

> The Parties affirm their existing rights and obligations with respect to each other under the General Agreement on Tariffs and Trade and other agreements to which such Parties are a party.

The United States objected to the very high tariffs on the basis that no new tariffs could be imposed under NAFTA. A panel was appointed under Chapter 20 of NAFTA to resolve the dispute, and it found in favour of Canada. As a result, Canada was able to maintain its very high tariffs.

The Canadian Wheat Board

The **Canadian Wheat Board (CWB)** is western Canada's exclusive exporter of wheat and barley. Because it is a government-backed producer, it is classified as a **state trading enterprise**. State trading enterprises are permissible under WTO rules as long as their practices are non-discriminatory and their sales or purchases are made in accordance with commercial practices. The operations of the CWB are based on three principles: single-desk selling, price pooling, and a government guarantee of the initial payment to producers. The US wheat industry has persistently claimed that the CWB is able to undercut commercially offered export prices in select markets or sell higher-quality wheat at discounted prices. However, the US industry has so far been able to offer only limited anecdotal evidence to support those claims with the result that complaints to NAFTA panels and to the WTO dispute settlement body have so far failed. Change may be looming on the horizon, however: a WTO framework agreement developed in the WTO Doha Round in 2004 calls for the end of "trade-distorting practices with respect to exporting State Trading Enterprises including eliminating export subsidies, government financing and the underwriting of losses."

Water

Environmentalists and trade analysts have differing opinions on whether water in its natural state is affected by NAFTA. Some view the agreement as opening the floodgates to unlimited transborder sales of fresh water to our thirsty southern neighbours, while others dismiss this concern as alarmist. Section 7 of the *NAFTA Implementation Act* states that natural surface and groundwater is excluded from the agreement but water packaged as a beverage or in tanks is not. A regime has been developed for prohibiting diversion of water from the Great Lakes basin and has been agreed to by the Great Lakes US states, Ontario, and Quebec with the participation of the federal governments of the United States and Canada. This regime deals only with diversion, however, not water management. The Canadian government attempted to get all Canadian provinces to agree to an accord prohibiting removal of water from major drainage basins. So far, Quebec and Ontario have done so. Parliament has also amended the *International Boundary Waters Treaty Act* to prohibit the bulk removal of water from boundary waters and the taking of it outside its basin. There remain, however, a number of issues of concern:

- *Water is a good to which the trade regimes of NAFTA and the GATT apply.* Water is included under the tariff classifications as a good; goods must be accorded "national treatment"; and exports cannot be subject to quantitative restrictions, such as an export ban. The Canadian government maintains, on the other hand, that water in its natural state is not a good, and only when it enters commerce as a saleable commodity does it become a good. The problem is: at what point between resource and commodity does water become subject to trade obligations? What is the status of diversion by channel or pipeline?
- *Both NAFTA and the GATT prohibit quantitative restrictions on exports unless there are critical domestic shortages.* NAFTA disallows the imposition of export duties and charges and requires that any cutbacks be proportional to historical levels. The fear is that once water contracts are agreed to within NAFTA, Canada may not then "turn off the tap."
- *Restrictions on goods may be acceptable under Article XX of GATT.* This provision allows a country to take measures "necessary to protect human, animal or plant life or health" and measures in relation to the "conservation of exhaustible natural resources." The worry is that these provisions may be very strictly interpreted by NAFTA or WTO panels because the measures must also comply with the "chapeau" or opening paragraph of Article XX, which states that such measures must not be applied in a manner that constitutes a means of arbitrary or unjustifiable discrimination or disguised restriction on international trade.

Cultural Industries

Culture as a component of international trade is increasing in value. Although it is difficult to compare national data on international trade in culture,

UNESCO issued a report in 2004 that indicated that world trade in all categories of cultural goods increased from US $39 billion in 1994 to US $59 billion in 2002 and represents approximately 1 percent of total world trade. As trade liberalization has increased, culture has been drawn in without the negotiating parties really agreeing as to how it should be handled. The difficulty originates with a fundamental difference of opinion as to the nature of culture and cultural goods. Some believe that culture includes only the "fine arts" and excludes books, magazines, films, television programs, and popular music. These items are considered to be commodities to be governed by market forces alone. Those with this view see cultural policies as barriers to trade that should be dismantled in a trade liberalization process. On the other side of the debate, culture is seen as extending beyond the fine arts, and cultural goods and services are seen as vehicles for transmitting intangibles such as ideas, values, identity, and a sense of shared experience and community. These different perspectives lead to conflicting views on whether domestic governments should support culture. In many countries, of which Canada is likely one, domestic markets are not large enough for cultural industries to achieve the economies of scale necessary to compete with large multinational entertainment industries. Many governments intervene to ensure access to local markets for indigenous cultural goods and services. Measures to support culture commonly take the form of public funding, controls on foreign access to distribution and retail services markets, and controls on foreign ownership. These measures are usually aimed at ensuring that local production remains viable, not at keeping foreign cultural goods out.

NAFTA contemplates a cultural industries exemption but the degree of protection it provides is debatable because NAFTA itself has no provision for cultural industries. Instead, it incorporates the provisions of the CFTA into the NAFTA text. The CFTA defined five types of cultural activity:

- printed publications;
- film and video;
- music recording;
- music publishing; and
- broadcasting.

The cultural exemption provides that cultural industries are exempt from the provision of the CFTA other than in certain specified situations, but then provides that another member country may retaliate against the use of the cultural exemption by taking actions of "equivalent commercial effect." Thus the protection provided is flawed and may, as one writer has described it, "be more diplomatic in nature than legal."[1]

A further complication is that NAFTA covers intellectual property and services—two areas that were not included in the CFTA. The result is that the import of the cultural protection provisions of the CFTA is an artificial ill-thought-out graft onto the later agreement. The weakness of Canada's position with respect to culture was seen in the *Split-Run Magazine* case in which the United States challenged Canada's position on protecting the advertising revenues of Canadian magazines. The challenge was brought, not to a NAFTA panel, but to a WTO panel. The WTO agreements contain no provisions for the protection of culture. Canada lost the case; the WTO found that Canada had violated the principle of national treatment.

Government Procurement

An entire chapter of NAFTA is devoted to government procurement (the purchase of goods and services by governments) because the value of government-purchased goods and services in the three NAFTA countries is substantial—approximately US$800 billion. Procurement is defined to include leases and rentals as well as the sale of goods and services. Governments and government-owned enterprises are affected by this provision. Member countries are committed to give providers of goods and services from other NAFTA countries treatment no less favourable than that extended to domestic providers. A transparent non-discriminatory process for tendering and bid review has been established. This includes advance publication of invitations to bid, requirements for qualification of suppliers, time limits for tendering, requirements on documentation, and a procedure for review of the bidding process by an independent body in each of the member countries.

One weakness of these provisions is that they do not clearly apply to subnational governments (provinces, for example) or their agencies as was illustrated in a recent Chapter 11 dispute, described below.

BOX 5.1   CANADIAN COMPANY FAILS IN NAFTA ACTION TO ENFORCE NON-DISCRIMINATION IN GOVERNMENT PROCUREMENT

ADF Group Inc. v. United States of America (NAFTA Arbitral Tribunal, 2003)

In the late 1990s, ADF, a subsidiary of a Canadian company, subcontracted to supply structural steel for the Springfield Interchange highway improvement project in northern Virginia. As contemplated by a combination of state and federal law that funds state highway projects, the

ADF subcontract contained a "Buy America" clause providing that only US steel could be used in the project.

ADF submitted a claim to arbitration against the United States in mid-2000, asserting that the "Buy America" law prevented it from fabricating the steel for the project in Canada and violated NAFTA's investment chapter. ADF claimed $90 million in damages.

In the unanimous award, the tribunal rejected ADF's claims under two NAFTA provisions because those provisions do not apply to government procurement such as the supply of steel for the Springfield Interchange project. Although on the face of it, the "Buy America" clause violated the Article 1106 provision prohibiting a government preference for the goods and services of the country's own territory, this provision was superseded by Article 1108 of NAFTA whereby these obligations do not clearly apply to all actions by state or provincial governments.

RULES RELATING TO TRADE IN SERVICES

The services provisions of NAFTA impose a general set of obligations on the governments of the member countries relating to the production, distribution, marketing, sale, and delivery of a service; the purchase of a service; and the presence in one member country of a service provider from another member country. The member countries have agreed to extend national treatment and most-favoured-nation treatment to each other's service providers. They have also agreed to waive any requirements for local presence—that is, they will not require that a service provider have a local office. Some quantitative restrictions will be tolerated. Existing non-discriminatory measures that limit the number of service providers or the operations of service providers may be protected by listing them in annexes to NAFTA.

Services Covered by the Agreement: Exceptions and Reservations

An important topic for a country such as Canada with a stronger tradition of providing public services than the United States or Mexico is the issue of protecting services that have traditionally been provided by the public sector. Under Article 1108 of NAFTA, the parties could list non-conforming measures under the jurisdiction of the federal or provincial governments that they wish to protect from the disciplines of the services provisions, provided that this was done within two years of NAFTA's date of entry into force. The result was a flurry of activity in this area prior to March 31, 1996. Annex I of NAFTA covers existing measures, and annex II allows new non-conforming measures if listed. Both the federal government and the provincial governments participated in protecting their respective areas of legislation. Because of the potential overlap in these areas, it was not always clear which government is responsible for listing the reservation. The question also remains as to whether a blanket exemption—that is, "any social service provided for a public purpose"—is sufficient. Successive Canadian governments have taken the position that our public health care system is protected and services that existed prior to the agreement are protected. What is less clear is what constitutes a "social service" or what determines whether a service has been established as a "social service." Provinces and the federal government routinely dictate the terms under which they will pay for various health and social services. In the past, the common proviso was that the supplier of such services be run on a non-profit basis. In today's economic and political environment, however, that assumption is no longer a given. We can no longer assume that services such as income security, welfare, social insurance, social services, public education, training, and health and childcare programs will be supplied exclusively by government. The transfer of such services to the private sector may in future lead to disputes as to whether the protection claimed in our reservations is sufficient. This becomes an issue in a climate where such services are transferred to the private sector by one government and a later government wishes to reverse the policy. This may raise the issue of compensation if the investors in such services are foreign investors. This topic will be addressed later in the chapter when we consider Chapter 11 of NAFTA. There may also be concerns if governments wish to expand the range of health care services.

Professional Licensing and Certification

Under NAFTA, professional licensing and certification must be based on objective and transparent criteria. They should be no more burdensome than necessary to ensure quality of service, and must not represent a disguised restriction on trade in services. Any citizenship or residency licensing requirements were to be removed by January 1, 1996. A major obstacle to free trade in services has been the inability of various professional communities to establish acceptable international standards for professional accreditations. Even the European Union (EU), which has been the most successful example of regional agreement and integration, has had problems in this area. Each of the NAFTA member countries has agreed to encourage its own professional bodies to develop mutually acceptable standards for licensing and provide for reciprocal recognition. The member countries have agreed to provide a fair review and a reply to any application for professional licensing by an individual from another member country. There is a provision for foreign legal consultants that allows lawyers licensed in one country to give advice on their own law in another NAFTA country.

Temporary Entry of Business Persons

Business persons are defined as citizens of a NAFTA member country who are engaged in trade in goods, services, or investment. There are several categories:

- business visitors engaged in international activities such as research and development, production, marketing, sales, distribution, or service;
- traders in goods or services between their own country and another NAFTA country;
- investors seeking to commit a substantial amount of capital who are employed in a supervisory, executive, or skilled capacity;
- managerial, specialist, or executive intra-company transferees; and
- specified professionals who meet professional qualifications.

The three countries have agreed to grant temporary entry to these business visitors on a reciprocal basis. NAFTA residents entering another NAFTA country on business must present the required documents, including a passport, and proper verification of the individual and the business purpose of the visit. Unlike the EU, these provisions do not create a common market for freedom of movement of labour within the area—that is, they do not give a resident of one country the right to take up residence and work in another member country.

Financial Services

The financial services provisions are found in Chapter 14 of NAFTA, which provides for activities relating to the financial institutions of the member countries, investment in financial institutions, and cross-border trade in financial services. Services covered include insurance, securities, and banking. The provisions apply to subnational governments (provinces, for example) and some self-regulatory bodies. A number of obligations have been created that include:

- the right to transfer profits;
- the right to fair treatment upon expropriation or acts tantamount to expropriation;
- limitations on imposition of special formalities; and
- an obligation to refrain from lowering standards in order to attract investment.

All countries were allowed to make reservations for non-conforming measures relating to financial services, and these reservations are listed in the annexes to NAFTA. General obligations have been agreed to that conform to similar obligations in the services agreement:

- *National treatment.* In addition to the normal requirement to give treatment no less favourable than that extended to domestic providers, NAFTA countries have agreed to provide equality of competitive opportunity.
- *Most-favoured-nation treatment.* This is the usual requirement of treatment no less favourable than is given in like circumstances to investors of other countries.
- **Right of establishment**. This is the right to establish a business in another country without establishing previous residency or citizenship in that country.

Although national service providers of the member countries may establish financial institutions in any other member country, that country has the right to require an investor to incorporate under the domestic law of the host country and may impose terms and conditions on that incorporation. This provision is significant to the banking industry where the objective of the United States was to obtain the right for its banks to establish branches in Canada and Mexico. Canada and Mexico have delayed such rights until the United States amends its laws to permit commercial banks to expand into all of the US market.

Also particularly relevant to banking are a number of concessions made by Canada to the United States in the CFTA. These commitments to the United States continue under NAFTA. They include:

- exemption from Canadian prohibition of non-resident ownership of more than 10 percent of shares in trust and insurance companies;
- exemption from prohibition of ownership limits on non-resident ownership of more than 25 percent of shares of a trust company, insurance company, or Canadian chartered bank;
- exemption from Canadian asset ceiling rules, which limit aggregate asset holdings of foreign banks to 12 percent of the banking sector; and
- permission for US investors to open multiple branches in Canada without approval from the minister of finance.

The government of Mexico has agreed to allow financial service providers incorporated in another member country to establish financial institutions in Mexico, subject to certain aggregate market capital restrictions for a six-year transitional period. After this period, temporary safeguard provisions may be applicable in the banking and securities sectors and may be imposed for a further seven years.

RULES RELATING TO INVESTMENT

The investment provisions are among the most important in NAFTA. They provide for:

- common rules for the treatment of investment by investors from other NAFTA countries;
- easing of existing investment restrictions; and
- resolution of disputes between investors and governments.

The definition of investment is broad. It includes a business; a share of a business; real estate or other assets acquired for business purposes; interests in construction contracts, turnkey projects, or concessions; and interests involving a commitment of capital in which remuneration depends on production, revenues, or profits. Specifically excluded from the definition of investment are claims to money arising from commercial contracts for the sale of goods or services and the extension of trade financing credit. The obligations undertaken by the NAFTA countries include the usual national treatment and MFN undertakings. The three governments have agreed to restrict investment-related performance requirements. With respect to **expropriation**—the taking of private property by government for government purposes—the three countries have agreed to treat investors in accordance with international legal concepts of minimum acceptable treatment. Expropriation may take place only for a public purpose, on a non-discriminatory basis, and in accordance with the principles of due process of law.

The relationship between social services and investment is addressed in NAFTA Article 1101(4), which states:

> Nothing ... shall be construed to prevent a Party from providing a service or performing a function such as law enforcement, correctional services, income security or insurance, social security or insurance, social welfare, public education, public training, health, and child care, in a manner that is not inconsistent with this [provision].

How effective this provision is to ensure that governments are protected in their provision of such services will depend upon the interpretation of this clause as well as the effects of reservations made by member countries.

RULES RELATING TO INTELLECTUAL PROPERTY

Intellectual property rights include patents, trademarks, and copyright. Owners of these forms of intangible property have exclusive rights to the use and protection of their property within the country that has conferred protection. Canada and the United States imposed obligations on Mexico in this area because it did not have a history of enforcement or the sophisticated legal rules to deal with infringement of these rights. NAFTA requires that its members amend domestic law to include specific enforcement obligations that are based on the following four international agreements:

- the Geneva Convention for the Protection of Producers of Phonograms, 1971;
- the Berne Convention for the Protection of Literary and Artistic Works, 1971;
- the Paris Convention for the Protection of Industrial Property, 1967; and
- the International Convention for the Protection of New Varieties of Plants, 1978 and 1991.

In addition, the parties agreed to the principle of national treatment with respect to recognition of rights and enforcement of rights.

PROTECTION OF THE ENVIRONMENT AND LABOUR: THE SIDE AGREEMENTS

A major reason for the negotiation of the NAFTA side agreements on labour and the environment was to help the Clinton administration (which did not negotiate NAFTA) to obtain congressional ratification of NAFTA in 1993. Canada's concern with the side agreements was that they could be used as a means to impose yet more trade sanctions to block exports from Canada to the United States and could provide one more tool for protectionist interests in the United States. Powerful US lobby groups have proved very creative in using any means available to them to protect US domestic industries.

For this reason, Canada would not agree to be subject to **contingency action**—that is, suspension of the benefits of tariff-free treatment, as a result of violation of agreed-upon rules. Canadian negotiators were successful in obtaining a special provision for Canada whereby no contingency action would be taken by the complaining country, but fines of up to $20 million may be assessed to be enforced by Canadian authorities.

The side agreements, known as the **North American Agreement on Environmental Cooperation (NAAEC)** and **North American Agreement on Labour Cooperation (NAALC),** contain lofty objectives such as fostering the protection and improvement of the environment in the territory of the parties, and the improvement of working conditions and living standards in each party's territory. The hope of achieving these objectives is, however, diminished by the principle that each country, while agreeing in principle to high standards, is free to retain the right to establish its own levels of environmental and labour protection and to enforce those domestic laws.

Two bodies have been established to oversee and enforce these agreements: the **North American Commission for Labour Cooperation (CLC)**, located in Washington, DC, and the **Commission for Environmental Cooperation (CEC)**, located in Montreal. Any party to the agreements—that is, one of the three country governments—may request a consultation if they allege a persistent pattern of failure of enforcement on the part of the domestic government of one of the three parties. Citizens or groups may also ask for an investigation if they believe that environmental laws in their country are not being enforced. If the parties cannot resolve the matter within an extendable period of 60 days, any party may request a special session of the CLC or CEC, as appropriate. The third NAFTA country may join as a complainant. The appropriate council then convenes an arbitral panel comprising 5 members chosen from a roster of 45 qualified individuals. If the panel finds in its final report a persistent pattern of failure to enforce effectively, the disputing parties are to agree on a mutually satisfactory action plan to conform to the determination and recommendations of the panel. If, after a prescribed period of time, the parties cannot agree on such a plan, any party may request that the panel reconvene and, at that stage, the panel may impose a monetary enforcement assessment. If the offending party fails to pay the monetary enforcement assessment within 180 days, the complaining party may suspend NAFTA benefits—that is, increase duty on goods to pre-NAFTA levels—in an amount sufficient to collect the monetary enforcement (contingency action). It is to this last provision that Canada negotiated an exception. If Canada is a "guilty party," the assessment is to be filed with a Canadian court and enforced by the Canadian authorities like any other court judgment. Thus, Canada is not vulnerable to increased duties on Canadian exports to NAFTA countries as a result of the provisions of the side agreements.

DISPUTE SETTLEMENT UNDER NAFTA

Trade disputes are bound to arise under any trade agreement. The disputes sometimes stem from problems unforeseen at the time of negotiation. More commonly, they are due to the diversity of political, economic, and social pressure experienced by member countries as they attempt to honour their multinational commitments, which curtail complete freedom of domestic policy. There are three main categories of dispute settlement methods provided for in NAFTA, excluding those in the side agreements:

- *Chapter 20.* General dispute resolution available only to governments (based on Chapter 18 of the CFTA).
- *Chapter 19.* Anti-dumping (AD) and countervailing duty (CVD) dispute resolution (based on Chapter 19 of the CFTA).
- *Chapter 11.* Investor–state dispute resolution (new to NAFTA).

Disputes relating to financial services are covered in Chapter 17.

General Dispute Resolution: Chapter 20

The NAFTA Chapter 20 process is available exclusively to the national governments of the parties; only they may request a Chapter 20 panel review. This provision applies to all disputes between the parties regarding the interpretation or application of the agreement and to situations where a party alleges that another party is contravening the agreement. It is also the provision used if a party alleges **nullification or impairment** of NAFTA's benefits. To establish this complaint, a party must show that a measure otherwise consistent with NAFTA has resulted in the impairment of an expected NAFTA benefit and that this outcome was not anticipated at the time the agreement was negotiated.

If a dispute arises that falls under Chapter 20, the parties have a duty to consult. If consultation does not result in agreement, the matter is referred to the **Free Trade Commission** (the Commission), which is composed of an equal number of cabinet-level representatives from each country. The Commission has a secretariat to assist it. If the Commission fails to resolve the dispute, either party may request that it refer the matter to compulsory binding arbitration or to a panel of experts (NAFTA binational panel). The provision for arbitration has so far not been employed by the NAFTA parties, but binational panels, comprising five members selected from a roster prepared by each country, have been used many times under NAFTA and the CFTA.

It is important to note that the decision of a panel under Chapter 20 is not binding. A Chapter 20 panel may produce an initial report that contains recommendations for the resolution of the dispute and provide an opportunity for the parties to present further views. There is no provision in this process for representation of anyone other than the parties; there is no contemplated role for private parties or for provincial or state participation in this process.

If any party disagrees with the panel's recommendations for resolution in the initial report, that party may present written comments within 14 days. The panel may then reconsider the report and issue a final report, which is due within 30 days of the issuance of the initial report. This procedure reinforces the intention that Chapter 20 panels function in an advisory role as well as an adjudicative one. Chapter 20 provides that the disputing parties "shall agree on the resolution of the dispute, which normally shall conform with the determination and recommendations of the panel." Whenever possible, the resolution should consist of either non-implementation or removal of a measure not conforming to the agreement or compensation. If the Free Trade Commission does not agree on the resolution of the dispute, the party that considers its fundamental rights or anticipated benefits under the agreement to have been impaired may suspend benefits of equivalent effect to the other party until there is a resolution of the dispute.

The Chapter 20 process combines elements of political negotiation with some **judicialization** of dispute settlement. Judicialization, or the use of adjudicative procedures, is characterized by impartial judges applying agreed rules or standards to the facts of a case. This represents a compromise of factors acceptable to the parties. The United States had the most to gain from the retention of negotiated settlements, which preserve sovereignty and reward political power, but Canada wanted dispute settlement to be characterized as much as possible by adjudicative procedures. Canada, with a smaller economy and a significant dependence on the United States as its largest customer, had a greater need to see the terms of the agreement honoured and the dispute settlement system work effectively.

See box 5.1 for a summary of the general dispute resolution mechanism established by Chapter 20.

BOX 5.1   CHAPTER 20—GENERAL DISPUTE RESOLUTION MECHANISM UNDER NAFTA

- a process available only to the national governments of the parties;
- parties must consult before referring the matter to a panel;
- the decision of a panel is not absolutely binding on the parties; and
- a process that combines political negotiation with adjudicative procedures.

Anti-Dumping and Countervailing Duty Dispute Resolution: Chapter 19

Anti-dumping (AD) and countervailing duty (CVD) dispute procedures were included in the CFTA at Canada's insistence. At the time of the negotiation of that agreement, Canada perceived that American **contingency**

protection laws were applied subjectively for the benefit of US industry. What Canada really wanted from the AD and CVD negotiations was agreement to a set of common rules on subsidies and dumping; however, the two countries were unable to agree on a bilateral regime providing for uniform provisions. It was agreed that each party would continue to apply its own AD and CVD law to goods imported from the territory of any other party. The provision was tempered by an agreement that appeals from the AD and CVD decisions of each country's administrative bodies would no longer be heard in the appeal courts of their own countries. Instead, binding binational panel proceedings would be substituted. This was an important compromise on the part of the two parties to the CFTA, and these provisions were incorporated substantially unchanged into NAFTA.

Binational Panel Review

Under NAFTA Chapter 19, each country promised to replace a judicial review of final AD and CVD duty determinations with a binational panel review. Under GATT/WTO rules, and under Canadian, United States, and Mexican law, AD and CVD duties cannot be imposed unless there is a finding of dumping or subsidy *and* a finding of material injury or threat of material injury to a domestic industry. NAFTA provides that review based on the administrative record of a final AD or CVD determination of a competent investigating authority may be requested in order to determine whether such determination was in accordance with the AD or CVD law of the importing party. "Competent investigating authority" is defined in Canada as the Canadian International Trade Tribunal (CITT) or the deputy minister of national revenue for customs and excise; in the United States as the International Trade Administration of the US Department of Commerce (Commerce) or the US International Trade Commission (ITC); and in Mexico as the designated authority within the Secretariat of Trade and Industry Development (SECOFI).

The panel appointed to review an AD or CVD may uphold the final determination of the competent investigating authority, or remand it (send it back) to the investigating authority for action consistent with the panel's decision. However, the panel does not have the power to substitute its own decision for that of the investigating authority; it may only agree with the decision or remand the case. Panels must apply the same domestic substantive law that the administering agency in the importing country must apply. This law is defined in Article 1904 of NAFTA as "relevant statutes, legislative history, regulations, administrative practice and judicial precedents." The standard of review has been defined by reference to specific legislation in each of the three countries with the intention that it be the same as would be applied by the reviewing court of the importing country.

COMPOSITION OF THE PANELS

According to Article 1901.2(1), the panels will be made up of five members who "shall be of good character, high standing and repute, and shall be chosen strictly on the basis of objectivity, reliability, sound judgment and general familiarity with international trade law." Each of the parties will maintain separate rosters of potential panelists. The CFTA did not include the specific preference for sitting or retired judges that NAFTA Chapter 19 does. Panel members must be citizens of one of the parties.

Unlike Chapter 20 panels, Chapter 19 panels are accessible by private parties. This is consistent with the fact that a Chapter 19 review is an extension of domestic proceedings. In addition, there is generally less government involvement with a Chapter 19 review than with a Chapter 20 review. In Chapter 19 reviews, decisions are intended to be binding upon the parties and there is no provision for political negotiations, as is the case with a Chapter 20 review. As Canadians have observed in the softwood lumber dispute, these provisions are not always honoured. The fact that private parties have standing in this review process also contributes to some of the intensive lobbying that we have seen from industry groups in the United States.

TIME LIMITS FOR PANEL DECISIONS

One of the objectives of the parties to NAFTA was to see disputes resolved in a timely fashion. For this reason, strict time limits were imposed. In most cases, there should be a final decision within 315 days of the date on which a request for a panel is made. Generally, panels have met these time limits, although there have been exceptions due to panelists stepping down to avoid any appearance of conflict and also due to the **remand** process, because successive remands may result in substantial delays before a final determination is made. Remand is the process by which a higher court or tribunal sends a case back to the original body to be dealt with again.

See box 5.2 for a summary of the AD and CVD dispute resolution mechanism.

Effect of Chapter 19 Panel Decisions

The decision of a panel is binding on the parties with respect to the particular matter that is before the panel. The finality of the panel's decision is further emphasized by the provision stating that a final determination by a panel may not be reviewed under the judicial review procedures of the importing party provided that the panel determination was requested within the time limits set out in NAFTA. *Thus, there can be no appeal from a panel decision to domestic courts.* A casual observer of this process, especially in

> ## BOX 5.2   CHAPTER 19—THE ANTI-DUMPING (AD) AND COUNTERVAILING DUTY (CVD) DISPUTE RESOLUTION MECHANISM UNDER NAFTA
>
> - originally insisted on by Canada under the CFTA as a substitute for common rules;
> - provides binational panel review of final AD and CVD determinations;
> - the panel issues a single, binding decision—it is empowered to remand the case to the national competent investigating authorities;
> - the interested parties may request a panel and have a right to be heard; and
> - a panel decision is binding subject to an **"extraordinary challenge."**

recent cases, could be forgiven for questioning the finality of panel decisions. Most of this uncertainty is due to the provisions that the "panel may uphold a final determination or remand it for action not inconsistent with the panel's decision." Some of the recent cases involving multiple remands resemble a ping-pong game between the panel and the determining agency. The question of the effect of successive remands to the determining agency was addressed by a panel in the first pork case (see below) when it concluded that it was required by Article 1904(8) of the CFTA to issue a "final decision"—that is, the CFTA did not contemplate or permit successive remands.

The history of decisions under the CFTA reveals a reluctance on the part of US competent investigating authorities to comply with certain panel decisions. In these cases, the panel's decisions included increasingly specific instructions to the agencies on remand and the tone of the decisions became somewhat antagonistic.

The Extraordinary Challenge Committee

The only exception to the rule of finality of Chapter 19 panel decisions is found in the extraordinary challenge procedure. The procedure provides for the establishment of an **extraordinary challenge committee (ECC)** made up of three members selected from a joint roster composed of judges or former judges. This provision allows an involved member government to request the extraordinary challenge procedure where it is prepared to make an allegation that

- a member of the panel was guilty of gross misconduct, bias, or a serious conflict of interest, or otherwise materially violated the rules of conduct; or

- the panel seriously departed from a fundamental rule of procedure; or
- the panel manifestly exceeded its powers, authority, or jurisdiction set out in this article—for example, by failing to apply the appropriate standard of review; and
- *any of the above actions* has materially affected the panel's decision and threatens the integrity of the binational panel review process.

If an ECC finds that the narrow grounds for an extraordinary challenge have been established, the ECC may vacate or remand the binational panel decision. The drafters of the extraordinary challenge process expected that it would be used infrequently. There have been significant tensions between Canada and the United States with respect to the proper role of an ECC.

Thus far, these challenges have arisen solely with respect to panel reviews of cases decided by US competent investigating authorities. The initial tension has been between a US desire for broader **appellate recourse** in cases it believes were wrongly decided by a panel and a Canadian desire to restrict extraordinary challenges to rare instances of systemic abuse, such as gross misconduct. Appellate recourse is the ability to appeal decisions. This issue has been addressed in a number of ECC decisions. In the first ECC decision, *In the Matter of Fresh, Chilled, or Frozen Pork from Canada*,[2] the Committee stated:

> As its name suggests, the extraordinary challenge procedure is not intended to function as a routine appeal. Rather the decision of a binational panel may be challenged and reviewed only in "extraordinary" circumstances. While the legislative history of the extraordinary challenge committee mechanism is lacking in specifics, it is clear that the extraordinary challenge procedure is intended solely as a safeguard against an impropriety or gross panel error that could threaten the integrity of the binational panel review process .... Notably, the legislative history states that an extraordinary challenge committee is intended as a review mechanism for "aberrant panel decisions" and that "the availability of or resort to extraordinary challenge committees should act to cure aberrant behavior by panelists."[3]

The Committee gave further reasons:

> As the procedural rules state, an extraordinary challenge committee is composed of three judges or former judges of a federal court of the United States or of a court of superior jurisdiction of Canada. The challenge committee's function is to determine whether a panel or panel member violated the three-prong standard of the extraordinary challenge procedure. In contrast, a binational panel is composed of five individuals with expertise in international trade law. The panel members' function is to

review the record evidence and the trade law issues that have been raised before the competent investigating authority. The committee and the panel have separate roles and different expertise; it is not the function of a committee to conduct a traditional appellate review regarding the merits of a panel decision. Another important procedural distinction and indicator of differences in review functions between the panel review mechanism and the extraordinary challenge mechanism is the disparate amount of time allotted to the two tribunals for review. Under the procedural rules, an extraordinary challenge committee typically is given only 30 days to issue a written decision, whereas a binational panel generally is given 315 days to issues a decision.[4]

The issue was also addressed by the second ECC, this time in the *Live Swine*[5] case:

> The ECC should be perceived as a safety valve in those extraordinary circumstances where a challenge is warranted to maintain the integrity of the binational panel process … . The ECC should address systemic problems and not mere legal issues that do not threaten the integrity of the CFTA's dispute resolution mechanism itself. A systemic problem arises whenever the binational panel process itself is tainted by failure on the part of a panel or a panelist to follow their mandate under the CFTA.[6]

The Pork Cases

The "pork cases" actually include a number of panel determinations, the specific details of which will not be presented here. For our purposes, these cases can be divided into two categories: the *Fresh Chilled and Frozen Pork from Canada* (*Fresh Pork* cases), and the *Live Swine from Canada* (*Live Swine* cases). Each of these cases involved panel reviews of CVD determinations by the US **Department of Commerce (DOC)** as well as findings of material injury by the **US International Trade Commission (USITC)**. Each of the cases involved multiple remands and each resulted in an appeal to the ECC.

These cases exposed weaknesses in the AD and CVD dispute settlement provisions and exerted considerable pressure on the system, severely testing the parties' commitment to it. They received a great deal of publicity at the time (1992-1993), especially in Canada, where the analogy of the "mouse in bed with the elephant" still strikes a resonant chord. To be fair, we may attach too much significance to the events in the pork cases. The issues in these cases were complicated, even for the panelists who were familiar with them; the texts that required interpretation were lengthy and the proliferation of cases was confusing. These cases presented, as did the later softwood lumber cases, a difficult tangle of sensitive economic, political, and legal issues for the panelists to resolve.

The Softwood Lumber Cases

Because of the difference in the two countries' methods of assessing timber-cutting costs, the softwood lumber industry has been a contentious area for Canada and the United States for more than 200 years. In the United States, such costs are established in advance by bidding on timber rights that are privately owned. In Canada, provincial governments own the timber rights and set stumpage fees, which are then paid to the Crown in right of the province by forestry companies. The situation became particularly volatile in the 1980s. In 1986 the two countries entered into a memorandum of understanding (MOU) in which Canada (under threat of countervailing duties) agreed to impose a 15 percent export levy on its own industry.

In 1991, the government of Canada, in conjunction with four provincial governments, undertook a joint study of the provincial stumpage systems, applying a methodology employed in certain instances by the US Forest Service. The joint study was said to have demonstrated that stumpage revenues in all four affected provinces exceeded the provinces' costs of administering their stumpage systems. On this basis, Canada concluded that the MOU had served its purpose and gave notice to the United States on September 3, 1991 that it intended to exercise its right to terminate the MOU effective October 4, 1991. On October 4, Canada ceased to collect the export charges provided for in the MOU. The result was a spate of softwood lumber cases, under both NAFTA and the WTO.

Protracted talks were held throughout 1996 involving the United States and representatives of a number of Canadian lumber-exporting provinces. A complex arrangement was cobbled together just before the talks were due to terminate in March 1996, with the United States threatening to impose substantial new duties on Canadian softwood lumber. Because the United States had amended the definition of subsidy in its legislation, the consensus of legal opinion was that Canada would lose a subsequent case on the issue of subsidy. Under the 1996 agreement (the Softwood Lumber Agreement, or SLA), Canada agreed to reduce its share of the US lumber market and impose a tax on lumber exports to ensure this outcome. The agreement was complex and difficult to administer, creating a nightmare of quotas and uncertainty for lumber producers. The SLA expired in 2001, setting off another round in the "softwood lumber war."

For a number of reasons, we will not review the actual softwood cases in detail here. First, because of the multiplicity of cases and remands, the history is tortuous, complex, and confusing even for a trade lawyer. Second, because such an account will be neither current nor accurate by the time this text reaches the reader. Third, because successive NAFTA panels have ruled in Canada's favour and the United States continues to ignore these decisions and pursue its case at the WTO where the rulings, while not condoning US actions, are somewhat equivocal. As one commentator recently stated, "Softwood is the NAFTA litmus test. And it has failed."[7]

Summaries of the NAFTA challenges to date are given below.

CANADA'S CHALLENGE TO THE DEPARTMENT OF COMMERCE
COUNTERVAILING DUTY DETERMINATION

The panel in this case was first established in 2002 and since that time, five decisions required the DOC to review its determinations in accordance with panel rulings that the DOC methodology was flawed. In November 2005, the DOC revised its finding in accordance with the panel's instructions and prescribed a CVD rate of 0.80 percent, which is a *de minimus* rate—that is, too small to be collected.

CANADA'S CHALLENGE OF THE DOC'S FINDING OF DUMPING ON
THE PART OF A NUMBER OF CANADIAN COMPANIES

The panel in this case was established in 2002, and there have so far been three remands to the DOC directing it to revise its findings to conform with the law as the panel sees it. The case remains open, with the DOC persisting in its finding of dumping.

CANADA'S CHALLENGE OF A FINDING OF THREAT OF INJURY
BY THE US INTERNATIONAL TRADE COMMISSION

The panel in this case was also established in 2002, and has issued three decisions culminating with a finding in August 2004 that the record did not support a threat of injury finding and ordering the USITC to issue a determination consistent with the panel finding. The USITC issued the finding, stating that it was doing so only because of the NAFTA dispute settlement process. In November 2004 the United States requested ECC review of the Panel Injury Decisions. In August 2005, the ECC unanimously upheld the panel ruling and denied the US challenge.

CANADA'S CHALLENGE OF DOC'S FINAL RESULTS IN
THE CVD ADMINISTRATIVE REVIEW

This challenge is important because it ensures that all duty deposits to date remain undistributed until the challenge is finished. This is significant because of the provisions of the Byrd Amendment, discussed in chapter 2 of this text.

CANADA'S CHALLENGE OF DOC'S IMPLEMENTATION
OF WTO RULINGS

In 2005, Canada requested three separate NAFTA panels to review the failure of the United States to implement WTO panel determinations on the illegality of "pass through"—that is, the direct payment of AD and CVD duties to industry complainants under the Byrd Amendment.

ECC CHALLENGES

There have been two challenges to the ECC thus far over softwood lumber. In 1994, an extraordinary challenge was brought against the final binational panel decision. The extraordinary challenge was brought on the grounds that the three Canadian members of the panel had exceeded the bounds of the panel's authority by deciding that neither of the subsidy programs at issue was countervailable and also that two of the three Canadians had failed to disclose that they worked for legal firms whose clients included lumber companies and the Canadian government. The ECC, the third in NAFTA history, was duly convened and its decision was in favour of Canada. This decision, announced in 1995, unlike those of the first two ECCs, was not unanimous and was split along national lines, the US judge dissenting from the two Canadians' majority decision.

Many Canadians saw this action as yet another attempt to convert the extraordinary challenge provisions into a normal appellate forum. Before accepting this conclusion too hastily, there are several factors to be considered. The first is the actual wording of article 1904(13), the extraordinary challenge provision:

> Where ... an involved Party *alleges* that ... a member of the panel was guilty of gross misconduct, ... seriously departed from a fundamental rule of procedure, or ... manifestly exceeded its powers ... and ... any of the actions ... has materially affected the panel's decision and threatens the integrity of the binational panel review process, ... that Party may avail itself of the extraordinary challenge procedure set out in Annex 1904.13. [Italics added.]

Note that the wording is not "where it can be demonstrated that" or "where there is evidence of" or other wording that would suggest an objective test as to whether the extraordinary challenge procedure is available. Instead, we have a clearly subjective test that imposes no limitation on the circumstances in which a party may make an allegation. Thus, Canadian observers should not be surprised when extraordinary challenges are brought, even in circumstances that do not appear to meet the ECC's three-prong test.

It is also worth noting that a private party cannot invoke the ECC process. It must be a party to NAFTA who makes the allegations. This provision should result in some control over the frequency of extraordinary challenges because a party cannot initiate a challenge but must convince its own government of the appropriateness of a challenge. In the case of the *Softwood Lumber (Subsidy)* case, these private interests were armed with "potent ammunition" in the words of the two American panelists.

The decision of the ECC in the *Softwood Lumber (Subsidy)* case was greeted with dismay by the US softwood lumber interests. In September

1995, the Coalition for Fair Lumber Imports filed a lawsuit alleging that rulings by the binational panels violated US sovereignty guarantees in the US constitution. The lawsuit was dropped in December 1995, but it serves to illustrate US reluctance to accept agreements that require any ceding of decision-making authority over Americans by multinational entities. The United States was very slow in releasing the more than $500 million in duties collected from the Canadian lumber exporters in the period between 1992 and 1995. This was eventually done at the end of 1995.

In November 2004, the US trade representative announced that the United States was requesting an extraordinary challenge of the unanimous threat of injury decision that found that Canadian lumber exports represented no threat to US producers. In this case, panels had rejected the USITC findings three times. In August 2005, the ECC unanimously confirmed the panels' findings and the United States lost its third extraordinary challenge.

WHY IS THIS ISSUE BEFORE THE WTO AND NAFTA PANELS?
This is an obvious question as the reader attempts to make sense out of media reports of decisions relating to softwood lumber emanating from the WTO and NAFTA. Why are cases being heard in both NAFTA and WTO forums and why are the decisions seemingly inconsistent? The reason is that the WTO agreement and Chapter 19 of NAFTA deal with different aspects of the situation and create different legal obligations.

The WTO agreement contains general rules for international trade that apply to WTO member states. These rules were considered in chapter 2. WTO panels adjudicate whether a WTO member has complied with these general rules. If a country is found to be non-compliant with WTO rules, it is expected to amend its law so that it becomes compliant. However, the fact that a WTO member meets all the WTO requirements that its laws be compliant with WTO principles does not mean that its own trade agencies have complied with that member's internal laws. This is where NAFTA comes in. Under NAFTA, each member country has agreed to retain its own AD and CVD laws, and to apply them in accordance with its own law. Under NAFTA, panels are established in place of each country's appeal courts to review whether a country has applied its own law correctly. The distinction is important, because it means that a country can comply with its WTO obligations, but contravene its own domestic legislation. This is what has occurred in the case of the threat of injury dispute. NAFTA panels have found that the US International Trade Commission contravened the domestic law of the United States in finding that Canadian lumber imports constitute a threat, in spite of an absence of evidence that this is so. The fact that the US legislation is WTO compliant is not the issue. The issue is whether the US agency is applying US law correctly.

As is obvious from the above short synopsis of the softwood lumber cases, they have served to cast considerable doubt on the ability of the binational panel system to resolve trade disputes objectively and to the satisfaction of the parties. The situation is a reflection of significant differences in the importance of the lumber trade in the two countries as well as the very real power that industry lobby groups in the United States wield, often to the detriment of the US consumer. Another significant factor in this difficult situation is the absence of a regular avenue of appeal from the binational panel process, such as is present in the newer WTO dispute settlement system.

As we know, the US lumber lobby is well funded and has a great deal of support in the US Senate. In April 2006, the US and Canadian governments reached an agreement to end the latest dispute. The deal is similar to deals that were agreed to in 1986 and 1996, and is to last for seven years with an option to renew for two additional years. Washington has agreed to lift the duties being charged at present in return for a complex arrangement. Theoretically, Canada may ship as much lumber as it wants to the United States, but if the price falls below $355 per thousand board feet, each region of Canada has to choose between paying a sliding export tax that rises as high as 15 percent as lumber prices fall, or paying a smaller charge and facing a regional quota. Canada will collect the export tax.

There is a surge mechanism that will impose more punitive taxes if annual exports exceed 110 percent of the share allocated to a specific region. The new arrangement contains the four elements that would have been in any deal:

- a fixed share of the US market for Canadian lumber, somewhere between 32 and 35 percent;
- an export tax imposed by Canada, or a tariff imposed by the United States on exports beyond that level;
- the reimbursement of $4 billion of the $5 billion collected by the United States as a result of their contingency action; and
- no more legal harassment from the US industry.

The latest lumber deal does reward bad behaviour and weakens NAFTA; it creates managed, not free trade, for Canadian lumber exports. But, at the end of the day, what were Canada's choices, given the history of our lumber dealings with the United States? As one commentator said:

> It may be the deal that Canada has to clench its teeth to endorse ... [but] given the power of the US softwood lobby, and given the US determination to appeal every nuance of every ruling, this week's agreement was the only responsible solution to this venomous and costly dispute.[8]

Investor–State Dispute Resolution: Chapter 11

The provisions of Chapter 11 were included in NAFTA to provide assurance of fair treatment for foreign investors making investments in any one of the three NAFTA countries. Historically, foreign investors have suffered at the hands of host governments in a number of ways that include seizure of property without compensation; lack of transparent laws and due process and unfair treatment by local courts; as well as the most important drawback, which is the traditional international law principle that individual persons may not sue sovereign states.

It is much easier to understand the provisions of Chapter 11 of NAFTA if we understand the history and proliferation of **bilateral investment treaties (BITs)**. When first developed, the principal purpose of a BIT was to protect the investments of firms from capital-exporting nations (developed nations), and they were typically negotiated between a developed nation and a less developed nation that wished to attract foreign investment and was prepared to provide assurances of fair treatment for investors. BITs have been the model for the investor–state protection provisions in NAFTA and most negotiations on investor–state protection. To date, more than 2,000 of these treaties have been concluded, most between a capital-exporting or developed country and a capital-importing or less developed country. What is significant about the incorporation of the provisions in NAFTA, and other more recent multilateral trade agreements, is that the provisions now apply between developed countries with active domestic policies, freedom of the press, and open and transparent judicial processes.

The Usual BIT Provisions

Generally, BITs were designed to address the fears of foreign investors and are, for this reason, very similar in terms of substantive provisions. They include rules on scope and coverage, general standards of treatment, performance requirements, transfer of funds, expropriation, and dispute settlement.

SCOPE AND COVERAGE

Provisions include rules that define "investment" and "investor," and that lay out the territorial and temporal scope of the agreement. There may also be provisions that exclude certain economic activities reserved to the state.

GENERAL STANDARDS OF TREATMENT

These provisions mandate the expectation of fair and equitable treatment, usually with a reference to the principles of customary international law. It is here that we find the requirements for national treatment and most-favoured-nation (MFN) treatment. The contracting states have ratified the

Convention on the Settlement of Investment Disputes between States and Nationals of Other States (ICSID Convention).

PERFORMANCE REQUIREMENTS

At one time it was common for host countries to impose restrictions on foreign investors such as local sourcing, local participation in ownership, and location requirements. These became less common in the 1990s and are now generally considered unacceptable. Modern BITs do not permit such restrictions and NAFTA prohibits specific performance requirements for both goods and services.

TRANSFER OF FUNDS

All BITs state that the host country must guarantee the free transfer of funds related to investments to investors of the other party.

EXPROPRIATION

Under customary international law, states are allowed to expropriate foreign investment as long as it is done on a non-discriminatory basis (that is, respecting the principles of national treatment and MFN treatment), for a public purpose, under due process of law, and with compensation.

DISPUTE SETTLEMENT

In traditional treaty practice, disputes between the contracting parties are settled under the general dispute settlement mechanism included in the treaty. Most BITs, however, include separate provisions for the settlement of investor–state disputes. At one time, a foreign investor was limited to bringing a claim against the host state in the host state's domestic courts, or to having its home state assume the investor's claim against the host state. BITs allow the investor to sue the host government directly and are thus remarkable for their extension of public international law to relationships between the state and private parties. Common practice in modern investment agreements is to provide the investor with the choice of referring the dispute to local courts, or to arbitration under the ICSID Convention. Most agreements also include an alternative form of arbitration, commonly under the United Nations Commission on International Trade Law (UNCITRAL) rules. In some cases, the International Chamber of Commerce is also available to resolve disputes. Under most BITs there is no requirement that local remedies must be pursued or exhausted prior to international arbitration. Under the typical BIT, the investor simply submits the notice of claim to the appropriate authority of the responsible government, which then responds by putting into motion the constitution of the appropriate arbitral tribunal. Thus the process is ad hoc, and the arbitrators are private agents, typically private lawyers or academics. Much has changed in the decade since NAFTA was signed and the explosion of BIT signing activity. This area, once the preserve of diplomats and state governments, is now the purview of the transnational adjudicator. Nuances and ambiguities of these treaties unimagined by the negotiators are now being plumbed by talented arbitrators as well as vocal members of the public.

One of the most common criticisms of the BITs by members of the general public is that the right to sue is determined by the investor's status as an alien. Although this special status was created in recognition of the particular vulnerability of the foreign investor, and reflects the long-standing concern of international law for the rights of aliens, it does result in the foreign investor having access to a process and remedy not available to domestic investors.

The investor–state provisions of Chapter 11 of NAFTA have proved to be controversial and have spawned considerable commentary in the popular press as well as in academic circles. Some observers decry the establishment of "secret tribunals and the serious weakening of national sovereignty,"[9] and believe that the provisions were drafted for the benefit of big business. The most widely expressed concern is that they create a regulatory chill that dissuades governmental authorities from pursuing social and environmental regulations for fear of challenge, thus effectively limiting government power to balance public and private interests. Proponents of the provisions take an opposite view, arguing that the rules allow Canadian businesses to operate fairly and freely abroad, to benefit from national treatment, and to be protected from unfair government actions. To receive these benefits, they argue, Canada must in turn treat foreign investments as fairly. Advocates see Chapter 11 as the culmination of a decade-long struggle to provide assurances of fairness for foreign investors, providing countries with cost-effective access to capital and encouraging increased efficiency of the market for goods and services in North America.

The Provisions of NAFTA Chapter 11

The difficulty with so much of the commentary on Chapter 11 is that it ignores the very significant contribution of the BITs to the substance of Chapter 11 and fails to recognize that these provisions are not nearly as revolutionary as either the proponents or detractors would have us believe. Table 5.1 illustrates the similarity between NAFTA Chapter 11 provisions and the provisions found in most BITs.

Table 5.1

Short Title BIT Provisions	Corresponding NAFTA Article	Nature of Obligation in NAFTA
Scope and Coverage of various public services	1101	Defines qualifying investors and investments. Parties reserve the right to exclusive performance of activities reserved to the state in annex III, and to provision
General Standards of Treatment		
National treatment	1102	Parties shall accord treatment no less favorable than accorded in like circumstances to its own investors
Most-favored-nation treatment	1103	Parties shall accord treatment no less favorable than accorded in like circumstances to investors of any other party or of a non-party
Standard of treatment	1104	Parties shall accord the better of national treatment and MFN treatment
Minimum standard of treatment	1105	Parties shall accord treatment in accordance with international law, including fair and equitable treatment
Performance requirements	1106	No party may impose or enforce performance requirements in connection with the establishment, acquisition, expansion, management, conduct or operation of an investment
Transfers	1109	Parties agree to permit all transfers relating to investment freely and without delay
Expropriation	1110	No party may directly or indirectly expropriate an investment or take a measure tantamount to expropriation, except for a public purpose, on a non-discriminatory basis, in accordance with the due process of law, and on payment of compensation
Dispute settlement	1115–1138	After consultation or negotiation, investor may submit claim to arbitration under ICSID Convention, additional facility rules of ICSID, or UNCITRAL arbitration rules

What Is All the Fuss About? Decided Cases Under Chapter 11

More than a decade after NAFTA's inception, we have the benefit of more decided cases than did some of the early commentators. We are in a position to take a more measured assessment of the effect of Chapter 11, as we no longer have to speculate as to the likely decisions of arbitral tribunals. While the decisions in the cases thus far are by no means consistent with each other, the record of this litigation has certainly not fulfilled the dire predictions of those who anticipated legislative paralysis as the result of opportunistic foreign investors preventing governments from pursuing legitimate social and environmental policy. Thus far, monetary damages have been awarded against Canada or Mexico in four cases, and no monetary damages have been awarded to date against the United States. In four cases, all allegations against the respondent governments have been dismissed. While recognizing that the common-law rule of precedent does not apply to Chapter 11 decisions or indeed to any arbitral decision, we cannot discount the influence that decided cases have as a subsidiary source of international law.

Of the six categories listed in the BIT discussion above—scope and coverage, general standards of treatment, performance requirements, transfer of funds, expropriation, and dispute settlement—the two most litigated and controversial areas under Chapter 11 of NAFTA have been the provisions relating to general standards of treatment and expropriation. The following two cases (boxes 5.3 and 5.4) are examples of how these issues have been decided by the tribunals.

What the decided cases illustrate generally is how narrowly the tribunals interpret their jurisdiction and generally how careful they are not to expand the effect of the investor protection provisions or to intrude into areas of domestic social and economic policy.

BOX 5.3   METALCLAD CORP. v. UNITED MEXICAN STATES
(BC Supreme Court, 2001)

Metalclad, a US firm, had obtained all necessary federal permits and assurances from the Mexican government to operate a hazardous waste disposal facility in the state of San Luis Potosi, but was denied a permit by the local municipality and by the state government, which declared the land in question to be an ecological preserve, once it became clear how much local opposition there was to the activities of the US company. Metalclad, no longer able to proceed with its planned operation, proceeded against the Mexican government under Chapter 11 of NAFTA, alleging a violation of Article 1105, failure to provide treatment of a foreign investor in accordance with international law, including fair and equitable treatment, and a violation of Article 1110, the expropriation section.

The tribunal, in a decision that has been widely criticized by legal observers, found that there had been a violation of Article 1105 because the Mexican government had failed to provide a "transparent and predictable framework" for the investor, and a violation of Article 1110 on the basis that the municipality's action amounted to an indirect expropriation.

The decision was reviewed by the BC Supreme Court (in accordance with the provisions of the arbitral rules) at the request of the Mexican government. The BC court disagreed with the tribunal's finding of a breach of Article 1105 and with the finding of indirect expropriation under Article 1110. The BC court did find, however, that the state government had effectively rendered the complainant's investment worthless by declaring the concession an ecological preserve and this amounted to a direct expropriation. Thus, although the outcome to the complainant was not changed by the BC court's review, it was made clear that the *Metalclad* tribunal had effectively turned a relatively straightforward direct-takings case into a more complex indirect taking. Any persuasive effect of this tribunal's decision was thus neutralized by the BC court's decision on appeal.

BOX 5.4   LOEWEN GROUP, INC. v. UNITED STATES OF AMERICA (ICSID Tribunal, 2003)

The investor, Loewen, a Canadian funeral home operator, claimed under Chapter 11 as a result of a judgment awarded against it in a Mississippi state court for approximately $500 million. The commercial transaction that was the subject of the litigation had been worth less than $5 million, but the jury, encouraged by various prejudicial comments about foreign multinationals versus "good ole Mississippi boys," awarded punitive damages "to teach" the foreign interlopers "a lesson." Loewen was unable to meet the bonding requirements for an appeal, which were 125 percent of the judgment and were thus set at $625 million. Loewen was forced to settle the case "under conditions of extreme duress" and agreed to pay $175 million to the plaintiff, O'Keefe. Largely as a result of this case, Loewen encountered financial difficulties and filed under US bankruptcy legislation and ceased to exist as a business entity. All of its business operations were reorganized as a US corporation. Immediately before going out of business, Loewen's interest in the NAFTA claim was assigned to Nafcanco, a Canadian subsidiary of the acquiring US corporation. The claim under NAFTA alleged that the trial court's failure to curb extensive prejudicial testimony and counsel comment was a violation of Article 1102 (national treatment), as well as Article 1105 (treatment in accordance with international law), and that the excessive verdict and judgment and the Mississippi court's arbitrary application of the bonding requirements were also a violation of the standard of treatment obligation (Article 1104)—specifically, fair and equitable treatment. Loewen also claimed a violation of Article 1110—the expropriation provision.

The tribunal found that the Mississippi court decision was "clearly improper and discreditable and not consistent with minimum standards of international law and fair and equitable treatment"; however, Loewen's case failed on the ground that all available domestic remedies—notably the Supreme Court option—had not been pursued. The tribunal also stated that the issues in the case were not properly the province of the tribunal because they were, in essence, local issues of justice administration. In consequence, the tribunal found that Loewen had failed to show a violation of customary international law and a violation of NAFTA for which the United States is responsible. For this reason it did not qualify for damages under Article 1105. A further reason that Loewen could not succeed, in spite of the findings of substandard treatment, was that the tribunal ruled that there must be continuous national identity at the time the claim arose and through the date of resolution of the claim. Because Loewen's business operations had been reorganized as a US corporation, it did not have the necessary standing and, for this reason, the tribunal had no jurisdiction under NAFTA to make a determination.

NOTES

1 Barry Appleton, *Navigating NAFTA: A Concise User's Guide to the North American Free Trade Agreement* (Scarborough, ON: Carswell, 1994) at 191.

2 ECC-91-1904-01 USA.

3 Ibid. at 8.

4 Ibid. at 12.

5 ECC-93-1904-01 USA.

6 Ibid. at 7.

7 Barrie McKenna, "Bush Sees the Big Picture with a Blind Eye to NAFTA," *Globe and Mail*, April 4, 2005, B16.

8 Editorial, *Globe and Mail*, April 29, 2006, A16.

9 One example is the program *Trading Democracy*, by Bill Moyers, aired on PBC, February 5, 2002.

REVIEW QUESTIONS

1. Explain why the provisions and general philosophy of NAFTA are so similar to the provisions of the GATT.
2. What is the significance of rules of origin and what is area treatment? Is it necessary for goods to be wholly obtained or produced in North America to qualify for area treatment? Explain.
3. What is the HS and why is it so important for the international trade in goods?
4. What is the significance of a valid certificate of origin?
5. How much progress has been made in achieving common technical standards in NAFTA? What is the basic principle that applies to the setting of these by each country?
6. Are the provisions on sanitary and phytosanitary measures in NAFTA significantly different from the provisions in the WTO?
7. Did Canada succeed in obtaining the provisions it sought with respect to AD and CVD rules in the CFTA negotiations? What did Canada want and why? What was the outcome and why?
8. What were the goals of Canada and the United States with respect to energy going into the CFTA negotiations? Is Canada obliged to supply the United States with all the energy that the United States wants in ordinary circumstances? Explain your answer.
9. How do the provisions of NAFTA affect trade in water?
10. The "protection" negotiated for culture by Canada is complicated. Explain why and state whether you think these protection provisions are likely to be effective.
11. Have Canadian social services been protected under NAFTA and, if so, how?
12. How is this issue connected to the Chapter 11 investor–state provisions?
13. Do we have complete freedom of labour movement in NAFTA as compared with the freedom in the EU? Explain your answer.
14. Describe the financial services provisions in NAFTA and compare these with the philosophy behind the investment principles in NAFTA and foreign investor protection generally (BITs). Why are these concepts related?
15. Explain why labour and the environment are protected in side agreements and explain how these agreements operate. Are the provisions the same for all three NAFTA countries?
16. Describe the characteristics of the three dispute resolution mechanisms under NAFTA. Provide an interesting example of a dispute under each.

DISCUSSION QUESTIONS

1. The NAFTA dispute resolution system is a failure as illustrated by the *Softwood Lumber* cases.
2. A Free Trade of the Americas Agreement (FTAA) would be in the best interests of
   a. the United States
   b. Canada
   c. Latin America
3. There is a strong possibility that the NAFTA region will catch up to the EU in terms of integration in the next decade.

FURTHER READING

Appleton, Barry. (1994). *Navigating NAFTA: A Concise User's Guide to the North American Free Trade Agreement.* Scarborough, ON: Carswell.

Fugate, Jeff. "NAFTA, 13 Years Later" (Spring 2005), *Yale Economic Review.* Available online at http://www.yaleeconomicreview.com/issues/index.

Romanow, Roy. (2002). *Building on Values: The Future of Health Care in Canada—Final Report.* Ottawa: Commission on the Future of Health Care in Canada. Available online at http://www.hc-sc.gc.ca/english/care/romanow/hcc0086.html. Chapter 11 of this report contains an interesting discussion of the interface between health care services in Canada and NAFTA.

Weintraub, Sidney (Ed.). (2004). *NAFTA's Impact on North America: The First Decade.* Washington, DC: CSIS Press.

Weisbrot, M., Rosnick, D., and Baker, D. (2004). *NAFTA at Ten: The Recount.* Washington, DC: Center for Economic and Policy Research. Available online at www.cepr.net/publications/nafta_2004_03.htm.

WEBSITES

Department of Foreign Affairs and International Trade, NAFTA Secretariat: www.nafta-sec-alena.org

Public Citizen: www.citizen.org
(for information on NAFTA, go to www.citizen.org/trade/nafta)

CHAPTER 6

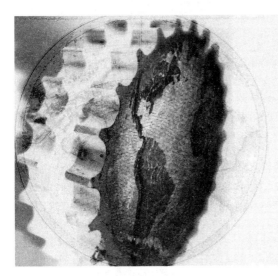

Canada's Response to Global Rules: Domestic Rules on Imports and Exports

INTRODUCTION

Canadian legislation governing imports and exports is influenced by a number of factors that include:

- protection of the health and safety of Canadian residents;
- maintenance of the economic well-being of Canada;
- compliance with the rules established under various international agreements including the WTO, NAFTA, and other trade agreements; and
- compliance with the provisions of treaties providing for environmental protection.

We now understand some of the more important provisions of the WTO agreements, and this

LEARNING OBJECTIVES

After reading this chapter you will understand:

- how Canada "imports" WTO law on dumping, subsidies, and safeguards into Canadian law
- what imports and exports Canada restricts or controls and why
- how Canada manages security and customs controls at its borders
- what services are available from the government of Canada and its agencies to support and assist Canadian exporters and importers
- how goods are valued for customs purposes and how applicable duties are assigned
- how Canadian trade remedy legislation is applied: the procedures, the rules, and the responsible agencies

understanding helps us to appreciate why we have some of the domestic legislation that we do, and why the legislation is drafted in the way that it is. As outlined in chapter 2, the WTO operates by developing agreements in which member countries agree to certain provisions. These provisions are then incorporated into the domestic law of the individual member countries by the passage of laws in each country. In Canada, for example, we take the WTO provisions concerning dumping and subsidies and incorporate them into our own legislation, the *Special Import Measures Act (SIMA)*.[1]

Although generally, Canada is an open market for the import and export of goods and services, we do control the import and export of certain products such as endangered species, protected cultural artifacts, uranium and nuclear-related material, and certain strategic and military goods. Some regulations are also generated by the NAFTA rules. The result is that numerous federal statutes in addition to SIMA regulate the import and export of goods and services. We will deal only with the most significant of these:

- the *Export and Import Permits Act* (EIPA),[2]
- the *Canada Border Services Agency Act*,[3]
- the *Customs Act*,[4] and
- the *Customs Tariff*.[5]

Most developed countries with open economies, like Canada, have relatively few import restrictions. Some countries, however, have extensive systems of import controls. This is changing as the world moves toward freer global trade. One example of a formerly restricted economy that has opened its doors to international trade is India. There was a time when India limited imports to industrial raw materials, capital goods, spare parts for maintenance, and essential consumer goods not produced or widely available in India. These restrictions supported India's goals of self-reliance and industrial development. Today, India is a leading example of a country that has benefited from globalization and the dismantling of barriers to trade in goods and services.

Some countries still protect their domestic industry by establishing barriers to imports on either an ongoing or a temporary basis. Some of the usual protective measures include:

- an absolute prohibition on the import of certain goods;
- an **embargo**, which is a prohibition against the import of goods originating in a specified country;
- a restrictive licensing regime for certain imports of goods or services;
- a system of quotas or quantitative limits on specified imports; and
- the imposition of extra duties on certain goods.

Before the creation of the GATT, customs duties or tariffs were an important source of revenue for the importing jurisdiction. Until World War I, for example, customs duties and excise taxes made up 80 percent of the federal government's revenue. This is no longer the case today because tariffs have been successfully lowered or eliminated as a result of successive WTO trade negotiations (rounds).

THE CUSTOMS ACT: RULES FOR IMPORTS AND EXPORTS

The *Customs Act* is Canada's primary legislation relating to imports and exports; it authorizes the Canadian government to control the import and export of goods and to levy duties. This statute operates in conjunction with two other important acts—the *Customs Tariff* and the *Special Import Measures Act*. It is the *Customs Act* that provides for import and export reporting, the calculation of duty, abatements and refunds, and enforcement of the legislation.

RESPONSIBILITY FOR BORDER SERVICES AND SECURITY

The events of September 11, 2001 had a dramatic effect on the attitudes of the United States toward border security. Washington is now focused on homeland security and on ensuring that US borders are as secure as possible. The ramifications of this for Canadian exporters, who send more than 80 percent of exports into the US market, are enormous, because secure, predictable, and speedy border crossings for goods and people providing services are of paramount importance to the Canadian economy.

Canada and the United States agreed on the Smart Border Action Plan in 2003, and, as part of that initiative, the **Canada Border Services Agency (CBSA)** was created. The CBSA is responsible for providing integrated border services that support national security priorities and facilitate the free flow of persons and goods—including animals and plants—provided they meet the requirements of the applicable legislation. The CBSA is responsible for ensuring that

- all people coming into Canada are admissible under Canadian laws and regulations;
- all commercial shipments comply with Canadian laws and regulations and that no illegal goods enter or leave the country;

- trade statistics are accurate;
- all applicable duties and taxes are paid;
- food safety and plant and animal health are maintained;
- any persons who pose a threat to Canada are detained, and that persons who have been determined inadmissible (for reasons such as international human rights violations or criminal activity) are removed; and
- measures for the prevention of money laundering are implemented.

Recognizing the importance of transborder commerce, the US Customs and Border Protection Agency (CBP) and the CBSA have established a number of programs to facilitate the flow of goods and services across the border:

- the **Canadian Partners in Protection (PIP)** program and the **American Customs Trade Partnership Against Terrorism (C-TPAT)**, and
- the bilateral **Free and Secure Trade (FAST)** program.

These programs are subject to change, and a prudent importer or exporter will avail himself of the current websites and consultants of federal and provincial trade advisory services.

PIP and C-TPAT

PIP and C-TPAT are industry–government partnership programs designed to improve the security of the goods and services supply chain. The program is open to importers, carriers, brokers, warehouse operators, and trade associates. Under the program, a participant from the private sector enters into an agreement with a government agency whereby the private sector party agrees to

- conduct a self-assessment of supply-chain security according to the prescribed guidelines;
- share this supply-chain security information with the government agency;
- develop and implement security enhancement programs; and
- participate in security awareness sessions.

Participation in these programs will result in decreased border examinations, and entitle the participant to certain administrative benefits and to participation in FAST.

FAST

The FAST program is a paperless cargo-release system that uses electronic data transmission, barcode technology, and transponder technology. It is a bilateral program established by the CBSA and the US CBP and it is open to importers, carriers, and drivers. Participants enjoy a number of benefits including a reduction in the information requirements for customs clearance, elimination of data transmission for each transaction, dedicated lanes for FAST clearance, reduction of the rate of border examinations, and the ability to verify trade compliance away from the border. The program does not operate at all border entry points, although the number of participating entry points is being expanded.

CANADIAN SERVICES FOR THE EXPORTER

The Canadian Trade Commissioner Service

The Canadian Trade Commissioner Service is the international segment of the Team Canada Inc. business service network (Team Canada) that comprises more than 20 Canadian federal government departments and agencies that work with provincial and municipal governments, industry associations, educational institutions, and the private sector to provide support to Canadian exporters. There are Trade Commissioner Service officers in Canadian embassies and consulates all over the world and these officers provide core services that include the following:

- assessments of potential prospects in the target market;
- searches for qualified contacts in the target market;
- information on foreign organizations, customers, and competitors;
- foreign visit information, including information on hotels, business support services, translators, and local transportation;
- face-to-face briefings with Canadian exporters in the target destination to discuss exporter's needs; and
- troubleshooting assistance (but officers do not act as brokers, agents, or legal counsel for a Canadian exporter).

Export Development Canada

Export Development Canada (EDC) is a Canadian Crown corporation created under the *Export Development Act*[6] whose purpose is to provide trade finance services to support Canadian exporters and investors. It is estimated that 90 percent of EDC's customers are smaller business enterprises. EDC provides a number of products and services, some of which are accounts receivable insurance, export protection insurance, performance security insurance, performance security guarantees, specific transactions insurance, and political risk insurance.

Accounts Receivable Insurance

Accounts receivable insurance is available to Canadian companies of any size operating in Canada in any sector of the economy. It covers up to 90 percent of losses for all accounts receivable. Risks that may be insured against include buyer bankruptcy or default; buyer rejection of goods shipped; cancellation of contract by buyer; war or insurrection in buyer's country; government cancellation of import or export permits; and foreign exchange control problems preventing buyer payment. The insurance premiums vary with the degree of risk, destination, and length of credit term.

Export Protection Insurance

Export protection insurance is single transaction–based accounts receivable coverage for losses up to US $250,000. Eligibility for this protection is more limited than it is for accounts receivable insurance. Only certain applicants, types of transactions, and destination countries are covered.

Performance Security Insurance

Performance security insurance covers up to 95 percent of an exporter's losses if a foreign buyer makes a wrongful call on an irrevocable letter of credit or letter of guarantee.

Performance Security Guarantees

A performance security guarantee, which is issued directly to an exporter's bank, covers 100 percent of losses if a foreign buyer calls or makes a demand against an irrevocable letter of credit or guarantee for any reason. The benefit to the exporter is that it makes it easier for the exporter's bank to issue the contract security without additional working capital from the exporter. Pricing of this coverage is based on policy liability, duration, risks of buyers, and country risks.

Specific Transactions Insurance

Specific transactions insurance covers up to 90 percent of an exporter's losses in relation to a specific export contract for service, capital goods, or projects. These are "one-off" transactions that represent unusual risk and will help the exporter obtain the participation of banks, or suppliers fearful of the types of risks outlined above under the description of accounts receivable insurance.

Political Risk Insurance

Political risk insurance protects an exporter's overseas assets—such as equipment, warehouse, and manufacturing operations—from the political actions of a sovereign state, and is not limited to specific transactions. Examples of political risks that may be covered are breach of contract; non-payment by a sovereign contracting party; expropriation or repossession of physical assets; political violence or terrorism; currency conversion problems; or the inability to transfer hard currency.

CANADIAN REGULATION OF EXPORTS

Export Permits

Who needs an export permit? The answer to that question may surprise you (see box 6.1).

The Canadian government, like other governments around the world, has passed legislation restricting the export of some types of goods from Canada. Much of this legislation is for the purpose of complying with multilateral agreements: to ensure that we receive the benefits from negotiated trade agreements, to control the movement of strategic or military goods and materials, and to ensure that environmental obligations are honoured.

BOX 6.1   WHO NEEDS AN EXPORT PERMIT?

Test your knowledge of permit requirements. Permits are required if goods and technology are:

1. destined for a country on Canada's Area Export Control List;
2. subject to a UN Security Council embargo;
3. on Canada's Export Control List;
4. of US origin;
5. designed for military application; or
6. all of the above.

The answer is all of the above.

Export Reporting and Documentation

The *Customs Act*, which is administered by the CBSA, imposes certain reporting requirements on exporters. Goods are classified for the purpose of reporting into one of three groups: (1) regular goods; (2) controlled, prohibited, and regulated goods; and (3) in-transit goods (goods shipped through the United States whose final destination is another country). The *Customs Act* does not require exporters to report the export of regular goods to the United States, Puerto Rico, or the US Virgin Islands, or regular goods having a value of less than Cdn $2,000 to non-US destinations. New regulations came into force in February 2005, with the result that all exporters, customs brokers, and carriers in Canada must report in writing to the CBSA the specifics concerning the particular goods destined for export and the location of export within prescribed time frames in advance of exportation, unless the goods are specifically exempt. Administrative monetary penalties have been established for non-compliance. The purpose of these new regulations is to enable the CBSA to minimize and manage risk and provide greater efficiencies for enforcement and targeting of exported goods by receiving information prior to the export of goods, and also to ensure that goods transiting Canada are not diverted while in Canada, as well as to comply with our commitment to manage controlled and/or embargoed goods. Canadian exporters doing business under a free trade agreement must fill out a certificate of origin in order for the importer in the participating country to claim the preferential tariff treatment.

Export Controls

The principal legislation providing for export controls is the ***Export and Import Permits Act* (EIPA)**, administered by the **Export and Import Controls Bureau (EICB)**, part of International Trade Canada (ITC). Violations of the EIPA are punishable by fines and imprisonment, and in some cases both the corporate exporter and its officers and directors may be prosecuted. The Act is enforced by the CBSA and the RCMP, who may charge suspected offenders, and detain or seize goods suspected of not complying with the requirements. There are two lists that are relevant to regulating exports: the **Export Control List (ECL)** and the **Area Control List (ACL)**.

The Export Control List

The ECL is a list of goods that are subject to export controls and that require an export permit prior to exportation. Exporters should always check the EICB's website before entering into serious contractual relationships, because the list changes from time to time. At present it includes:

- some agricultural products—for example, sugar and peanut butter;
- textiles and clothing;
- military and dual-use goods that may have a strategic purpose;
- nuclear energy materials and technology;
- missile, chemical, or biological goods for which proliferation is a concern;
- softwood lumber, unprocessed logs, and other forest products;
- goods of US origin;
- certain goods with medical value;

- goods subject to a UN Security Council embargo or action; and
- goods subject to re-export controls by foreign governments.

The Area Control List

The ACL is a list of countries to which the export of any good or technology requires an export permit. At present, this list contains the name of only one country, Myanmar. Because the list can be changed by regulation on short notice, an exporter should check the list periodically, particularly if contemplating trade with a country under a questionable regime with issues of terrorism or human rights violations.

Different Types of Export Permits

There are two types of export permits: an **individual export permit (IEP)** and a **general export permit (GEP)**. The IEP is for specific goods to be exported to a specific destination by a specific exporter. A GEP does not specify the exporter, but provides a general authorization for the export of specific goods to specific destinations. An example is General Export Permit no. Ex. 30, which permits the export of a large number of specified goods on the ECL to a specified list of countries, all of which are industrialized democracies with adequate record-keeping capabilities. GEPs may also limit exports—for example, the export of US-originating goods to Cuba, North Korea, Iran, and Libya.[7]

Export Controls and US Legislation

Exporters should be aware that although the US government prohibits trade with Cuba, there is no such prohibition in Canada. In fact, Canadian law prohibits a Canadian subsidiary of a US corporation from complying with the extraterritorial application of US law restricting trade with Cuba. Canada takes the position that extraterritorial application of laws adopted by other governments is a violation of international law, and Canada's *Foreign Extraterritorial Measures Act*[8] prohibits a Canadian company from honouring such US legislation.

Export Controls Imposed by Other Government Departments

Most controls of exports originate with International Trade Canada; however, other governmental departments may require authorizations for export. Current examples include Heritage Canada, Health Canada, Agriculture Canada, Natural Resources Canada, the Canadian Wheat Board, Environment Canada, and Fisheries and Oceans Canada.

CANADIAN REGULATION OF IMPORTS

Procedure and Documentation for Imports

All carriers are obliged to report the arrival of imported goods at the nearest border point. The goods must be accompanied by a customs invoice or equivalent commercial invoice that describes the transaction and identifies both the vendor and the purchaser, consignee, or importer. The representative of the Department of National Revenue will review the documentation and determine:

- the value for duty of the goods;
- the tariff classification of the goods;
- the origin of the goods; and
- the applicable tariff rate.

After applying the appropriate tariff rate to the dutiable value of the goods, the customs officer will add any applicable sales tax, anti-dumping (AD) duties, and countervailing duties (CVD). AD duties and CVD are discussed later in this chapter.

Dutiable Value of the Goods

In 1985 the *Customs Act* was amended to bring Canada's customs valuation procedures into conformity with the valuation code adopted at the Tokyo Round of the GATT. Our valuation procedures are now similar to those of the United States, the European Union, Japan, and Australia. Our former rules were based on "fair market value" whereas the GATT Valuation Code requires an assessment of "actual value." The GATT Code precludes the use of arbitrary or fictitious values, and attempts, wherever possible, to use actual transaction values as the basis for customs valuation.

The transaction pricing system we have adopted provides for six methods of determining the value for duty: transaction value; transaction value of identical goods; transaction value of similar goods; deductive value; computed value; and residual value.

Transaction Value

The transaction value method is the primary valuation method. It is used to value approximately 75 percent of all imports. The transaction value is the price actually paid or payable for the goods—that is, the invoice price. Thus, it is not suitable for use in **non-arm's-length transactions** because pricing may be dictated by the intercorporate relationship rather than the market. Nor is this method suitable for goods on consignment or under lease. There is also provision for adjustments to this value to take into account costs incurred by the importer but not included in the invoice, such as royalties, licensing fees, packing costs, and commissions.

Transaction Value of Identical Goods
When the transaction value method is not suitable, the first alternative is to use the transaction value of identical goods. The sales used as a comparative base must be export sales and not sales in the domestic market of the country of export.

Transaction Value of Similar Goods
Where there are no transactions involving identical goods, the transaction value of similar goods is used.

Deductive Value
The deductive value is obtained by starting with the resale price in Canada and working backward to an export price for the good, relying solely on information available in this country.

Computed Value
The computed value takes the costs of producing the goods and allows an amount for profit and general expenses. This method requires the foreign manufacturer to provide information on the costs of production of the goods.

Residual Value
When it is not possible to value goods under any of the above methods, the one determined to be most suitable is flexibly applied, but only on the basis of information available in Canada. This is the good's residual value.

Tariff Classification
The *Customs Tariff* is the Canadian domestic legislation that provides for implementation of GATT tariff obligations. The *Customs Tariff* provides for differing rates of duty on the thousands of tariff items listed in schedule A to the *Customs Tariff*. The items are listed with an identifying number and description according to the International Convention on the **Harmonized Commodity Description and Coding System (HS)**.

The schedules to the *Customs Tariff* are very long and complex. This complexity discourages importers from contesting the classification of their goods by a customs officer because, in any appeal against the classification of an item, the onus is on the importer to establish that an error of classification has been made.

Canada and the United States have recently adopted the uniform system of customs classification developed by the **Customs Co-operation Council**

(CCC). The CCC is an international organization concerned with the technical aspects of customs law and administration. The organization is based in Brussels and has a membership of approximately 100 countries.

The CCC developed the HS. This system enables countries to bring tariff rates and trade statistics into conformity with each other. The HS contains 21 sections divided into 99 chapters, with 1,241 headings and 5,019 subheadings. A good's basic identifying number consists of six digits, with the first four digits representing the heading and the additional two, the subheading. In Canada, we add an extra four digits for our own tariff and for statistical purposes, so that the complete Canadian tariff classification number is 10 digits long.

Under the HS, goods are grouped according to their raw material, industrial sector, and degree of processing. Identification is by observable characteristics such as material composition and not by the importer's intended use of the goods.

One of the major goals of the HS is to facilitate the electronic transmission of information concerning goods. Direct computer transmission of entry data from the importer to Canada Revenue Agency is accomplished under the **Customs Automated Data Exchange System (CADEX)**. As a result, Canadian transactions have become more adaptable to international commerce. Companies can now use HS numerals in their records for internal as well as external statistical purposes.

Rules of Origin of Goods

Once the imported item is "classified" by description and assigned the appropriate number, a tariff rate is prescribed according to the country of origin of the goods. An importer is legally obliged to furnish evidence of the country of origin upon entry of the goods into Canada. The decision of the minister of revenue as to the origin of the goods, once made, is not reviewable.

Rules of origin are the rules that govern the assignment of nationality to goods being imported. The general rule of origin under the *Customs Tariff* provides that goods originate in a country if the whole of the value of the goods is produced in that country. This general rule is subject to numerous other regulations under the Act, because many of the items imported are composite products whose components are manufactured in various countries and assembled and finished in still others. The result is a myriad of complicated regulations used for determining origin. These of course affect the documentation required for proof of origin.

The basic principle is that a minimum percentage of the cost of production of the goods must have been in a given country in order for that country to be deemed the country of origin. Another commonly used rule is "substantive transformation" or a tariff classification change. (A tariff classification change occurs when a good is processed or altered sufficiently to move it from one subheading number to another.) In some cases the rules are combined, as under NAFTA where the basic approach is tariff classification change with an additional condition in some cases that a certain value–content threshold be met. There is also provision for an accumulation of costs among more than one country enjoying the particular tariff status claimed (for example, MFN, GPF, British preferential). This wide variety of highly specific but uncoordinated rules makes the subject of tariff classification and rules of origin a sometimes impenetrable morass and creates a ready market for the services of customs brokers and consultants. The most widely used approach in case of doubt is to declare the country of origin to be the country where the goods assumed their final form.

There is broad international recognition and it is likely that the growing adoption of the HS as the basis for national tariff laws will give an advantage to tariff classification change as the foundation for a harmonized rule of origin. The primary basis for defining substantial transformation in the European Union and in the NAFTA region is tariff classification change.

Canadian Tariff Schedules

Once the dutiable value, the tariff classification, and the country of origin of the goods are determined, the appropriate tariff rate is applied. The *Customs Tariff* prescribes different tariff schedules as follows:

- *The most-favoured-nation tariff*—this is the tariff rate that applies to WTO members and to other nations with whom we have agreed to extend favourable rates. This rate applies to the majority of Canada's trading partners.
- *The NAFTA tariff*—this tariff rate reflects the provisions of NAFTA. Other countries with whom we have negotiated free trade agreements will have tariff rates that are similar to these.
- *The general preferential tariff*—lower than the most-favoured-nation rate, this is a favourable tariff rate extended to developing countries to help them increase their trade with Canada. This rate is applicable, however, at Canada's discretion and can be withdrawn by the Cabinet of the federal government if Canadian producers appear to be adversely affected.
- *The general tariff*—this is the highest tariff rate in the *Customs Tariff* and applies when there is no treaty or agreement between Canada and the exporting country.

Import Permits

Import permits are required in a number of areas. Although the details of these areas will change from time to time, the major ones are:

- *Items where Canada is allowed to limit imports under the WTO agreement*—for example, goods in the dairy and poultry sectors. As you will recall from previous chapters, Canada's poultry and eggs industry operates under an orderly marketing system that is designed to match supply with demand. This regulation requires the ability to control supply from all sources—international as well as domestic. After the Uruguay Round, Canada was obliged to convert its existing agricultural quantitative import controls (quotas) to a **trade restrictive quantities (TRQs) system**. The TRQs determine the tariff at which a specific agricultural product will be imported according to the status of previous quantities of the specific good that have already been imported. Under the TRQs, imports are subject to low "within access commitment" rates of duty up to a predetermined limit—that is, until the import access quantity has been reached. Imports over this limit are subject to significantly higher "over access commitment" rates of duty.
- *Food and drug safety*—the *Food and Drugs Act* and regulations set requirements for the production and sale of food and drug products.
- *Restricted goods*—for example, explosive goods and hazardous wastes.
- *Clothing and textiles*—as of April 2005, only those clothing and textile products eligible for tariff preference levels established under NAFTA or another trade agreement are subject to import permit requirements.
- *Packaging and labelling*—Canada has special packaging and labelling requirements, particularly for pre-packaged goods. The relevant legislation is under federal jurisdiction and includes the *Consumer Packaging and Labelling Act*, the *Food and Drugs Act*, the *Hazardous Products Act*, the *Trade-marks Act*, the *Pest Control Products Act*, the *Textile Labelling Act*, the *Customs Tariff*, and the *Precious Metals Marketing Act*. Much of this legislation specifies the manner in which basic information is placed on the product container, even down to specifying the lettering size. The requirement for country of origin, and information identifying the Canadian distributor for products, is common. In addition, because Canada is bilingual, certain information must be provided in both English and French. If a product is to be sold in Quebec, the French version must be displayed no less prominently than the English version.
- *Safety of non-food items*—non-food items may have to meet standards set by the Standards Council of Canada or Canadian Standards Association.

CANADIAN TRADE REMEDY LEGISLATION

The two primary remedies available to Canadian firms wishing to protect their industry from unfair importing practices are anti-dumping (AD) duties and countervailing duties (CVD). Anti-dumping duties are duties imposed by an importing country over and above the usual import duties when the goods are being dumped into the importing country. Dumping refers to selling an imported good at a price lower than the price at which it is sold in the exporting country. Countervailing duties are duties imposed by an importing country over and above the usual import duties when the goods have been subsidized by the country in which they are produced. The major users of these measure, which are authorized by the WTO Anti-dumping Agreement and the WTO Agreement on Subsidies and Countervailing Measures, have been, until recently, developed countries such as Canada, the United States, Australia, and, collectively, the countries of the European Union. Increasingly, less-developed countries are also protecting their domestic industries in this way. WTO members are obliged to adopt legislation that conforms to the WTO rules, and all assert that they have done this. The WTO case involving the Byrd Amendment (discussed in box 2.7 of chapter 2) is an example of the ability of the WTO to assess whether a country is adhering to the WTO rules and shows how a country will be eventually "persuaded" to comply with those rules.

The Canadian rules on dumping and subsidies are found in SIMA. The CBSA and the **Canadian International Trade Tribunal (CITT)** are jointly responsible for the administration of SIMA.

The Canadian International Trade Tribunal (CITT)

The CITT is the principal decision-making body for Canadian legislation affecting imports and exports. Located in Ottawa, it has nine members, each appointed for a term of five years. It is an independent, quasi-judicial body with rules and procedures similar to those of a court of law, but tempered with more latitude than exists in regular courts. It has the authority to

- conduct inquiries into whether dumped or subsidized imports have caused, or are threatening to cause, material injury to a domestic industry;
- hear appeals of decisions made under the *Customs Act*, the *Excise Tax Act*, and SIMA;
- conduct inquiries and provide advice on economic, trade, and tariff issues referred by the governor in council or the minister of finance;
- conduct inquiries into complaints concerning procurement under NAFTA, the **Agreement on Internal Trade**, and the WTO Agreement on Government Procurement; and

- conduct safeguard inquiries to determine whether increased imports are causing, or threatening to cause, serious injury to domestic producers.

Anti-Dumping Rules in Canada

Dumping is governed by the WTO Anti-Dumping Agreement. It is important to realize that care must be taken in assuming that dumping has occurred. Considerable confusion is created by the generally adopted colloquial meaning of "dumping" as disposing of excess, unwanted, or simply cheap, goods. This is not dumping as defined by the WTO. Consider the simplified scenario in box 6.2.

Retaliation in the form of AD duties may be taken only if the dumping causes or threatens to cause material injury to an established industry in an importing country or inhibits the establishment of a domestic industry in the importing country. One of the objectives of the GATT/WTO rules is to promote the judicialization of anti-dumping procedures. Judicialization involves dispute settlement by the objective application of rules to the facts of the situation.

BOX 6.2   WHAT IS DUMPING IN THE EYES OF THE LAW?

A Brazilian shoe manufacturer is able to manufacture ladies' sandals in Brazil and sell them to a wholesaler in Brazil for a price equivalent to Cdn$18. This price is sufficient for the manufacturer to cover all costs and recover his usual percentage of profit. The same manufacturer sells the sandals to a wholesaler in Canada. The extra cost of export to Canada (covering packing, shipping, insurance, customs duties, and handling) is Cdn$2 per pair. An equivalent pair of sandals manufactured in Canada and sold to the wholesaler with the usual allowance for profit to the manufacturer is $25, and appears in retail shoe outlets priced from $30 to $35. Consider whether dumping has occurred in the following examples.

Example 1. The Brazilian manufacturer sells the sandals to the Canadian wholesaler for Cdn$17 per pair. These sandals eventually appear in Canadian retail shoe outlets priced at $23.

Example 2. The Brazilian manufacturer sells the sandals to the Canadian wholesaler for Cdn$20 per pair. These sandals eventually appear in Canadian retail shoe outlets priced at $25.

Has dumping occurred in both example 1 and example 2? No, dumping has occurred in example 1 only. The test is whether the imported product is being sold at a price lower than that in its country of origin, not whether the good is later sold at a price below that of goods manufactured in Canada.

Margin of Dumping

The WTO rules provide for the imposition of AD duties based on the philosophy that the remedy or retaliation should be no greater than is necessary to compensate for the injury. There is no intention to punish the "dumper," but simply to restore conditions of fair trade. This is the purpose of calculating the "margin of dumping," which is the idea that the duty imposed should be the difference between the normal value and the "dumped price." The normal value is generally considered to be:

- the comparable price in the ordinary course of trade for like products when destined for consumption in the exporting country; or
- the highest comparable price for the product when exported to any third country in the ordinary course of trade; or
- the cost of production of the product in the country of origin plus a reasonable addition for selling costs and profit.

A different approach to price comparisons must be taken where a government monopoly exists in the exporting country and the WTO provisions make allowance for this. Once the normal value is established, it may be adjusted to allow for other variables, such as quantity discounts, quality, structure, design or material differences, and freight allowances if an allowance for these has not already been made.

Once determined, the normal value is compared with the export price. Care must be taken at this stage to ensure that no relevant facts are overlooked—such as a non-arm's-length relationship between the parties or some arrangement that affects the prices of the goods—such as rebates after sale.

Subsidy and Countervailing Duty Rules in Canada

A subsidy is any financial or commercial benefit given to a producer, manufacturer, grower, distributor, importer, or exporter by any government. A subsidized good will be countervailable—that is, subject to the importation of CVD—if a substantial portion of the industry in the importing country can prove material injury. The rules on subsidies are established by the WTO Agreement on Subsidies and Countervailing Measures. Subsidies are not subject to outright prohibition under the WTO. It is recognized that subsidies can be an integral part of the economic development programs of developing countries, in particular, and such subsidies may be acceptable when they are consistent with the development needs of such countries. Generally, if subsidies are available to all industries within a jurisdiction, and do not adversely affect international trade by conferring a competitive advantage, they are not countervailable.

Historically, state activity in the market has been more politically acceptable and more open in Canada than in the United States, where, despite the substantial use of subsidies, they are seen as undesirable and are not generally openly acknowledged. The difference in attitudes in the two countries helps to explain some of the Canada–US disputes over entities like the Canadian Wheat Board, and issues such as the softwood lumber dispute. The procedures for imposing countervailing duties in Canada are found in SIMA and are virtually identical to those used for dumping allegations.

Dumping and Subsidy Investigations and Rulings in Canada

The first issue in a dumping or subsidy case is whether dumping or subsidy has in fact occurred. The second and necessary requirement is to show that the dumped or subsidized imports are causing or threatening to cause injury to the Canadian industry. Injury is most commonly shown by reduced prices, lost sales, lost market share, decreased profits, and other similar difficulties. The decision whether to impose duties to compensate for dumping or subsidy is two-fold—it is divided between the Anti-dumping and Countervailing Directorate of the CBSA and the CITT.

The first stage in the investigation is usually the lodging of a complaint by a Canadian producer of goods that are identical or similar to the competing imports. Quite often the complaint will be generated by an association of producers. This is important, because there must be evidence of sufficient support by the Canadian industry for an investigation to be launched, and the general rule is that complaining producers must represent at least 25 percent of Canadian production to support a complaint. In addition there must be more support than opposition to the complaint within the Canadian industry.

It is the CBSA's job to evaluate the complaint and, if appropriate, start a formal investigation to determine whether the goods imported into Canada are dumped or subsidized. Usually, questionnaires are sent to exporters, importers, and, in subsidy investigations, to the foreign government involved. If necessary, representatives of the CBSA will meet directly with these parties to examine the information provided.

When the CBSA initiates an investigation, a copy of the complaint is sent to the CITT, which assumes responsibility for the question of injury to the Canadian industry and conducts an inquiry into the issue. The Tribunal holds public hearings to provide interested parties, which would normally include Canadian producers and importers, as well as foreign exporters, an opportunity to present evidence and argue in favour of their position.

The process normally takes at least seven months until a final decision on injury is made. Each body (the CBSA and CITT) usually makes a preliminary decision and a final decision.

If the preliminary decision is negative, any further investigation and hearings will be cancelled. If the preliminary decision supports the allegations, temporary duties on imports of dumped or subsidized goods will be imposed, usually within three months of the preliminary decision. If the final decision is that the goods were not dumped or subsidized, or that there was no material injury, these duties will be refunded. Sometimes, proceedings are suspended because the exporter or foreign government makes an undertaking—that is, an agreement—to change their pricing or subsidizing practices to eliminate the harm to Canadian industry.

The following two examples illustrate the use of anti-dumping and subsidy law in Canada. The *Hyundai* case, described in box 6.3, is an excellent illustration of the limitations of anti-dumping law for protecting producers against unfair competition where there is globalization of production.

BOX 6.3   THE HYUNDAI CASE
(Canadian Import Tribunal, 1988)

In this case, decided by the Canadian Import Tribunal, or CIT (CITT's predecessor) in March 1988, the complainants were General Motors of Canada and Ford of Canada. Hyundai was importing its entry-level vehicle, the Pony, into Canada where it was competing with the Ford vehicle, the Escort, and the GM entry-level vehicle, the Chevy Nova. The director of investigation and research of the Competition Bureau was an intervenor representing the public interest. There had been a preliminary finding of dumping by the deputy minister of national revenue. The case was complex and required four weeks of hearings. The Canadian auto producers based their request for ongoing anti-dumping duties on:

- present and past material injury, which was causing price suppression and margin erosion; and
- future material injury, which would result in reduced production, reduced employment, and reduced utilization of capacity, as well as continued price suppression and margin erosion.

The Competition Bureau's submission stated that, from a competitive point of view, Hyundai was a positive influence on the marketplace and did not cause injury to domestic production. The Bureau also argued that globalization was an important factor to consider in evaluating whether there was material injury in this case.

The Tribunal accepted that there was dumping of automobiles into the Canadian market, and asked: Was there material injury that would justify the imposition of ongoing AD duties?

The Tribunal found that the dumping of cars as defined in the preliminary determination had not caused, was not causing, and was not likely to cause material injury to the production in Canada of like goods.

The CIT decided that final AD duties would not be imposed and gave the following reasons for its ruling that Hyundai's dumping had not caused material injury to Canadian domestic producers:

1. Many of the industry's cars were manufactured for export and, therefore, there was insufficient evidence of injury to domestic production for domestic consumption.
2. Some apparent loss of production of Escorts was due to the life cycle of the product, costs of necessary retooling, falling demand in the North American market, and a downturn in the North American economy.
3. World capacity increases had led to more competition and the pricing environment was, therefore, too dynamic for one firm to have much control. Models and variations were proliferating too rapidly and Hyundai was but one part of an increasingly complex set of alternatives; thus the argument on price suppression was rejected.
4. Profitability in the Canadian market was a function of many factors, such as transfer-pricing policies, exchange rates, economic conditions, and the stage in the production cycle of new products.

The application of subsidy law in Canada is well illustrated by the ongoing Canada–US dispute over grain corn. A major case was decided in 1987 (see box 6.4) and a recent case was decided in 2006 (see box 6.5).

BOX 6.4   GRAIN CORN CASE
(Canadian Import Tribunal, 1987)

The case began with a complaint brought by Canadian grain corn producers against the export to Canada by the United States of grain corn, which the Canadians believed to be subsidized. The complainants alleged that there was material injury to the production in Canada of like goods.

The CIT asked: Was the American subsidization of grain corn causing and likely to cause material injury to the Canadian grain corn industry?

The Tribunal found that the import of grain corn (with the exception of corn for consumption in British Columbia and dent corn for use in the manufacture of snack foods and tortillas) had caused, was causing, and was likely to cause material injury. Countervailing duties could therefore be imposed.

The CIT gave the following reasons for its decision:

1. The United States was currently the only viable source for imports of grain corn. Canadian production was less than 4 percent of the US output and, given the ready access of buyers in Canada to US supplies, domestic prices in Canada were determined in large measure by prices and events in the United States.
2. Canadian domestic corn must be priced competitively with the cost of landed corn from the United States because buyers and sellers look to the Chicago Board of Trade in deciding whether to buy or sell domestic or US corn.
3. The price decline experienced by domestic grain corn producers was of sufficient magnitude to constitute material injury, both directly to producers and indirectly by the increased financial burden on domestic government support programs.
4. World production of grain corn had exceeded world consumption.
5. The major factors contributing to the recent growth in surplus United States stocks were the target price and loan rate policies in the US 1981 Farm Bill, which inhibited US corn production adjustments to reflect the changing realities of the international situation.
6. The United States was able to transfer its farm policies to international markets. The drastic decline in the international price for grain corn was in very large measure a direct consequence of the policies of the 1985 US Farm Bill.
7. Because of the open nature of the Canadian market, these lower prices were transferred to Canada, with substantial adverse effects on Canadian producers. Accordingly, the subsidization of US grain corn had caused and was causing material injury.
8. There was every indication that present conditions would persist for some time. Prices could not be expected to show much improvement and therefore the subsidization of United States grain corn would continue to be a cause of material injury.
9. The issue was not whether imports had taken place, but whether they would have increased substantially in the absence of a price response by domestic producers to the subsidized US grain corn. Although imports into Canada had been at modest levels, much higher levels of imports would have been a certainty given the open nature of the Canadian market.

> ### BOX 6.5   2006 GRAIN CORN CASE
> **(Canadian International Trade Tribunal, 2006)**
>
> In September 2005 the Canadian Grain Corn Producers initiated a complaint to the CBSA alleging that US government programs had subsidized American corn producers and also that US corn had been dumped into the Canadian market.
>
> The CBSA made preliminary and final determinations that US government programs had subsidized American corn growers, and that US corn had been sold at a cost below the US sale price or cost of production in Canada. Interim duties were imposed.
>
> The CITT ruled in April 2006 that the complainants had failed to prove that US subsidies or alleged dumping were in fact causing injury to Canadian producers.
>
> This case was significant for the Canadian food processing industry because CVD and AD duties would result in higher costs for Canadian manufacturers and producers of corn-derived or -dependent products, such as corn chips, soda pop, beer, pork, and beef. A total of 15 parties appeared in opposition to the Canadian Grain Corn Producers.

Safeguards

Under the WTO Agreement on Safeguards, member countries may impose safeguard measures on imports of goods if the domestic industry is being seriously injured by increased imports. The standard for serious injury is higher than the material injury standard used in dumping and subsidy determinations. The safeguard measure is applied through an **emergency safeguard mechanism (ESM)**, which may be described as a "safety valve" to protect a country that is experiencing hardship arising from intensified international competition in its domestic market as a result of trade liberalization obligations. The measure usually takes the form of an import surcharge and or a quantitative limitation. Safeguards are intended to be temporary measures that can be invoked only under carefully prescribed conditions. Like AD and CVD actions, an emergency safeguard measure is generally applied following a complaint from a domestic industry and an investigation has concluded that the domestic industry is being seriously injured by increased imports. These provisions provide policy flexibility to governments to respond to unanticipated challenges of intensified competition and provide considerable comfort to countries signing multilateral trade liberalization agreements. Canada has not applied a safeguard measure since it did so in the frozen beef case in 1993.

One current issue with respect to ESMs is the question whether they should apply to trade in services. The General Agreement on Trade in Services does not currently provide for the use of ESMs. Canada is presently content with this situation because our services exporters could be adversely affected by the use of ESMs by our trading partners. Canada does not have a great deal to gain from ESMs in the services sector because our service sector is a relatively open regime to imports.

NOTES

1   *Special Import Measures Act*, RSC 1985, c. S-15.
2   *Export and Import Permits Act*, RSC 1985, c. E-19.
3   *Canada Border Services Agency Act*, SC 2005, c. 38.
4   *Customs Act*, RSC 1985, c.1 (2nd Supp.).
5   *Customs Tariff*, SC 1997, c. 36.
6   *Export Development Act*, RSC 1985, c. E-20.
7   General Export Permit No. 12—United States Origin Goods, SOR/97-107.
8   *Foreign Extraterritorial Measures Act*, RSC 1985, c. F-29.

REVIEW QUESTIONS

1. What are some of the major reasons that Canada restricts imports and exports?
2. What are some of the more common methods that countries use to impose barriers against imports?
3. What changes in border security occurred in Canada and the United States after the events of 9/11?
4. Describe two services provided by the Canadian government to assist Canadian exporters.
5. In what circumstances do you need a permit to export goods from Canada? How would you ensure that your information on permit requirements is current?
6. What is the difference between the export control list and the area control list?
7. What is the difference between an individual export permit and a general export permit?
8. Describe the process by which the CBSA determines what duties apply to goods being imported into Canada.
9. What types of goods are subject to restrictions or limitations when being imported into Canada?

10. Describe what is meant under the WTO rules by dumping and subsidy.
11. Describe how dumping and subsidy cases are processed in Canada.
12 Describe the emergency safeguard provisions of the WTO and explain how they differ from the provisions on dumping and subsidies. Do the safeguard provisions apply to trade in services? What is the Canadian position on this?

DISCUSSION QUESTIONS

1. Some observers take the position that current AD and CVD rules under the WTO are outdated and should be replaced by global competition rules. Discuss this, using the Hyundai case and the grain corn cases as examples of the way that AD and CVD rules play out. Do these rules protect domestic producers or domestic consumers?
2. Identify some of the areas of trade friction between Canada and the United States. Describe current cases and the issues for producers and consumers in each country.
3. Have students, individually or in teams, choose a product to be exported from Canada to a designated country and do the necessary research to identify what permits, if any, will be required.

WEBSITES

International Trade Canada:
www.dfait-maeci.gc.ca/eicb/general/impcan-en.asp

The Canadian Food Inspection Agency (CFIA) Automated Import Reference System (AIRS):
http://airs-sari.inspection.gc.ca/AIRS/airs-sari.asp

Canadian Association of Importers and Exporters:
www.importsource.ca/gol/importsource/site.nsf

Anti-dumping and Countervailing Directorate, Canada Border Services Agency:
www.cbsa-asfc.gc.ca/sima

CHAPTER 7

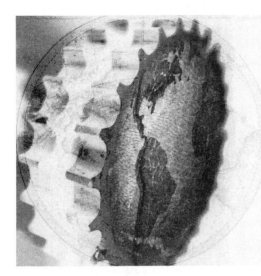

Negotiating the International Sale of Goods

INTRODUCTION

At the beginning of this book, we stated that knowledge of the global business environment is an important foundation for the effective business strategist and manager. Equally important to pursuing effective strategies, managing risk, and maximizing profit is an understanding of the legal principles of contract and tort. Some readers will be familiar with these concepts and may treat this section as a review, but for those readers without any previous knowledge of law, the following is a necessary foundation.

Contracts are fundamental to all that we do in business because they set out the rights and obligations of business parties. Some knowledge of tort law is also necessary because society may impose rights and obligations on business

After reading this chapter, you will understand:
- the essential elements of a valid contract and of tort in the common law tradition
- the importance of product liability and the different approaches in Canada, the United States, and the EU
- the importance of anticipating problems and including necessary terms when the primary contract is negotiated
- the trade terms used in international sale contracts, and Incoterms
- contractual problems and how to avoid them
- the importance of the Convention on the International Sale of Goods and how its provisions may vary from Canadian domestic sale of goods law
- the end of the international transaction: performance, breach, and frustration
- how a countertrade transaction differs from an international sale of goods

parties that are independent of any contracts that are made. This review of law is from the perspective of the Anglo-American, or **common law** tradition—that is, it applies generally to the domestic law of Canada, the United States, the United Kingdom, Australia, New Zealand, Ireland, Singapore, and other countries that have a history of colonial ties with the United Kingdom. We do not discuss the rules of other important legal systems, particularly the civil law system, which is used in most continental European countries. A review of the civil law is beyond the purview of this text, although references and comparisons will be made where relevant to specific topics.

The common law is often referred to as "judge-made" law and was originally a case-based system that had as its foundation the principle that similar disputes should have similar legal outcomes. This was achieved by the principle of ***stare decisis***, that is, "to stand by a previous decision." As society became more sophisticated, common law countries began to change or supplement the case law with statute law with the result that we now have a mixed system of cases and statutes as the source of law in common law countries. In modern society, governments frequently enact statutes to change or overrule the common law.

The **civil law** tradition is far more prevalent around the world than is the common law system. We find this tradition in all of continental Europe, Central and South America, parts of Asia, the Middle East, and Africa. The civil law is code based, originating with the Justinian Code of the Roman Empire. Civil law countries may have large comprehensive statutes or specific legislation in specialized areas known as codes. Over time, civil law countries have modified and shaped their code law with court decisions. As a result, the civil law and the common law are growing more alike.

THE LAW OF CONTRACT

Essential Elements of a Valid Contract

In both the common law and the civil law traditions, there are four essential elements for a valid or enforceable contract:

1. There must be an intention on the part of each party to create a legal relationship. Situations where this might not be the case would include promises made in a family, or in social relationships.
2. There must be an offer and an unequivocal acceptance of the offer. Advertisements or displays of priced products on shelves, although they may appear to be offers, are actually invitations to do business. If an acceptance alters the terms of an offer in any way, it is merely

a counteroffer and must be accepted before a contract is formed. A counteroffer also operates to terminate the original offer.

3. The parties to the contract must have the legal capacity to make a contract. The parties, if corporate, must be properly incorporated and acting within their corporate powers; the parties, if individuals, must not be diminished by alcohol, drugs, or mental infirmity.

4. The contract must be for a legal purpose. Agreements that clearly violate moral or legislative rules, such as antitrust, currency control, anti-corruption, or workers' compensation provisions, will not be enforceable by the parties.

The requirements described above are shared by the common law and civil law traditions.

The Common Law Requirement for Consideration

An important additional requirement of the common law is that every contract must be supported by **consideration**. If there is no consideration supporting the contract, it will not be enforceable by the courts. This requirement is not shared by the civil law. Consideration is the idea that a contract must be characterized by an exchange of value moving from each party to the other. The concept is often described as the **"bargain theory" of contract**, whereby each party trades one thing to get another. The reciprocal promises do not have to be equal in value because the courts do not consider whether the consideration is adequate or whether the parties made a good bargain; it is enough that consideration is present. An agreement that is not supported by consideration is referred to as a **gratuitous promise** and is not enforceable. The requirement for consideration can be avoided by having the parties sign the contract under seal. This is accomplished when a seal is placed on the contract, before or at the time that it is signed. There are a number of legal exceptions and rules in the common law that have developed as a result of problems arising from the requirement of consideration, but these will not be explored in this brief overview. Because the civil law does not use the concept of consideration, these complications are avoided. We will see examples of this when we consider some of the provisions of the Convention on the International Sale of Goods (CISG), later in this chapter.

Enforceability of Contracts

It is possible that a contract may meet the above requirements and still not be enforceable because of defects that have arisen in the course of negotiating the contract. These defects include undue influence, duress, mistake, and misrepresentation.

Undue Influence

Undue influence usually involves special personal relationships where a person in a position of power dominates a weaker person with whom he or she makes a contract. The relationship is typically between a parent and child, doctor and patient, or caregiver and infirm patient. Undue influence can also arise in contracts between lawyer and client or trustee and beneficiary. In such cases, the contract may be set aside if it is demonstrated that the stronger party benefited from his or her position to obtain a contractual benefit from the weaker party. Because undue influence usually arises only in personal relationships where there is an imbalance of power, it is unlikely to arise in international contracts.

Duress

Duress arises where one party uses economic or physical threats to extract contractual promises. When duress occurs in the making of international business contracts, it is often in countries that lack the legal infrastructure or rule of law to enforce the rights of the innocent party.

Mistake

Mistake is a complex and uncertain area of the law. Mistake may arise if the parties do not have the same objective in mind in agreeing to the contractual terms. Where the parties "are not on the same page," there is a chance that the contract may be set aside by a court on the basis of mistake.

Misrepresentation

Misrepresentation occurs where one party makes a statement that is material—that is, that can reasonably be expected to influence the decision of the other party to enter the contract, and the statement turns out to be false, or misleading. Misrepresentation can be innocent, negligent, or fraudulent and the remedies available to the innocent party will depend on the character of the misrepresentation. At the very least, the innocent party may have the right to have the contract set aside.

Breach of Contract and Remedies

Privity of Contract

If the terms of a contract are not honoured, or fully or adequately performed, the innocent party may sue for damages. However, in common law countries, under the principle of privity of contract, only the parties may sue for breach. If the contract was to benefit a third party—that is, a person not a party to the contract—that person cannot normally sue for damages if the contract is breached. This principle has been amended for specific situations in Canada, such as insurance contracts, and has been altered more broadly by legislation in the United Kingdom and Singapore. Most civil law countries do not have this restriction.

Breach of Warranty and Breach of Condition

A breach of contract in the common law may be a **breach of condition**— that is, a breach of an important or essential term of the contract—or a **breach of warranty**—that is, the failure to perform a less important or non-essential term of the contract. A breach of condition entitles the innocent party to walk away from the contract with no further obligation to perform and sue for damages. A breach of warranty only entitles the innocent party to sue for damages for the reduced value of the contract; the innocent party is not excused from the obligation to perform under the contract. Box 7.1 describes a scenario in which a breach of condition occurs and a scenario in which a breach of warranty occurs.

BOX 7.1

Indo Canada Exports Ltd. agrees to ship 10,000 one-kilogram bags of grade A wild rice to an importer located in Mumbai. The written contract was made in May 2006, and Indo Canada agreed that the rice would arrive in Mumbai no later than September 30 of the same year. The contract specified that the rice would be packaged in white paper bags with the importer's shop name and logo in its usual colours of saffron and green.

Scenario A: Indo Canada ships the 10,000 bags of grade A rice on time, but the rice is packaged in brown paper, rather than white. The importer's shop name and logo conform to the requirements of the contract. Although the Mumbai importer may be annoyed and disappointed that the bags are brown, rather than white, it is likely that this is simply the breach of a non-essential term of the contract. The importer is not entitled to reject the shipment of rice without itself committing a breach of contract. If the Mumbai importer can show that it has suffered any damages as a result of the bags being brown rather than white (such as a small reduction in sales), it will be entitled only to damages for the loss that it has suffered.

Scenario B: Indo Canada ships the grade A rice in white bags with the shop name and logo as required, but the shipment does not leave Canada (by sea) until September and does not arrive in Mumbai until October 31. In this situation, Indo Canada has breached an important or essential term of the contract, and the Mumbai importer is entitled to reject the rice and discharge the contract, freeing itself from any obligation to pay Indo Canada.

Mitigation of Damages

In the event that one party injures another through breach of the contract, the injured party must **mitigate**, or reduce, the loss if possible. A party that simply lets damages mount and claims for the full amount when some damages could have been prevented, will not succeed in recovering the full amount of damages suffered.

TORT LAW

The Purpose of Tort Law

The word "tort" originates from the French word meaning "wrong," and is an important instrument for apportioning loss in a society. Historically, tort law has developed to compensate victims for harm suffered from the activities of others. Its purpose is compensation, not punishment, which is left to the criminal law. A modern society faces difficult issues in determining who should bear a non-contractual loss arising from normal activities: should it be the victim, the person whose act caused the harm, or those who benefit from the overall activity—often all of society? Early tort law imposed the burden of compensation on the person who had caused an injury, without consideration of whether he or she was blameworthy. This is referred to as **strict liability**, or liability without fault. Gradually, the law evolved to require fault as the basis for liability in most tort situations.

Elements of a Tort Action

The general rule in common law tort law is that a plaintiff who wishes to recover in tort must prove three things:

1. that the defendant owed the plaintiff a duty of care;
2. that the defendant breached that duty; and
3. that the defendant's conduct caused the injury.

Failure to prove any one of these elements to the satisfaction of the court will result in failure by the plaintiff to obtain a damage award.

Product Liability

A major concern of the international business person is the tort of product liability—that is, liability for a defective product and the consequential damage that may occur as a result of a defective product. Liability for defective services, such as financial or consulting services, may also be of concern; but, in the majority of these cases, liability is based on contract, not tort, because the courts have imposed limitations on tort liability to third parties for professional or financial services. Because the distribution of products is so widespread, the potential for a defective product to harm a third party is enormous. For this reason, most developed countries have special rules relating to product liability.

Product Liability in Canada

In Canada, product liability is based on fault. Most cases involve proof of a manufacturing defect, proof of a design defect, or a failure by the manufacturer or distributor to warn of an inherent danger. The development of class actions is increasing the potential liability of manufacturers and has resulted in more judgments based on economic loss. A recent case of significance is the Supreme Court of Canada decision in *British Columbia v. Imperial Tobacco Canada Ltd.*[1] The Supreme Court upheld the constitutionality of BC legislation authorizing civil action by the province to recover health-care expenditures from the tobacco manufacturers. The tough new legislation puts an onus on the defendant to prove that its breach of duty did not give rise to disease; allows claims to be pursued on an aggregate basis (that is, against various parties in the tobacco industry); apportions liability on the basis of market share; and dispenses with the **limitation period**. This is a landmark judgment by the Supreme Court of Canada and greatly expands product liability of a manufacturer, albeit limited to the tobacco industry.

Product Liability in the United States

Many, but not all, product liability claims in the United States are based on the doctrine of strict liability. This strict liability applies to sellers of defective and unreasonably dangerous products. Such sellers will be responsible for any damage caused by their products, even without proof of negligence. Products identified by US court decisions thus far include food, furniture, appliances, airplanes, industrial machinery, and building materials. Even if a product is not defective or unreasonably dangerous, the manufacturer may be liable if the consumer was not adequately informed of potential hazards arising from the product's reasonably foreseeable use. To avoid liability, manufacturers have taken pains to include detailed instructions and warnings with their products (see box 7.2).

Product advertising can also contribute to liability for manufacturers and distributors because consumers who have suffered injury while using a product for the purpose for which it was advertised may successfully claim for breach of warranty. This has resulted in advertisements with lists of adverse effects for products almost as long as the positive attributes that are being promoted. (Typical of these are US television advertisements for

> **BOX 7.2   SOME WARNINGS ISSUED BY US MANUFACTURERS**
>
> - Do not put any person in this washing machine!
> - This blanket should not be used as protection from a tornado.
> - Wearing of this garment does not enable you to fly.
> - Eating rocks may lead to broken teeth (on a novelty rock garden).
> - This product not intended for use as a dental drill (on an electric rotary tool).
> - The contents of this bottle should not be fed to fish (on a bottle of pet shampoo).
>
> Source: Jeremy G. Zimmermann, Wiggin & Dana, LLP. (2003). *Recent Developments in U.S. Product Liability Law.* Available online at www.wiggin.com/pubs/pubs.asp.

prescription drugs in which the list of adverse effects can be longer than the list of symptoms that the product is meant to relieve.) One defence available to manufacturers and distributors of products in the United States is the "learned intermediary" defence, which can be used where products are sold to doctors or other intermediaries whose expertise places them in a better position to communicate warnings to the ultimate users. The most worrisome aspect of US product liability law to the business community is the punitive damage awards for which the American legal system has become famous. For example, in 1994, a woman who sued after spilling a cup of hot McDonald's coffee in her lap was awarded $2.7 million in punitive damages. (The award was subsequently reduced to $480,000.)

The growth of class actions in the United States is an important development and not without controversy. What began as a procedure for aggregating multiple claims in complex civil litigation has become a complicated and unwieldy form of litigation, in which individual class members may receive a very small share of a very large damages award, with the attorney taking as much as one-third of the entire judgment. There is no such system in the European Union (EU), and the system in Canada is much less developed. Because of the growing size of punitive damages awards and the increasing number of class action lawsuits, the issue of tort reform in the United States is an important one for US business.

Product Liability in the European Union
Since the adoption of the Directive on Liability for Defective Products[2] in 1985, the European Union has applied the principle of liability without fault for a manufacturer or producer in cases of damage caused by a defective

product. The result is that product liability claims in the EU have increased substantially. A "producer" includes the importer of the defective product; any person putting his or her name, trademark, or other distinguishing feature on the product; and any person supplying a product whose producer cannot be identified. Because the Directive provides for liability without fault, it is not necessary to prove the negligence or fault of the producer or importer. It is necessary to prove only the actual damage, the defect in the product, and the causal relationship between the damage and the defect. Factors to be taken into account when determining whether a product is defective include the presentation of the product, the use to which it could reasonably be put, and the time when the product was put into circulation. An injured person must bring his or her claim within three years from the time of injury. The adoption of the Directive has made EU and US law very similar with respect to liability for defective products, with the important difference being that there is no provision for class actions or punitive damages in the EU.

In 1999, the EU expanded the scope of the Directive to primary agricultural products such as meat, cereals, fruit and vegetables, and game products. This expansion occurred in the aftermath of an outbreak of bovine spongiform encephalopathy, or "mad cow" disease.

INTERNATIONAL CONTRACTS FOR THE SALE OF GOODS

This section will consider only the international sale of goods and the law relating to the sale of goods.

The Importance of the Primary Contract

An import or export transaction is simply a contract for the sale of goods; however, because goods are being shipped from one jurisdiction to another, we need to consider more than just the relevant domestic sale of goods law. For simplicity, we will refer to these transactions as export transactions, although one party's export transaction is another party's import transaction.

Because goods are being transported over long distances and across national boundaries, certain considerations may become just as significant in negotiations as the usual questions of price, quality, date of delivery, and payment terms. The various factors to be considered are illustrated in the scenario described in box 7.3.

It is important to address and answer all of these questions at the negotiation stage of an international sales transaction because the likelihood of

> ### BOX 7.3   A TYPICAL CANADIAN EXPORT CONTRACT
>
> Canequi Inc., a Canadian equipment manufacturer based in Toronto, is negotiating with Wanco Ltd., a purchaser in Hong Kong. In addition to agreeing on specifications for the equipment, price, and delivery dates, the parties must consider how the goods will be packaged for international shipment, what mode of transportation will be used, who will be responsible for all stages of the transportation process, storing, delivering, and clearing customs at the Canadian exit point, loading, shipment, trans-shipment, unloading, clearing customs at the entry point, possible storage, and land transportation. Who will be responsible for any necessary export or import authorization? Do the parties need to provide for an inspection of the goods before they are shipped long distances to ensure that the goods conform to the contract? Who will pay for the goods and where? When, by what means, and under what circumstances? Which party bears the risk of the loss of the goods?

problems increases with the longer distances involved and the different business customs, practices, and laws of each country. These problems may be exacerbated by communication issues, especially if there is a language barrier. It is also more likely in an international transaction that the parties do not know each other, either by previous dealings or by reputation in the local business community, and this too may contribute to a lack of trust, which may further compound any problems that do arise. The significance of these risks becomes even greater when you consider the difficulties of enforcing your rights against a contracting party in another jurisdiction.

Because of the greater complexity of an export transaction, contracts of sale used for these transactions may incorporate terms not frequently used in domestic trade. These trade terms have evolved from customs universally accepted and used in international commerce, and have, to some extent, simplified and standardized transactions for the international sale of goods.

Parties entering into negotiations involving an international sale should be aware that more than one contract may be necessary. The primary contract is the prime focus for initial negotiations and deals with the sale of goods. The contracting parties in this central or primary contract will be the seller/exporter and the purchaser/importer.

In box 7.3, the central or primary contract is between Canequi Inc. and Wanco Ltd. Other contracts will be necessary to deal with transportation, insurance, and financing, and these contracts will likely be with third parties. Remembering the principle of privity of contact, *it is essential that the obligations of the two main contracting parties for matters such as transportation, insurance, and financing be clearly stated in the central or primary contract because the failure to meet any of these obligations may be just as serious to the parties as a breach of the sale of goods obligations.*

Trade Terms Used in Export Sales

Specialized trade terms specify the method and place of delivery of the goods. They also indicate what is included in the calculation of the purchase price. A review of some of the terms reveals the reason for the considerable variation in purchase price according to the trade term adopted.

Although terms such as FOB, FAS, and CIF have been the most widely used instruments of the export trade for almost two centuries, they do not have exactly the same meaning in every country of the world. Various bodies such as Unidroit, UNCITRAL, and the International Chamber of Commerce (ICC) have made attempts to standardize trade terms to promote certainty and predictability in international transactions. The standard terms developed by the ICC represent the most successful of these attempts.

The **Incoterms** were first drawn up in 1936 and have been periodically amended, with the latest set agreed upon in 2000. The purpose of the terms is to provide a set of international rules for the interpretation of the most commonly used trade terms. Use of the terms is optional and generally the contract must specify that they apply: by simple reference to one of the trade terms expressly stating that it should be interpreted according to Incoterms—for example, "CIF Incoterms 2000—Incoterms will be included in the contract."

Incoterms deal exclusively with the obligations of buyers and sellers and stipulate which party bears the risk of loss during transit. It is important to realize that Incoterms relate only to the contract of sale, not to the separate contracts for carriage, insurance, and financing. The terms deal with:

- the seller's obligation to place goods at the disposal of the buyer or deliver them to a carrier or to a destination;
- the distribution of risk to the parties at the various stages of production, carriage, and delivery; and
- the buyer's obligation to take delivery and acknowledge that the seller's obligations are fulfilled.

Incoterms do not cover:

- transfer of ownership and property;
- breach of contract and consequences of such breach; and
- exemption from liability.

The terms fall into four main categories:[3]

- *"E" Terms.* Departure Term. This represents the seller's minimum obligation. Example: Ex Works.
- *"F" Terms.* Shipment Contracts (Main Carriage Paid). Examples: FCA, FAS, and FOB.
- *"C" Terms.* Shipment Contracts (Main Carriage Paid). Examples: CFR, CIF, CPT, and CIP.
- *"D" Terms.* Arrival Contracts. Examples: DAF, DES, DEQ, DDU, and DDP.

A Review of Commonly Used Incoterms

Because trade terms carry rights and obligations, international business persons should not rely on their memory in choosing the correct Incoterms for a contract. Unless they are completely familiar with the terms and have used them many times, they should always check any terms proposed for use in a new contractual arrangement. The appropriate set of rules should always be consulted before a final commitment on price is given. A brief overview of 14 commonly used Incoterms follows.

The "E" Terms

EX WORKS—EXW

This term represents the minimum obligation for the seller. The seller delivers when it places the goods at the disposal of the buyer at the seller's premises or another named place. The seller is not obliged to clear the goods for export or load them onto a collecting vehicle. The buyer bears all costs and risks involved in taking the goods from the seller's premises.

The "F" Terms (Shipment Contracts—Type 1)

FREE ON BOARD—FOB

This Incoterm is applicable only to waterborne transport. The seller delivers when the goods have been cleared for export and have passed the ship's rail at the named port of shipment. The buyer bears all costs and risks of loss from that point.

However, if FOB is not specified as an Incoterm, its meaning is interpreted under the common law and governed by a large body of established law and practice affecting the legal obligations between the parties. The Americans use the term in a somewhat different way. For this reason it is necessary to specify the legal system governing the term FOB and pay careful attention to the obligations undertaken by each party. Unless "FOB Incoterms" is specified, the term will be defined by the law of the contract, which, in the case of a transaction having some connection to Canada, may well involve common law precedents.

One potential problem is that the American and British use of the term FOB differs. In the United States, FOB is generally used as FOB destination, which denotes free delivery at that place; whereas common British practice is to use the term FOB to denote FOB vessel. For this reason, it is important for the parties to be very clear which definition applies. The set of legal rules being used should be clearly stated in the contract to avoid any misunderstandings between the parties.

The term FOB originated with maritime transport, but is sometimes used in connection with container and air transport. There is considerable potential for confusion in this area, so it is important that the parties clarify what is meant by such terms as "FOB Container Collection Depot," or "FOB Airport," sometimes referred to as FOA. The Incoterms are useful here because they set out the obligations of seller and buyer in detail.

In a straightforward FOB contract, it is the responsibility of the buyer to arrange the freight and marine insurance. This situation is often inconvenient for a buyer who is not familiar with firms or practices in the country of origin. The seller often has much better resources for arranging these matters than does the buyer. For this reason, the FOB contract with additional services has developed. In such a contract, the seller undertakes to arrange freight and insurance. In this case, the seller may take out the bill of lading in its own name or as an agent of the buyer.

One area of potential conflict with respect to FOB contracts is the question of examination of the goods. The parties should agree on a location for the examination of the goods. In the absence of specific arrangements, the buyer is not normally obliged to inspect the goods at the point of shipment unless the custom of the particular trade requires it. The buyer is entitled to postpone inspection of the goods until they reach their destination and, if the goods are found to be defective, the buyer may exercise its right of rejection. This practice may create problems for both parties and, for this reason, a more common and advisable practice is to agree on a pre-shipment inspection.

Other important "F" terms are Free Carrier [named place] (FCA), FOB Airport, and Free Alongside Ship (FAS).

The "C" Terms (Shipment Contracts—Type 2)

COST, INSURANCE, AND FREIGHT—CIF

Under Incoterms, CIF is applicable only to waterborne transport. The seller delivers when the goods pass the ship's rail (that is, are loaded onto the ship) in the port of shipment. The seller must pay the costs and freight necessary to bring the goods to the named port of destination, but the risk of loss and additional cost arising from events occurring after delivery are borne by the buyer. Although the buyer bears the risk of loss, the seller must obtain marine insurance on the buyer's behalf.

CARRIAGE PAID TO—CPT
The seller delivers the goods to the carrier chosen by him, but must also pay the cost of carriage to the named destination. The buyer bears all risks and other costs occurring after the goods have been delivered.

COST AND FREIGHT—CFR
According to the Incoterms, the seller must pay the costs and freight necessary to bring the goods to the named destination, but the risk of loss of or damage to the goods, as well as of any cost increases, is transferred from the seller to the buyer when the goods pass the ship's rail in the port of shipment.

These "C" contracts are the most widely used in international trade because they offer the flexibility needed to deal with goods that are often purchased and resold several times before they are delivered to their ultimate destination. These contracts also conform best to international banking and financing practices.

Consider the hypothetical situation described in box 7.4, which illustrates the flexibility of the "C" terms.

The traditional CIF contract was often referred to as a "sale of documents relating to goods." It is not so much a contract to deliver goods to a specific buyer as an agreement that the seller will do the following:

1. ship the goods complying with the contract of sale;
2. arrange for a shipping contract to the destination;

BOX 7.4   FLEXIBILITY OF THE "C" TERMS

Recall our scenario involving Canequi and Wanco in box 7.3. Imagine that the contract was made on January 1 and that the goods are due in Hong Kong on June 1 of the same year in three separate shipments. Wanco then contracts with three other Asian purchasers, Singapore Widgets, Taiwan Gizmos, and Thai Tools, to sell each of them one-third of the goods, with each to take delivery in Hong Kong on June 1. In a case such as this, it would be cumbersome for Wanco to take possession of the goods and then transport them to Singapore Widgets, Taiwan Gizmos, and Thai Tools, so the contract will stipulate that a "C" term be used, allowing Wanco to transfer the right to collect one-third of the shipment to the three subsequent purschasers using the documents only.

3. insure the goods on the voyage; and
4. tender the documents relating to the goods for payment.

The buyer's goal in a CIF sale is often to obtain the right to resell the goods, because frequently the original buyer never takes possession of the goods. The documents referred to above include:

- the bill of lading or other transport document, depending on the type of transport used.
- the **insurance policy** or **certificate of insurance**. This document is issued by the insurance company or underwriter, is dated on or before the date of shipment, and is effective on that date. It should be in an amount at least equal to the CIF value of the goods plus 10 percent and be in the currency of the credit.
- the **commercial invoice**. The commercial invoice is the accounting document by which the seller charges the goods to the buyer. It normally includes the date, names, and addresses of buyer and seller, order number, quantity and description of goods, their weight, the number of packages, terms of delivery, and payment and shipment details.
- other documents specified in the contract of sale.

Clarifying responsibility for goods and insurance
The seller's responsibility for goods under a CIF contract ends when the goods are delivered into the carrier's custody. Once with the carrier, the goods are the responsibility of the carrier. The parties must take care to ensure that the goods are adequately insured during each stage of the journey until they are in the buyer's possession.

Right of rejections of goods
The goods are deemed to be delivered, and property in the goods passes, when the bill of lading is delivered to the buyer or the buyer's agent. When property in the goods passes with the delivery of the bill of lading, it is a conditional property right only, and is subject to the goods reverting to the seller if they do not conform to the contract.

Box 7.5 illustrates that the responsibility of the seller for representations and warranties may continue until the goods have been examined and accepted.

Payment is due upon presentation of the documents
Payment of the purchase price of the goods normally becomes due when the documents conforming to the contract are tendered to the importer or its representative. The presentation of documents is considered to be a condition of the sales contract and significant delay in presenting these documents may entitle the buyer to rescind the contract.

BOX 7.5 SELLER'S RESPONSIBILITY FOR THE QUALITY OF GOODS

Assuming a CIF contract, Canequi manufactures the goods and arranges for their transportation and insurance. The goods are delivered by Canequi to the shipping firm (or freight forwarder) and the bill of lading, the insurance policy or certificate, the commercial invoice, and any other specified documents are assembled. These documents are then forwarded by Canequi (or its bank) in Canada to Wanco (or its bank) in Hong Kong. In this case, Wanco may have specified that there be three separate shipments (each with supporting documents) as it may have anticipated the three ultimate purchasers.

Once Canequi delivers the goods to the shipping firm, it is relieved of any immediate responsibility for the goods. It remains responsible under the contract of sale, however, for any representation or warranties relating to the goods. For this reason, the title of the goods will revert to Canequi if the goods are ultimately examined by Singapore Widgets, Taiwan Gizmos, and Thai Tools and they are found not to conform to the original sales contract between Canequi and Wanco.

Importance of anticipating problems and clarifying terms

Business persons may be surprised to learn that the port of shipment and the port of destination may be considered to be conditions of the contract; therefore, the breach of either of these terms will entitle the buyer to refuse to accept the documents tendered. For this reason, it is advisable to include in the contract a clause protecting the seller if dispatch of goods from the intended port becomes impracticable or impossible.

Consider the scenario described in box 7.6, which illustrates the importance of clarifying the port of shipment in the initial negotiations.

BOX 7.6 EXPORTER CHANGES SHIPPING ARRANGEMENTS

Suppose that the sales contract between Canequi and Wanco provided that shipment be made from Toronto to Hong Kong. It is considered a condition (that is, an essential term) of the contract that this be adhered to exactly. Suppose, however, that there was a strike affecting shipment from Toronto and Canequi could make alternative arrangements for transshipment of the goods from Toronto to Halifax and by sea from Halifax to Hong Kong, still meeting the June 1 deadline. Although this makes good commercial sense, unless there is a clause in the contract allowing for such deviation, Wanco can claim a breach of condition and use this as an excuse to avoid the contract.

Good are lost or destroyed

If the goods are shipped and lost, the seller is still entitled to tender proper shipping documents and claim the purchase price. The buyer's normal remedy in this situation is to claim against the carrier or the insurer. Consider the scenario described in box 7.7, which illustrates a relatively straightforward case of loss of goods.

BOX 7.7   VESSEL SINKS AND CARGO IS LOST

Suppose that Canequi's goods are shipped and the vessel on which they are carried is destroyed by fire. Unless the contract provides otherwise, Wanco is still obliged to pay the purchase price. Wanco may then collect the value of the shipment from the insurer, if the goods were fully insured, or make a claim against the carrier.

The "D" Terms (Arrival Contracts)

The "D" terms are becoming increasingly common. As more countries develop sophisticated infrastructures and reliable and transparent rules, sellers have become more willing to undertake an obligation in the country of the importer. A number of variations are available. Four of them are described as follows.

DELIVERED EX SHIP—DES

Under Incoterms, this means that the seller makes the goods available to the buyer on board the ship at the destination named in the sales contract. The seller must bear the full cost and risk involved in bringing the goods to the destination.

DELIVERED EX QUAY—DEQ

Under Incoterms, this means that the seller makes the goods available to the buyer on the quay (wharf) at the destination named in the sales contract. The seller must bear the full cost and risk involved in bringing the goods to the destination. There are two "Ex Quay" contracts in use: "Ex Quay (duty paid)" and "Ex Quay (duty on buyer's account)," in which the liability to clear the goods for import is to be borne by the buyer instead of by the seller. Parties are always recommended to use the full description of these terms in their contracts because there may be uncertainty as to who is to be responsible for the liability to clear the goods for import.

DELIVERED AT FRONTIER—DAF

Under Incoterms, this means that the seller's obligations are fulfilled when the goods have arrived at the frontier, but before "the customs border," of the country named in the sales contract. This term is primarily intended to be used when goods are to be carried by rail or road but it may be used irrespective of the mode of transport.

DELIVERED DUTY PAID—DDP

While the term "Ex Works" signifies the seller's minimum obligation, the term "Delivered Duty Paid," when followed by words naming the buyer's premises, denotes the other extreme—the seller's maximum obligation. Under Incoterms, this means that the seller's obligations are met when the goods are made available at the destination named in the sales contract. The seller must bear the full cost and risk in bringing the goods to the destination, including duties, taxes, and any other charges. The term "Delivered Duty Paid" may be used irrespective of the mode of transport. If the parties wish that the seller should clear the goods for import but that some of the costs payable upon the import of the goods should be excluded—such as value added tax (VAT) and/or other similar taxes—this should be made clear by adding words to this effect (for example, "exclusive of VAT and/or taxes").

Choice of Terms

At first glance, it would seem best that each of the contracting parties would try to limit its obligation as much as possible. The seller would try to negotiate an ex works contract while the buyer would try to convince the seller to deliver the goods duty paid to the buyer's premises (DDP). In practice, however, the situation is not that simple. A seller or a buyer cannot easily make a better contract merely by shifting functions, costs, and risks to the other contracting party. The parties involved will probably be guided by other criteria in their choice of trade terms.

MARKET FACTORS

In a highly competitive market, the seller may wish to offer prices to the buyer that are comparable to prices offered in the buyer's domestic market. Because additional costs and risks accepted by the seller are always reflected in the price, the seller would undertake to deliver the goods using terms such as "Ex Quay" or "Delivered Duty Paid." As a minimum, the seller would be obliged to arrange and pay for transportation by using such terms as CFR, CIF, or Freight & Carriage Paid.

ACCESS TO RELIABLE TRANSPORT AND INSURANCE

In some instances, an exporter of large and regular volumes of goods will usually be in a position to obtain better terms from carriers and insurers than the "occasional" importer. It may be comparatively simple to arrange the transport in the country of exportation, and the risk of something going wrong is minimal. In such cases there is really no reason why the seller should limit its obligations under ex works, FAS, or FOB agreements. Under normal conditions of trade between countries with well-organized container ports and peaceful labour conditions, the risk of political disturbances, congestion in the ports, strikes, or interruptions of trade may be minimal. In such cases, the seller may elect to assume the risk during transport, and to choose a term in which its responsibilities extend to the arrival of the goods at the destination (a "D" or "arrival contract"). A seller who thinks that such risks may be difficult to ascertain and therefore difficult to include in the calculation of the price might prefer to have the buyer assume the risks during international transport and use an "F" or "shipment contract."

GOVERNMENTAL INVOLVEMENT

Directly or indirectly, government authorities may guide or even instruct parties in their country to sell on CIF terms and to buy on FOB terms. There are two main reasons for this:

- Trade terms constitute an important tool for directing the flow of goods to national shipping lines or other national carriers.
- It is possible to save foreign currency. A seller who has undertaken to pay for carriage and insurance will include these costs in its price for the goods and thereby obtain more foreign currency. On the other hand, a buyer who has assumed these costs will pay less for the goods, and may sometimes be able to pay for transportation and insurance services in domestic currency.

AVOIDING COMPLEXITIES OF INTERNATIONAL SALE

Where goods are sold "ex works" or "ex factory," the overseas buyer or its agent must collect the goods at the seller's factory, warehouse, or office. This arrangement is the simplest for the seller and would, therefore, be appropriate for a seller who does not wish to be involved in the complexities of arrangements for international shipping, insurance, and financing. The arrangement is unlikely to be attractive to an overseas buyer, who must make necessary arrangements for international shipping, insurance, and financing in the unfamiliar environment of the seller's country. This term is not attractive to sellers eager to capture new export sales, but it has obvious advantages for the seller who decides to export (perhaps on a once-only or occasional basis) and wants to keep the transaction as similar as possible to a local transaction.

CONVENTION ON CONTRACTS FOR THE INTERNATIONAL SALE OF GOODS

The **Convention on Contracts for the International Sale of Goods (CISG)** applies to all contracts of sale of goods when the parties have their places of business in different contracting states. It will automatically apply unless the parties "opt" or contract out of it. The CISG applies only to commercial sales of goods and does not apply to household or domestic goods, goods sold by auction, or sales of securities, electricity, or aircraft. One area that may present difficulties is a contract for a "turn-key" operation or similar contracts for completed installations. Are these contracts for goods or for services? The answer probably lies in an assessment of the predominant part of the contract; if the contract is predominantly one for services, the CISG should not apply. There are, at present, no definite guidelines available as to what proportion is required to be "predominant."

Many attempts were made at achieving a uniform law of sales in international transactions before the adoption of the CISG. This Convention, which first came into force in 1988, appears likely to achieve the goal of widespread acceptance and use. As of 2006, more than 30 countries had ratified the Convention and it is becoming an international standard for international sales contracts. See Table 8.1 for a list of contracting countries (or states). Note the absence of Japan and the United Kingdom.

Because the sale of goods falls within provincial jurisdiction in Canada, it was necessary for each province to adopt the Convention by passing its own legislation. There is thus a provincial statute incorporating the CISG into the laws of each province. This Convention came into force in Canada in May 1992 and now applies uniformly to international sales contracts made by businesses in all parts of Canada, provided that the other contracting party is also located in a country that has ratified the CISG.

Opting Out of the CISG

Parties may specifically opt out of the CISG. Why would they wish to do so? If the parties have an established and successful relationship based on a contract that is founded on, say, the common law, or the US **Uniform Commercial Code (UCC)**, they may see no reason to change the contractual basis of the relationship. Similarly, if the parties have no history between

---

BOX 7.8   LIST OF CISG SIGNATORIES, 2006

Argentina	Ecuador	Kyrgystan	Russian Federation
Australia	Egypt	Latvia	Saint Vincent &
Austria	Estonia	Lesotho	Grenadines
Belarus	Finland	Liberia	Singapore
Belgium	France	Lithuania	Slovakia
Bosnia-Herzegovina	Gabon	Luxembourg	Slovenia
Bulgaria	Georgia	Mauritania	Spain
Burundi	Germany	Mexico	Sweden
Canada	Greece	Moldova	Switzerland
Chile	Guinea	Mongolia	Syria
China (PRC)	Honduras	Netherlands	Uganda
Colombia	Hungary	New Zealand	Ukraine
Croatia	Iceland	Norway	United States
Cuba	Iraq	Paraguay	Uruguay
Cyprus	Israel	Peru	Uzbekistan
Czech Republic	Italy	Poland	Yugoslavia
Denmark	Republic of Korea	Romania	Zambia

---

themselves, but each is accustomed to similar contracts based on a familiar system of law, they may wish to stay with the system that is familiar to both.

Parties may also opt out of the CISG on the advice of their lawyers. Many lawyers have pointed out that the Convention is new and untried, and that there is little in the way of Canadian judicial precedent to guide parties in the interpretation of CISG provisions. It is likely to be many years before there is a reliable body of case law to guide businesses, and it will take time for practitioners and traders to becomes completely familiar with all the ramifications of the CISG's many provisions. As Professor Jacob Ziegel, a recognized Canadian authority in this area, has said in his much-quoted conclusion on this dilemma, "One's clients should not serve as guinea pigs upon whom to try out the convention."[4]

If the parties do decide to opt out of the CISG, in whole or in part, the wording of the exclusion must be clear and unambiguous. It is not sufficient to state, for example, "Ontario law shall apply to this contract," since Ontario law will result in the application of the CISG. A safer clause would be, "The parties specifically exclude the application of the provisions of the Convention on Contracts for the International Sale of Goods and agree that the domestic sale of goods law of Ontario shall apply to this contract." Businesses may find that many of their assumptions about the law that applies are no longer correct. Consider the scenario described in box 7.9.

BOX 7.9   SALES MANAGER ASSUMES THAT CANADIAN LAW APPLIES TO "HIS" CONTRACTS

An Ontario firm has developed a camera stabilizer that enables an operator to take excellent moving pictures of sports and other action events. The company manufactures the equipment and also functions as a service company, providing consultants to customers to help them obtain sharp pictures in challenging situations. This firm has entered into the following four major contracts this year:

1. a contract to deliver one unit to a film company in New York state;
2. a contract to deliver one unit to a ski instruction school in British Columbia;
3. a contract to deliver two units to the Japanese Institute of Sporting Films in Tokyo; and
4. a contract to send two consultants to help the French Broadcasting Network film skiing events in Davos, Switzerland in January of next year.

The individual who arranged for these contracts is the sales manager of the company. He is focused on selling the company's product and has no time for expensive lawyers and their interference in his dealings, so the contracts were simple ones. They contained all the essential terms, such as price, packing and shipping arrangements, dates for delivery, insurance, and payment obligations. There was no thought given to settlement of disputes or what law would apply to the contracts. The sales manager assumed that Ontario law would apply because all the contracts were signed in Toronto on a standard form prepared by the Ontario company.

Problems have arisen under each of these contracts and the company has come to you seeking legal advice. Is the sales manager correct in his assumption that the law of Ontario applies to each of these contracts? What law do you think applies to each of these contracts?

Advantages of the CISG

The CISG has been described as very readable, practical, and balanced. There has been genuine progress made in harmonizing the common law and the civil law rules relating to contracts for the sale of goods. The purposes of this Convention have been described as follows:

1. to define a "default law," which will apply where parties have failed to designate any other law applicable to the agreement;
2. to provide a sales law regime for developing countries and for countries with regulated economies that lack private sales laws of their own; and

3. to balance the interests of buyer and seller and avoid some of the rigidities and anomalies that have developed in many national laws.

The Provisions of the CISG

The CISG governs the formation of the contract of sale and the rights and obligations of the seller and the buyer; however, it does not deal with the validity of the contract. Issues such as fraud, minority, or other problems of capacity are not covered by the Convention. Nor does the Convention deal with questions of title to the goods. Also excluded from the Convention are questions of product liability.

One of the differences that those having a background in the common law will notice is the "codification" in the Convention of principles that are familiar to us but have been established, not by a written code, but by previous cases decided by our courts. In some cases, rules familiar to residents of common law countries are eliminated. For example, the CISG provides that "where a court must determine a party's intent, due consideration should be given to all relevant circumstances including the negotiations leading up to the contract, the practices the parties have established between themselves and the parties' conduct after they have agreed to the contract." Note that this provision has the effect of doing away with the difficult common law **parol evidence rule**. This common law rule prevents parties from successfully bringing evidence before a court to contradict the terms in a written contract and prove that changes to the contract had been agreed upon before or at the time that a written contract was signed.

Similarly, the CISG provides that

> the parties are bound by any usage to which they have agreed and by any practices which they have established between themselves ... or are considered to have impliedly made applicable to their contract a usage ... which in international trade is widely known to and regularly observed by parties to contracts of the type involved in the particular trade concerned.

Has a Valid Contract Been Formed?

One of the most important considerations for an international negotiator is to ensure that a valid, enforceable contract has been formed. A number of rules that relate to contract validity have evolved in various countries and must be taken into account when assessing the terms of a contract. The most important of these will be examined in this section.

Requirement of Writing

The sale of goods laws of Canada, the United Kingdom, the United States, and most other countries require that commercial contracts for the sale of goods having any significant value be in writing to be enforceable in court. This is also a requirement in Muslim countries because the Koran requires that commercial contracts be in writing. In contrast, the civil law countries of Europe do not have a tradition of requiring sales contracts to be in writing. The exception is Eastern Europe, where certainty in contract has been highly valued under Iron Curtain influence, although the changes occurring in these countries are such that no uniform statement may be made as to their present rule on such contracts. It is likely that these countries will adopt the approach of their fellow Europeans and the CISG, which states that a contract of sale need not be evidenced by writing and is not subject to any specific requirement as to form, but may be proven by any means, including witnesses.

Consider the scenario described in box 7.10, which illustrates the potential difficulties associated with the rule that contracts must be in writing to be enforceable.

BOX 7.10 INFORMATION TECHNOLOGY USED TO FORM AN INTERNATIONAL CONTRACT

Apex Limited of Edmonton is a manufacturer of heavy construction equipment and has recently entered into four contracts using the Internet, with subsequent confirmation of the details, including requirements and arrangements for delivery, by telephone. The first contract is with a firm in Minnesota, the second with a firm in France, the third with a firm in Saudi Arabia, and the fourth with a firm in Australia. If problems were to arise under these contracts, and Apex wished to enforce them in court, would there be any obstacles to Apex's actions?

What Constitutes an Offer?

THE COMMON LAW

Many negotiations do not result in a completed contract. It is very important to be able to ascertain with certainty whether a party has made an offer or merely a quotation or invitation to do business. The first contract between the parties will often take the form of an advertisement, a catalogue entry complete with description and price, or simply a letter of inquiry. It is a natural assumption on the part of a party to regard a quotation or an advertisement as an offer; however, under the common law, such activities are viewed as mere invitations to do business and it is the buyer who must make an offer based on the information contained in the advertisement or quotation. It is important that the information contained in an advertisement or quotation be correct because it may well form the foundation of the contract and, if incorrect, could result in an unprofitable contract or a misrepresentation for which the party in error could later be found to be liable in damages.

Some quotations may contain all the elements of an offer and may be considered by the courts as such. This is the exception rather than the rule. The test used by the courts in these cases is the intention of the person submitting the quotation. There must be evidence of a clear intention that the quotation was meant as an offer.

THE UCC

The UCC provides that an offer should contain all the essential elements of a contract and is a statement that the offeror intends will result in a binding contract if accepted unaltered by the offeree. The essential elements of an offer are usually the following:

1. A clear description of the goods.
2. A statement of the purchase price and terms of payment.
3. A list of all details of delivery, including details concerning packing, invoicing, transportation, and insurance.

THE CISG

Article 14 of the CISG provides that a proposal addressed to one or more specific persons is an offer if it is sufficiently definite and indicates the intention of the offeror to be bound. A proposal is sufficiently definite if it indicates the goods and expressly or impliedly fixes, or makes provision for determining, the quantity and price.

Although the provisions of the three systems are similar, the CISG is the most flexible because it does not demand any provisions for the terms of delivery in a valid offer.

Consider the scenario described in box 7.11, which illustrates the importance of knowing whether a communication is an offer or simply an invitation to do business.

BOX 7.11 WELL-DESIGNED CATALOGUE RESULTS IN RESPONSE FROM CANADA

A Canadian buyer of specialty items sees a catalogue prepared by a Bulgarian manufacturer of chess sets that reads, "Beautifully carved chess sets of Bulgarian semi-precious stone, US $200 per set, ex works, if 20 or more are ordered, payment cash on collection, sets ready for collection within 60 days of order received." The Canadian buyer sends a letter stating,

"We hereby accept your offer p. 65 of current catalogue for 30 chess sets, US $200 per set, ex works, contact our agents, ABC Shippers, based in Sofia, for collection arrangements within 60 days. They are authorized to pay and collect on our behalf and they are instructed to make all shipping and insurance arrangements."

The Bulgarians do not respond to the letter, although the Canadian buyer can prove that it was received. Six months have elapsed. The Canadian buyer made contracts in Canada with various gift shops, which were to resell the chess sets, and is now facing disgruntled customers and possible lawsuits in Canada. The Canadian buyer now wishes to sue the Bulgarians for breach of contract. Is the Canadian buyer likely to succeed? Why or why not? What law applies to the contract? Would your answer be different if any other law applied?

Revocation of an Offer

THE COMMON LAW

Under the common law, the doctrine of consideration prevents an offeror from making a simple offer irrevocable. Thus, an offer can be revoked at any time before it is accepted, as long as the revocation is communicated to the offeree. This is true even in cases in which the offeror has stated that the offer will remain open for a specific period of time. Under the common law, there are two special circumstances in which a commitment to leave an offer open for a specified time will be legally binding. The first is where the offer is made under seal and the second is where the offeree pays (thereby creating consideration) for the privilege of the certainty of what is then an option period.

THE CISG

The CISG follows the civil law tradition, which does not use the concept of consideration in contracts and generally regards a firm offer to be binding for the period specified. The CISG, reflecting the civil law view, states in Article 16(2) that a firm offer will be binding and cannot be revoked if it indicates by stating a fixed time for acceptance or otherwise that it is irrevocable, or that it was reasonable for the offeree to rely on the offer being irrevocable. Such promise of irrevocability does not have to be signed or in writing.

THE UCC

The UCC takes a middle course on the issue of revocation. It provides in s. 2-205 that a firm offer for the purchase or sale of goods stated to be effective for a limited period given by a merchant in a signed writing can be enforced by an offeree who has relied on the offer.

Consider the scenario described in box 7.12, which illustrates the difficulties that can arise when a Canadian firm assumes it can revoke an offer with no legal ramifications.

BOX 7.12   MANITOBA FIRM RENEGES ON OFFER

On February 1, a Manitoba seller sent a Michigan buyer an offer by fax to sell 5,000 carpets for Cdn $200 each. A complete description of the goods, together with all relevant payment and delivery terms, was included with the offer. The fax stated that the offer was binding and irrevocable until February 28 of the same year. On February 14, the Manitoba seller sent another fax to the Michigan buyer stating, "Ignore our fax of February 1. We have miscalculated and we withdraw our offer." On reading this, the Michigan buyer decided that the price must have been a good one and faxed the Manitoba seller on February 15 stating, "We accept your offer of February 1."

Is there a contract? Under what law? Why?

Requirements for a Valid Acceptance

Generally, a contract is formed and the parties are bound by its provisions once the offer to buy or sell the goods is accepted. This concept is common to all legal systems.

THE COMMON LAW

The acceptance of an offer must be unconditional and unqualified. If the acceptance alters the original offer in any way, it is considered a counter-offer and must be accepted by the original offeror before a contract is formed. This is referred to as the "mirror image" rule, which means that the acceptance must be an exact "reflection" of the offer.

THE UCC

The strict approach taken by the common law has been modified in the American UCC, which states that an acceptance containing minor additional or different terms will be valid, but the minor additional or different terms will not become a part of the contract. Terms that "materially alter" the offer are not considered "minor terms" under this rule. This rule is helpful in the common situation in which parties negotiate with each other on the basis of their own standard form, which may contain provisions in the small print that even the parties are unaware of. If this rule did not exist, a confirmation in response to, say, a purchase order, on a form differing slightly from the original offer, would result in no contract. The UCC thus attempts to uphold the intention of the parties that there be a binding contract in spite of small discrepancies between the standard forms of the parties. The approach of the UCC to this situation is thus pragmatic, freeing business persons from the time-consuming task of reading the small print on each other's forms to ensure there are no discrepancies. Many business persons have remarked that if businesses read the back of each other's forms, all business would come to a halt.

THE CISG

The CISG also takes a more practical approach than the common law to the issue of acceptance. The Convention states that an acceptance containing new terms that do not materially alter the terms of the offer constitutes a valid acceptance unless the offeror promptly objects to the change. If the acceptance contains additional or different terms that materially alter the terms of the offer, it will not be effective until it is accepted by the other party. The CISG clarifies this provision by listing the elements that are considered to materially alter the contract: price, payment, quality, and quantity of good, place and time of delivery, extent of the parties' liability to each other, and settlement of disputes (Article 19).

The potential for differences between an offer and its acceptance increases greatly when each business uses its own standard form.

The Battle of the Forms

Providing for a common set of terms and conditions that apply to most transactions in which a firm engages is a good business practice. Buyers and sellers may each wish to have the advantage of familiar and tested provisions and hence will attempt to impose terms upon other parties with whom they do business. As a result, it is not uncommon for the seller to send the buyer an offer on a form that incorporates the seller's general conditions and for the buyer to accept on a form that incorporates its general conditions. It is unlikely that the sets of conditions will be identical. The outcome is sometimes referred to as the "battle of the forms." These impasses can often be avoided by the offeror sending with the offer a confirmation slip that must be signed and returned by the offeree.

If the offeree does not use the offeror's confirmation slip, but accepts on its own form containing its own terms and conditions, a strict application of the mirror image rule would result in no binding contract under the common law. This, however, may not be the intention of the parties, each of which believes an enforceable contract was established. In these situations, there is an advantage in the more flexible rules of the UCC and the CISG because these systems allow for minor variations between offer and acceptance. There is evidence that even the common law is becoming more flexible in this area. In the United Kingdom, an influential common law jurisdiction, there have been decisions in which the courts have held that, where there was a clear intention to create a contractual relationship and the parties have considered themselves bound, contradictory minor terms that are at variance may not prevent the formation of a valid contract. Such a contract between the parties will be deemed to exclude the terms at issue between the parties.

A scenario in which a battle of the forms arises is described in box 7.13.

BOX 7.13 A BATTLE OF THE FORMS

A Nigerian company, Lagos Computers Ltd., requested that an Ontario company, Oakville Computers Inc., advise on specific conditions of sale (CIF) on a specific model of computer to be delivered to Lagos on or before January of the following year. Oakville replied using its own standard form containing its conditions of sale, including a price escalation clause and a clause stating that the laws of Ontario would apply. On the bottom of this form was a printed tear-off portion stating that the order was accepted by the buyer "on the terms and conditions stated above and on the reverse." Lagos signed this form and added the words "subject to deletion of Clause 14." Clause 14 was the clause that provided for price escalation in the event of unforeseen increased costs.

Upon receipt of the tear-off acceptance slip, Oakville entered the order in its order book without noticing the amendment and immediately began arranging to manufacture the computer for Lagos. Oakville advised Lagos accordingly.

Unfortunately, due to an unanticipated rise in the cost of component parts from Japan, the cost of manufacture of the computer rose 50 percent in the relevant six-month period. Oakville notified Lagos of this development, advising it that the price escalation clause would be operative in the circumstances and that the purchase price would rise from Cdn $2 million to Cdn $3 million. Lagos protested that it was not liable to pay the increase in price and would hold the Canadian company responsible for delivering the computer for Cdn $2 million. Each of the parties is now contemplating legal action, Oakville to compel Lagos to honour the commitment for Cdn $3 million, and Lagos to compel Oakville to deliver the computer for Cdn $2 million. What is the likely outcome of this action, assuming it is heard by an Ontario court applying Ontario law?

The Question of Missing Terms

THE COMMON LAW

Under the common law, an agreement to agree is not a binding contract. However, there are situations in which the parties wish to be bound to a contract but certain details have not been settled. The approach of the common law courts is to refer to the intention of the parties and to examine the reason for the absence of the missing term. The more important the missing term, the less likely it is that the parties have a completed contract. The court will also take into account the reason for the missing term. Perhaps certain information was not available at the time of negotiations but is ascertainable at the time of performance. In such a case, if the contract provides for an established or agreed method of providing the missing term, there may well be a binding contract. This is possible even if the missing term concerns a significant issue, such as price. It is not uncommon for the parties to rely on some external market factor to determine price.

THE UCC

The UCC provides that in appropriate circumstances, if price is not specified, then a "reasonable price" will be presumed.

THE CISG

The CISG states that an offer is sufficiently definite if it indicates the goods and expressly or impliedly fixes or makes provision for determining quantity and price. The CISG goes even further and provides that where a contract has been validly concluded but does not impliedly fix or make provision for price, in the absence of any express indication to the contrary, the parties are considered to have made reference to the price generally charged in comparable circumstances in the trade concerned.

The scenario described in box 7.14 illustrates a situation in which an important term is omitted from a contract.

BOX 7.14   PRICELESS BREAKFAST AT SASKATCHEWAN WEDDING

Banquo Banqueting Inc., a Saskatchewan firm, made a contract with a wealthy customer to cater a wedding breakfast of lobster and champagne for 300 people. Banquo had neither the lobster nor the champagne in stock, so it faxed orders to a lobster supplier in Maine for 300 large American lobsters and to a wine exporter in France for 20 cases of its finest champagne. The price was not specified in the communications with either the lobster supplier or the wine merchant. The lobster and the wine arrived on time and the breakfast was a success. Subsequently, invoices arrived from both the lobster supplier and the wine merchant, and Banquo believes that the prices quoted by each are inflated. What recourse does Banquo have? Is there a contract in each of these cases? What law would apply to these transactions? Are there any additional facts you require in order to answer these questions?

Verbal Variations of Written Contracts

At the time a contract is being negotiated, parties will often take exception to particular provisions in the general conditions of the other party. As a result, it is not uncommon for one party to agree verbally to vary a provision but not record the variation.

THE COMMON LAW

This situation is one in which the parol evidence rule would apply under the common law. This rule provides that no evidence will be admitted that would have the effect of adding new terms to the contract or changing or contradicting the terms of a clear and unambiguous written agreement. The party attempting to bring evidence of the oral variation made at the time of the formation of the contract would likely be unsuccessful and would be bound by the terms of the written contract. The application of this rule is limited to the contract. Any verbal agreement made by the parties after the written agreement is formed to alter or even cancel the agreement is valid. It must be borne in mind, however, that there may be serious problems of proof and it is never advisable to vary or rescind a written agreement except in writing.

THE UCC

This Code, based on the common law, provides that a written contract cannot be contradicted by parol evidence but may be explained by it. A court may not consider "prior" or "contemporaneous oral understanding" when interpreting a writing that the parties intended as a "final expression of their agreement."

THE CISG

Many legal systems do not employ the parol evidence rule and the CISG reflects these systems. The Convention provides that when a court is to determine the intention of the parties to a contract, due consideration may be given to all relevant circumstances including the negotiations leading up to the contract.

A typical scenario in which the parol evidence rule arises is described in box 7.15.

BOX 7.15   JAPANESE OBJECT TO NOVA SCOTIA LAW IN CONTRACT

A company in Nova Scotia entered into a contract with a Japanese company in which the Nova Scotians agreed to supply the Japanese with regular shipments of dried fish. The parties used the standard form prepared by the Nova Scotia company but the Japanese company objected to the provision that the laws of Nova Scotia would apply to the contract. The Japanese insisted that the CISG govern the contract and the Nova Scotians verbally agreed at the time that the contract was signed that this was acceptable, although no change to the printed form was made. The parties subsequently had serious disputes under the agreement and it was necessary for a Nova Scotia court to determine what law applied to the contract. What is the court likely to decide?

Suppose that the parties entered into the contract on June 1, 1996, and on January 1, 1997 agreed orally to vary the price, providing for an increase of 10 percent. Assume that the Japanese later denied such agreement but the Nova Scotians were able to provide compelling evidence of the oral variation. Would the Japanese be bound by the variation?

Performance of the Contract

A number of factors are significant in assessing whether or not the contracting parties have fulfilled their obligations under the contract. In this section, we will consider many of the most common trouble spots for international contracts.

Invoices

Correct invoicing is essential in an international sales transaction because it affects not only the obligations between the buyer and seller but also, in most cases, financing arrangements made through the parties' bankers. Invoices must also contain detailed instructions to ensure that they conform to import and customs regulations in the buyer's country. The prudent buyer will often request a pro forma or "sample" invoice in order to be sure that the invoice meets all import and customs regulations. The requirements of foreign countries vary greatly as to what must be included in invoices. An example of the type of regulation that may be encountered is described in box 7.16.

The details normally found on the commercial invoice include the names and addresses of the seller and buyer, the date and reference number of the buyer's order, a description of the goods sold, details of packages (including the weight of every bale or case), any identifying marks or numbers on

---

BOX 7.16   MEXICO'S INVOICE REQUIREMENTS FOR IMPORTS

Mexico is very strict in its examination of all documents accompanying shipments of goods. Any discrepancy, even a trifling one, can lead to delays, penalties, and even confiscation of goods being shipped. An invoice accompanying a shipment to Mexico must contain all of the following information:

- Place and date of issuance.
- Complete name and address of Mexican buyer or importer.
- Complete name and address of exporter.
- A detailed description of the merchandise, including brand name, model, marks, serial numbers, motor numbers, manufacturer's imprints, product characteristics, material of manufacture, intended use, etc. (These details are particularly important because they determine the duty rate payable. If merchandise is not properly classified, the highest possible rate may be charged.)
- FOB unit value and total value of each item listed on the invoice or itemized charges making up the CIF value to the Mexican port of entry, or, in the case of rail and truck transportation, all charges to place the goods at the Mexican border.
- Seller's name, position, and signature.
- Shipper's invoice number and customer's order number.

This documentation must be presented in its original form, with up to 11 copies, and a Spanish translation must accompany the English original.

---

packages, and the price. Details of shipping are sometimes included. If this is the case, care must be taken that these details correspond with the actual shipping documents.

The invoice price must be stated exactly in accordance with the sales contract—for example, FOB, FAS, or CIF. In some cases, regulatory agencies in the buyer's country may require more detail, such as the cost price and further charges specified.

In a transaction in which payment is to be made by letter of credit, the commercial invoice is an essential document in the transaction. The details contained in the invoice will have been provided by the buyer to its financing institution and will have been passed on to the corresponding institution in the seller's country. If the details in the invoice presented by the seller do not correspond exactly to the details in the financing instructions, the bank will reject the documents and refuse to pay the seller. In addition, the details in the invoice must correspond exactly with the general description of the goods in the other documents tendered to the bank.

REQUESTS FOR PHONY INVOICES

It is not uncommon in international transactions for the buyer to ask the seller to provide an invoice that does not accurately reflect the true bargain between the parties. This is often an attempt by the buyer to circumvent import duty or currency exchange control regulations in its own country, which are tied directly to the contract price. The wise seller will resist all such requests because they are frequently based on an improper—if not illegal—motive. Under the common law, a contract in which the parties have agreed to a false invoice may not be enforceable. It is the policy of common law courts to refuse to assist a party who has entered into a contract having an illegal purpose. For this reason, a seller who agrees to provide a false invoice for the benefit of a buyer, who then defaults on its obligations under the contract, may find itself without any legal recourse against the defaulting buyer.

The scenario described in box 7.17 is typical of these cases.

The seller can often save itself difficulties in this area by clearly stating in its general conditions of business that it will not under any circumstances participate in false invoicing.

BOX 7.17   SOUTH AMERICANS IN BREACH OF "FISHY" CONTRACT

Winnipeg Exports Ltd. negotiated a contract for the sale of frozen goldeye fillets to a South American company located in a country with strict currency exchange control regulations. The parties agreed that the laws of Manitoba would apply to the contract. At the request of the South American buyer, the value of the fish was doubled for the purpose of the written agreement and an oral arrangement was made between the parties in which Winnipeg Exports would deposit half the total price stated in the contract to a Canadian bank account in the name of an agent for the South American buyer. This arrangement enabled the South American buyer to obtain permission for more hard currency to leave the country, contrary to the regulations of that country.

Winnipeg Exports exported the fish according to the contract and invoiced the South American company as had been agreed. The South American company refused to pay, although the fish had been received in good condition. Winnipeg Exports sued the South American company, which gave evidence as to all the arrangements that the parties had made. Is the Manitoba court likely to find in favour of Winnipeg Exports?

Packing

It is normally the duty of the seller to pack the goods in a manner that will ensure their safe arrival in good condition, unless the parties have agreed otherwise in the sales contract. Failure to pack the goods properly may be considered a breach of condition and may entitle the buyer to reject the goods. Under the common law, the packing of goods often forms part of the description of the goods.

It is customary that FOB and CIF prices include packing charges; therefore, if the seller intends to charge extra for this, it should be clearly stated in the quotation or confirmation.

The type of packing chosen will depend on a number of factors. The way goods are packed will affect the freight charges applicable. If the goods are being shipped by sea, packing will vary depending on whether the goods are being shipped on deck or stored in the holds of the ship.

The shipment of goods overseas is a complex matter requiring specialized knowledge not only of packing requirements but also of insurance contracts and the transportation industry. For this reason, the services of freight forwarders may be required. (Freight forwarders are discussed in chapter 8.)

Insufficient packing may, in certain circumstances, be regarded as inherent vice of the goods and deprive the assured of the protection of all-risks coverage under a marine insurance policy.

Finally, there are special requirements for the packing and labelling of dangerous goods in transit. These regulations vary for sea, rail, air, and road and the services of a transportation specialist are recommended.

Timelines for Delivery

The principal legal systems take slightly different approaches to the obligation of timeliness of delivery. The common law system (including that of the United States) generally regards timelines of delivery as a condition of the contract. Therefore, the innocent party has the right to treat the contract as repudiated once a reasonable time for delivery has expired. Although the provisions of various civil law countries vary, a feature of many is a provision whereby if a delivery is delayed, the buyer must demand delivery and allow the seller a reasonable time for performance, even though the seller has delayed delivery in an apparent breach of the contract. The contract cannot be treated as repudiated until the additional time given for delivery has expired. This concept is variously referred to as *mise en demeure, delai de grace*, or *Nachfrist*. This approach is also taken in the CISG, which provides for a **Nachfrist notice**. Such notice allows either party to fix an additional period of time for the other to perform and thus covers a situation of failure of delivery or one in which unacceptable goods have been delivered. During the extended period of time, the granting party may not resort to any remedy for breach of contract. If the notified party fails to perform within the additional period given, the granting party may treat the contract as repudiated, whether the breach was important (that is, of a condition) or not. A further provision of the Convention encourages flexibility and the maintenance of the contractual relationship even in the face of difficulties. This provision allows the seller to make good its promise to deliver goods even after the specified delivery date, if it can be done without causing the buyer unreasonable inconvenience (Article 48). If a seller requests an extension of time for delivery from the buyer, the buyer is obliged to respond within a reasonable time, or the seller may perform within the additional requested time.

Consider the scenario described in box 7.18, which illustrates the different assumptions that may be made by parties as a result of their experience under different legal systems.

BOX 7.18   FREDERICTON COMPANY AFFECTED BY ALUMINUM SHORTAGE

A company from New Brunswick, Fredericton Pre-Fab Ltd., made a contract with a Thai company, which the parties agreed would be governed by the CISG rules. Under the contract, Fredericton agreed to supply 20 prefabricated houses for a construction project in the north of Thailand by August 1 of that year. Fredericton had problems obtaining sufficient sheet aluminum and was unable to meet the completion date for the houses. Fredericton advised the Thai company of its difficulties and the Thai company granted an extension of the delivery date for the houses to October 1 of the same year. The Thai company later had second thoughts and decided that, because Fredericton was in breach of its delivery date, the contract was at an end. Accordingly, the Thai company arranged with another supplier to ship prefabricated houses to Thailand from Saudi Arabia by August 15 of that year. The Thai company notified Fredericton in September in writing that they no longer required the Canadian product. By this time, the houses had been manufactured and shipped from the New Brunswick plant and were en route to Thailand. What is the legal position of Fredericton?

Loss of Goods in Transit

The loss of goods through fire, theft, or other misadventures can occur at any time prior to the delivery of the goods, during their transit, while they are being inspected, or after delivery. Which party bears the loss? Usually, the loss is covered by insurance and the question is which of the parties is entitled to collect the insurance proceeds. In many countries, this will depend on whether title or property in the goods has passed from seller to buyer at the time of the loss. The traditional common law rule, derived from sale of goods acts, was that the risk of accidental loss of goods passed when the property passed to the purchaser.

The laws of England, the United States, France, Belgium, Italy, and Portugal provide that the property in goods sold passes when the parties intended it to pass, whether the goods have been delivered or not. The laws of the Netherlands, Spain, Germany, Argentina, Brazil, Chile, and Colombia, however, provide that property in the goods does not pass unless there has been actual delivery of the goods. The differences in the domestic laws of major trading nations on this important point provide a good illustration of the need for a common set of rules acceptable and familiar to traders all over the world. Fortunately, great progress is being made in this area with the increasing adoption and use of the CISG, which provides that the risk passes on delivery of the goods.

The parties should clarify the time of passage of risk between themselves and also with their insurer. The use of accepted trade terms goes a long way in limiting any problem as to who bears the loss. Generally, most defined trade terms provide that the risk will pass when the goods leave the custody of the seller—that is, in ex works contracts when they are collected by the buyer, and in FOB and CIF contracts when the goods are delivered to the carrier.

Acceptance and Rejection of Goods

An international seller is often required by contract to provide a certificate of quality from a recognized expert. Some are certificates of standard quality addressed to any person interested while others are addressed and prepared specifically for the parties to the contract. Depending upon the subject matter of the contract, these certificates may be issued by a scientist, a consultant, a trade association, a classification organization, or an inspection organization.

In negotiating requirements for such certificates, parties should be aware of the distinction between the quality of the goods and their condition when they arrive. To avoid disputes later, it is important to express clearly what is covered by the certificate.

A certificate of inspection is not the same as a certificate of quality because it states only that goods have been inspected and found to be in good condition. If more is expected of the inspection certificate, this must be clearly stated in the sale of goods contract as well as in the contract with the inspection organization.

Pre-shipment inspection is very important in international trade. If goods are inspected before they are delivered to the carrier and are found not to conform to the contract, costly shipping charges and transnational legal disputes can be avoided.

Disputes concerning whether any loss or damage occurred before or after shipping can also be avoided, thereby clarifying responsibility between the seller and the insurer. Some countries go so far as to insist on pre-shipment inspection of any imported goods entering their jurisdiction. Others go even further and will not grant import licences unless an inspection organization has issued a clean pre-shipment certificate as well as a statement that the price charged is comparable to prices charged by other suppliers for similar goods. A requirement such as this creates an opportunity for third-party interference in an agreement in which the parties have already agreed on the price of the goods. For this reason, a seller should be reluctant to agree to a pre-shipment certificate verifying price. If such a certificate is agreed to, the sales contract should provide clearly for the rights of the parties in the event that the certificate verifying price is not obtained.

Under the common law, a buyer who is dissatisfied with the goods must indicate its intention to reject them within a reasonable time. In the absence of specific terms, the rejecting buyer is not obliged to return the goods to the seller, but the buyer becomes a bailee of the goods and must take reasonable care of them. Normally, the buyer's right to reject the goods is reserved until the goods arrive and the buyer has an opportunity to inspect them.

This rule can present problems when applied to CIF contracts, where so often the shipping documents are sold or pledged before the buyer has the opportunity to inspect the goods. The question then arises: Does the buyer retain the right to reject the goods even after disposal of such shipping documents as the bill of lading? Precedents indicate that in a CIF contract, the sale of documents by the buyer to a third party before the goods have been received passes only conditional title to the goods (the condition being that the goods conform to the contract). Thus the property in the rejected goods revests in the seller when the rejection is accepted by the seller.

Under the UCC and the CISG, inspection of the goods and notice of any breach of contract are required. The CISG provides that the buyer must examine the goods within as short a period as is practicable. The buyer must then give notice of lack of conformity within a reasonable time after the lack of conformity has been discovered or ought to have been discovered (no more than two years).

Consider the scenario described in box 7.19, which illustrates the importance of the importer notifying the exporter of the rejection of the goods.

BOX 7.19   DANES REJECT CANADIAN HERB SHIPMENT

A Danish company ordered a quantity of Canadian herbs from an exporter in PEI. When the herbs arrived in Copenhagen, they were found to be mildewed and were unusable. Because the Danish company had already paid for the herbs by letter of credit, it did not bother to advise the PEI company of the unacceptability of the shipment but instead contacted the insurance company, which contacted a lawyer, who proceeded to sue the PEI company for breach of contract. The PEI company first became aware of the problem when documents were served on it in Charlottetown 18 months after the herbs had been shipped. What is the legal position of the PEI company? What should the Danish company have done in the circumstances?

Implied Warranties

The law with respect to implied warranties in Canada is determined by the sale of goods legislation in each province. The common law provinces of Canada impose certain implied warranties that are the responsibility of the seller. These implied warranties are that

- the seller has the right to convey title to the goods to the buyer;
- the goods supplied will correspond with the description given by the buyer when ordered;
- the goods supplied for a particular purpose will satisfy the purpose where the buyer has made known the purpose and has relied on the seller's skill and judgment in meeting those needs;
- the goods purchased by description will be of merchantable quality in order to meet the usual or general use of such goods; and
- if the sale is based on a sample, the goods will be of the same quality as the sample and free of any hidden defects.

The provisions of the CISG are similar to those of the common law. The seller must deliver goods that are of the quantity, quality, and description required by the contract and that are contained or packaged in the manner required by the contract. Unless the parties have otherwise agreed, the goods do not conform with the contract unless they

- are fit for the purposes for which goods of the same description would ordinarily be used;
- are fit for any particular purpose expressly or impliedly made known to the seller at the time the contract was made;

- possess the qualities of goods that the seller has held out to the buyer as a sample or model; and
- are contained or packaged in the manner usual for such goods.

The provisions of the UCC are similar to the provisions of the CISG. The UCC differs from the CISG in its provision that any exclusion or modification of warranties must be specific and conspicuous to be effective. Case law in Canada and the United Kingdom also establishes this principle. By contrast, any provision of the Convention may be modified and there is specific mention of exclusion in Article 35(2), "except where the parties have agreed otherwise." There is thus no requirement or limitation governing how clearly any exclusion must be expressed to be effective under the Convention. Traders must be vigilant when signing contracts in which the applicable law is that of the Convention. It is important to remember here, however, that the Convention does not apply to questions of product liability.

Payment

Payment will be due at the time and in the currency provided for in the contract. This will often be determined by the trade term chosen. Over the years, standardized methods of payment in international trade have been developed, the most common of which is the letter of credit (discussed in detail in chapter 8). It is generally recommended that the seller include in its contract a provision stating that if the buyer sells goods for which the seller has not been paid, the buyer does so as agent of the seller and the buyer will be a trustee of the proceeds of the sale for the benefit of the seller. Such clauses are common and generally effective, although if the clauses are very complex, the parties may choose to register them under the personal property security rules of their jurisdictions.

Breach of Contract and Damages

The remedies available under the common law, the UCC, and the CISG are generally similar where there is a clear or acknowledged breach of contract. Damages under the common law will encompass an amount designed to compensate for the breach and may include an amount for lost profits that are a reasonably foreseeable result of the breach. The UCC provision is similar, although US courts differ in their approach to calculation of the damages. The CISG provides that damages will consist of a sum equal to the loss, including loss of profit that was foreseeable at the time of the conclusion of the contract.

Avoidance of the Contract

When does a breach of contract by one party release the other party from its contractual obligations? The different legal systems have resolved this question in slightly different ways.

Under the common law, whether or not the innocent party is released from the contract by the breach of the other depends on the seriousness of the breach. If the breach is of a serious or important term of the contract—that is, a condition—the innocent party is released from further obligation under the contract. If the breach relates to a less serious term—that is, a warranty—the innocent party must continue to honour the contract, but is entitled to recover damages to cover the diminished value of the contract.

Under the UCC, a buyer may reject goods if the goods or the tender of their delivery fails in any respect to conform to the contract. Once the goods are "accepted," the buyer may refuse to keep them only if the "non-conformity substantially impairs their value."

Under the CISG, a buyer may avoid a contract in two situations. The first is the familiar situation in which the seller commits a fundamental breach. The second is less familiar to North Americans, although it is a common feature of continental law, that of a Nachfrist notice. This is a fixing by the buyer of an additional period of time of reasonable length for performance by the seller of its obligations. This period must be definite and, once this period has run, the buyer has the right to terminate the contract.

Specific Performance

Specific performance is a remedy sought by the innocent party to a contract that has been breached in which the court orders the defaulting party to perform the obligations under the contract. The common law and the UCC limit the granting of this remedy to cases in which the goods are unique or other circumstances in which damages are inappropriate. The civil law, on the other hand, applies the principle much more readily, on the basis that the buyer wants what was ordered, not just compensation for the consequences of the failure to deliver. The CISG reflects this civil law tradition, but qualifies it in Article 28, which provides that performance should be limited to cases in countries in which specific performance would be allowed by the domestic law of the land.

Frustration of Contract

All legal systems recognize that sometimes the commercial object the parties had in mind when the contract was concluded may be defeated by circumstances completely beyond the control of the parties. Such events may be an excuse for non-performance of the contract in certain circumstances. Each legal system has different rules governing when non-performance is excused and accepted without liability on the part of the non-performing party.

ENGLISH AND CANADIAN LAW

English and Canadian law have the concept of frustration of contract. Frustration occurs when, after the conclusion of the contract, a fundamentally different situation unexpectedly develops that makes performance of the contract under its original terms impossible. It is not sufficient if such development has merely rendered the performance of the contract more difficult or expensive. Only if the change is of such magnitude that it creates a fundamentally different situation will it qualify as a frustrating event. Difficult questions arise because frustration may often be a matter of degree, particularly when the facts involve dramatically increased costs or delays in delivery. Much clearer are situations that involve the destruction of the subject matter of the contract, or the outbreak of war, or change of government policy involving the ability to import or export goods.

Self-induced problems will never qualify as frustration. The failure of one party to apply in a timely fashion for necessary export or import authorization would not qualify as frustration.

The effect of frustration is that the contract is terminated, leaving both parties free from any further obligation under it.

THE UCC

Under the UCC, "commercial impracticability" is recognized as a valid excuse for non-performance of the contract. This concept has been explained as follows: "a thing is impossible in legal contemplation when it is not practicable; and a thing is impracticable when it can only be done at an excessive and unreasonable cost." This doctrine is not often used because of the difficulty in determining how much extra cost is unreasonable. For the majority of cases, inflation and even dramatic fluctuations in market prices are events expected to be anticipated by the parties, and do not permit a claim of commercial impracticability.

The American courts also recognize the common law concept of frustration. The courts may accept the excuse of frustration in the following circumstances:

1. *Impossibility.* Performance of the contract has been rendered physically or legally impossible.
2. *Frustration of purpose.* The underlying purposes of the contract no longer exist.
3. *Commercial impracticability.* A change in the surrounding circumstances has rendered the contract commercially or financially impracticable.

However, the whole concept is not well received in American courts, and judges have favoured the more practical approach of keeping the contractual relationship alive. This approach is reflected in the UCC, which provides as follows:

1. Where without fault of either party the agreed berthing, loading or unloading facilities fail or an agreed type of carrier becomes unavailable or the agreed manner of delivery otherwise becomes commercially impracticable but a commercially reasonable substitute is available, such substitute performance must be tendered and accepted.

2. If the agreed means or manner of payment fails because of domestic or foreign regulation, the seller may withhold or stop delivery unless the buyer provides a means or manner of payment which is commercially a substantial equivalent. If delivery has already been taken, payment by the means or in the manner provided by the regulation discharges the buyer's obligation unless the regulation is discriminatory, oppressive, or predatory.

THE CISG

The CISG provides that a party is not liable for a failure to perform any of its obligations if

- it was due to an impediment that was unavoidable or beyond the party's control;
- the impediment was not reasonably foreseeable at the time the contract was concluded; and
- notice was given to the other party of the impediment and its effect on the contract.

Consider the case described in box 7.20, which illustrates the uncertainty in judging whether frustration has occurred.

BOX 7.20 SUEZ CANAL DISPUTE AFFECTS SHIPMENTS TO IRAN

A British shipping company contracted with an American company to ship a cargo of wheat from the southern United States to Iran in 1956. Several days after the ship sailed from the United States, the government of Egypt declared war on Israel and passage through the Suez Canal was closed to all shipping. As a result, the ship had to sail around the Cape of Good Hope on the tip of the African continent. The British shipping company sued the American company for the extra expense, claiming it had contracted only to take the cargo through the Suez Canal, which was the usual route to Iran. Do you think that the British company was successful? On what grounds? Will your answer depend on whose law applies?

Drafting the Contract

Most businesses engaging in regular international sales of goods will operate under general terms of business, which will be carefully drafted by corporate counsel to protect the business in foreseeable situations. These terms and conditions will usually be printed on price lists, catalogues, estimates, and offers as well as acceptances. The incorporation of these terms saves lengthy negotiation time between parties and eliminates the need to settle afresh for every transaction the duties and responsibilities of the parties on relatively straightforward or predictable matters. Where forms are not lengthy enough to duplicate all the general conditions, there should at least be a clear reference to the fact that such conditions will apply to any sale and the conditions should be included with the correspondence or communication.

The seller/exporter should include the following provisions when drafting the general terms and conditions of a contract:

- A general statement to the effect that every contract of sale will be subject to the seller's general conditions.
- A provision that title to the goods will be retained by the seller until the purchase price is paid in full in cash. In addition to this protection, there should be a provision that, if the buyer sells the goods, such sale is made only as agent for the seller.
- Provision for price escalation based on increased prices of raw materials, components, or labour.
- Provision that any amounts owing to the seller shall bear interest at a specified rate (usually tied to bank prime).
- A **force majeure** clause to protect the seller from liability for delays or failures beyond its control. This clause should always be included.
- Provision for settlement of any disputes between the parties. Arbitrations should be specified, if this is desired, and the law applicable to the contract should be specified, usually the law of the seller's own jurisdiction.

Many organizations have developed standardized terms appropriate to specific types of contracts and it may well be that such a standardized set of general conditions is available and will greatly ease the conduct of international transactions.

FORCE MAJEURE CLAUSES

It is not always easy for the parties to know if the contract has been frustrated. Because of this uncertainty as to when or whether the parties can be released from their contractual obligations when unforeseen circumstances interfere with the anticipated performance of the contract, it is advisable for the parties to anticipate problems that may arise and make provision in the contract for their respective rights and obligations in the event of interfering or catastrophic events. These clauses are referred to as *force majeure* clauses.

The term "*force majeure*" has a specific meaning in law, and is confined to events beyond the control of the parties. Catastrophic events such as war, blockades, fire, acts of governments, the failure to obtain import or export licences, acts of God, terrorist acts, transportation failures, strikes, or labour slowdowns are contemplated and may be specifically spelled out in a *force majeure* clause.

Drafting a *force majeure* clause is not a task for amateurs. It should only be undertaken by experienced legal advisers who can draft a suitable clause for your particular needs. This clause may then be used in your general form of contract, doing away with the need to reconsider the details for every new situation. Care should always be taken, however, when your firm deviates from the usual type of transaction for which the clause was drafted. In such a case, the *force majeure* clause should be carefully reviewed to ensure that it will cover any additional risks presented by the new situation.

In practice, most *force majeure* clauses do not end a contract or excuse the parties entirely from their rights or obligations under the contract, but merely suspend them for the duration of the *force majeure*. A popular and practical form of *force majeure* clause provides for two stages: the first is for a defined period, say, 30 days, during which obligations under the contract are suspended, and the second stage entitles each party to cancel the contract if the precipitating event continues after the initial period.

Because *force majeure* clauses need to be tailored to the specific needs of particular types of trade, it is common for various trading associations to develop clauses suitable for the needs of their particular trades.

Consider the hypothetical case described in box 7.21, which illustrates the difficulty of determining whether there is a breach or frustration of a contract in the absence of a *force majeure* clause.

BOX 7.21   EXPORT PLANS FOILED BY FAILURE TO OBTAIN IMPORT LICENCE

A Sri Lankan company, Chalpal Textiles, made a contract with a British Columbian manufacturer of textiles, B.C. Textiles Ltd., to buy a large number of used textile-finishing machines. Under the terms of the contract, Chalpal agreed to use its best efforts to obtain the necessary import licence for the equipment. One month after the contract was made but the week before Chalpal filed its application for the import licence, the

Sri Lankan government decided to limit import licences for used equipment in an attempt to encourage its nationals to buy only "state of the art" equipment. Chalpal notified B.C. Textiles of the difficulty and advised it that, although it had made every reasonable attempt to obtain an import licence, the freeze on licences for used equipment appeared to be in effect for the foreseeable future.

B.C. Textiles wishes to sue for breach of contract and Chalpal claims frustration of the contract. Assuming that BC law applies, what will be the outcome? Would the outcome be any different under the CISG?

A *force majeure* clause that itemized failure to obtain the necessary import licence would have settled the issue. These facts raise another potential difficulty between the parties: the issue of the level of effort one party might reasonably expect of the other in meeting an obligation.

BEST EFFORTS CLAUSES

It is not uncommon in international contracts that one party must take on an obligation to obtain an approval from a government official, a specific import permit, or financing on specific terms or from a specific body. Difficulties may arise when the parties attempt to describe this obligation in the contract. One method is to enumerate in detail the specific acts to be performed and provide benchmarks, deadlines, or targets for performance. A second, very common method, is to state that the party obliged will make "all reasonable efforts" to achieve this goal. Another phrase commonly used is that the party obliged will use its "best efforts" to satisfy the objective. While the courts have been reasonably consistent in interpreting the phrase "reasonable efforts" as those that a reasonable person would make in the circumstances, judicial interpretation of "best efforts" has been less satisfactory. The courts generally impose a higher standard of performance for a best efforts clause and have gone so far as to require the party obliged to exert itself "to the extent of its total capabilities." Another court found the phrase to mean that the party must "leave no stone unturned." Such interpretation may mean that financial difficulties or economic hardships are not a sufficient excuse. For this reason, it is unwise to agree to a best efforts clause. It is wiser to accept an obligation to expend reasonable efforts or to spell out in detail the actions required and their expected completion dates.

COUNTERTRADE

Although countertrade is not, strictly speaking, a contract for the purchase and sale of goods, it is appropriate to discuss it here. Most transactions for the import or export of goods are based on the concept of the sale of goods—that is, the exchange of goods for money. A contract that provides for an exchange of goods for goods is not a contract of sale in the proper legal sense. It is properly referred to as a barter contract. Contracts for barter are not governed by the same rules as those that apply to sale of goods contracts. Countertrade is defined as a transaction where a sale to an importer is conditional on a reciprocal purchase or undertaking by the exporter.

Countertrade had been frowned upon by the General Agreement on Tariffs and Trade and the Organisation for Economic Co-operation and Development because it is not consistent with their model of open, cash-based, multilateral trading relationships. It is now accepted, however, that these arrangements will continue to be part of the global trading environment. There are good reasons why countertrade continues. Less-developed countries (LCDs) and other countries that are short of hard currency are the chief proponents of this form of business transaction.

The reasons for these countries' adoption of countertrade are well documented. Some of the reasons are:

- *To preserve hard currency.* Countertrade enables a country to import "non-essential" goods without using up any of its short supply of hard currency, which it can then reserve for its most essential imports.
- *To improve the trade balance.* By obliging the foreign supplier to buy goods in return for goods exported, the importing company can stimulate its own export market.
- *To obtain technology and investment.* By paying for plants, capital equipment, and technical expertise with goods produced from newly established facilities, countries are able to acquire such new plants without expending scarce currency reserves.

Many Canadian exporters have been able to avoid countertrading arrangements because most of Canadian output, at present, goes to the United States, Japan, or developed countries in Europe. In the past, exports such as agricultural goods or raw materials were less likely to generate countertrade requirements. As trading patterns broaden, however, and Canadian exporters seek to acquire new markets—particularly in the fields of telecommunications, resource extraction, processing equipment, and other high-technology products—we can expect to see more Canadian exporters having to deal with a "countertrade or no trade at all" situation. Indeed, the most common industries involved in countertrade transactions are the industries on which our export growth depends, such as transportation equipment, telecommunication facilities, resource and energy extraction and processing equipment, agriculture and forestry equipment, and engineering and consulting services.

Some countertrade arrangements may simply be the "price" of obtaining the sale or contract.

The exporter involved in a countertrade transaction must take care that it can:

- specify the goods that will be supplied as payment by the importer and be assured of their quality;
- dispose of the countertrade goods easily in a readily available market; and
- dispose of the goods at a price that will ensure a profit for the exporter, even after deducting the cost of hiring a third party (such as a trading house) to arrange the sale.

It should be apparent that the countertrade adds considerable risk to the export sales transaction and should not be undertaken lightly by the exporter. A careful calculation of ensuing costs must be done to ensure the overall profitability of the transaction. The Canadian trader must be careful to begin negotiations with a "countertrade price." In addition, financing arrangements will become more complex. A bank will insist that the initial sales agreement be free of any conditions linked to the counterpurchase. Thus each contract must have its own financing arrangements. No financing assistance will be available from Export Development Canada if payment is to be in goods.

Types of Countertrade Transactions

There are many different forms a countertrade transaction may take. In fact, one might say that the number of forms is limited only by the ingenuity of the parties. Some of the more common and recognizable forms are discussed below.

Reciprocal Sales Agreements

This is the most common form of countertrade; it involves two parallel contracts of sale and a third agreement that links them together. The first contract is the agreement by the importer to buy goods or services from the Canadian exporter. The second is the agreement by the Canadian exporter to purchase goods from the importing country, either for the same value, or, in some cases, part of the value. Each party normally pays cash for the other party's goods or services. The two contracts are linked by an agreement called a framework agreement or countertrade agreement. This agreement should be a proper contract enforceable in law, and should clearly state the obligations of each party. It is important to specify the countertraded goods or services and state their value. The agreement should always provide that the exporter's obligations may be performed by a third party nominated by the exporter.

It is common for these obligations to be transferred to a trading house. If brought in early, a trading house can, for a fee, assist with bid preparations and countertrade cost estimates. The exporter should be wary of provisions that limit the markets in which the counter-sold goods can be traded. The exporter must also ensure that its counterpurchase obligations become effective *only* when the first contract has been completed or a performance guarantee is provided.

Sometimes parties will be urged to accept a letter of intent or a "protocol of intent" rather than an enforceable framework agreement. This is not advisable because expressions of intention are not enforceable in the courts and this introduces an element of uncertainty into the transaction. The framework agreement should contain all the usual clauses contained in an international sales agreement, such as a provision for the law applicable to the contract and provision for the settlement of disputes.

Barter

The term "barter" is sometimes used to refer to all types of countertrade but its precise meaning includes only a simple exchange of goods of supposedly equal value between the parties or payment "in kind." No value is placed on the goods exchanged, and no monetary payment is involved. Partial payment by barter, with the balance in hard currency, is a more common arrangement than simple barter.

The major problem with simple barter is that goods available for barter arrangements do not usually have a ready market. As well, LDCs will often insist on paying for imported goods with not one product but several, depending on what products are available on the performance date. Thus, the services of a third party will nearly always be required by the acquiring exporter, which may have neither the expertise nor the desire to deal with a shipment possibly as varied as bananas, sandals, and children's toys.

There is another form of barter—the so-called valued barter. In such a contract, the goods are valued and arrangements are made for a "settlement account" into which a settlement balance will be paid by one of the parties to the barter. This arrangement allows the parties to deal with the question of the valuation of the goods. Quality and quantity must be addressed and specified in the contract. A drawback to valued barter is that it may be difficult to achieve an exact balance in value of goods, particularly when there are fluctuations in the prevailing world price of commodities.

Product Buy-Back Agreements

Product buy-back agreements are most often seen in situations in which a Canadian exporter is supplying machinery and equipment—and sometimes know-how—to be used for a new or upgraded production facility, and the exporter agrees to buy back goods produced by that facility. The Canadian exporter/contractor will then agree to pay all or part of the purchase price when it buys back goods produced by the new or upgraded facility. Care must be taken that the buy-back terms are detailed enough to ensure the Canadian company an acceptable price. An equitable provision would be one that promises the Canadian exporter/contractor the most favourable price charged to any customer purchasing the goods in comparable conditions. The duration of a buy-back agreement will usually be lengthy—ranging on average from 4 to as many as 15 years.

Advance Purchase

This is a contract in which the exporter agrees to purchase goods or services from the LDC in advance, thus generating sufficient hard currency for the LDC to pay for the exporter's goods. The price paid for the LDC's goods is placed in an "escrow" account outside the LDC. This method is often used in transactions with countries with a high debt load or to circumvent difficult foreign exchange regulations. The Canadian exporter must satisfy itself that the arrangement is legal (otherwise it will risk the disadvantage of having entered into an illegal contract). A continuing problem with these arrangements is identifying suitable products for advance purchase.

Negotiation of Countertrade Agreements

The services of a lawyer or experienced countertrade specialist are recommended to any business person negotiating a countertrade arrangement. Recall that there will usually be three agreements in connection with the transaction: two sales agreements and one agreement tying the two sales agreements together, called the framework agreement. A checklist, which may be helpful in assessing your arrangements, follows:

- Ensure that the goods you are buying are specified and properly described, and that provision is made for determining their value.
- Ensure that the framework agreement is a proper agreement enforceable in law and that it clearly states the obligations of each party. This agreement should contain all the usual protective clauses normally insisted on by Canadian traders, such as a choice of law clause and an arbitration clause.
- Ensure that there are provisions that allow the exporter's obligations to be performed by a third party.
- Ensure that the markets in which the goods bought by the exporter are to be sold are not geographically limited.

- Consider the possibility of arranging a "performance guarantee." This is a type of letter of credit and is arranged through a bank or international financier.

NOTES

1 *British Columbia v. Imperial Tobacco Canada Ltd.*, [2005] SCJ no. 50 (QL).

2 Directive 85/374/EEC.

3 These categories are used by Castel, Graham, de Mestral, Hainsworth, and Warner in their discussion of Incoterms in their book *The Canadian Law and Practice of International Trade* (Toronto: Emond Montgomery, 1997), 129.

4 Jacob Ziegel, "Canada Prepares to Adopt the International Sales Convention" (1990), 2 *International Business and Trade Law Newsletter* 6.

REVIEW QUESTIONS

1. Briefly describe the difference between the common law and the civil law traditions. Provide an example of three countries where you would expect to find a common law tradition and three countries where you would expect to find a civil law tradition. Can you think of any countries where you would find both traditions?

2. What are the four essential elements of a valid contract in the common law tradition? How do the requirements for a valid contract differ in the civil law tradition?

3. What are the three elements of a successful tort action in the common law tradition?

4. How is product liability related to tort, and why is modern law on product liability a good example of the ways in which the common law can be changed by legislation?

5. Describe generally how product liability law in Canada differs from that in the United States and the European Union.

6. Which organization has led the way in developing an acceptable set of trade terms for use in international trade? Where are these terms found and how do traders make use of them? Briefly describe the four categories of trade terms.

7. In what circumstances does the CISG apply to a sale of goods transaction?

8. What is the importance of knowing how the Canadian domestic sale of goods law, the UCC, and the CISG differ in the following areas: requirement of writing; what constitutes an offer; when an offer can be revoked; requirements for a valid acceptance; a battle of the forms; missing terms?

9. Why is it important to address the format of invoices in the negotiations for an international sale?
10. Describe the difference between the CISG and the common law with respect to delivery on time.
11. Can an importer reject goods that are not satisfactory, even though the goods have been paid for before receipt under a "C" or "D" contract?
12. Do the common law, the UCC, and the CISG differ in their approach to specific performance and frustration of contract?
13. Why should a *force majeure* clause always be included in an international sales contract?
14. Briefly describe countertrade and the usual situations in which it is used.

FURTHER READING

Klotz, James M. (2000). *Going Global? Power Tools for Negotiating International Deals.* Toronto: Global Business Press.

DiMatteo, L., Dhooge, L., Greene, S., Maurer, V., and Pagnattaro, L.A. (2005). *International Sales Law: A Critical Analysis of CISG Jurisprudence.* New York: Cambridge University Press.

WEBSITES

Pace Law School:
www.cisg.law.pace.edu
(an excellent website for up-to-date information on the CISG)

International Chamber of Commerce:
http://www.iccwbo.org/incoterms/id3045/index.html
(information on Incoterms)

CHAPTER 8

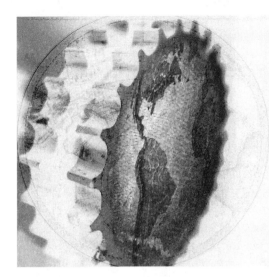

Ancillary Contracts for the International Transaction: Financing, Transportation, and Insurance

INTRODUCTION

In the last chapter we considered some fundamental legal principles as a basis for negotiating an international contract, particularly a contract for the international sale of goods. We now turn our attention to the important ancillary contracts—that is, additional or supporting contracts that are essential to these commercial transactions. These are separate contracts between one of the main contracting parties and a third party, and they are most often in the areas of financing or credit arrangements, transportation, and insurance. Remembering the rule of privity of contract, it is

LEARNING OBJECTIVES

After reading this chapter you will understand:

- how a documentary credit is structured and how it works
- the international rules for documentary credit transactions and why international business persons need to know these rules
- the difference between documentary credits, standby letters of credit, and surety bonds
- the significance of autonomy of credit and strict documentary compliance
- the significance of a draft or bill of exchange in a documentary credit transaction and the implications of a negotiable instrument
- international transportation arrangements and the significance of the documentation that is provided by shippers and carriers
- insurance arrangements in international transactions; insurable interests; marine insurance; and subrogation

important to incorporate the obligation of the parties to conclude these separate contracts with third parties into the primary contract as a *condition*, so that if a party fails to make these separate contracts as promised, the innocent party is relieved of its obligation to perform under the primary contract, and the failure is actionable as a breach of the contract between the two principal parties.

FINANCING THE INTERNATIONAL TRANSACTION

Understanding the Letter of Credit Arrangements

Once the parties to a negotiation for an export of goods or services have settled the description of the goods or services and the delivery or performance terms, the most important matter will be the payment arrangements. The payment arrangement most often agreed upon by Canadian parties doing business in countries other than the United States is the **letter of credit (L/C)**. Box 8.1 presents a typical international sales transaction in which a letter of credit will be used.

Let us consider the expectations of each party to this transaction. The Taiwanese exporter will want payment as quickly as possible and will not be willing to wait until the pots have arrived in Canada and have been accepted by the Canadian importer. The most favourable term for the exporter would be payment before shipment. However, such a provision is not common and is only agreed to by an importer in special circumstances, such as an order that requires some retooling on the part of the exporter. Less satisfactory

---

BOX 8.1   CANADIAN IMPORTER MAKES CONTRACT WITH TAIWANESE FIRM

A representative of Canadian Import Ltd. of Toronto attends a trade show and sees an attractive line of stainless steel cookware at reasonable prices. He negotiates with the representative of the manufacturer, T.I.E. Steel of Taipei, Taiwan, with a view to importing the products to Canada in time for autumn when, according to market research, Canadians are most interested in such items. The two representatives agree on the purchase by the Canadian company of 400 sets of stainless steel pots at US $80 per set. They also agree on a date by which the pots must be shipped CIF (cost, insurance, and freight) to Toronto. These parties have had no prior dealings with each other.

from the exporter's point of view, but most common and thus acceptable, is assurance of payment as soon as the goods are shipped. The exporter's major concern is to protect itself in a situation where valuable goods are being shipped far away, out of reach of the exporter's legal system, and the exporter has not been paid for the goods. The exporter will not be prepared to relinquish the title documents for the goods until it has been paid, and will also want to receive payment at its own bank or at least through another bank in Taiwan.

The Canadian importer, on the other hand, will wish to postpone payment as long as possible—at a minimum, until the title documents are delivered to the importer or the importer's agent. Canadian Imports wants some assurance that the goods will be shipped in time, and will not want to pay until it is certain that the Taiwanese manufacturer has performed its obligations fully. Thus, for the importer, payment after the goods have been received is the most satisfactory arrangement. Less satisfactory is payment at the time of shipment, and even less satisfactory is payment in advance. Each of the parties may need advice and assistance in dealing with a complex international transaction in which specific procedures must be followed to ensure prompt payment for the exporter and a managed cash flow for the importer/purchaser.

The services of international bankers can go a long way to overcome the problems of long-distance, unfamiliar parties, and different legal systems. In most international sales transactions, the services of banks in the importer's and exporter's country will be necessary. In particular, an issuing bank and a corresponding or nominated bank will be required. The issuing bank issues the letter of credit—a written undertaking by the bank given to the exporter (seller) at the request of and in accordance with the instructions of the importer (purchaser) to effect payment up to a specified amount, against stipulated documents, and within a prescribed time limit. The stipulated documents are likely to be the commercial invoice, a certificate of origin, an insurance policy or certificate, and a transport document.

In these credit arrangements, payment is usually made by a bank in the exporter's country when the documents that represent the goods are presented by the exporter to the **corresponding bank** or **nominated bank**. The corresponding or nominated bank is the bank with which the issuing bank makes arrangements for payment to the exporter in the exporter's country. Convenience, confidence in the banking and letter of credit laws and practices of financial institutions in the exporter/seller's own country, and unwillingness to take the credit risk on unfamiliar foreign financial institutions motivate the exporter/seller to request that the L/C name a familiar institution in its own country as the corresponding or nominated bank.

The corresponding or nominated bank may be an advising or confirming bank, depending on the wording of the credit agreement. A **confirming bank** undertakes a direct obligation to the exporter to pay on the proper presentation of documents under the L/C. The confirming bank is then entitled to reimbursement from the issuing bank, provided it has paid on a proper presentation of documents under the L/C. An **advising bank** undertakes only to examine and forward the documents to the issuing bank; it is not obligated or authorized to negotiate a draft or pay the seller. Thus, if an advising bank refuses to pay on the tender of the documents, the exporter may be compelled to institute legal proceedings abroad, a situation that is avoided if the corresponding or nominated bank is a confirming bank. For this reason, an exporter will prefer an L/C in which there is a confirming bank, although this will increase the cost of the L/C to the importer.

The presentation of these documents often occurs well in advance of the importer receiving the goods in the country of destination. Once the importer receives the documents it can then transfer title in the goods to a third party, even in advance of receiving the goods.

If the documents presented by the exporter do not comply with the documents described in the letter of credit, there are a number of possibilities. The documents may be corrected if the exporter (seller) or shipping company is able to remedy the deficiency within the period of time for presentation of documents. If this cannot be done, the exporter (seller) may request authority from the issuing bank to negotiate the draft despite the discrepancy. Depending on the seriousness of the discrepancy, the issuing bank may have to await the importer's decision whether or not to accept the discrepancy. Sometimes an exporter who requires prompt payment will have no alternative but to provide the paying bank with an indemnity by which the exporter undertakes to repay the bank if the L/C is not honoured by the importer.

If the L/C is an irrevocable L/C, the commitment of the issuing bank is a binding one and, provided that the correct documents are tendered before the expiry of the L/C, the bank must pay the amount agreed on. Even if the importer/purchaser gives subsequent instructions to the bank not to pay the exporter/seller, the bank will not accept a revocation of the L/C.

An L/C that does not state otherwise is irrevocable. This rule was changed under the most recent UCP 500 (**Uniform Customs and Practice for Documentary Credits**), which came into force on January 1, 1994. A revocable L/C may be withdrawn at any time and is thus a very insecure method of payment. Its advantage over the irrevocable L/C is that it is much cheaper.

Figure 8.1 illustrates the various parties and the mechanics of the letter of credit transaction.

FIGURE 8.1   MECHANICS OF THE LETTER OF CREDIT TRANSACTION

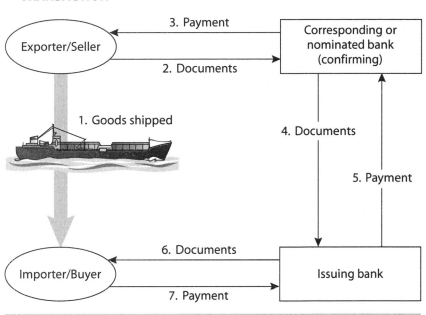

It will now be clear to the reader that a letter of credit arrangement is built on separate contractual undertakings by different parties:

- the contract between the importer/purchaser and the exporter/seller whereby the importer agrees to obtain the L/C for the benefit of the exporter;
- the contract between the importer and its bank whereby the bank agrees to provide the L/C on the importer's behalf; and
- the undertaking by the importer's bank, the issuing bank, to pay a specified sum when the specified documents are presented to the importer's bank or its agent, usually the corresponding or nominated bank.

The undertaking of the issuing bank in the letter of credit is primary and must be honoured without any claim, setoff, or defence that the issuing bank or the importer/purchaser may have against the seller. This independence of the letter of credit from the underlying transaction between the importer and the exporter is a characteristic special feature of a documentary letter of credit transaction.

Negotiation of the Letter of Credit Arrangements

The terms of the credit financing to be obtained by the importer are very important for the exporter. For this reason, the requirements for the letter of credit must be spelled out and made a condition of the sales contract. Making the terms of the credit financing a condition in the sales contract means that if any of the provisions of the credit financing are not met, the exporter is not required to proceed with the contract. Important provisions that must be anticipated and agreed on by the parties include the following:

- It must be decided whether the L/C will be revocable or irrevocable. Irrevocable L/Cs are now the norm under the UCP 500 rules. According to Article 6, a credit is deemed to be irrevocable unless specifically stated to be revocable.
- The terms of payment must be specified. Will payment be immediate on presentation of the documents or will it be deferred, say, for 60 days or 90 days? Other possibilities are acceptance or negotiation by the importer's bank.
- The party on whom drafts are to be drawn must be specified. Will this be the issuing bank or the importer?
- The goods must be described, and the information to be included in the commercial invoice must be anticipated and settled.
- Details of freight costs must be settled. Will freight be prepaid?
- The documentation required must be settled. In addition to the usual transport document, insurance document, and commercial invoice, many countries will require certificates of origin or inspection certificate. Packing lists are frequently required.
- Embarkation and destination points for the goods must be settled. Will the parties make any provision for variation of these due to strikes, plant closures, unforeseen events, etc.?
- It must be decided whether transshipment is permitted or prohibited. The last permissible date for shipment of the goods must be specified. This clause is very important for the protection of the importer, who will be relying on the goods arriving within a certain period of time.
- The L/C must state whether partial shipments are permitted.
- The L/C must specify the period of time within which the documents must be presented for payment, acceptance, or negotiation.
- The L/C must state whether it is transferable. This may be very important to the parties.
- The date and place and expiry date of the credit must be specified.
- The method by which the L/C will be "advised" or communicated (mail or teletransmission) must be specified.

Once the parties have discussed and agreed on these matters, they are in a position to include terms in the sales agreement providing for the requisite letter of credit. The importer will then arrange with its bank to issue a letter of credit conforming to the parties' agreement.

International Rules for Letters of Credit

The set of internationally agreed on rules that governs letter of credit transactions is the Uniform Customs and Practice for Documentary Credits. These rules were adopted by the International Chamber of Commerce in 1933 and are used by banks in most countries. The rules have been revised from time to time to reflect changing commercial practices. The current set of rules, reflecting rapid advances in information technology, is known as the UCP 500, which was adopted in 1993, and came into force in 1994.

The advantage of this system is that it provides a form of security for each of the parties involved, ensuring that the goods will be shipped by a certain date and that the exporter will be paid, provided that the terms and conditions of the L/C have been fulfilled. It is important to realize, however, that payment is based on documents only and not on the merchandise or services that are the subject of the sales or service contract. It is, therefore, of utmost importance that the importer or purchaser of services be sure of the reputation and reliability of the provider of the goods or services.

Documentary Credit and Standby Letters of Credit: Important Differences

Originally, letter of credit law and practice was limited to the use of letters of credit in commercial sale of goods transactions. Letters of credit were used exclusively to provide sellers who were unwilling to rely simply on a promise of the buyers to pay with assurance that they would be paid once the goods were delivered to the carrier. Increasingly, letters of credit are now being used to provide insurance to a purchaser of large-scale services or owners of large-scale projects in the event that the contract or project is not completed. A **standby letter of credit** anticipates the possibility that something will go wrong or a negative event will occur, such as the failure of the applicant to make a payment under a loan agreement or the failure of the applicant to perform some contractual obligation. A standby letter of credit is payable only if things go wrong in the underlying transaction. The **documentary credit**, or commercial letter of credit, is a method of payment that anticipates a positive event—the consummation of the underlying transaction. It is a means of implementing the performance of the buyer and the seller. A letter of credit is referred to as documentary because it requires the presentation of documents as a condition of payment. A standby letter of credit may or may not be documentary.

There are, at present, three major sets of rules governing credit transactions, all of which have been adopted by the International Chamber of Commerce (ICC):

- *Uniform Customs and Practice for Documentary Credits (UCP 500).* This is by far the most common and widely used set of rules and is routinely used in both domestic and international letters of credit and bank guarantee transactions. The UCP regime was primarily drafted to deal with documentary credits used in the sale of goods context, but it does specifically include standby letters of credit within its scope. It is often criticized in this regard because it has a number of provisions that are inapplicable to standby letters of credit and bank guarantees.
- *Uniform Rules for Demand Guarantees (URDG).* This set of rules is not widely used because it is intended to apply to independent guarantees, but standby letters of credit are also included in its scope.
- *International Standby Practices (ISP98).* This set of rules is the latest set of rules adopted by the ICC and specifically addresses international standby letters of credit. It is intended to bridge the gap when the UCP has not been fully suitable for standby letters of credit.

In addition to these three sets of rules there is also the UNCITRAL (United Nations Commission on International Trade Law) Convention on Independent Guarantees and Stand-by Letters of Credit, but this Convention has not yet had the necessary number of ratifications to be widely relied on.

The Importance of Standby Credit in a Global Environment of Expanding Trade in Services

Increasingly, international contracts are complex and high-risk endeavours that involve a mix of trade in goods and services and many subcontractors from a number of different countries. The failure of any one of these players to fulfill its obligations, or the occurrence of any one of the many risks associated with such projects is a daunting prospect to many project owners and countries. To mitigate these risks, many of them have sought financial protection. Some of the risks contemplated are:

- physical risks such as adverse weather, earthquakes, floods, tornados, tsunamis, heat, cold, altitude, and humidity;
- labour risks such as strikes, work slowdowns, and riots;
- human risks such as corruption, vandalism, theft, work accidents, and disease;

- design and technology risks, such as problems with new technology, materials, or processes;
- site risks, such as changes to subsurface conditions, environmental contamination, harm to endangered or protected species, and archeological or anthropological discoveries that prevent further use of the site;
- logistical difficulties, such as urban congestion and remote access problems;
- regulatory risks, such as complex and uncertain government authorization;
- financial risks, such as the cost of borrowing, inflation, and taxes; and
- political risks, such as war, terrorism, and government change or intervention.

These risks are in addition to the usual risks associated with foreign projects such as problems with currency exchange, international double taxation, barriers to repatriation of profits, and the difficulties of conducting a legal dispute involving multiple jurisdictions.

The Difference Between Standby Letters of Credit and Performance Bonds

While the challenges outlined above also affect large domestic projects and contracts, owners usually protect themselves in the domestic context by requiring that the contractor provide a **performance bond** issued by a surety company. In the event of a contractor default, the surety company stands behind the performance of the contractor and acts as a guarantor of the project owner for full performance of the underlying contract. Depending on the wording of the bond, the surety may be required to

- finance a contractor and keep an insolvent contractor afloat so that the project may be completed;
- engage another contractor to finish the project; or
- allow the owner to finish the project on its own, by paying the owner the amount of liability assumed by the surety.

In international contracts, the more common protection employed is the standby letter of credit. A standby letter of credit is quite different from a performance bond, in that the beneficiary can obtain payment very quickly and relatively easily. Under a US-style performance bond, or surety, the project owner will have to convince the surety of the contractor's default before the surety will take action on the bond. To receive payment on a letter of credit, the beneficiary need only make a presentment to the issuing bank that conforms to the requirements of the credit. These requirements will vary depending on the agreement between the parties, but can be the presentation

of a **sight draft** without any further documentation of the applicant's/
contractor's default or non-performance of the underlying transaction.
Such an instrument is known as a "clean" or "suicide" credit. Wise contracting
parties will require certification from an independent third party attesting
to the contractor's non-performance.[1] An important characteristic of the
standby letter of credit is the ease and speed with which the seller can
obtain payment, in contrast to a performance bond or surety, which may
require the project owner to convince the surety of the contractor's default
before the surety will take action on the bond.

Principles of Letter of Credit Transactions

Letter of credit transactions are characterized by two fundamental characteristics: the "autonomy" of the credit and the doctrine of strict compliance.

It is advisable that any business person using a letter of credit in an
international transaction fully understand these concepts before negotiating the main or principal contract for the sale of goods or services.

The Autonomy of the Letter of Credit

Autonomy of the letter of credit provides that the credit is separate from
and independent of the underlying contract of sale or other transaction. This
means that payment for goods or services is made on the basis of satisfactory
document presentation and not on the basis of delivery of goods or services
that conform to the contract. This principle is enshrined in the UCP, which
has become the accepted code for international bankers. The rules of the
UCP have been confirmed by judicial decisions in both common-law and
civil-law jurisdictions with the result that it has become a uniform law of
international trade financing. The following excerpts from the UCP express
the principle very clearly:

> **Article 3**
>
> Credits, by their nature, are separate transactions from the sales or other
> contract(s) on which they may be based and banks are in no way concerned
> with or bound by such contract(s) even if any reference whatsoever to
> such contract(s) is included in the credit.

> **Article 4**
>
> In credit operations all parties concerned deal with documents, and not
> with goods, services and/or other performances to which the documents
> may relate.

The importer should be aware of the risk that it may be obliged to pay in full
for shoddy goods or unsatisfactory services under a letter of credit if proper
procedures are not established, independent of the letter of credit, to protect
the interests of the importer/purchaser. This risk exists because it is possible

for an exporter to comply with the terms of a letter of credit by producing documents that apparently conform to the requirements while at the same time breaching the contract for the sale of goods or services. The best protection is knowledge of the absolute reliability of the exporter; however, this is a luxury enjoyed by few international traders. Some protection may be obtained by pre-shipment inspection of goods, suppliers' warranties, and protective clauses in the sales contract, but the latter may be expensive to enforce and lack the simplicity of merely stopping payment for unsatisfactory goods or services. The risk inherent in the letter of credit should always be borne in mind when negotiating the principal sales contract.

A case that provides a stark illustration of the principle of "autonomy of credit" is the American black bean caper case, described in box 8.2.

BOX 8.2 GUATEMALANS LOSE OUT IN CONTRACT WITH CHICAGO CON ARTIST
(United States Court of Appeals for the Seventh Circuit, 1988)

Indeca, an agency that purchased food for Guatemala, made a contract with Rumex for 6,000 tons of black beans for US$5 million. Banco de Guatemala was Indeca's bank and issued a letter of credit in favour of Rumex. The deal had been put together by a Chicago commodities broker, Bell, and her attorney, and they arranged for the credit to be confirmed by the Continental Bank in Chicago. The letter of credit provided that payment would be made upon receipt of documents showing that the beans had been loaded on board a ship in Hong Kong.

Documentation was presented by Rumex, the exporter, to the Continental Bank and was initially rejected because it did not conform to the requirements of the letter of credit. The documents were revised and resubmitted with the result that the Continental Bank paid Rumex on the letter of credit and sent the documents to Banco de Guatemala, the issuing bank, in order to be reimbursed. Banco de Guatemala duly reimbursed the Continental Bank under the UCP rules. It then looked to its client, Indeca, for reimbursement under the terms of the letter of credit. The documents were forged, however, and Indeca never received the black beans.

Although the appropriate party for Indeca to sue was Rumex and/or its principal, Bell, this was not practical because Bell had been convicted of wire fraud and submitting false documents to a bank and was in no position to pay a judgment. Indeca therefore decided to sue the Continental Bank in the United States on the basis of negligence, alleging that Continental should have known of the fraud and protected Indeca from loss, even though Continental had no contractual relationship with Indeca. The lower court absolved Continental of any actual knowledge of the fraud and found that Continental had not acted recklessly or care-lessly. The plaintiff, Indeca, then appealed, alleging that Continental had a duty to Indeca to act more carefully.

The decision of the appeal court in this case was to confirm the lower court's finding that the confirming bank owes its duty of care in inspecting the documents solely to the bank that issues the letter of credit, and not to the buyer or importer. Thus Indeca was out of luck; it had spent its money and received neither beans nor restitution.

The Doctrine of Strict Compliance

Article 13 of the UCP states:

> Banks must examine all documents stipulated in the Credit, with reasonable care, to ascertain whether or not they appear, on their face, to be in compliance with the terms and conditions of the Credit. Compliance of the stipulated documents on their face with the terms and conditions of the Credit, shall be determined by international standard banking practice as reflected in these Articles. Documents which appear on their face to be inconsistent with one another will be considered as not appearing on their face to be in compliance with the terms and conditions of the Credit.

The bank will not assume any responsibility for knowledge of usages or practices of any particular trade. The doctrine of strict compliance requires that documents tendered must be in strict conformity with the terms of the credit or the bank will refuse to accept them, even if the goods or services conform to all the parties' requirements.

The meaning and application of the words "strict compliance" have troubled banking institutions and courts in several countries for many years. The question is, how strictly must the documents conform to the terms of the credit? The Uniform Commercial Code (UCC) adopts the strict compliance standard, while the International Standby Practices does not expressly recognize a strict compliance standard. The ISP states that rules must be interpreted in the context of standard standby practice. The UCP states that banks must use "reasonable care" when examining documents and their compliance with the terms, and that conditions of the credit are to be determined by international standard-banking practice as reflected in the UCP articles. The difficulty is that no absolute uniform banking practices actually exist. On a practical note, issuing banks may well attempt to limit their liability to customers by including in their standard form agreements wording such as

> The issuer is obliged to pay the beneficiary only if the documents presented strictly comply with the credit, but the applicant is obliged to reimburse

the issuer when the issuer has paid against documents that only substantially comply, or do not comply at all.[2]

Common discrepancies and errors in documents that may lead to rejection by the bank are:

- an unclean bill of lading;
- a shipment made between ports different from those named in the L/C;
- incorrect insurance documents;
- insurance coverage expressed in different currency;
- underinsurance;
- insurance not effective from the date-of-transport document;
- documents inconsistent with each other;
- description of the goods on the invoice differs from that on the L/C;
- amounts on invoice and bill of exchange differ;
- absence of documents called for in the L/C;
- absence of required signatures on documents;
- credit amount exceeded; and
- credit expired.

In many cases, these discrepancies and errors can be corrected, but they may create an opportunity for the paying party to avoid the contract. In a situation where prices have fallen between the making of the sales contract and the presentation of the documents, the importer may not be prepared to provide the written waiver that the bank will require.

How Canadian Courts Apply the Rules

THE ANGELICA CASE

A landmark Canadian case in which the Supreme Court of Canada dealt with the principle of strict compliance is the *Angelica* case, decided in 1987. There are two issues in this case that are relevant to our discussion. The first issue is what constitutes documentary compliance and the second issue is that of the fraud exception. The facts of this case are given in box 8.3.

BOX 8.3   THE ANGELICA CASE
(Supreme Court of Canada, 1987)

Angelica Whitewear, a Canadian clothing merchandiser, made a contract with Protective Clothing of Hong Kong whereby Angelica would import uniforms from Protective Clothing and pay them by letter of credit. The Bank of Nova Scotia, at Angelica's request, opened a confirmed irrevocable letter of credit in favour of Protective Clothing of Hong Kong, in the amount of the proposed purchase of uniforms. The Shanghai Bank was Protective Clothing's bank and was acting as a confirming bank.

The letter of credit provided that shipments were to be made in installments from Taiwan to Montreal and that the foreign supplier could recover payment for each installment by making partial draws against the letter of credit. Each draw was to be made by presenting a draft for the price of each shipment together with a bill of lading, a commercial invoice, a Canadian customs invoice, an insurance certificate, and a quality inspection certificate. The L/C included the not-uncommon undertaking by the issuing bank to honour drafts presented by the negotiating bank with conforming documents.

The first and second shipments were made and invoiced for $107,000 and $67,000, respectively. At the time of the first shipment, the Shanghai Bank presented a draft with conforming documents to the Bank of Nova Scotia and that draft was honoured. After payment on the first draft, but before payment on the second draft, Angelica discovered that the inspection certificate for the first shipment contained a forged signature. Angelica therefore requested that the Bank of Nova Scotia withhold all further payments on the letter of credit.

When the second draft was presented, Angelica informed its bank that the inspection certificate referred to the wrong letter of credit, that the commercial invoice specified a different quantity than the inspection certificate, and that the bill of lading specified freight prepaid to Vancouver rather than CIF Montreal as required by the letter of credit. Angelica instructed its bank not to pay. Meanwhile, the Shanghai Bank was insisting upon payment of the second draft. The Bank of Nova Scotia sought legal advice and, based on this advice, paid the second draft and reimbursed itself by debiting the account of Angelica. Angelica challenged its bank's action and the bank sued its customer to recover the moneys paid under the L/C.

Documentary Compliance Issue

As stated previously, there are two important issues in this case. The first is the issue of strict documentary compliance. Had there been documentary compliance in this case within the rules of the UCP? The Supreme Court of Canada held that the reference to the wrong letter of credit on the inspection certificate did not violate the principle. The Court also stated that the quantity discrepancies between the invoice and inspection certificate were not sufficiently material to justify refusal of payment. On the third issue of documentary compliance, however, Angelica won its case against the bank. The Court found that the bank had violated the principle by accepting a bill of lading on the second shipment that specified freight prepaid to Vancouver rather than CIF Montreal as required in the L/C instructions. This non-compliance obliged the bank to refuse the documents tendered. (It did not matter that the freight had in fact been paid to Montreal by the seller as required by the underlying contract.)

Fraud Exception Issue

The second important issue is whether the fraud exception was applicable in this case. In Canada, the United States, and the United Kingdom there are court precedents that indicate that an exception to the strict rule of documentary compliance exists where there is fraud in the transaction. This rule means that, in some cases where there is strict documentary compliance, the bank can be prevented from paying out on the credit if there is sufficient evidence of fraud. The problem with the rule is its potential for creating serious uncertainty and lack of confidence in the operation of letter of credit transactions. At the same time, it is important that application of the rules of strict documentary compliance and autonomy of credit not serve to encourage or facilitate fraud in these transactions.

In *Angelica*, the Supreme Court of Canada confirmed that this rule does apply in Canada in a case where there is fraud in the underlying transaction. It is not confined to cases of fraud in the presentation documents. The fraud must be committed by the beneficiary of the credit. The rule does not extend to fraud committed by a third party where the beneficiary is innocent. The Court made some important distinctions with respect to the onus of proof, which is on the importer seeking to prevent the bank from paying out on documents when there is a suspected fraud. Such an importer has two options in this situation. One option is to attempt to convince the bank of the existence of the fraud. The standard that is required is that *the evidence of fraud must be clear and obvious* to the bank. The second option is to obtain an injunction ordering the bank to withhold payment. A court will grant an **injunction** if a strong *prima facie* case of fraud is established against the beneficiary.

If no injunction is obtained, the rule of strict compliance is applied and the issuing bank must honour the letter of credit unless the fraud is made clear and obvious to the bank before the letter of credit is drawn. The issuing bank does not normally owe a duty to its customer to satisfy itself by independent inquiry that there has been no fraud upon presentation of documents that appear regular on their face. A court, on the other hand, has a duty to examine evidence and has the mechanisms to ensure that the evidence presented is reliable and that both sides of a case are heard. Applying these principles to this case, the Supreme Court of Canada held that the bank was not put on inquiry by its knowledge that the first inspection certificate had been forged. The beneficiary's fraud was not disclosed on the face of the presentation documents and had not been clearly established by Angelica at the relevant time. Therefore, Angelica did not succeed in its argument that the fraud exception applied to this case.

THE BANCO DE CUBA CASE

The *Banco de Cuba* case, which was decided after *Angelica*, is another important Canadian case that deals with the issues of strict documentary compliance and the fraud exception (see box 8.4). The court in this case considered and adopted the reasoning of *Angelica*. *Banco de Cuba* is also interesting because it involved a documentary requirement for a quality certificate, but did not clarify what was meant by that description. The case is a good example of the legal difficulties that can arise when the parties are not precise in their description of the documents required.

BNC's case was based on its argument that these circumstances were sufficient to put Scotiabank on inquiry and Scotiabank should not have accepted the certificate. The decision of the Court dealt with two issues: (1) whether there had been strict documentary compliance, and (2) whether the facts were sufficient to bring the fraud exception into play.

BOX 8.4   THE BANCO DE CUBA CASE
(Ontario High Court of Justice, 1988)

Cuba Export, a Cuban purchaser of coffee, made a contract with Hava-Cu Enterprises, a seller of coffee, whereby Hava-Cu was to ship coffee of a specified quantity and quality to Cuba Export, which would pay by letter of credit. Cuba Export arranged for its bank, Banco Nacional de Cuba (BNC), to issue a letter of credit for Cdn$8,775,000 in favour of Hava-Cu Enterprises, which was located in San Martin. Hava-Cu's banker was Scotiabank and arrangements were made for Scotiabank in Toronto to be the corresponding bank.

Hava-Cu Enterprises presented documents to Scotiabank in Toronto that purported to conform to the L/C. These documents consisted of a bill of lading, a master's receipt, a shipping telex, a "quality certificate," a weight certificate, and an invoice. Scotiabank paid Hava-Cu on the basis of these documents, sent them to BNC, and was reimbursed. The coffee was never received in Havana with the result that Cuba Export was unwilling to pay its bank. BNC then sued Scotiabank for paying out on the documents, alleging that Scotiabank had erred in accepting the "quality certificate."

The L/C required a quality certificate in duplicate issued by any supervising enterprise. The certificate presented was in Spanish and did not contain the words "Quality Certificate" on the document. These words were added by Scotiabank employees who were responsible for scrutinizing the documents. The document, which was headed "Secretariat of State for Agriculture, Dominican Republic, Department of Coffee" and contained the subtitle "Quality Control Laboratory," gave information about the shipment in question, including the colour, size of grain, toast, and classification (grade). The statement was signed by the coffee inspector and two tasters. BNC alleged that this was not a quality certificate under the L/C because it was not so labelled.

BNC also alleged that Scotiabank was put on notice of fraud by the following facts:

- Scotiabank received calls from persons with whom the bank had no dealings.
- The beneficiary appeared very anxious to be paid.
- The proceeds were requested in cash.

Documentary Compliance Issue

Was there strict documentary compliance in this case? Specifically, was the certificate presented a "quality certificate" in spite of the fact that it did not bear this title? The Court reviewed the contents of the certificate in question, considered the dictionary definition of the word "quality," and decided the only reasonable conclusion was that the document appeared to be, on its face, a certificate dealing with quality and therefore came within the generic description of a quality certificate. The Court stated:

> The absence of any instruction concerning the quality certificate, other than that it was to be of any supervising enterprise, of necessity presented the paying bank with the problem of deciding whether the particular document tendered was one which fell within the descriptive words. It was a decision upon which the paying bank risked millions of dollars. Giving due reflection to the frailty of human nature, it is improbable that any such decision could ever be made without hesitation or doubt.

Fraud Exception Issue

The second issue before the Court in this case was whether sufficient evidence of fraud had been brought to the attention of Scotiabank to bring the fraud exception into force, even though there may have been documentary compliance. In this respect, the Court decided in favour of Scotiabank. In making this decision the Court noted that the statement of claim contained an extended list of particulars of negligence said to have been committed by Scotiabank and the defendants, Brodie and Solankee, dealing with the L/C transaction. At trial, evidence was adduced of a number of circumstances which were said to be, and in some instances were admitted to be, unusual. Brodie received telephone calls about the transaction from persons with whom he had had no dealings. Some of these were not mentioned in the L/C. The beneficiary appeared anxious to be paid. Brodie was asked to have Scotiabank confirm the L/C payment of a large portion of the proceeds, exceeding $2 million, was requested in cash—a request which was refused. The argument on behalf of BNC was that these and other unusual circumstances should have put Scotiabank on inquiry and should have called for particular scrutiny of the documents and possibly some communication with the issuing bank. In my view, these suspicious circumstances, admitting for the purpose of argument that they were suspicious, were of no legal consequence.

Onus of Proof for Fraud Exception

The Court in this case also considered the onus of proof when the fraud exception is raised, and confirmed the conclusions of the *Angelica* case. Mr. Justice Anderson of the Ontario High Court of Justice stated:

On the issue raised by this appeal, I would draw a distinction between what must be shown on an application for an interlocutory injunction to restrain payment under a letter of credit on the ground of fraud by the beneficiary of the credit and what must be shown, in a case such as this one, to establish that a draft was improperly paid by the issuing bank after notice of alleged fraud by the beneficiary. A strong *prima facie* case of fraud would appear to be a sufficient test on an application for an interlocutory injunction. Where, however, no such application was made and the issuing bank has had to exercise its own judgment as to whether or not to honour a draft, the test in my opinion should be the one laid down in Edward Owen Engineering—whether fraud was so established to the knowledge of the issuing bank before payment of the draft as to make the fraud clear or obvious to the bank. The justification for this distinction, in my view, is the difficulty of the position of the issuing bank, in so far as fraud is concerned, by comparison with that of a court on an application for an interlocutory injunction. In view of the strict obligation of the issuing bank to honour a draft that is accompanied by apparently conforming documents, the fact that the decision as to whether or not to pay must as a general rule be made fairly promptly, and the difficulty in many cases of forming an opinion, on which one would hazard a lawsuit, as to whether there has been fraud by the beneficiary of the credit, it would in my view be unfair and unreasonable to require anything less of the customer in the way of demonstration of an alleged fraud.

Practical Conclusions for Canadian Importers
and Purchasers of Services

On the basis of this discussion, we can come to certain practical conclusions. The first is that banks will accept no responsibility for contractual compliance of the sales agreement between the vendor and purchaser in an international sale of goods or services. The second is that any serious discrepancies in documentation will require a waiver by the buyer or the L/C will not be honoured. This can present an opportunity for the purchaser to renege on the payment obligations of the contract. The third conclusion is that, when there is strict documentary compliance but the buyer has strong evidence of fraud on the part of the seller or its agent, there is an exception to the bank's obligation to pay on the documents. It is impractical, however, to attempt to convince the bank of the fraud. The level of proof required is very high. For this reason, an importer's best action in these circumstances is to inform the bank of the details of the fraud and advise the bank that it is instructing counsel to apply for an interim injunction. As a practical matter, it is probably easier to satisfy a court of the need to issue an injunction to prevent the bank from paying on the documents to the detriment of the importer than it is to produce proof of fraud sufficient to overcome the bank's duty to pay on conforming documents and honour its obligation to other banks under the rules of the UCP.

Negotiable Instruments: Their Role in Letter of Credit Arrangements

As we discussed above, the usual stipulated documents for an L/C transaction include the commercial invoice, certificate of origin, insurance policy or certificate, and a transportation document. In addition, a draft or bill of exchange may be included in the L/C requirements as part of the mechanism for ensuring that the exporter/seller is paid. The initiative for drawing the bill of exchange lies with the creditor (the seller or banker). Wanting to be paid, the exporter/seller prepares the document in which the debtor acknowledges its indebtedness and agrees to pay according to the terms stated in the instrument. A sample bill of exchange for the contract between T.I.E. Steel and Canadian Import (discussed in box 8.1) is given in figure 8.2.

What Is the Significance of a Negotiable Instrument?

A negotiable instrument is a document whose ownership may be transferred by endorsement and delivery; it may confer on the person receiving it greater rights than the transferor had. The most common examples of a negotiable instrument are cheques and bills of exchange or drafts. These instruments have great advantages over contracts that must be assigned in

Figure 8.2 Sample Bill of Exchange in Connection with L/C

Drawn under Canabank
LIC 601/80002

June 18, 2006

AT SIGHT

PAY TO THE ORDER OF _____*T.I.E. Steel of Taipei*_____

THE SUM OF _____*Thirty-Two Thousand*_____ 00/100 _____*U.S. Dollars*_____

VALUE RECEIVED _____*Covering shipment of 400 sets of Stainless Steel*_____
_____*Cookware from Taiwan to Toronto, per CT Freight Inc.*_____

TO: CANABANK
200 KING ST. WEST
TORONTO, CANADA

T.I.E. Steel of Taipei
Signed: _____*Jamie Frame*_____
President

writing with notice to the debtor and that confer only those rights that the assignor possesses. Endorsement is simply signing the instrument itself and delivery is the act of handing over the instrument.

The Development of the Bill of Exchange

Negotiable instruments were developed as early as the 12th century to meet the requirements of international transactions. In those days, a merchant in London could buy goods from Florence and arrange for payment in Florence, thereby freeing the parties from the difficulty of transporting heavy coinage or gold from London to Florence. Mechanisms were developed to enable the London merchant to pay the appropriate sum to a London "financial institution" (in those days, often simply a "money-changer"), which would then draw a "bill" (a forebear of our bill of exchange) on a cooperating money-changer in Florence, instructing the Florentine money-changer to pay the Florentine supplier on a certain date. Once he was paid, the Florentine supplier would give up the title documents for the goods and the goods would be shipped to London.

The early international financial industry grew up around such transactions, as trade increased among the principal European cities. At first, credits collected in Florence would be offset by similar credits in London from goods sold by English merchants to Florentine buyers. Gradually, the money-changers in the principal trading cities of Europe developed a more sophisticated system of meeting and tallying the bills that they had honoured on a multilateral basis. Accounts were tallied and payments were made to settle with those having a favourable balance. Thus, in our example, if the Florentine had a creditor in France, he might use the written promise of the London money-changer to satisfy the French debt. This written promise or "bill" would then be settled through the developed mechanism for international bills. Because the French creditor would be in no position to check the authenticity of the transaction giving rise to the original bill, the custom developed that the promisor on the bill (in our case the London merchant) was required to honour any instrument presented for payment by a bona fide transferee of it (in our case the French creditor), provided that the bill was not a forgery. This assignment from one creditor to another was called "negotiation" and the written promise to pay became known as a "negotiable instrument." Over time, rules evolved to deal with the complexity of these transactions. These rules determined what sort of written promises would qualify for the special treatment accorded to negotiable instruments. They became an important part of the *Law Merchant*, a set of common rules for commerce, which was developed and shared by all the trading nations of the medieval world, and which was eventually incorporated into the common law and into the commercial codes of civil-law countries. In England, a large body of precedent or case law relating to negotiable instruments developed and the various rules were consolidated into a single statement of the law by the *Bills of Exchange Act* of 1882.

Contemporary Law Governing Bills of Exchange

Our own legislation in Canada, the *Bills of Exchange Act*, follows the UK Act very closely and our laws in this area are very similar to those of the United Kingdom. A "bill of exchange" is defined in Canada as an *unconditional* order *in writing*, requiring the person to whom it is addressed to pay *on demand*, or at a *fixed or determinable time*, a sum certain in money to or to the order of a *specified person* or bearer.

In the United States, bills of exchange or drafts are governed by the *Uniform Commercial Code* (UCC). (Note that the words "bills of exchange" and "drafts" are interchangeable for the purpose of the general description of the written promises under discussion.) The law relating to bills of exchange in many other countries is governed by legislation that conforms to the 1930 Convention Providing a Uniform Law for Bills of Exchange and Promissory Notes. Many European countries, as well as Japan and Brazil, have this Convention as the basis of their law.

Negotiation of Bills of Exchange

There are certain obligations inherent in initiating a bill of exchange that may come as a surprise to many business persons. These involve the liability of the drawer of a bill. As we have stated, the bill of exchange is usually drawn by the exporter, who prepares the document as part of the L/C arrangements. There are three original parties to a bill of exchange: the drawer, the drawee, and the payee. Note that the drawer and payee are often the same party, as in the sample bill of exchange in figure 8.2, above.

Liability on a Bill

All three original parties normally are liable to honour the bill, the drawer by drawing it, the drawee by accepting it (that is, writing its acceptance on or across the bill), and the payee by endorsing the bill when negotiating it. The drawer or endorser who does not wish to maintain further liability on the bill may reject liability by adding the words "without recourse" to its signature. While this will protect the drawer or endorser from liability on the bill, it will also increase the risk to the transferor and will therefore reduce the value of the bill.

Until an instrument is delivered, the drawer is not liable. Delivery is the term used for transfer from the payee to a new holder, and for later transfers to successive holders. Negotiation is normally made by endorsement and delivery. A typical situation in which negotiation occurs is illustrated in box 8.5.

Negotiation normally includes both endorsement and delivery. Only when the instrument is payable to bearer is endorsement not necessary. Bearer instruments are not common in modern international trade, because they can be negotiated by delivery alone and can thus be negotiated by someone who has acquired possession of them unlawfully (for example, by theft).

Rights of the Transferee

The negotiable instrument is a very special type of assignable contract and is not subject to the ordinary rules applicable to the assignment of contract.

BOX 8.5   EXAMPLE OF NEGOTIATION

Canadian Auto Parts is a manufacturer based in Winnipeg that has sold parts to an Italian automaker and is being paid by letter of credit in the amount of Cdn $62,000 payable 60 days after sight (presentation to the bank or other payor). The draft has been accepted as of March 15, 2006. However, Canadian Auto Parts is indebted to Canada Steel Inc. for $56,000 and this account is due no later than March 24, 2006. In order to satisfy this indebtedness, Canada Steel Inc. agrees to allow Canadian Auto Parts to negotiate the bill by endorsement (signing) and delivery. Canadian Auto Parts signs the bill, adds the words "payable to Canada Steel Inc.," and delivers the bill to Canada Steel Inc. on March 23, 2006.

In the example in box 8.5, Canada Steel Inc. has become a holder in due course (see below) and, as such, is entitled to collect payment according to the terms of the bill even though the promisor or original debtor has not been notified. Indeed, Canada Steel Inc., as transferee, may be in a better position to enforce its rights under the bill than was the original payee, Canadian Auto Parts. All this has been achieved by the simple act of signing and delivering the bill to the endorsee/transferee. Because of the transfer of the negotiable instrument, certain defences that could be used successfully against the original drawer/payee are no longer available to the debtor. The two most important of these defences, sometimes referred to as personal defences, are lack of consideration (a very common and important defence) and the right of setoff. Other defences, referred to as real defences, are good against any holder, even a holder in due course. These defences include failure of contract due to incapacity, cancellation of instrument, forged signatures, incomplete instrument, and fraud as to the true nature of the instrument.

To ensure that the endorser has the maximum rights available, the endorsee/ transferee must be a **holder in due course**. A holder in due course is a holder who took a bill, which is complete and regular on its face, in good faith and for value, without notice of any defect in the title of the person negotiating it, before it was overdue, and without notice that it was dishonoured. Similarly, a subsequent holder who acquires its title through a holder in due course and who is not a party to any fraud or illegality affecting the bill has all the rights of a holder in due course. Not all endorsees/transferees are holders in due course. Personal defences are not effective against a holder in due course but real defences are.

Applying these principles to our example in box 8.5, let us suppose that the goods supplied by Canadian Auto Parts to the Italian importer were substandard in quality and did not conform to the description in the contract of sale. This would be a failure of consideration and would be a valid defence for the Italian importer in a lawsuit brought by Canadian Auto Parts against the Italian company to enforce payment of the bill. This defence, however, being a personal defence, is no longer available against the party to which the bill has been negotiated for value (in this case, Canada Steel Inc.), provided that, in all other respects, Canada Steel Inc. qualifies as a holder in due course. This situation is significant in international trade because often the bill is held and enforced by a party other than the original payee.

Dishonour of a Bill

Dishonour is the failure or refusal of the party who is primarily liable on the bill to pay the debt according to the terms of the instrument. This may occur when the drawee refuses to accept the bill or later, if, after acceptance, he or she refuses to pay as acceptor.

A bill payable on demand, or sight bill, is dishonoured if it is not paid on presentation. A time bill is dishonoured if it is not accepted by the drawee when presented for acceptance or not paid when the time has expired. The law of Canada and the United Kingdom allows three days' grace unless the bill provides otherwise. The grace period has been abolished in most other jurisdictions and is not a feature of bills in Convention countries.

An endorser is liable to any holder for the amount of the bill if the party primarily liable fails to pay, provided that the endorser receives prompt notice of the dishonour from the holder.

The drawer of the bill is liable if the bill is dishonoured and must compensate the holder or any endorser who is compelled to pay and must also compensate that holder for any necessary proceedings taken by reason of the dishonour.

The liability of the endorser and the drawer depends on prompt notice of dishonour. Prompt notice is interpreted to be no later than the next business day following the day of dishonour. If the bill is drawn or payable or accepted in Quebec or outside Canada, notice of dishonour must be in the special form known as protest. This is accomplished using the services of a notary public or justice of the peace, who prepares the protest in a prescribed form and delivers it to the endorser.

INTERNATIONAL TRANSPORTATION CONSIDERATIONS

A detailed discussion of international transportation is beyond the scope of this book. However, some general guidelines on managing transportation risks are outlined below. International transportation is complex and highly specialized, and a business person lacking experience in international shipping would be unwise to embark on a contract of significant value without the services of a qualified transportation specialist.

Freight Forwarding Services

In the past it was common for an exporter to rely on a single mode of transportation to move a shipment. Increasingly, however, carriers are combining the strengths of different modes of transportation service to offer intermodal services. An exporter may also be faced with the fact that the shipment contemplated is not of sufficient size to secure a favourable transportation handling rate. Transportation choices and decisions are complex matters involving very specialized knowledge. The small or medium-sized exporter may be well-advised to obtain the services of a freight forwarder.

Freight forwarders offer a variety of services, but act primarily to forward goods on behalf of shippers or cargo owners who do not possess their own export organization or shipping department. Depending on the contracted service, the freight forwarder will act as a principal or agent, or both. Examples of services commonly provided are:

- full-service documentation;
- export packaging and container stuffing;
- marine insurance;
- letters of credit analysis and negotiation;
- consolidation services; and
- deconsolidation services.

International freight forwarders may be ocean freight forwarders or air freight forwarders. Ocean freight forwarders often act as principal in consolidating small shipments into full-container loads. In this situation, the bill of lading is issued between the forwarder and the carrier. The forwarder is then responsible for deconsolidation and distribution to designated recipients.

Air freight forwarders act as principal in the situation where consolidation of small shipments into airline-approved unit load devices (ULD) is undertaken. The bill of lading is issued by the air carrier, and the forwarder is shown as the shipper. The freight forwarder, in turn, provides each small shipper with a "house" bill of lading. These in-house bills of lading provide little protection to shippers or owners of goods, and are not popular for this reason. Most have now been replaced by the International Federation of Freight Forwarders Associations multimodal transport bill of lading approved by the ICC and incorporating the UNCTAD-ICC Rules for Multimodal Transport Documents. This model bill of lading is used by most international freight forwarders all over the world. Sometimes freight forwarders are registered with the International Air Transport Association and can act as official airline agents. In this case, the carrier, not the forwarder, assumes liability for the shipment, and the contract of carriage is between the air carrier and the shipper. These details become significant when the parties are applying for documentary credit because the detailed description of the documents to be presented to a financial institution must be accurate.

Transportation of Goods

Unimodal

When goods are carried by only one mode of transport, the international transportation is unimodal. In these cases the contract of transport will be evidenced by a document that is particular to the mode of transport being used: if the goods are transported by sea, an ocean bill of lading or an ocean waybill is used; if the goods are transported by air, an air waybill or an air consignment note is used; and if the goods are transported by rail, a rail consignment note is used. These documents are issued by the carrier at the departure point, contain the terms of the transport contract, usually refer to any applicable international convention or national law that regulates the particular mode of transport, and may limit liability.

Multimodal
When goods are carried by more than one mode of transport, the transportation is multimodal. This may be evidenced by the issue of a series of separate single-mode transport documents or by a combined or multimodal transport document. Each successive carrier is subject to different rules concerning liability, which may create problems in the event of damage or loss if it is difficult to ascertain at which stage of the carriage the goods were damaged or lost.

Carriage of Goods by Sea
Shipments by sea occur in two ways. In the case of small shipments, the goods are transported as part of the ship's general cargo under a contract of carriage by sea, evidenced by an ocean bill of lading. In the case of large shipments, the entire ship may be hired under a charterparty.

THE OCEAN BILL OF LADING
When the exporter delivers the goods to a ship FOB, or CIF, a **bill of lading** will be issued as evidence of the contract of carriage. Note that this is merely *evidence* of the contract of carriage and not the contract of carriage itself. The named parties to the bill of lading will usually be the shipper, the carrier, and the consignee or importer/purchaser, or the bill will be made out "to order." Carriers generally make their standard form bills of lading available and the shipper usually provides one of these in draft form to the carrier's agent. The shipper guarantees the accuracy of the information supplied. If there are no problems, the bill of lading will be "clean"; if not, it will be "claused" or "unclean"—meaning that the shipment does not completely correspond to the description of the bill of lading. If a letter of credit is involved, this will create serious problems because banks usually require clean documents of transport. The number of duplicates of the bill of lading varies from one country to another: in Canada they are issued in triplicate, in the United Kingdom, in duplicate, and in some jurisdictions, in quadruplicate. The bill of lading will be included in the set of documents delivered to the advising or nominated bank in a letter of credit transaction, or it will be forwarded directly to the consignee or agent.

BILL OF LADING

The term "bill of lading" presents some problems because it is derived from movement of goods by sea. In many countries, the use of the term is restricted to the movement of goods by sea; however, in North America we use the expressions "rail bills of lading" and "truck bills of lading." In other English-speaking countries, the expressions "goods receipt" or "shipping contract" may be used.

Generally speaking, the bill of lading serves three purposes:

1. as a receipt to the shipper acknowledging that specific goods have been received for shipment;
2. as a memorandum of the terms and conditions of the contract between the shipper and the carrier for the transportation of the named goods to the specified destination; and
3. as evidence of title to the goods. (This is limited to common-law countries and must be an "order bill of lading.")

It is this last characteristic, the evidence of title to the goods, that, combined with its negotiability, makes the bill of lading unique in international trade as it enables the property in the goods to pass on delivery or endorsement and delivery of the bill. (Please refer to the earlier discussion in this chapter for a review of negotiability.) Thus goods may be sold or pledged to secure an advance while they are still in transit. Not all bills of lading are negotiable; in the common law, a bill made out "to order" or "to order or assigns" is negotiable, but a bill made out exclusively to a named consignee is not. In the United States and in most civil-law systems, generally, the holder of a negotiable document of title to goods is the owner of the document and the goods.

OCEAN WAYBILLS

Ocean waybills are non-negotiable contracts of carriage of goods by sea; they are contracts of carriage and receipts and not documents of title. A waybill consignee cannot obtain delivery of the goods by merely presenting the ocean waybill. It must prove that the consignee is the person named in the waybill.

CONTAINER TRANSPORT

Container shipments may be unimodal or multimodal and may be door-to-door or consolidated. A door-to-door container shipment occurs when the exporter/consignor is able to fill a full container load, usually filled at the exporter's place of business and sealed by the carrier when collected. The container is then delivered to the importer/consignee's place of business.

Where the exporter's goods will not fill a full container load, they are taken to a container freight station for consolidation with the goods of other exporters, and the goods will be separated and delivered to the various importers once they have arrived at the destination container freight station.

The Incoterms 1990 provide a trade term that deals with cargo in containers and multimodal transport. The trade term is "free carrier (named place)," or "FCA."

Intermodal Bills of Lading

If the exporter itself arranges for shipment with several carriers, each carrier will issue a bill of lading for its segment of transportation. Each party will be responsible for its portion of the journey and the terms and conditions appearing on each of bill of lading will apply to that portion of the transportation process. Because this transport fragmentation may represent excessive administrative time and uncertainty, the exporter may arrange for multimodal transport of the goods through an intermediary—a "combined transport operator." In this case, the operator will act as principal and assume full responsibility for the shipment, including liability for loss or damage, and will issue a combined transport document.

Carriage of Goods by Air

AIR WAYBILL

An air waybill is a non-negotiable document and is used for the transportation of individual shipments and consolidated shipments, in which case it may be a "house" air waybill. The air waybill must contain an indication of the places of departure and destination. Among the clauses appearing in fine print on the back of a bill of lading will be terms and conditions that set limits on liability and specify carrier exemptions. These terms and conditions are regulated by each country's domestic legislation as well as international conventions applicable to each mode of transport. The air waybill is *prima facie* evidence of the conclusion of the contract, of the receipt of the cargo, and of the conditions of carriage. Air waybills are not usually negotiable, but there is nothing in the Warsaw-Hague Convention, which governs international carriage of cargo by air, that prevents the issue of a negotiable air waybill.

LIABILITY OF THE AIR CARRIER

The air carrier is liable for damage sustained in the event of the destruction of, loss of, or damage to any cargo, if the occurrence that caused the damage took place during the carriage by air. This includes the period during which the cargo is in the custody of the air carrier, preloading, and after landing within the airport. The carrier is also liable for damage due to delay in the carriage of the cargo. The air carrier may avoid liability if it proves that all necessary measures were taken to avoid the damage. The liability of the carrier is limited unless the parties have otherwise agreed.

IATA UNIVERSAL AIR WAYBILL

The International Air Transport Association (IATA) has developed a common form of air waybill and conditions of contract for interline and online carriage. This is known as the IATA Universal Air Waybill. The document provides a receipt to the shipper at the time of delivery to the carrier, indicates the charges for the carriage, enables the carriage of the shipment on more than one carrier to be recorded on the same document, provides for settlement of charges between carriers, specifies the conditions of the contract, complies with the requirements of the Warsaw Convention, and enables data processing and document transmission.

Exemptions to Liability

The various documents described here may contain significant exemptions from liability for the carrier. In addition to statutory provisions limiting the liability of carriers, there are four basic exemptions allowed by the common law:

1. act of God, such as an accident due solely to natural causes, without human intervention and which could not have been prevented by reasonable foresight or care;
2. enemies of the Queen or state, such as incidents of terrorism, insurrection, or war;
3. defect or inherent vice of goods, such as fermentation or evaporation of liquid or failure of animals to eat; and
4. act or default of the shipper, such as poor or inadequate packaging.

The exporter should remember that liability can always be extended beyond statutory limits, for a price. In negotiating transportation contracts, careful inquiries should always be made about the amount of liability and insurance coverage for damage and loss of goods. Adequate coverage should never be assumed.

Electronic Transmission of the Bill of Lading

The electronic transmission of documents presents some challenges arising from the characteristics of the bill of lading, particularly the fact that it is a transferable document of title to the goods described in the bill. When the

bill of lading as a paper document is eliminated and replaced with electronic data transmission, significant legal problems arise. These problems
have not yet been fully addressed or clarified internationally. If a negotiable
bill of lading is transmitted through a network and printed out at several
different locations, can each of the printouts be considered an original and
therefore negotiable? Are all the printouts copies? Which is the original?
Some international rules have evolved. The UCP 500 allows the use of documents produced by reprographic, automated, and computerized systems
and for electronic signatures. Incoterms 1990 have been revised to be fully
compatible with electronic data interchange. What has not yet been achieved
is clarification of the electronic equivalent to a bill of lading that fulfills all
its traditional functions. This is relevant to trade payments, electronic funds
transfer, and collections systems, so that care must be exercised to ensure
that the methods of transmission used by the parties conforms to the wording of the contracts between them, because the law is not clear in the absence
of specific provisions by the parties.

INSURANCE

Insurance for international transactions is a highly specialized area. Expert
and reliable insurance advice is necessary in setting up any one export transaction or in developing an exporting policy for the small or medium-sized
business embarking on an export program. The following is a brief overview
of the insurance of goods against losses occurring during their international
transportation by sea or by air. It is important to use the services of highly
competent insurance brokers. This is necessary to ensure that the exporter
is able to make satisfactory arrangements for insurance to protect its interest in the goods while they are being transported. The material in chapter 6
relating to Canadian services for the exporter should also be reviewed in this
context. Most relevant to the international exporter is marine insurance.

Marine Insurance

Marine insurance is unique from a legal and constitutional point of view
because insurance normally falls within provincial jurisdiction in Canada
under s. 92 of the *Constitution Act, 1867* as "property and civil rights in the
province." However, because marine insurance was developed several centuries before other forms of insurance, the Supreme Court of Canada ruled
in 1983 that marine insurance falls within federal jurisdiction under s. 91,
which deals with "navigation and shipping."[3] Some power remains within
provincial jurisdiction, with the result that there is concurrent jurisdiction

in this area. The Supreme Court decision did, however, enable Parliament to pass the federal *Marine Insurance Act*, which entered into force in 1993.

Marine insurance is an essential part of letter of credit arrangements for an export transaction and can be extremely comprehensive because it covers marine losses including losses from incidental air or land peril and losses incidental to the building, repair, or launch of a ship. It may be extended to cover goods from the time they leave the warehouse at the point of shipment until they are delivered at the destination named in the policy. This insurance overcomes the difficulty caused by the liability of ocean shipping companies being strictly limited by international conventions.

A marine insurance policy or certificate is usually made out to the order of shippers or drawers, like bills of lading, so that they may be endorsed and the loss collected by subsequent holders of the policy or certificate.

Most exporters will use the services of a qualified marine insurance broker, who will act as an agent of the insured, although the broker will be paid by the insurer. The terms of the contract of sale or the trade term will indicate whether the buyer or the seller is responsible to pay the cost of the marine insurance. Both the Incoterms and the UCP specify who pays for the insurance and the amount of insurance required. The parties to the contract of sale should always specify what risks are to be covered as well as the value of the insurance coverage. Care should be taken to consider whether the goods will be shipped on deck and whether goods will be insured against exposure to the elements, and also whether pilferage will be covered.

Many exporters who ship recurring shipments will arrange for an open cover policy—that is, a contract whereby the insurance company agrees to protect all shipments made by the insured from the moment the shipment leaves the factory or warehouse until delivery to the destination. The insured in these circumstances agrees to report all shipments to the insurance company, periodically, usually monthly, and pay premiums on the shipments made in accordance with the agreed schedule of rates in the policy. If an exporter is dealing with individual shipments of lower value, a blanket policy may be preferable because the insurer does not have to advise the insurer of each shipment, but pays a lump-sum premium to cover all shipments made.

The insured must have an insurable interest in the goods insured at the time of the loss, but not necessarily at the time that the insurance is arranged. An **insurable interest** is not confined to a strict legal right of property, but is any interest that would be recognized by a court of law or equity, such as possession of goods or the right to immediate possession. A contract of marine insurance, like all insurance contracts, is a contract of utmost good faith, meaning that the insured must disclose to the insurer, at the time the contract is made, every material circumstance that is known to the insured. A material circumstance is one that would influence the judgment of a prudent insurer on determining whether to issue the insurance and assessing the risk to determine the appropriate premium.

Settlement of Losses

Normally the insurer is liable for any loss caused by a peril that has been insured against. Any loss attributable to the willful misconduct of the insured will not be covered, nor losses caused by delay, ordinary wear and tear, leakage and breakage, inherent vice, or loss due to rats and vermin. Losses may be total or partial. A total loss occurs when the subject matter insured is destroyed or damaged so as to cease to be a thing of the kind insured, or where the insured is irretrievably deprived of the subject matter of the insurance. A unique characteristic of marine insurance is the concept of "average," which is used to indicate partial loss or damage. **General average** is unique to maritime carriage. It is a loss arising out of a voluntary and reasonable sacrifice made of any part of the cargo or of the ship in an attempt to prevent the loss of property or the ship, and made for the benefit of all persons with an interest. Examples of this include jettisoning part of the cargo, cutting away part of the ship, or incurring water damage as a result of fighting a fire. The law provides that a person who incurs a loss in such a situation is entitled to receive from the other interested person a pro rata contribution in respect of their loss. Because this can be a very difficult and complex calculation involving possibly hundreds of different shippers or consignees, the adjustment of such claims is carried out by general average adjusters. A **particular average** is a partial loss or damage that is not a general average loss. It is a partial loss suffered by a particular shipment from an accidental cause, not related to saving the ship or the contents of the ship. Marine insurance often does not cover partial losses, and these policies are described as free of particular average (FPA). The form of clause usually reads, "free of particular average unless the vessel is stranded, sunk, burnt, on fire, or in collision." This means that the insurance does not cover partial losses, unless caused by one of these particular causes mentioned. Marine insurance thus falls into three main types:

1. *free of particular average*, in which losses are recoverable only if the vessel has been stranded, sunk, burnt, or in a collision;
2. *with average*, in which partial damage is covered if it amounts to 3 percent of the value of the shipment; and
3. *all risks*, which protects against physical loss or damage from external causes but does not cover war, strikes, riots, or detention unless by special endorsement.

Subrogation

Under the principle of subrogation, once the insurer pays for a total loss, the insurer becomes entitled to assume the interest of the insured and may pursue all the rights and remedies of the insured and sue for any loss incurred.

NOTES

1 Readers will find the material provided by EDC helpful here. Go to www.edc.ca/english/bonding.htm and click on Performance Security Guarantee.

2 For an excellent discussion of this issue, see David J. Barru, "How to Guarantee Contractor Performance on International Construction Projects: Comparing Surety Bonds with Bank Guarantees and Standby Letters of Credit" (2005), 37 *Geo. Wash. Int'l Rev.* 51.

3 *Triglav v. Terrasses Jewellers Inc. et al.*, Supreme Court of Canada 1983.

REVIEW QUESTIONS

1. Describe the contractual relationships that are likely to result when a Canadian importer buys a sizeable quantity of consumer goods from a manufacturer in Hong Kong. Assume that the goods are being shipped from Hong Kong CIF to Halifax, and are being paid for by documentary credit.

2. Eastern Industries Ltd., a manufacturer/exporter in Canada, is entering into negotiations with Brazilian Telecom, a potential buyer/importer in Brazil. The product is subway cars. What contracts do you anticipate will arise if the negotiations are successful? Who will be a party to the contracts?

3. What is the difference between a confirming bank and an advising bank? What terms describes both these kinds of banks?

4. List at least 12 issues that must be addressed by parties negotiating payment by letter of credit.

5. What institution is responsible for developing internationally agreed-on rules governing letter of credit transactions? How recent is the current version of these rules?

6. Describe the differences between the usual documentary credit, a standby letter of credit, and a surety bond and describe a typical situation in which each would be most commonly found.

7. Describe the two fundamental characteristics of letter of credit transactions and describe the precautionary measures that you would take to avoid any losses due to these characteristics.

8. Describe the two important issues in the *Angelica* case and report how the Supreme Court of Canada decided upon each issue.

9. What was the major issue in the *Banco de Cuba* case and what is its contribution to our understanding of the Canadian law relating to documentary credit?

10. What is the role of a bill of exchange in a letter of credit arrangement? What is particularly significant about a negotiable instrument? What is a holder in due course and what rights does the holder have? What is the significance of this for the drawer, and the holder of the bill?

11. Give at least two reasons why it is important to have some knowledge of the differences among various forms of documentation issued by ocean carriers.

12. What are the three purposes that a bill of lading may have? How does an air waybill differ from a "traditional" bill of lading?

13. What particular legal issue arises as a result of electronic transmission of a bill of lading? Why is this knowledge important to international traders negotiating documentary credit transactions?

14. The liabilities of an ocean carrier are different from those of a surface or air carrier. What are the three main types of marine coverage and what do they insure against?

FURTHER READING

Documentary Credits

Baxter, Ian F.G. (1992). *Law of Banking*, 4th ed. Scarborough, ON: Carswell.

Busto, Charles del. (1994). *ICC Guide to Documentary Credit Operations for the UCP 500*. Pub. no. 515. New York: International Chamber of Commerce.

Institute of International Banking Law and Practice. (1998). *International Standby Practices ISP 98*. Pub. no. 590. New York: International Chamber of Commerce.

Schütze, Rolf A., and Fontane, Gabriele. (1998). *Documentary Credit Law Throughout the World*. Pub. no. 633. New York: International Chamber of Commerce.

Uniform Customs and Practice for Documentary Credits (UCP 500). (2002). Pub. no. 500-2. New York: International Chamber of Commerce.

Marine Insurance

Gold, E., Chircop, A., and Kindred, H. (2004). *Maritime Law*. Toronto: Irwin Law.

Strathy, G.R., and Moore, G.C. (2003). *The Law and Practice of Marine Insurance in Canada*. Markham, ON: LexisNexis Canada.

WEBSITES

International Chamber of Commerce:

www.iccwbo.org/policy/law
(information on commercial law and practice)

www.iccwbo.org/policy/banking
(information on banking technique and practice)

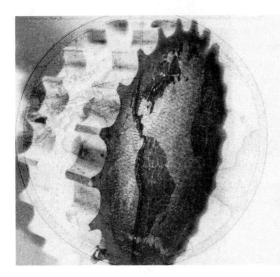

CHAPTER 9

Intellectual Property and International Business

INTRODUCTION

Intellectual property has been defined by the World Intellectual Property Organization (WIPO) as

> creations of the mind: inventions, literary and artistic works, and symbols, names, images, and designs used in commerce.

It is divided into two categories: Industrial property, which includes inventions (patents), trademarks, industrial designs, and geographic indications of source; and Copyright, which includes literary and artistic works such as novels, poems and plays, films, musical works, artistic works such as drawings, paintings, photographs and sculptures, and architectural designs. Rights related to copyright include those of performing artists in their performances, producers of phonograms in their recordings, and those of broadcasters in their radio and television programs.[1]

The breadth of this definition underscores the importance of intellectual property as a necessary component of economic growth and the financial success of businesses. In fact, many businesses expand into other countries by licensing intellectual property rights, and the proportion of world economic activity that is based on intellectual property is growing at an exponential rate.

Intellectual property reflects the work of the human mind, and because of its intangible nature, its legal protection is both important and sophisticated. This source of wealth is difficult to protect because information resources are not bound to a specific geographic location or jurisdiction, and are not easily controlled by governments whose jurisdiction is traditionally only within their own borders. As one writer has commented, "A person with the skills to write a complex software system can walk past any customs officer in the world with nothing of value to declare."[2]

Developed and developing countries have very different perspectives on the importance and appropriateness of protecting intellectual property. This makes the task of agreeing on common international rules very difficult. Because developing countries are not major producers of intellectual property, they have little incentive to protect this form of property. From their perspective, weak protection is desirable and justified because the developing world needs maximum access to intellectual property for its development. Many in developing countries believe that such knowledge is the "common heritage of humankind," and should be freely available to all. From the perspective of the developed world, information is a valuable resource upon which its economic well-being depends. For some developed countries, the licensing of intellectual property, or "transfer of technology," as it is often described, represents the major component of their income and it is expected that this trend will increase. It is generally accepted that without sufficient intellectual property protection on a global basis, international business will be limited, because creators will not be prepared to divulge any detailed information relating to their research and development to third parties for fear of losing their proprietary rights. The result would be less dissemination of ideas, fewer trading opportunities, and, ultimately, a poorer world. The task of developing an acceptable international intellectual property protection regime is a daunting one: negotiators from different countries must agree on what property will be protected and what limits or exceptions are acceptable on a multilateral basis. One example of this conflict relates to the extent of patent protection for the developers of drugs to treat HIV/AIDS. Many countries with high rates of HIV/AIDS among their citizens argue for limited patent protection so that generic drugs can be made available quickly to treat infected persons.

WORLD INTELLECTUAL PROPERTY ORGANIZATION

The World Intellectual Property Organization and the World Trade Organization (WTO) are the two major international organizations concerned with the protection of intellectual property rights. WIPO is the older of the two institutions, having been created in 1967 as a successor to earlier intellectual property bureaus. It is a specialized agency of the UN with a mandate to maintain and increase respect for intellectual property throughout the world. As part of this mandate, it administers the major international intellectual property agreements. Of the many agreements, the two broadest and most important are the Paris Convention for the Protection of Industrial Property (protection of patents and trademarks), and the Berne Convention for the Protection of Literary and Artistic Works (protection of copyright). WIPO's activities fall into three areas:

- registration of intellectual property rights ownership;
- promotion of intergovernmental cooperation on intellectual property; and
- provision of legal and technical assistance to countries to enhance intellectual property rights protection.

The treaties that WIPO administers fall into three groups:

- treaties that establish international protection, such as the Paris Convention (patents and trademarks), the Madrid Agreement (trademarks), the Lisbon Agreement (appellations of origin), and the Berne Convention (performers, phonograms, and broadcasting);
- treaties that facilitate international protection, such as the Patent Cooperation Treaty (PCT), the Madrid Agreement, and the Lisbon Agreement; and
- treaties that establish classification systems, such as the International Patent Classification Agreement and the Nice Agreement.

THE WTO AND INTELLECTUAL PROPERTY

The Agreement on Trade-Related Aspects of Intellectual Property Rights

The Agreement on Trade-Related Aspects of Intellectual Property Rights (TRIPS Agreement) builds on existing multilateral treaties for the protection of intellectual property; where these treaties provide adequate protection, their standards form the basis for some of TRIPS's substantive provisions.

One of the most important achievements of the Uruguay Round was the conclusion of the TRIPS Agreement. During the protracted negotiations in this round, the issue of intellectual property protection contributed to the seven years of deadlock. A satisfactory outcome on this issue was very high on the agenda of the United States for which intellectual property is a particularly valuable resource. Developing countries, on the other hand, had little interest in ensuring better protection for intellectual property, and indeed many perceived that their interests were best served by resisting attempts at better global protection for this form of property.

In spite of the conflict, the TRIPS Agreement was negotiated and agreed on. For the first time in the history of the world trading system (the GATT contained no rules on intellectual property protection), countries must undertake to abide by comprehensive rules for the protection of intellectual property rights. These rules set minimum standards for the protection and enforcement of intellectual property rights in the areas of

- patents,
- trademarks,
- copyright and related rights,
- geographical indications,
- industrial designs, and
- layout designs of integrated circuits.

All members of the WTO agreed to comply with the standards by providing for them in national legislation within the time periods prescribed in the agreement. These time periods were shorter for developed countries, and longer for developing countries. The general principles of the agreement include a commitment to national treatment, and most-favoured-nation treatment. This agreement established a comprehensive intellectual property regime standardizing both substance and procedure on a global basis. The agreement represents a significant departure from the previous situation, which left the substance and procedure for protection up to each sovereign nation with the result that intellectual property rights varied enormously from one country to another. The agreement provides for broader intellectual property protection by ensuring national treatment, establishing minimum terms for protection, imposing significant local enforcement and dispute settlement requirements, and authorizing trade sanctions against non-compliant nations.

Settlement of Intellectual Property Disputes under the WTO

The TRIPS Agreement established a Council for Trade-Related Aspects of Intellectual Property Rights to monitor and manage administrative issues surrounding the agreement, ensure member compliance, and provide assistance to members in dispute settlement matters. Importantly, the TRIPS Agreement now falls within the Dispute Settlement Understanding of the WTO, rather than the previously applicable WIPO arrangements. This provision for the integration of intellectual property dispute settlement within the overall world trade dispute settlement mechanism was an important step and indicative of the importance of intellectual property in the world trading system.

PATENTS

The Defining Characteristics of a Patent

The development of an equitable patent protection regime represents a challenge, because a patent is essentially a compromise. The need to encourage and reward innovation must be balanced against the necessity of ensuring that innovation will benefit a society as a whole. While it is important to reward and encourage innovation, it is also important to ensure that ideas are diffused for the common good.

A patent is an exclusive right granted for an invention, which is a product or a process that provides a new way of doing something, or offers a new technical solution to a problem. In order to be patentable, the invention must fulfill the following conditions:

- It must have an element of novelty—that is, some new characteristic, or one that is not presently known in the body of existing knowledge (sometimes referred to as "prior art").
- The invention must show an inventive step that could not be deduced by a person with average knowledge of the technical field.
- The subject matter of the invention must be patentable under law. This varies because in some countries scientific theories, mathematical formulas, plant or animal varieties, discoveries of natural substances, commercial methods, or methods of medical treatment (as opposed to medical products) are not patentable.

Ideas cannot be patented, and theoretically they belong to everyone. It is when we attempt to apply this principle that difficult questions may arise. It is easy to state that mathematical models and scientific theories are not patentable because they are ideas. However, the techniques that spring from these ideas are patentable in certain countries. For example, in the United States, surgical techniques are patentable, but not in Canada. There are also serious issues that arise with respect to "business methods" (that is, the exclusive right to a particular way of doing business). They are patentable in the United States, but in Canada business methods must meet certain criteria in order to be patentable. The Canadian Patent Office has issued guidelines that state that to be patentable a business method must be performed by some physical agent upon some physical object and produce on such object some change either of character or condition, and must produce an essentially economic result in relation to trade, industry, or commerce. Thus, in Canada, a business method must have a relationship with a physical object such as a computer. For example, a computer method or system that is directed to a "useful" end result has been considered to be patentable. This is illustrated by a case decided by the Federal Court of Canada, which found that a software program that was a method of playing poker was patentable as it (1) had a commercially useful result, (2) was a practical application of an idea, and (3) was a new and innovative method of applying a skill or knowledge.[3] Similarly, there is a principle in Canada and in other countries that naturally occurring substances are not patentable. For example, US and EU authorities recently overturned patents on the medicinal use of the turmeric spice and the neem plant after India helped establish that the plants' medicinal properties were already widely known in that country. The issue of patenting organisms that have been modified is one that was faced by courts having to decide whether the "Harvard Mouse," a genetically altered mouse developed specifically for cancer research, was patentable. The mouse has received patent protection in the United States and Europe, but the Supreme Court of Canada rejected a patent claim on the mouse itself. It did, however, recognize a patent on the mouse's genes—a decision that had the same effect of protecting the owner of the invention. A similar issue arose in the *Schmeiser v. Monsanto* case decided by the Supreme Court of Canada (see box 9.1).

Obtaining a Patent

Patent protection is usually for a period of 20 years, and provides the patent owner with the exclusive right to make, use, distribute, or sell the patent rights. The patent owner may grant permission or a right to a third party to use the rights. This is referred to as a licence. Once a patent expires, the protection ends, and the invention enters the public domain, and the owner no longer has exclusive rights to the invention. A patent is granted by a national patent office or by a regional office established by a multilateral treaty or agreement among countries. There is, at present, no such thing as a world or international patent. The process of obtaining a patent therefore involves filing an application in each country in which patent protection is desired, or a

BOX 9.1   SCHMEISER v. MONSANTO
(Supreme Court of Canada, 2004)

This was a difficult case for the Court and the judges were not unanimous in their decision with 5 judges in favour of the plaintiff and 4 dissenting.

Monsanto, an agricultural company, sued farmer Percy Schmeiser for collecting and using seeds of Monsanto's patented Roundup Ready canola without paying the licensing fee to Monsanto. Roundup Ready seeds are engineered to survive the herbicide Roundup, making weed control for canola crops much easier. Schmeiser's neighbours had paid for and planted the Monsanto seeds, and some of these seeds blew onto Schmeiser's land, where they germinated and survived. Schmeiser claimed to be an innocent bystander merely collecting seeds from his own crop and re-planting them the next year.

The Court found that Schmeiser had deliberately cultivated, segregated, and bagged Monsanto's seeds and sowed them. It found that through his husbandry, he acquired over 1,000 acres of Roundup Ready canola, which would otherwise have cost him $15,000. The Court found in favour of Monsanto on the ground that Schmeiser was not an "innocent" bystander, although, as Justice Louise Arbour wrote in her dissent: "a truly innocent infringer may be able to rebut the presumption of use."

regional office, if available. As of February 2004, a new WIPO system allows firms and inventors to file requests for global patent protection by electronic mail. Managed by the UN's copyright and patent agency, the applications may be filed in almost any language. Prior to the creation of this electronic system, applications had to be filed on paper.

Procedural and substantive requirements and fees may vary from one country to another, but generally the patent application will describe the invention, indicate its technical field, and include the background and a description of the invention clearly and in enough detail that an individual with an average understanding of the field could use or reproduce the invention. Such descriptions are usually accompanied by visual material and contain the claims that will determine the extent of protection of the patent. The first step taken before a patent is filed is a search of the relevant national and regional databases to determine that an application has not been pre-empted by a prior patent application. This is a highly specialized process, and it is recommended that a patent seeker consult a lawyer who specializes in intellectual property or the intellectual property offices of the countries in which the patent seeker wishes to obtain patent protection.

International Patent Protection Prior to TRIPS

The Paris Convention

International harmonization of domestic legislation on patent protection began more than 100 years ago in 1883 with the adoption of the Paris Convention. This Convention requires members to protect inventions and trademarks and to take effective measures to prevent unfair competition. More than 100 nations belong to this Convention, which, while stressing the independence of national patent systems and the territorial limitations of rights granted under these national systems, sets out some basic norms, including the principle of national treatment, the right of priority, the prohibition of the forfeiture of a patent because of importation of the patented product, and time limits. Under the Paris convention, a separate filing must be made in each country; however, priority is given to an application filed in any member country within one year from the date on which an application is initially filed in any other member country. The weakness of this Convention was that it laid down few substantive rules on what could be patented, and it did not provide rules with respect to minimum term of protection or the exclusive rights to be conferred on owners. The result of this laxity was that countries were free to exclude certain inventions to serve their interests. For example, a number of less-developed countries excluded pharmaceuticals from patent protection. The Paris Convention has not been revised since 1979.

The Patent Cooperation Treaty

It is important to understand that the Patent Cooperation Treaty (PCT) is a treaty that *facilitates* international patent protection. It does not *establish* international patent protection. The importance of this treaty, established in 1970, is that it provides member countries with a centralized procedure for filing an international patent application in which the applicant can designate the member countries in which protection is sought. This was a significant improvement over the previous situation where an applicant had to file a separate foreign application for each individual country. Instead of a number of separate foreign applications, only one international application is filed, saving costs associated with multiple filings and ensuring that one common filing date is obtained. The application is filed and is automatically subjected to an international search by a WIPO-designated International Searching Authority. Then, once the search report is received, the applicant can make its final decision on whether or not to pursue foreign patent protection in the designated countries. An applicant under the PCT has 30 months to make that decision from the date of the initial filing, unlike the Paris Convention (described above) where the decision must be made within 12 months.

TRIPS Patent Provisions

The establishment of the WTO and the conclusion of the TRIPS Agreement dramatically changed the landscape with respect to global protection of intellectual property rights. All members of the WTO are now obliged to abide by comprehensive rules for protecting intellectual property. As we know, the Paris Convention laid down very few rules, and there was no requirement for members of the GATT to ratify the Paris Convention. The TRIPS Agreement thus represented an important victory for developed countries such as the United States, members of the European Union, and Japan, who wished to protect valuable sectors of their economies. The TRIPS Agreement (Article 27(1)) requires member states to make patent protection available for

> any inventions, whether products or processes, in all fields of technology, provided they are new, involve an inventive step and are capable of industrial application. Patents shall be available and patent rights enjoyable without discrimination as to the place of invention, the field of technology and whether products are imported or locally produced.

According to Article 33, patents under TRIPS must be granted for a term of at least 20 years from the application filing date. Patents must confer on their owners the exclusive rights to prevent third parties from making, using, offering for sale, selling, or importing patented products without consent (Article 28). There are, however, some limits to this protection:

- protection of the undisclosed information for the purpose of obtaining government approval of the patents;
- protection is to be applied in a manner conducive to social and economic welfare and a balance of rights and obligations; and
- protection does not apply where a necessary action is taken in time of war or other emergency in international relations, or for the maintenance of international peace and security.

In addition, the TRIPS Agreement includes provisions that allow members to permit parallel imports, and to authorize use of the patented invention without the patent owner's consent (known as compulsory licensing). However, these provisions are restricted by Article 30:

> [T]hese limitations must not unreasonably conflict with a normal exploitation of the patent and not unreasonably prejudice the legitimate interests of the patent owner, taking account of the legitimate interests of third parties.

This phrase was considered by a WTO dispute settlement panel in a case involving Canadian provisions for pharmaceuticals (see box 9.2).

> **BOX 9.2   CANADA AND PATENT PROTECTION OF PHARMACEUTICAL PRODUCTS: BOLAR PROVISIONS (WTO panel, 2000)**
>
> Canada passed legislative provisions described as **Bolar provisions**, making an exception to patent rights on certain pharmaceuticals. The provisions allowed generic drug manufacturers to engage in the pre-marketing, testing, and stockpiling of generic drugs before the expiration of the patent period. The WTO Dispute Settlement Body found that the pre-marketing testing provision, which allowed generic manufacturers to conduct the tests needed to prepare their products for regulatory approval during the term of the patent, and thus enabling them to market the generic products immediately on expiration of the patent, was not inconsistent with the TRIPS Agreement, but the stockpiling provision was a violation of the agreement.

Patent Protection in Individual Countries

Patent Protection in Canada

Fundamental changes were made to Canada's *Patent Act* in order to modernize Canada's patent system and enable Canada to ratify the PCT. This legislation became effective in 1989. Some features of the amended *Patent Act* are:

- *The change from a "first-to-invent" to a "first-to-file" system.* This brings Canada's legislation into line with most other industrialized countries. Under the first-to-file system, when two or more applications for the same invention are pending at the time the patent is granted, the patent is granted to the person who was the first to file an application.
- *A requirement for "absolute novelty."* This requirement avoids situations in which people attempt to patent inventions that are already in the public domain.
- *An early publication system.* Under the old system, the Patent Office made the contents of a patent application available to the public only *after* the patent was granted. The reason behind this change is the desire to make new technology available to business as quickly as possible.
- *Protection for the inventor.* The patent holder can sue for reasonable compensation for any infringement that occurs, beginning from the date the application is opened (assuming the patent is granted). Furthermore, to protect an inventor in a situation where someone learns

of the invention and files for the patent independently, there is a rule that only an inventor is entitled to a patent. Therefore, provided the true inventor can prove in a court of law that the invention is his or hers, he or she is protected.

- *A system of maintenance fees.* In order to keep the patent in effect, a maintenance fee is payable annually. If the patent holder decides to discontinue the maintenance fee, the patent will lapse.
- *Deferred examination.* The Patent Office will not examine applications until requested to do so up to a maximum of seven years. This is intended to give inventors more time to assess the marketability of their inventions.

Patent Protection in the United States

As Canada's biggest market for goods and services, the American patent provisions are of immense importance to Canadians because it is common for a Canadian inventor to protect his or her property in that important market. US patent law is significantly different from patent law in Canada and the European Union. To protect an invention in the United States, a Canadian inventor must obtain a US patent. A US patent cannot be enforced outside of the United States. Two significant differences between the US system and that of Canada and the European Union are:

- The US system is a first-to-invent system. Where there are competing patent applications for the same invention, the United States awards the patent to the person or organization that can show it was the first to invent.
- The US system allows a grace period between disclosure of the invention and the formal filing date. This grace period allows companies to assess market interest in the invention before applying for patent protection. This is unique to the United States and does not apply in Canada or the European Union. In fact, divulging details of a patent in the United States before the patent is filed in Canada or the European Union can destroy a patent application in the other jurisdictions.

In 1999, the United States made some changes to its patent law to allow ratification of the PCT,[4] but just enough to make it possible for US patentees to participate in the international system; it was unwilling to change its basic patent regime to conform to that of most of the rest of the world. Patents in the United States have a normal life of 17 years, but there are a number of provisions that make it possible for patent holders to extend the life of the patent beyond this period.

Patent Protection in the European Union

Two important characteristics of the EU patent system are that it is a first-to-file system, like Canada and unlike the United States. The second important characteristic is that enforcement of the patent is still carried out in individual EU countries. Thus, there is no single pan-European patent system, because protection must still be obtained in each member country. The PCT and the regional European Patent Organization do, however, provide procedures and processes that simplify the patent filing process in the European Union. Typically, non-EU owners decide to take out patents in large EU markets such as Germany, the United Kingdom, France, and Italy. Although many people have advocated the adoption of a single European patent, member countries have, so far, been unable to agree on the details of a European patent system. One important area of disagreement is the choice of which languages may be used in patent applications.

Once a decision is made to file for patents in the European Union, inventors may:

- file directly with the national patent office in individual member states;
- apply for patent protection through the European Patent System (the European Patent Organization's European Patent Office); or
- apply for patent protection through the International Patent System (established under the PCT and administered by WIPO).

TRADEMARKS

Characteristics of a Trademark

A trademark is a distinctive sign, word, name, device, or any combination of these that identifies certain goods or services as those produced or provided by a specific person or enterprise. A trademark provides protection to the owner of the mark by ensuring the exclusive right to use it to identify the goods and services, and hinders the efforts of unfair competitors to use similar distinctive marks to market inferior or different products or services.

International Trademark Protection

Almost all countries in the world register and protect trademarks. National offices in various countries maintain a register of trademarks and provide the opportunity to register and renew, examine, search, and oppose a trademark application. Registration is effective only for the country in which it is made.

The Madrid System for International Registration of Marks

This registration system was established in 1891 and functions under the Madrid Agreement of the same year and the Madrid Protocol of 1989. It is administered by the International Bureau of WIPO located in Geneva, Switzerland. A number of countries, including Japan, the United Kingdom, and the United States, have not ratified the Madrid Agreement because it requires that an applicant obtain a home registration before filing an international application and provides a short examination period for national trademark offices to consider incoming international applications. The Madrid Protocol, however, allows countries that are not members of the Madrid Agreement to adhere to the Madrid system of international registration, allows the filing of international applications at the same time as home applications, and gives member countries up to 18 months to consider applications. Under the Madrid system a trademark owner may file one application directly with his or her own national trademark office, designating the countries in which registration is desired. The application must contain a clear reproduction of the sign filed for registration, including any colours, forms, or three-dimensional features. The application must also contain a list of goods or services to which the sign would apply. The rights applied for cannot be the same as, or similar to, rights already granted to another trademark owner. A search and examination is conducted by each national office designated by the applicant, and if there are no similar or identical rights previously granted, and if there is no opposition to the trademark by third parties, registration will be granted in each of the designated countries. The international mark so registered is equivalent to an application or registration effected directly in each of the countries designated by the applicant. This system greatly simplifies both the initial application for a mark and also subsequent changes or renewals of registration. More than 68 countries have become parties to the Madrid Protocol, including the members of the European Union, the United States, and the United Kingdom.

Unfortunately, Canada is not a party to this system and Canadian trademark applicants cannot enjoy its advantages. This situation reflects the fact that Canada's position on trademarks is ambivalent because we are a net importer of trademarks, and for us the Protocol could serve as a vehicle for multinationals to flood the Canadian registry with applications for defensive purposes. One result of Canada's position, however, is the fact that it puts Canadian-based applicants for copyright in other countries at a disadvantage because the rights they can secure abroad can be no greater than what the applicant may secure in its home country.

The Nice Classification System

This is a list of over 10,000 goods and services, categorized into 34 classes of goods and 8 classes of services, developed to help determine whether a chosen mark might be registered and used in any particular field of activity. This uniform classification system for the registration of marks was made official in 1957, at a diplomatic conference in Nice, which adopted the "Nice Agreement concerning the International Classification of Goods and Services to which Trademarks are applied." The agreement has been revised since 1957 and, as of January 1, 1995, the countries that are parties to the Nice Agreement are known as the "Nice Union." The classification system is used by the Madrid Agreement parties and by over 50 other countries that are party to neither Nice nor Madrid.

The Paris Convention

The Paris Convention was discussed earlier in the context of patent protection. This Convention also applies to trademarks and establishes fundamental concepts to be enjoyed by trademark owners in member countries around the world. With respect to trademarks, the two fundamental provisions are the requirement for national treatment and the creation of the "priority right." The latter allowed a single first filing for a trademark in one member country to establish a filing date that would be effective in other member countries. A condition for this is that subsequent filings in other countries must be effected within six months of the original priority date. Thus, the only priority date is the first date upon which an application for the mark is made in any member country in the world. Canada is a signatory to the Paris Convention.

TRIPS Provisions on Trademarks

The TRIPS Agreement defines what types of signs are eligible for protection and the minimum rights conferred on owners. Trademarks may be one or a combination of words, letters, and numerals or they may consist of drawings, symbols, three-dimensional signs, shapes, packaging, sounds, fragrances, or colours, provided these are used as distinguishing features.

Trademark Protection in Individual Countries

Trademark Protection in Canada

Trademarks may be filed in Canada based on the following: prior use of the trademark in Canada; proposed use in Canada, or a prior application for registration of the mark in a foreign country that is a party to the Paris Convention. A Canadian applicant can initiate trademark filings in other signatory countries with a single application in Canada. Acceptance of the mark for registration, however, requires the filing of a statement of actual use of the mark in Canada. The application period under the Paris Convention is six months from the date of the first Paris Convention filing. A registered trademark in Canada gives the owner the exclusive right to its use in Canada for 15 years from the date of registration and this right may be renewed every 15 years without limitation. A trademark may be cancelled for non-use, but not if the owner can furnish evidence of use at any time during the three years preceding the notice of cancellation proceedings.

An interesting trademark case in Canada illustrating the limitations of trademark protection is the *Barbie* case (see box 9.3).

It is important to note that in Canada, as in the United States, we recognize a priority right arising on first use of a trademark, but this right can be defeated by a foreign applicant who seeks a Canadian registration based on a foreign priority right. Canada and the United States impose as a precondition to a trademark registration by their nationals the requirement that a mark must be "used" in the country in order for a trademark registration to issue. This creates problems with multiple international filings because the obvious reason for filing is to reserve the right to use a mark in a market in

---

BOX 9.3   MATTELL INC. v. BARBIE'S RESTAURANTS
(Supreme Court of Canada, 2006)

A small Montreal restaurant chain named Barbie's tried to register its name for use across the country in the restaurant, takeout, and catering business. The name had been chosen by the proprietors of the restaurant in 1992 as a play on words because the restaurant sells barbequed food. Mattell Inc., the toy manufacturer, challenged the registration on the grounds that Mattell had the exclusive right to use the Barbie name.

The Court ruled unanimously, 8–0, that Barbie's restaurant could register the name.

The Court found that Mattell does not have the exclusive right to use the Barbie name. It stated that while Barbie has achieved a distinctiveness within the doll world, that does not give Mattell the right to prevent very different businesses from using the name. The Court observed that the two businesses occupy entirely different "channels of trade" and deal with largely different clienteles. It found that there was unlikely to be any confusion in the minds of consumers as to any possible connection between the source or any association between a doll marketed to little girls and a restaurant whose clientele is exclusively adults.

which it is not yet in use. Anticipating this situation, the Paris Convention requires member countries to register a mark nationally without imposing a requirement of use if the applicant has already obtained a registration in the applicant's home country for the same mark. Because the phrase "country of origin" is loosely applied to mean any country where the applicant has a real and effective establishment, a foreign registration can be obtained by relying on registrations already obtained in any other country of the Paris Union where a company maintains an office. Thus a foreign applicant actually has an advantage over Canadian and US nationals in their own country. This is because they can become registered without the need of actually using the trademark. Remember that trademark filings are still subject to the procedure and substantive law of each country in which registration is sought.

Trademark Protection in the United States

As noted above, the United States has ratified the Madrid Protocol, so its trademark applicants have the advantage of that system. A trademark in the United States can be registered based on the applicant's intention to use the mark. The mark must then be used within six months although it is possible to extend this period. Trademark owners must be cautious because a non-use during the initial two-year period following registration gives rise to a presumption of abandonment and shifts the burden of proof of use of the mark to the trademark owner. The life of a trademark in the United States is 10 years, but re-registration is available at the end of the 10-year term, provided there is evidence of prior use.

COPYRIGHT

Characteristics of Copyright

Copyright is defined as the right to produce or reproduce a work that can be fixed in a tangible medium for the purpose of communication. A copyright owner is the only person who may produce or reproduce his or her work or permit someone else to do so. It has been suggested that copyright has become the intellectual property right of primary importance in the Internet age.[5] Governments are faced with the challenge of balancing the rights of creators with the rights of Internet users.

Copyright protects the author's form of creative expression, but not the ideas expressed by the author. The laws of almost all countries provide that copyright protection automatically begins as soon as the work is created. It is, however, advisable to register copyright in any work having commercial value.

International Protection of Copyright

The Berne Convention

Primarily a creation of civil law negotiators, the Berne Convention is one of the two major copyright conventions. Under this Convention an author does not have to register a work in order for it to be protected. However, registration establishes the date for the copyright and the content of the material in the event of a future dispute. This Convention first came into effect in 1887, and now has more than 80 members, including Canada, the United States (only since 1988), the United Kingdom, Japan, and China. Revisions to this Convention have been made regularly. The Convention establishes a "union" of countries that are responsible for protecting artistic rights. Fundamental principles of this convention include:

- agreed-upon minimum standards for copyright;
- reduction of formalities required for copyright to be established, although the country of origin may make protection conditional on registration or contract;
- protection of moral rights of authors;
- the principle of national treatment—that is, works of foreign authors must receive as favourable treatment as do the works of authors who are nationals;
- protection is independent of protection in the country of origin—thus authors who are nationals of non-member countries may obtain protection within the Berne Union by publishing their work in a member country;
- rules for minimum standards for granting copyright that are common to all member states; and
- minimum duration of copyright for a written work is the life of the author plus 50 years.

The Universal Copyright Convention

The Universal Copyright Convention came into force in 1952, and was revised in 1971. It came into being largely as a response to the failure of the Berne Convention to obtain universal acceptance. (Note that the United States did not join the Berne Convention until 1998.) The rules of the Universal Copyright Convention are less strict than those of the Berne Convention. Under the Universal Copyright Convention, members may establish formalities (or their own additional requirements) as a prerequisite for protection and to make exceptions to the common rules, provided the exceptions are consistent with the spirit of the Convention. The principles of national treatment and protection independent of protection in the country of origin are maintained. Because many countries are members of both conventions, special rules were included to resolve any conflicts between the obligations of the two. In the case of conflict between two countries that are both members of both conventions, the provisions of the Berne Convention will prevail. It is unlikely that the Universal Copyright Convention will be revised again because there are simply too many different interests to achieve consensus on revision, and the momentum for change in this area is with WIPO.

The Rome Convention

The Rome Convention, agreed to in 1961, protects live performances, recordings, and broadcasting. It prohibits the unauthorized recording of live performances, the unauthorized reproduction of recordings, and the unauthorized rebroadcast of broadcasts. A later agreement, the Phonogram Privacy Agreement, signed in 1971, provides protection to performers, producers of phonograms, and broadcasting organizations against unauthorized duplication of their phonograms.

TRIPS Provisions on Copyright

The Berne Convention became the foundation for the 1994 TRIPS Agreement on copyright.[6] Parties to the WTO are required to comply with the substantive provisions of this Convention in its latest version, with the exception that not all are obliged to protect moral rights[7] as stipulated in Article 6b of the Convention. An important innovation of TRIPS was to provide that computer programs would be protected as literary works under the Berne Convention and to set out the criteria necessary for databases to be protected by copyright. Other important additions related to rental rights and protection from unauthorized recording and broadcasts. Two important additional treaties have been negotiated under the auspices of TRIPS: the WIPO Copyright Treaty and the WIPO Performances and Phonograms Treaty. Each of these treaties creates substantial new intellectual property protection for digital technology and Internet software and have given rise to the phrase "digital rights management,"[8] (also called "electronic rights management," and called "technological protection measures"[9] in Europe). These treaties prevent or restrict acts not authorized by the rights holders and require parties to protect pre-existing works that have not fallen into the public domain in the country of origin from other member countries. This is an obligation that is also contained in both the Berne Convention and the TRIPS Agreement. Each of these treaties was negotiated in 1996, but did not come into force until the requisite number of ratifications occurred in 2002.

WIPO COPYRIGHT TREATY

The WIPO Copyright Treaty (WCT), in force as of 2002, raised global minimum standards for copyright protection, largely at the insistence of negotiators from the United States. Under Article 11, member states are required to provide

> adequate legal protection and effective legal remedies against the circumvention of effective technological measures that are used by authors in connection with the exercise of their rights under this Treaty or the Berne Convention and that restrict acts, in respect of their works, which are not authorized by the authors concerned or permitted by law.

Thus, under Article 12, any person commits an offence who knowingly

- removes or alters any electronic rights management information without authority, or
- distributes, imports for distribution, broadcasts, or distributes to the public works or copies of works knowing that electronic rights management information has been removed or altered without authority.

In addition, Article 12 of the Treaty requires member states "to provide adequate and effective legal remedies against any person who knowingly commits the above offence."

WIPO PERFORMANCES AND PHONOGRAMS TREATY

The WIPO Performances and Phonograms Treaty (WPPT), in force as of 2002, protects the intellectual property rights of performers and producers of phonograms (devices for the fixation of sounds and aural performances). The Treaty extends to four kinds of rights: the right of reproduction, of distribution, of rental, and of making performances available. The term of the protection is at least 50 years and the Treaty obliges contracting states to provide legal remedies against circumvention of technological measures used to protect these rights.

It has been observed that these two WIPO treaties (WCT and WPPT) marked the beginning of a strategy by the United States to improve the property rights of copyright owners to a level beyond that specified in the TRIPS Agreement, and in effect, to use international law as domestic leverage to achieve results that might not have been achievable in the more open debate of congressional hearings.[10] (See discussion of the US *Digital Millennium Copyright Act*, below.)

It is important to remember that these provisions are treaty provisions only; they do not become law in any specific country unless that country's government passes legislation making the treaty provisions part of domestic law.

Copyright Protection in Individual Countries

Copyright Protection in Canada

Copyright generally is protected in Canada under the federal *Copyright Act*. The Act provides that the author of a work shall be the first owner of the copyright to the work and these rights have a life of 50 years after the author's death. Creators of works can assign or license others to copy their work. Infringement of copyright occurs when someone uses or assists in using copyrighted material without the owner's consent. Remedies for copyright infringement are similar to those for breach of contract and include damages, an accounting to disclose profits made by illegal use, and, where appropriate, an injunction to restrain violation of the copyright. There is also provision for criminal penalties under the *Copyright Act.*

Although Canada negotiated and agreed to the two WIPO treaties, it has so far failed to ratify them because the relevant domestic laws have not yet been passed. In 2005, the Canadian government introduced Bill C-60, which was an attempt to bring Canadian legislation into conformity with the WIPO Copyright Treaty and enable Canada's ratification. The legislation failed to pass in the House of Commons and was criticized by both creators and users. Creators as owners, particularly the recording industry and entertainment lobbies, saw the legislation as too weak and insufficiently similar to the US legislation (see below). Advocates of file sharing and open source access, on the other hand, saw the legislation as being too restrictive of rights of free expression by users.[11] The result is that Canada has not been in a position to ratify the WIPO 2002 treaties, and is said to be behind Europe and the United States in recognizing and protecting technology protection measures.

Copyright Protection in the United States

As mentioned, the United States took the lead in the negotiations for the two new WIPO treaties and was one of the first countries to pass domestic legislation to implement the provisions of the treaties. The *Digital Millennium Copyright Act* (DMCA) was signed into law in 1998 and creates two new prohibitions: the first on circumvention of technological measures used by copyright owners to protect their works, and the second on tampering with copyright management information. These obligations serve as technological adjuncts to the exclusive rights granted by copyright law. They provide the legal protection that the international copyright community wanted for the safe and efficient exploitation of works on digital networks. The measures are divided into two categories: measures that prevent unauthorized *access* to a copyrighted work, and measures that prevent unauthorized *copying* of a copyrighted work. Making or selling devices or services that are used to circumvent either category of technological measure is prohibited except for a small category of fair-use circumstances, including law enforcement; intelligence and other government activities; non-profit library, archive, and educational institutional use; reverse engineering; encryption research; protection of minors; personal privacy; and security testing. Each of these exceptions has its own set of conditions as to their applicability in specified circumstances. The US legislation makes it a criminal offence to violate the substantive provisions of the DMCA and provides for civil actions in federal court that can result in a range of equitable and monetary remedies.

Copyright Protection in Europe
Europe adopted the norms of the WIPO Copyright Treaty by passing Directive 2001/29/EC, which requires the harmonization of the national copyright laws of all member states, especially with respect to online and digital use of copyrighted works. As you will remember from our discussion about the European Union, an EU directive does not create provisions to which citizens of individual countries normally appeal to directly, but rather addresses the legislative bodies of each member state and obliges them to implement the norms dictated in the directive into local legislation. The provisions in individual member states will not be identical; they must, however, achieve a common result. The directive addresses copyrighted material such as texts, music, and films and excludes software from its scope. The directive requires member states to protect technological measures that prevent copyright infringement—that is, any measure that allows the rights holder to control the use of a work. In addition, the directive requires laws prohibiting the manufacture, distribution, and sale of devices or services that are for the purpose of circumvention. There are a number of potential exemptions (26 in all). The major ones relate to reproductions made by public libraries, schools, and museums; reproductions for teaching or for scientific research; uses for the benefit of people with a disability; and uses for public security or administrative or judicial procedures.

PROTECTION OF COMPUTER SOFTWARE AND INTEGRATED CIRCUIT TOPOGRAPHIES

What Are Integrated Circuit Topographies?
Semiconductor integrated circuits are at the very heart of modern information, communications, entertainment, manufacturing, medical, and space technologies. Integrated circuit products are constructed from a complex series of layers of semiconductors, metals, insulators, and other materials on a

substrate. The three-dimensional configuration of these layers is referred to as an "integrated circuit topography." Thus, the Canadian legislation is entitled the *Integrated Circuit Topography Act* and provides protection to owners against the copying of their registered topographies, but does not prevent others from developing integrated circuit products that use other topographies to provide the same electronic functions. Some integrated circuit products, such as random access memory (RAM) and read only memory (ROM), may be used to store sets of instructions for electronic processors. These sets of instructions may be subject to protection under the *Copyright Act*, and may in some cases be patentable as industrial methods. Other aspects of integrated circuit products may also be patentable, such as the structure and method of operation of electronic circuits embodied in integrated circuit products, or industrial processes used to manufacture integrated circuit products. This is a highly specialized subject and not one that can be adequately covered in a general review such as this. Businesses whose products fall into these categories should ensure that they obtain qualified and current legal advice regarding the protection of these products, because the law is adapting rapidly to the demand for protection of this type of property, and the law can vary widely from one country to another.

Protection in Canada

The *Integrated Circuit Topography Act* was passed in 1993. This legislation protects the original design of a registered topography, whether embodied in an integrated circuit product or not. A topography must qualify as original—that is, it must be developed through the application of intellectual effort, and not be produced by the mere reproduction of all of, or a substantial part of, another topography.

The *Integrated Circuit Topography Act* provides owners of registered topographies exclusive statutory rights to exclude others from

- reproducing a protected topography or a substantial portion thereof;
- manufacturing an integrated circuit product that incorporates the topography of a registered topography; and
- importing or commercially exploiting a product that embodies a protected topography.

Topographies are protected for up to 10 years from the date of the application for registration. The exclusive rights are subject to some exceptions. Three of the most significant are:

- Once there is a legitimate sale of the product, the topography owner has no statutory right to control its use, rental, resale, or redistribution. This exhaustion of rights exception applies to products legitimately put on the market anywhere in the world with the authorization of the owner of the rights.

- Unauthorized copying of a protected topography is allowed if it is for the sole purpose of analysis or evaluation or for the sole purpose of research or teaching relating to the topography.
- Reverse engineering is permitted. This is the process of taking apart an integrated circuit to design a new and original topography.

The remedies provided by the legislation include injunctions, damages, and punitive damages. If a Canadian court concludes that there has been an importation of an integrated circuit product in contravention of the legislation, Customs authorities may stop the entry of the product.

Protection in Other Countries

Protection in other countries is very important if significant market opportunities are foreseen, or where significant foreign competitors have manufacturing facilities. More than 20 countries currently have protection for semiconductor chips. These countries include the United States, Japan, Australia, and those of the European Union, where the protection of technological measures that are applied to software products is governed by Directive 91/250/EEC. Canada has negotiated reciprocal rights for nationals and residents of Canada in countries that offer protection comparable to that of Canada. At present reciprocal rights exist for Canadians in the United States, Switzerland, Japan, and Australia.

INDUSTRIAL DESIGNS

An industrial design is the ornamental or aesthetic aspect of an article. The design may comprise three-dimensional features, such as the shape or surface of an article, or comprise two-dimensional features, such as patterns, lines, or colour. The industrial design must appeal to the eye. Because industrial designs add to the commercial value of a product and increase its marketability, many countries provide the design owner protection against unauthorized copying or imitation of the design. In most countries the industrial design must be registered in order to be protected and must be new or original. The term of protection is generally 5 years, renewable for further periods up to, in most cases, 15 years. Depending on the country and the character of the design, it may also be protected under copyright law or competition law.

The Hague Agreement Concerning the International Deposit of Industrial Designs provides a procedure for the international registration of an industrial design. The Agreement allows an applicant to file a single international deposit either with WIPO or the national office of their country, provided it is a party to the WIPO Copyright Treaty.

GEOGRAPHICAL INDICATIONS

What Is a Geographical Indication?

A geographical indication is a sign used on goods that have a specific geographical origin to indicate that they possess qualities or a reputation that derives from that place of origin. Most commonly, geographical indications consist of the name of the place of origin of the goods and often apply to agricultural products because qualities are influenced by specific local factors, such as climate and soil. Geographical indications are not, however, limited to agricultural products. They may indicate specific qualities of a product owing to human factors, such as specific manufacturing skills and traditions—for example, "Swiss made." To qualify for a geographical indication, a product must derive its qualities and reputation from the geographical place; it is necessary for a specific link to exist between the products and their original place of production. Sometimes a geographical term has come to be used as the designation of a kind of product, rather than an indication of the place of origin of that product. An example of this is "Dijon mustard." While this is a style of mustard that originated in the French town of Dijon, it now denotes a type of mustard that can be made anywhere in the world. Once this generalized adoption of the name occurs, the term becomes generic and is no longer subject to protection as a geographical indication.

What Is an Appellation of Origin?

An appellation of origin is a special kind of geographical indication, used on products that have a specific quality that is exclusively or essentially due to the geographical environment in which the products are produced. Thus, the concept of geographical indication encompasses appellations of origin, which are at present usually used to indicate the origin of wine.

How Is a Geographical Indication Protected?

National laws of individual countries are the primary means of protecting geographical indications. These national laws are passed under various regimes, such as laws against unfair competition, consumer protection laws, laws for the protection of certification marks, or special laws for the protection of geographical indications or appellations of origin. The essence of the protection is to prevent unauthorized parties from using the description to mislead the public as to the true origin of the product.

Protection at the International Level

A number of treaties administered by WIPO provide for the protection of geographical indications, including:

- the Paris Convention for the Protection of Industrial Property;
- the Lisbon Agreement for the Protection of Appellations of Origin and Their International Registration; and
- the TRIPS Agreement (Articles 22 to 24).

WIPO has a Standing Committee on the Law of Trademarks Industrial Designs and Geographical Indications, which explores new ways of enhancing the international protection of geographical indications.

NOTES

1 WIPO website, www.wipo.int/about-ip/en.

2 Walter Wriston, "The Twilight of Sovereignty: How the Information Revolution Is Transforming Our World," 1992, as cited in Giunta and Shang, "Ownership of Information in a Global Economy" (1993-94), 27 *Geo. Wash. J of Int'l L & Econ.* 340.

3 *Progressive Games, Inc. v. Canada (Commissioner of Patents)* (1999), 3 CPR (4th) 517 (FC). Available online at www.canlii.org.

4 Substantive revisions of patent law were consolidated with provisions intended to curtail cyber squatting and to amend the law relating to satellite home viewing and rural local television signals in the *Intellectual Property and Communications Omnibus Reform Act, 1999.*

5 Sunny Handa, remarks made at *Colloquium,* "Digital Copyright Reform in Canada: An International Perspective," Centre for Innovation Law and Policy, Rotman Business School, University of Toronto, March 3, 2006.

6 The Trips Agreement is annex 1C of the Marrakesh Agreement Establishing the World Trade Organization, signed in Marrakesh, Morocco on April 15, 1994.

7 Moral rights are the rights of the originator of a copyright to prevent any person, even a subsequent holder of the copyright, from distorting, mutilating, or otherwise modifying the work in a way that is prejudicial to the reputation of the original creator of the copyrighted work.

8 "Digital rights management" refers to a number of technologies used to control access to digital data—for example, software and music.

9 Technical protection measures are technologies that control or restrict the use of and access to digital media content on electronic devices with digital rights management (see note 6) installed.

10 Carolyn Hotchkiss, "Free Trade Agreements and Copyright Law: Closing the Door on Legislative Change?", paper delivered at the ALSB Annual Conference, Ottawa Ontario, August 2005.

11 For an excellent discussion of this perspective, see the numerous articles written by Dr. Michael Geist of the University of Ottawa. See www.michaelgeist.ca.

REVIEW QUESTIONS

1. How did the inclusion of intellectual property provisions in the WTO agreement after the Uruguay Round affect WIPO? What activities does WIPO now undertake?

2. What was the significance of the TRIPS Agreement and what did it achieve?

3. What body now hears intellectual property dispute cases?

4. Generally, under TRIPS, what three conditions must be met before a patent can be granted?

5. Can ideas be patented? Discuss this issue, using examples of actual cases.

6. What are the major differences between US and Canadian patent law? What is the danger of divulging details of a patent in the United States before a patent is filed in Canada or the European Union?

7. What was the major weakness of the Paris Convention with respect to patent law? What was the significance of the PCT?

8. Is there a system that provides for a single European patent? Explain your answer. Are the rules for patents in the European Union more similar to those in Canada or the United States?

9. What is the significance of the Madrid Protocol with respect to trademark protection? The Paris Convention? Is Canada a member of either system? Explain the reasoning behind Canada's policy.

10. Explain the problem that arises for international registration as a result of the rule on the priority right for first use of a trademark as applied by Canada and the United States.

11. What are the major differences between the Berne Convention and the Universal Copyright Convention with respect to copyright protection? How has the signing of the TRIPS Agreement affected copyright?

12. Describe how legislative measures with respect to digital rights management differ in the United States, the European Union, and Canada.

13. How are the rights to computer software and integrated circuit topographies protected in Canada? Is the Canadian approach similar to those of other developed countries?

14. What is an industrial design and what international agreement facilitates international protection for this form of intellectual property?
15. What is a geographical indication and how is it protected internationally?

CLASS ACTIVITY

There are a number of emerging issues concerning intellectual property (IP) that affect international business. Assign the following topics to student teams to research and present. Many of these topics are suitable for a debate format.

- IP issues in private sector agricultural biotechnology.
- Copyright issues related to the downloading of music from the Internet.
- IP protection of biotechnology versus public policy in agriculture.
- Patent protection and access to HIV/AIDS, anti-malarial, and anti-tuberculosis drugs for developing countries.
- IP and genetic resources and developments: for example, the controversy surrounding the patentability of the "Harvard mouse."
- IP and traditional knowledge and folklore: for example, attempts to patent traditional herbal remedies.
- IP and e-commerce issues: for example, the responsibility of ISPs for protecting IP rights; another interesting topic is Turnitin.com, an anti-plagiarism website.
- The effect of TRIPS-mandated IP protection on economic activities in developing countries.

FURTHER READING

Bird, Robert C. "Defending Intellectual Property Rights in the BRIC Economies" (2006), 43 *Am. Bus. LJ* 317.

Dam, Kenneth W. "The Growing Importance of International Protection of Intellectual Property" (1987), 21 *The International Lawyer* 627.

Harris, Lesley. (2000). *Canadian Copyright Law*, 3rd ed. Toronto: McGraw-Hill.

Oman, Ralph. "Intellectual Property–Our Once and Future Strength" (1993-94), 27 *Geo. Wash. J of Int'l L & Econ.* 301.

Vaver, David. (2000). *Copyright Law*. Toronto: Irwin Law.

Vaver, David. (1997). *Intellectual Property Law: Copyright, Patents, Trade-Marks*. Toronto: Irwin Law.

WIPO Guide to Intellectual Property Worldwide, 2nd ed. WIPO Publication no. 479E.

WIPO Intellectual Property Handbook: Policy Law and Use. WIPO Publication no. 489E.

WEBSITES

World Intellectual Property Organization:
www.wipo.int/about-ip/en

WTO—TRIPS Agreement:
www.wto.org/english/tratop_e/trips

Canadian Intellectual Property Office:
http://cipo.gc.ca or http://strategis.ic.gc.ca

CHAPTER 10

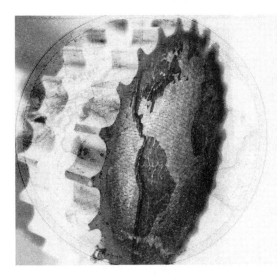

Legal Aspects of Different Foreign Market Entry Strategies

INTRODUCTION

With globalization has come an enormous increase in the **global value chain**, or worldwide dispersion of production. Falling transportation costs, lower barriers to trade and investment, and improvements in information and communications technology have made it easier for firms to locate parts of their businesses around the world. Different functions can be shifted to the most efficient site—for example, design in North America or Europe, manufacturing in China, and after-sales service in India. Businesses may also expand into foreign markets so that they can be closer to their customers.

Whether a business is a "born global" firm or an established business in Canada wishing to expand into foreign markets, it must determine the method by which foreign and domestic markets will be accessed, used, and expanded. A business may opt to enter into various contractual agreements, short of acquiring a foreign business in another jurisdiction, or it may choose to make a direct foreign investment by establishing or purchasing a firm in the targeted market. The decision will vary depending on the type of business, the chosen market, and the resources that the business is able to allocate to a foreign presence.

There are many forms that such an increased presence can take. We will review several business forms that are most commonly used in today's global business environment. These are:

- outsourcing,
- agency,
- distributorship,
- licensing agreement,
- franchising agreement,
- joint venture, and
- direct investment.

It is often apparent which business form a business should use to increase its presence in a country or region. However, some business arrangements are suited to only some aspects of a business form, while others require a combination of forms. Therefore, the parties must understand the characteristics of these forms of entry to ensure that they are establishing viable and enforceable association arrangements. This knowledge should help the parties ensure that adequate thought has been given to the structure of any new arrangement, which may involve a number of contracts with differing parties. Careful attention should be paid to ensure that the parties

- clarify their expectations,
- anticipate any possible problems, and
- adopt proper legal safeguards for the protection of each party.

OUTSOURCING

We will begin with **outsourcing**, a relatively new form of business in foreign markets and one that is particularly relevant in a globalized world where the greatest growth is in trade in services.

Understanding Outsourcing: The Global Supply Chain

Outsourcing of services globally is commonly understood as the practice of companies sending service functions abroad, where they can be done more cheaply or efficiently. For many years, organizations have had core, mission-critical aspects of their business such as manufacturing or accounting done by others. Technology now makes it possible for a broader ranger of services to be done abroad. Services ranging from human resource management, entire information technology operations, back-office operations, call-centre functions, medical diagnostics, and stock market research, to software development can be done around the world with significant benefits to the service outsourcer in terms of cost and time. One example of this is Sun Life Financial's decision to develop a project in India, described in box 10.1.

As the Sun Life experience suggests, Canada benefits both ways from the current trend to outsource services to other countries. We are not only an outsourcer, but we are also a provider of outsourcing services and a prime destination for companies attracted by Canada's proximity to the United States, lower costs, stable government, and well-educated, mainly English-speaking population.

The practice of outsourcing is not without controversy, as we witnessed in the emotional debates in the US election campaign of 2004, where candidates promised to prohibit outsourcing to ease fears among the electorate that service and knowledge workers would be displaced by workers in developing countries, as had occurred much earlier with manufacturing workers. Their fears may not be well founded: some commentators report that total

---

BOX 10.1 SUN LIFE FINANCIAL OUTSOURCES SOME UNDERWRITING TO INDIA

Sun Life Financial has embarked on a major expansion of its life insurance business in India, and in addition has opened a service and technology centre in Bangalore where local Indian managers will oversee IT services and some underwriting (evaluating people who are applying for insurance coverage) for the Canadian insurance market. Sun Life, which also operates an outsourcing centre in Ireland, has stated that the decision to outsource more of its IT and insurance administrative functions to India was motivated more by time than by cost, despite the fact that India's labour market is young, highly skilled, and inexpensive. Given the time difference between the two countries, it is possible to work on a file in Canada during the day, and then pass it on to the Indian operations where it can be handled during the night. Sun Life points out that this division of labour can flow in both directions, enabling the Canadian office to help the Indian office with underwriting assignments during busy periods.

Source: Sinclair Stewart, "Sun Life Tests Underwriting in India," *The Globe and Mail*, November 16, 2005, B4.

global service outsourcing accounts for less than one-quarter of 1 percent of all world services trade.[1] Other observers point out that the outsourcing of services is a normal development in the global supply chain, where each element of a product or service is sourced where it can be produced most efficiently.

Legal Aspects of the Outsourcing Arrangements

Major Considerations

Two major considerations that a firm must bear in mind in structuring an outsourcing transaction are the protection of intellectual property and the protection of privacy of personal data.

INTELLECTUAL PROPERTY RIGHTS OF THE OUTSOURCER

In most cases of outsourcing, a key component of the process is allowing the supplier access to legally protected rights such as copyright, patents, trademarks, trade secrets, and industrial designs. The issue of moral rights must also be respected by the supplier (see the discussion in chapter 9). The outsourcer must pay particular attention to how the supplier will handle the rights that it is given access to. Contractual provisions obligating the employees of the supplier must be included, and, if any subcontracting is to be done by third parties or by affiliates of the supplier, there must be an obligation that they also be covered by agreements protecting the intellectual property rights of the outsourcer.

PROTECTION OF PERSONAL INFORMATION

Canadian law, both federal and provincial, requires companies to protect personal information. The *Personal Information Protection and Electronic Documents Act* (PIPEDA)[2] is federal legislation that applies to the private sector across Canada, and restricts the collection, use, and disclosure of personal information. There is provincial legislation in Quebec,[3] Alberta,[4] and British Columbia[5] that also limits the use of personal information. In addition, we have the federal *Privacy Act*,[6] which covers government use of personal data. Generally, this legislation protects the privacy of individuals with respect to personal information held by companies and institutions and provides individuals with a right of access to that information. These legislative requirements must be honoured by Canadian companies even when data is being processed out of the country.

The Process of Establishing an Outsourcing Arrangement

When considering outsourcing arrangements, the usual parameters of careful preparation for negotiations and entering into a contract apply. These include developing the business case for the outsourcing clearly and carefully to ensure that the reasons the outsourcing is being undertaken are explored and understood and that the required parameters for success are clearly established. The case must be founded on business reasons and must be vetted and approved by all constituents in the organization. The appropriate team should be assembled to manage the contracting process, and, more important, the ongoing governance of the process. The outsourced service must be very carefully defined, and detailed operational, functional, and technical specifications must be prepared at the outset. In some cases, a company will be transferring assets and employees to an outsource provider, which makes the arrangements even more complicated. Because every outsourcing situation is different, using a standard form contract or following another company's template is not likely to provide a firm with supportive, viable legal arrangements. It is important to realize that the structuring of an outsourcing arrangement can be complex, requiring contracts not only with the outsourcing supplier, but also with third parties to cover situations where people are transferred or other pre-existing contractual arrangements are affected. There may also be tax issues. It is important to bear in mind the rule relating to privity of contract—that is, you cannot create obligations with third parties without making a direct contract with them. This is also important when addressing the issue of the privacy obligations of the outsourcer.

THE REQUEST FOR INFORMATION

A request for information from potential outsource providers is the usual starting point for most companies embarking on outsourcing. The request expands the information about outsource providers and helps narrow the candidates to ensure that the best supplier is identified. The firm that decides on a single source without comparing it to others risks choosing a less suitable supplier and loses the bargaining advantage of a competitive procurement.

THE REQUEST FOR PROPOSAL

Once the company has narrowed down a list of suppliers, it sends a request for proposal to each. The request for proposal (RFP) is the technical document that describes what a company wants to outsource and what it is seeking from the supplier. The document is important because it sets the stage for the outsourcing contract that will follow. Caution must be exercised in embarking on this process in Canada. The outsourcer must ensure that the terms of the RFP are the final terms, because our law creates certain legal obligations on the part of the issuer of the RFP. In the absence of special language, the RFP cannot be substantially altered after responses come in.

THE NON-DISCLOSURE STATEMENT

Parties to the negotiation process must agree on a non-disclosure statement that obliges the possible outsource supplier to protect the confidential information of the company. It is important to ensure that there is no end date for this undertaking because a limited period for this obligation could result in the company's confidential information becoming public knowledge long after the proposal process is over.

THE CONTRACTS

As with all important contracts, attention must be paid to the details of the contract to ensure that it truly reflects the intention of the parties. In addition, the contract should include

- detailed operational requirements with a clear governance framework;
- personnel controls including key person requirements;
- performance standards related to specific industry norms;
- quality control methods including those for subcontractors and affiliates;
- provision for continuous improvement including benchmarking and technology renewal;
- performance verification including reporting, inspection audits, and detailed recordkeeping;
- performance milestones including dates and connection to payment;
- provision for remedies for breach;
- provision for change management including contract amendment;
- termination provisions including provisions for transition and repatriation of work; and
- dispute settlement provisions including a provision for arbitration.

AGENCY

Some Canadian manufacturers may initially be content to ship their goods or sell their services in various parts of the world and have no desire to increase their involvement or presence in the countries to which the goods are shipped or services sold. The pressure of intensive international competition and need to expand markets, however, may make it necessary to establish a stronger link in the foreign market. One of the simplest ways to achieve this increased presence is to appoint an agent in the foreign market. The common commercial reasons for appointing an agent, thereby increasing local participation in the target market, may be the result of:

- a need for more committed and indigenous marketing of the product or service;

- a need for more local sourcing of parts or personnel for political or competitive reasons;
- a desire to service the products in the country of sale; and
- a need for more local influence in the development of the product or service.

The appointment of an agent may represent an interim step between direct sales into a country and licensing or franchising in that country; although, in many cases, the Canadian firm's need for a presence in the foreign market will be satisfied with an agency agreement.

Common Characteristics of an Agency Relationship

An **agency** is a relationship between one person who is a supplier of services or a manufacturer of goods (whom we will refer to as the principal) and another person who carries out a specific task on the principal's behalf, usually to sell the principal's product or service. This person is usually located in the foreign country, is familiar with local requirements, may have special knowledge with respect to the product or service, and may provide additional technical services, such as installation and repair. This person is properly referred to as an agent. Agents often represent principals with high-cost or somewhat customized goods or services, or principals who need to enter into specialized contracts. Agents often travel within their assigned territory to develop business for the principal. Characteristics of an agency arrangement may vary, but usually

- the agent does not buy or sell for his or her own account;
- the agent is compensated by commission, which is usually related to sales;
- the agent takes orders on behalf of the principal (supplier), but submits these orders to the principal for approval or rejection;
- the agent is unable to bind suppliers unless he or she has express or implied authority to do so;
- the economic risk for failure of delivery of the goods or service and the risk of non-payment remains with the principal;
- the principal retains ownership of the product until it is sold to the end user; and
- there is no transfer of technology from the principal to the agent.

Although agents may sometimes be responsible for warehousing and distributing the goods, this is not usually the case. This is an arrangement more commonly reserved for distributors.

Figure 10.1 illustrates a typical agency relationship. The contracts that are negotiated by the agent, Australian Technical Products, with the third-party customer, Adelaide Communications, are intended to be contracts

Figure 10.1   Canadian Firm Appoints Australian Agent

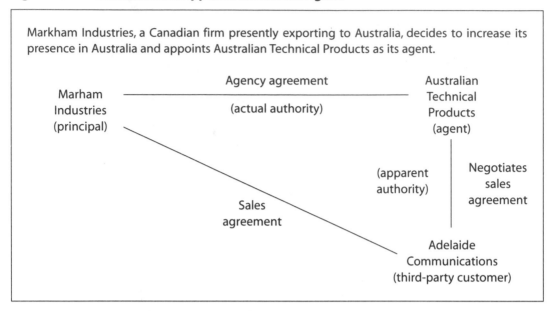

Markham Industries, a Canadian firm presently exporting to Australia, decides to increase its presence in Australia and appoints Australian Technical Products as its agent.

between Markham Industries and the customer. The agent is simply the facilitator. As long as the agent has negotiated the contract on behalf of its principal, Markham Industries, within the scope of the authority given, only Markham Industries and the third-party customer are bound by the contract.

Actual Authority and Apparent Authority

In the eyes of the law, there are two different types of authority present in an agency relationship: actual authority and apparent authority. These two types of authority co-exist but come from different sources. The agency agreement will describe and define the authority given to the agent and this is the source of the agent's real or actual authority. Actual authority is defined by the contractual relationship between the principal and the agent. The third party is not a party to this agreement nor is he or she likely to be informed of its terms. Apparent authority is part of the legal relationship between the third party and the principal and is created by the representation made by the principal to the third party that the agent is representing the principal. It is simply the authority that the agent appears to have. This situation is clearly described by Lord Diplock, in his reasons for judgment in a famous case decided in England in 1964:

> In ordinary business dealings the contractor at the time of entering into the contract can in the nature of things hardly ever rely on the "actual"

authority of the agent. His information as to the authority must be derived either from the principal or from the agent or from both, for they alone know what the agent's actual authority is. All that the contractor can know is what they tell him, which may or may not be true. In the ultimate analysis he relies either upon the representation of the principal, that is apparent authority, or upon the representation of the agent, that is, by permitting the agent to act in some way in the conduct of the principal's business with other persons. By doing so, the principal represents to anyone who becomes aware that the agent is so acting, that the agent has authority to enter on behalf of the principal ... into contracts ... of the kind which an agent so acting ... has usually "actual" authority to enter into.[7]

Thus the principal will be bound by acts done by the agent that are within his or her apparent authority. If the principal has limited the agent's authority in any way that is not usual in the industry, the principal should make sure that any potential customers are informed of the limitation. Consider the scenario described in box 10.2.

BOX 10.2   AGENT'S ACTUAL AUTHORITY LIMITED BY PRINCIPAL

Monster Road Equipment Inc., a Canadian company headquartered in Winnipeg, has been very successful in the Australian market. Exports of its heavy road-building equipment have been increasing at a very healthy rate. However, the constant travel to Australia to attend to the marketing and sale of its products has taken its toll on the marketing manager of Monster and is diverting too much time away from the development of other overseas markets. Monster decides to appoint an agent in Australia so that it can continue to expand its market in Australia while reducing the need for its employees to travel there. Monster identifies a suitable individual in Sydney, a Mr. Foster. The average cost of a single unit of Monster equipment is Cdn $100,000. Wanting to authorize Mr. Foster to make contracts on Monster's behalf but not wanting to authorize him to make commitments that would unduly stretch the company's resources, Monster decided to limit Mr. Foster's authority to contracts having a value of less than Cdn $400,000. The agreement between Mr. Foster and Monster provided for this limitation.

Mr. Foster had been Monster's agent for more than two years and the relationship had been very satisfactory to both sides when Mr. Foster was approached by Outback Construction Co., which had just been awarded a contract to build a new highway to Alice Springs and required a number of specialized units to complete the job. They negotiated a contract with Mr. Foster for eight units at a total cost of Cdn $824,000. Mr. Foster was delighted that he had obtained such a large order, but

Monster was already operating at peak capacity and was unable to deliver the units to Outback on time. The result was that Outback fell behind in its contractual obligations to complete the new highway on time, and sued Monster for breach of contract—that is, failure to perform to agreed-on deadlines. Monster defended the case on the basis that there was no contract, because Mr. Foster had exceeded his actual authority in agreeing to such a large order. Monster took the position that Mr. Foster was solely responsible for the damages for breach of contract because he knew about the limitation in the agency agreement.

In this case, Outback would succeed in its claim for damages against Monster, because Mr. Foster was acting within his apparent authority and Monster had done nothing to inform Outback, as a third party, of the limitation of authority. Monster would have a good chance of suing Mr. Foster successfully for breach of a condition of the agency agreement, but Mr. Foster might not have the resources to pay a large judgment.

What do you think Monster could have done to avoid this unfortunate situation?

Termination of the Agency Agreement

An agency agreement is automatically terminated on the death, dissolution, or bankruptcy of the principal, or by notice, or as otherwise provided in the agreement. When an agency agreement is terminated by the parties, the principal must be sure to give notice to third parties, because customers may otherwise assume the existence of the relationship and the principal may continue to be bound on the basis of the agent's apparent authority.

An Agency Agreement Is a Contract of "Utmost Good Faith"

The agency relationship must be based on honesty and trust, because the contract carries important responsibilities: choosing customers, disposing of the principal's goods, determining customer credit terms, and often receiving the purchase price for the goods or services. Careful inquiries into the personal reputation and financial standing of the agent are essential, as is personal contact, which should be maintained between the principal and agent throughout the relationship.

The agency relationship falls within that category of contracts in the common law referred to as **contracts of utmost good faith**. In such contracts, the parties have a high standard of duty toward each other, requiring them to reveal all relevant information and to always put the interests of the other party first. The effect of this rule is that the agent must always place the interests of the principal first and must always keep the principal fully informed of all relevant facts known to the agent. The agent may not act for both the principal and the third party in a transaction without express permission from each. If the agent obtains a commission or benefit from the third party without disclosing this to the principal, the agent is not entitled to a commission on the sale. The principal is also entitled to recover any such secret profit made by the agent. The agent has a duty to seek the most favourable price on a sale, which may conflict with an agent's desire to obtain a quick commission.

Preparing the Agency Contract: Duties of Principal and Agent

In negotiating an agent's contract, the duties imposed on the parties by the common law should be borne in mind. The duties of the principal include:

- paying the agent a reasonable fee or the fee agreed on; and
- indemnifying the agent for any reasonable expenses.

The duties of the agent include:

- obeying the lawful instructions of the principal;
- keeping information obtained as an agent confidential;
- keeping in constant contact with the principal and informing the principal of relevant or important developments;
- maintaining the standards applicable to the performance of an agent in the particular industry or sector;
- accounting for any goods or money belonging to the principal; and
- placing the principal's interests first in all transactions subject to the agency agreement (as discussed above).

In addition, the agent is not normally free to delegate any of his or her duties to a third party unless this is expressly permitted by the agency agreement.

The agency agreement should always be a properly drawn written contract stating the rights, duties, and reasonable expectations of the parties. The most common sources of problems are:

- the failure to consider the full effect of the provisions agreed to;
- the omission of important provisions; and
- the failure to define the relationship clearly.

It is important that the principal maintain a relationship with the agent that is sufficiently "arm's length" to ensure that the agent is an independent contractor and not an employee. Care must be taken to ensure that the agent is responsible to the principal only for the end result of its activities, not for the manner in which they are carried out. Extensive supervision of the agent's activities may result in the agent being considered legally an employee, with the consequent social insurance, income withholding, employment insurance, and workers' compensation responsibilities. In short, the agent must be left free to manage his or her own business.

Special Protection for Agents in Other Countries

In Canada, the United States, and other common law countries, the parties are free to develop the agency relationship as they wish within the framework of the common law and are unencumbered by legislation that limits their freedom of contract, particularly in the areas of compensation and termination. Nevertheless, principals should check any applicable legal provisions, because some provinces and states have passed legislation providing for compensation to agents when an agency agreement is terminated.

Principals who wish to enter into an agency agreement with an agent who is located in a country other than Canada or the United States should exercise caution because many countries, particularly those with civil law systems, have special laws to protect the agent, and these laws will supersede any written contract entered into by the principal and agent. There are provisions in a number of countries that grant the agent an indemnity if the contract expires or is terminated for reasons other than a default attributable to the agent. Under German, Swiss, and Dutch law, such indemnity may be considered compensation for goodwill created by the agent, which benefits the principal after termination. French law, on the other hand, characterizes the indemnity payment as compensation for the loss suffered by the agent as a consequence of termination of the contract (that is, commissions that would have been earned had the contract lasted longer). There are, however, other countries that make no legal provision for compulsory payments to agents upon termination of an agreement. Algeria bans the use of agents altogether. Many countries require agents to be citizens. Registration of all agency contracts is also a common provision.

For parties within the European Union, the EU Directive on Self-Employed Commercial Agents[8] is relevant. This Directive requires each EU member to pass national laws consistent with the Directive's terms. The Directive sets out the following mandatory provisions for an agency contract:

- An economic conditions alarm is to be included, whereby the principal must notify the agent if it expects the volume of business to decrease significantly.
- Payment of commission is required not only on contracts negotiated by the agent but also on contracts concluded between the principal and a party that the agent had previously acquired as a customer.

- Payment of commission is required whenever the principal makes a sale in the territory designated for the agent even if the agent has not participated in the sale.

In response to to the difficulties created for international traders by the variation in national laws governing agency relationships, the International Chamber of Commerce (ICC) has developed a model form, which is an attempt to find a balanced solution to the conflicting agency rules in national states. This model form incorporates the prevailing practices in international trade as well as the principles generally recognized by the domestic laws on agency.

Some of the major areas dealt with by the model form are the following:

- *Provisions for indemnity on termination.* Because of the different national rules relating to indemnity on termination, the model form gives the parties the choice of including a provision with or without the indemnity.
- *International arbitration.* Because the goal of the model form is to avoid the direct application of conflicting domestic legislation, the form provides for disputes to be settled by international commercial legislation. However, this may present problems for jurisdictions whose national laws assume all agents to be employees and provide for specialized labour jurisdiction for disputes arising from such agreements (for example, France, Belgium, and Italy).

This model form is designed to be used only for international agency agreements with self-employed commercial agents acting for the sale of goods.

Competent legal advice is recommended before entering into any agency agreement, particularly in civil law countries.

Checklist for Negotiating an Agency Agreement

Box 10.3 contains a checklist of important matters to be considered when negotiating an agency agreement. These matters should be fully explored by the parties, and the terms should be clearly spelled out in the written contract.

BOX 10.3   AGENCY AGREEMENT CHECKLIST

- Definition of specific important terms, such as territory, products, market segment, net selling price, and commissionable accounts.
- Nature of the appointment: Is it exclusive or non-exclusive?
- Term (time period) of the agreement, including provisions for renewal.

- Rights and obligations of both principal and agent.
- Payment provisions, including the rate, the basis of computation, and when payment is due and payable.
- Requirements for the agent's personnel: qualifications and training.
- A non-competition covenant upon termination of the relationship. (This may not be enforceable in all jurisdictions. The usual rule is that the covenant must be reasonable in time and geographic area and not deprive the agent of the right to earn a living.)
- Termination for "cause." This should be provided for and defined. In the case of termination without cause, sufficient protection for the parties should be included. This is particularly important with respect to payment of post-termination commissions.
- General clauses, such as those concerning proprietary rights to improvements, non-assignability, manner of giving notices, protection of principal's trade secrets, law selection, and arbitration. The parties should not neglect these important clauses.

DISTRIBUTORSHIP

Companies that wish to expand their presence into foreign markets must appoint a **foreign intermediary** to act on their behalf. As we have seen in the previous section, this is often an agent. Sometimes, companies instead choose to establish a **distributorship** and appoint a distributor. The choice of whether to establish an agency or a distributorship is usually determined by the type of business or industry. As stated above, the agent tends to travel and represent the firm, selling more specialized products to customers with whom an individual contract may be negotiated. Distributorships are more common in the case of standardized goods, such as cars, appliances, and consumer products, and are often used where after-sales service and parts and a permanent location are expected. In a distributorship, the distributor usually purchases goods on its own account from the foreign supplier for resale to customers in its own market. The distributor may be an individual or an incorporated entity. A distributor often has rights for subdistribution and may sometimes have a licence to use a brand name, technology, and know-how to install or service the product. Sometimes the distributor will bear the economic risk of payment and carry the customer credit.

The distributor is normally free to select its customers, determine pricing, incur expenses, and control its operations. Compensation is normally by way of a mark-up of the goods, less any expenses incurred in bringing the product into the market. A distributor will often provide installation and maintenance services for the product sold but the manufacturer normally provides the warranty.

Foreign Protective Legislation Affecting Distributorships

Just as many countries have enacted legislation to protect agents on termination, there is often legislation protecting foreign distributors in two major areas: minimum notice requirements and compensation for termination. Some of these provisions extend beyond termination to the non-renewal of the relationship or the failure to renew. The philosophy behind the legislation derives from the perception that foreign suppliers may take advantage of a foreign distributor who has no comparative advantage in negotiating the terms of the original representation contract. The goal of the foreign supplier is the development of goodwill and a customer base in a country or region for its products or services. Once the penetration of the market is at an acceptable level, the foreign supplier may be tempted to terminate the distributor and move into the country or region through an affiliate, branch, or subsidiary, just as the distributor was close to realizing a return on its investment of time and money. This is perceived as unjust and, for this reason, a common provision of the protective legislation is to prohibit a termination or failure to renew unless "just cause" can be shown by the foreign supplier.

International Distribution Agreements and Competition Law

Canadian business people must be aware of the importance of the competition laws of the country of distribution whenever they enter into a new distribution arrangement, whether as a Canadian supplier to a distributor in a foreign jurisdiction, or as a Canadian distributor of foreign products or services in Canada. Canadian competition law has provisions that may lead to criminal charges when there is evidence of price discrimination, price maintenance, predatory pricing, conspiracy, or bid rigging. Also prohibited, but leading to less serious charges, are refusal to supply, exclusive dealing, and tied selling.

Competition laws in foreign countries cannot be assumed to be similar to those in Canada, either as to their substantive provisions or as to the spirit with which they are enforced. The amount of the penalties may be much higher than those in Canada and may come as a very unpleasant shock to the poorly informed Canadian business.

The European Union in particular has very strict provisions for the prevention of anti-competitive measures; enforcement can best be described as "enthusiastic" and penalties can be very large by Canadian standards. Unlike in Canada, where larger companies are more likely to be charged, small-, medium-, and large-sized companies are considered equally important in the EU "war" against anti-competitive behaviour. The cases[9] in boxes 10.4 and 10.5 illustrate the risk.

BOX 10.4 DISTRIBUTOR AGREES TO EXPORT BAN IN EUROPEAN UNION

Parker Pen Ltd. had established exclusive distributors in several European countries. In an exclusive distribution agreement with its German distributor, a Parker marketing director had inserted a clause prohibiting the distributor from exporting the pens outside the territory assigned to it without Parker's written consent. The marketing director had inserted the clause on his own initiative and apparently without seeking legal advice. He had done so in order to prevent "parallel imports" of Parker pens into territories in which Parker had agreed to give "exclusive" distribution rights to another party. (Parallel imports are imports of identical goods, manufactured by the same manufacturer, but brought in through channels other than the official exclusive distributor for the territory.)

A would-be unofficial distributor of Parker pens based in the Netherlands filed a complaint with the Commission of the European Communities. It was unhappy because it had been unsuccessful in persuading the German distributor to export sizeable quantities of pens at the lower "export prices" to it in the Netherlands. The Commission undertook an investigation, conducting a hearing, and fined Parker ECU 700,000 (approximately Cdn $1,204,000). The German exclusive distributor was fined ECU 40,000 (Cdn $68,800) for having signed the exclusive distribution agreement that contained the export ban.

The Commission reasoned that European competition law is clear on this point: export bans are always restrictions on competition. A long line of case law existed on the topic and "it was not possible for Parker to be unaware of this fact." Furthermore, the Commission said it made no difference that the clause was put into the agreement by a manager with no authority to do so. The company was liable for infringing the competition law.

BOX 10.5 HEAVY FINE FOR DISTRIBUTOR'S UNWRITTEN AGREEMENT TO EXPORT BAN

The products in question were various types of sports equipment. Exclusive distributors had been appointed in various countries in the European Union. Perhaps knowing that "export bans" were prohibited in distribution agreements under the EU competition law, the manufacturer avoided putting the "export ban" in writing in its agreement. There was, however, a verbal agreement by both parties to each distribution agreement, and proved later by letter. The unwritten clause undertook to protect the exclusive distribution by having each distributor agree, verbally, not to export the goods out of his or her exclusive territory. This was, in fact, the very essence of an "export ban." Keeping the clause out of the written agreement did not save the parties. When a third party complained to the Commission, the decision was that the behaviour of the manufacturer and the particular distributor about whom the third party had complained (that is, the German distributor) had infringed the European Community's competition laws. The manufacturer was fined ECU 5,000,000 (approximately Cdn $8,600,000), and the distributor was fined ECU 150,000 (approximately Cdn $250,000). The fines assessed were high in this case because of the manufacturer's defiant failure to cooperate. When first contacted by the Commission and forewarned that it was contravening the competition laws, the manufacturer had protested and attempted to justify what it was doing. It had blatantly signed another "infringing" distribution agreement with a new distributor while arguing with the Commission.

LICENSING

What Is Licensing?

Some knowledge of intellectual property law rules is essential to understanding licensing, because an important part of most **licence agreements** is the grant of the right to use intellectual property rights held by the licensor. In simplest terms a licence is the right to use something that belongs to someone else. The owner of the right (the licensor) grants a licence allowing the other party (the licensee) to use the owner's right as under the conditions imposed by the licence agreement. These agreements are sometimes referred to as **technology transfer agreements** because they usually involve the transfer of knowledge and information relating to a product or process. The phrase "technology transfer" is misleading because it suggests that the technology is "transferred" or sold, leaving no residual rights for the transferor. This is not the intention of most potential licensors, who intend only to allow some limited use of their property. This knowledge and information may be subject to statutory legal protection, such as patents, trademarks, copyrights, or industrial designs, or it may have to be protected solely by contract, as is the case with trade secrets and know-how.

Reasons for Licensing

One of the major advantages of a licensing agreement is the ability to establish a manufacturing base and/or a market for a product in a foreign country without any capital investment. By finding a foreign licensee, a firm avoids the risk and expense of foreign direct investment. If the foreign licensee has experience in manufacturing similar products, manufacturing capacity, and an established marketing network, the arrangement can be very attractive for the Canadian licensor. Another common reason for a Canadian firm to seek a licensee abroad is the cheaper labour costs in the foreign country.

Licensing agreements do not always involve a Canadian firm seeking a licence abroad. There are many situations in which a Canadian manufacturer will seek a licence for manufacture and sale in Canada of a product that belongs to a foreign firm.

Potential Problems

How Effective Is Intellectual Property Protection in the Host Country?

From the point of view of the licensor, the major risk associated with licensing is the loss of control of the trade secrets relating to the technology and the risk of establishing effective competition in the global marketplace. For less-developed countries, licensing remains a means of acquiring manufacturing knowledge relating to technology without having to wait years to develop it. The attitude of the government of the licensee's country becomes very important when assessing the possibility of licensing arrangements abroad. The first question should be: does the country have effective intellectual property laws and, if so, are these laws fairly and effectively enforced? Some countries have adequate legislation protecting intellectual property rights but fail to enforce them. See box 10.6.

Host Country Approval Requirements

Many foreign governments assert their right to monitor all foreign licensing agreements to ensure that they do not cause a drain on valuable foreign exchange. Licence agreements that involve rights to beneficial and up-to-date technology are more likely to be approved than agreements that involve less-essential products, such as consumer products or products that have become obsolete or outmoded in their home market. Regulatory schemes for technology transfer agreements can take the form of a requirement for prior approval, which means the licence is not valid until approved, a requirement for registration of the licence, or simple notification. A requirement for registration may mean that licences are available for public inspection. This can involve a serious compromise of confidential information. Early consultation with local lawyers is advisable for the Canadian firm intending to grant a foreign licence.

BOX 10.6   "DON'T EXPECT HUGE GAINS IN CHINA'S BATTLE AGAINST PIRACY"

This is the title of a recent article on intellectual property rights and enforcement in China.*

The author describes a recent agreement where some of Beijing's biggest retail landlords signed a memorandum to protect brand names. The agreement was made with 23 international brands and it promised that counterfeit products will not be tolerated and tenants breaking the law would be evicted.

Although China agreed to implement acceptable intellectual property protection legislation as part of its obligations leading to its accession to the WTO, applying that law in China has never been easy or certain. The economy is massive and chaotically regulated. The scope of piracy is enormous, estimated by consultants A.T. Kearney in a recent study to account for some 8 percent of China's GDP. China has only recently and somewhat reluctantly recognized physical property rights, so intellectual property rights, a more complex area, may not be easy to enforce in the short term.

*   Tom Grimmer, *Globe and Mail*, June 14, 2006, B10.

For persons considering acquiring a licence from a foreign firm to manufacture or sell in Canada, there are few legal impediments. Canada has no regulatory scheme governing licensing arrangements and there are no requirements for registration or public disclosure. The *Investment Canada Act*,[10] which requires a review and approval of some foreign acquisitions of businesses in Canada, does not apply to licensing agreements unless it relates in some way to control of a large Canadian enterprise. Furthermore, Canada does not impose restrictions on licence agreements granting exclusivity in relation to products or territory, unlike the European Union, the United States, and other jurisdictions.

Competition Law and Licensing

Businesses that are negotiating licensing agreements must also consider potential competition law problems in the country of manufacture and distribution, and the issue of disclosure of confidential information as a part of the negotiating process. Each of these issues requires the advice of competent counsel experienced in intellectual property or licensing law. Some of the preliminary considerations will be discussed here.

LAWS FOR THE PROTECTION OF COMPETITION

Laws for the protection of competition can have the effect of curtailing the freedom of intellectual property owners to deal freely with their rights when imposing conditions on licensees. The United States and Canada appear to be moving in the direction of tougher competition law enforcement, so caution must be exercised when designing agreements in the NAFTA region. Some of the danger areas to be aware of are:

- arrangements in which the licensor and licensee make up more than 25 percent of the market;
- exclusive licensing arrangements that prevent the licensee from using competing technologies;
- agreements that tie the licensed technology or product to another product or products;
- arrangements that create "innovation markets"—that is, combine firms working at the forefront of research and development in respect of particular technologies;
- agreements for non-use or suppression of protected technology;
- arrangements that corner a market through acquisition or restrictive licensing; and
- demands for grant-backs of improvement packages from the licensee.

EARLY DISCLOSURE OF CONFIDENTIAL INFORMATION

It is often necessary for the potential parties to the licensing agreement to exchange confidential business and/or technical information to enable them to decide whether or not they will continue with the negotiations. The parties need this information to assess their potential compatibility. It is essential that the terms of such a disclosure be documented, in order to protect the asset from unauthorized exploitation and to protect the person to whom the disclosure is made from false claims. The parties should be prepared to have a customized document tailored for their specific situation and not use another firm's "confidentiality agreement," which may be designed for quite different circumstances. It is recommended that the customized disclosure agreement describe the information revealed and that the specific secrecy measures required be stated. The very common but relatively meaningless "X will use its best efforts to ensure the secrecy of the information" clause should be avoided. The duration of the secrecy requirement should also be stated. Some examples of measures to ensure secrecy are:

- physical security of areas where access may be gained to the confidential information;
- security measures for electronic storage and transmission of data;

- controls on access to any computer facility and tape or disk storage where confidential information is kept;
- provisions for visitor control;
- controls over photocopying confidential information;
- control systems for employees and agents who have a need to know sensitive dates; and
- confidentiality agreements with employees, agents, or invitees who are permitted access to the confidential information.

Typical Licensing Situations

Like many legal contracts, licensing agreements may vary in their format, depending on the situation. Four common situations are presented below.

1. A Canadian firm has a product it wishes to have manufactured and sold by a licensee in another country. If this is the Canadian firm's first experience with licensing, it should take great care to enter the negotiations with a complete checklist, having considered all factors important to the firm as well as any problems likely to arise. It is advisable to involve an experienced licensing lawyer well before an agreement in principle is finalized because often no amount of ingenious drafting on the part of the lawyer will rescue the firm from concessions or points ceded in earlier negotiations. It will also be necessary to consult lawyers in the licensee's country to ensure that the firm's interests are protected and information relating to local law is accurate.

2. A Canadian firm wishes to negotiate with a potential licensee in another country, and the Canadian firm has previously licensed others in other countries. In this situation, the Canadian firm will have the advantage of a previous agreement that suits its business. This previous agreement may be used as a "basis" for negotiation of agreements in other countries, provided it is carefully reviewed to ensure that it is appropriate. Amendments are made to reflect any variations in the arrangement between the parties and any differences in the laws of the contemplated host country.

3. A foreign firm wishing to acquire a Canadian licensee presents a form, designated as a standard form, to the Canadian firm and advises that there is little room for Canadian renegotiation of individual terms. In such a situation, the Canadian firm must satisfy itself that a profitable and enforceable business arrangement is possible under such standard contract, which, once signed, will in normal circumstances be binding. Again, care should be taken to ensure that the agreement is reviewed by a Canadian lawyer familiar with licensing.

4. A foreign firm wishing to make an agreement with a Canadian licensor presents a version of a contract recently entered into in another jurisdiction. In this situation, there is likely ample room for negotiation and the Canadian firm should not be afraid to counter-offer with its own draft agreement based on its own requirements and legal advice.

A Checklist for a Licensing Agreement

Before entering into negotiations for a licensing agreement, you should know how the finished agreement is likely to be drafted or structured. This will assist you to clarify your negotiating goals, help you to review a draft agreement, and save time and money when instructing your legal advisers. A typical licensing agreement will be divided into five main sections as described below.

Description of the Parties

A clear and correct description of the parties is very important. Corporate names should be written exactly as they are shown on incorporation documents. Remember that a corporate division cannot be a party to a contract because, unlike a corporation, it is not considered a legal person.

Recitals

This is the part of the agreement that often begins with "Whereas" and proceeds to describe why the parties are entering into the agreement and what the agreement is intended to accomplish. Recitals are useful to clarify the thinking of both parties and make the agreement easier for an uninitiated reader to understand. Recitals have no legal effect unless they are later referred to in order to clarify some uncertainty or ambiguity in the agreement.

Defined Terms

Although this section of the agreement may appear to be overly legalistic to the layperson, it is an excellent way of simplifying a potentially complex document. For example, suppose that you are licensing know-how that is in the possession of your company. It will be necessary to define very carefully what that know-how consists of. This definition may be extensive—one paragraph of text or more. A definition section enables you to define know-how only once and state that every time the word "know-how" is used, it refers back to the definition given. Once a term is defined in this way, it must be consistently used. Other common examples of defined terms are "licensed product," "licensed patent," "licensee," "gross sales," and "term."

Schedules

Schedules are useful devices for simplifying an agreement by separating out technical or complicated information, such as technical specifications, royalty escalation formulas, or minimum sales scales. A schedule may also be called an appendix or exhibit. Care should be taken that any attached schedule is dated and signed and incorporated into the agreement together with any agreement for its periodic amendment.

The Grant

The grant is the heart of the licence agreement—the very reason the parties are making an agreement—yet it is not uncommon for overenthusiastic parties to leave it out altogether. This should be the first operative clause of the agreement—the one that states what rights are being granted. When negotiating this part of the licence agreement, the parties should ensure that it includes provisions addressing the following issues:

- *Territory.* The grant of rights should be confined to a specific area. It is not uncommon that different considerations may apply to geographical limitations on manufacturing, selling, and sublicensing. Care must also be taken not to breach the antitrust laws of the licensor's home jurisdiction.
- *Exclusivity.* The nature of exclusivity or non-exclusivity should be clearly spelled out. For example, there may be an exclusive right to manufacture and a non-exclusive right to sell. What about export sales? These questions should be addressed in order to avoid disputes later.
- *Sublicensing.* Whether sublicensing will be allowed or prohibited should be stated.
- *Term.* A licensing agreement is a long-term arrangement; however, some provision should be made to establish a term. A common practice is to provide for an initial term of a specific number of years and provide for one or more renewals unless, within some specified period, one party gives notice to the other of its intention to terminate. Provision should also be made for automatic termination in the event of bankruptcy or of specific violations of the agreement. Consideration should be given to the inclusion of minimum performance requirements, which would give the licensor the right to terminate the licensee if minimum performance requirements are not met.
- *Future improvements.* A decision must be made as to who acquires the rights to future improvements of the technology. The licensor may require a "flow-back" clause, which requires that the licensee relinquish rights to any improvements it has made to the technology. If, on

the other hand, the licensee negotiates to license its improvements in the technology to the licensor, a "grant-back" clause will be required.

- *Royalties.* These are the periodic payments made to the licensor based on the use of the licensed rights. The various ways of relating payment to use will vary considerably from one industry to another. Some of the most common alternatives are royalties based on percentage of sales, on production, or on net profit. Occasionally, royalties take the form of lump-sum payments. Once the appropriate base is determined, the parties must agree upon the royalty rate. Most licensors will open negotiations with a suggested rate based upon industry norms. When determining the royalty base, it may be necessary to establish a point at which the product is considered manufactured or sold. Another common royalty provision is an escalation clause tied to some published index. Finally, and most important, the currency of payment must be specified and any necessary conversion formula should be tied to an internationally recognized rate of exchange.

- *Protection of the licensed rights.* Both parties have a common interest in protecting the licensed rights against violations by third parties. A licensee will want the right to begin legal action in the name of the licensor should the licensor not be willing to do so. The parties should be sure to discuss their respective responsibilities in this area and provide for responsibility for expenses.

- *Title retention.* It is advisable for the licensor to require a clause acknowledging that the trade secrets and know-how that are the subject of the licence are valuable assets and that any breach of the secrecy provisions by the licensee will render the licensee liable for damages to the licensor.

- *Confidentiality clause.* The agreement should contain a clause stating that the licensee agrees not to disclose the information, know-how, or trade secrets acquired from the licensor, and that the licensee will require any affected employee, sublicensee, or subcontractor to make a similar covenant of secrecy and confidentiality.

- *Quality control.* Because the licensee's output is usually identified with the licensor's own products and corporate name, care must be taken that the licensee maintains quality standards that are consistent with those of the licensor. Quality control clauses may therefore include obligations such as manufacturing the product in accordance with specifications and directions supplied by the licensor, providing the licensor with samples for inspection, making any requested changes in manufacturing procedures or raw material reasonably requested, and, most importantly, permitting inspection of manufacturing facilities by the licensor.

- *Language.* The language in which the licensed property is to be provided should be specified. Trademarks licensed in a foreign jurisdiction usually must be translated into the local language, and the licensor should ensure that both the English language version and any translation are available for registration. If the licence is for computer software, it may be necessary to translate programs and supporting documentation. Licences are frequently prepared in two languages. For this reason, there should be a provision that one version in a particular language, say English, will be the official version and will prevail in the case of conflict.
- *Assignability.* The parties should address the question of whether the licensee may freely transfer the licence to another party. Often, the parties will reach a compromise whereby the agreement cannot be assigned without the licensor's consent but that consent will not be unreasonably withheld.
- *Settlement of disputes.* Parties should ensure that a choice of law is included, and a Canadian licensor may wish to include a choice of forum clause in favour of its own jurisdiction or another acceptable jurisdiction. The most important provision is, however, the provision that any disputes be referred to arbitration. In addition, the place for the arbitration and the arbitral rules that will apply must be specified.
- *Official notices.* Names and addresses to which official notices should be sent should be clearly stated together with the method by which notices are to be sent (for example, fax, mail, or personal courier).

FRANCHISING

Franchising is a form of licensing in which the franchisor grants to the franchisee the right to use a trademark or logo, provided that strict quality standards are maintained and the business is run in the manner and style prescribed by the franchisor to ensure that the business conforms to the franchisor's corporate image. Franchising seldom involves significant patent law or a transfer of technology in the true sense. Typically, almost every aspect of the business is controlled by the franchisor to preserve strict uniformity between franchisees and the original business. The franchisee, however, owns the business and risks his or her franchise's own capital.

Characteristics of a Franchise Agreement

A franchisor will require strict control over every aspect of the franchisee's business. Failure to comply with any of the detailed requirements for the conduct of the business may carry the penalty of termination. Agreements are usually for a fixed term of years during which the franchisee will expect to recover his or her original investment and make a profit. The question of renewal is an important one and the franchisee will wish to negotiate to secure favourable renewal rights. Retention of the franchise is often conditional on the franchisee meeting certain marketing quotas. The franchisee will want exclusive rights within a certain geographical area, whereas the franchisor may be reluctant to commit so fully to one franchisee. Royalties, as in pure licensing agreements, are generally tied to sales.

Franchising and Competition Law: The EU Example

A franchisor planning an entry into the European Union must consider the EU's competition law. The European Union originally took a very negative stance toward franchising when these agreements began to appear in Europe. EU officials believed that the typical limitations imposed on the franchisee were an unacceptable interference with the free market. A great deal of lobbying was carried out on behalf of large franchising firms in the late 1970s with the result that the European attitude has moderated. In a landmark case, *Pronuptia*, the European Court of Justice held that a franchising agreement, the purpose of which was to protect the know-how, standards, and identity of the franchisor, did not violate Article 85(1) (now Article 81) of the Treaty of Rome prohibiting concerted market behaviour in itself, but that clauses limiting or dividing markets geographically could constitute restriction of competition and would not be tolerated. This case is described in box 10.7.

BOX 10.7   EUROPEAN COURT OF JUSTICE ALLOWS FRANCHISE AGREEMENT

(European Court of Justice, 1986)

The franchisor, Pronuptia, which specialized in the sale of bridal wear, sued the German franchisee for franchise fees owed. The franchisee claimed no money was due because the agreement violated Article 85 of the Treaty of Rome. The agreement provided that the franchisee would

- not grant the rights to any third party to use the Pronuptia trademark in the territory (part of Germany);
- not open any other Pronuptia shops in the territory;
- not provide goods or services to third parties in the territory;
- sell products only in the shop equipped mainly for selling of bridal fashions in accordance with the brand image of Pronuptia;
- purchase 80 percent of its wedding dresses and accessories from Pronuptia; and

- purchase the remaining dresses and accessories exclusively from suppliers approved by Pronuptia.

In 1984, the West German court ruled in favour of the franchisee and stated that Pronuptia could not require the franchisee to buy most goods from Pronuptia or to stay within the defined retail territory.

Pronuptia appealed to the European Court of Justice. In such cases, the European Commission makes recommendations to the Court. The Commission, in this case, argued that the franchisor needed to enforce certain rules to maintain uniform standards of quality for customers.

Did this agreement violate Article 85, which prohibits agreements between undertakings, decisions by associations of undertakings, or concerted practices that may affect trade between the member states of the EC and that have as their object or effect the prevention, restriction, or distortion of competition within the Common Market?

The Court held that the clauses in the franchise agreement that appeared to limit competition were necessary to protect the company name, identity, and know-how. The Court stated:

> Franchising is a contractually governed form of commercial cooperation between independent undertakings, whereby one party, the franchisor, gives one or more other parties, the franchisees, the right to use his trade name or mark and other distinguishing features, in the sale of products or of services. The sale takes place on the basis of an exclusive marketing concept (system or formula) developed by the franchisor; in return, the franchisor receives royalties. The use of those rights by the franchisee is supervised by the franchisor in order to ensure uniform presentation to the public and uniform quality of the goods or services. ... It would appear ... the main advantage (for the franchisee) is ... the fact that it gives him (usually exclusive) access to products of high quality the market for which is already established.

The Court also agreed with the suggestion of the Commission and the French government that a block exemption for franchise agreements was desirable.

In 1987, shortly after the decision in the *Pronuptia* case, the European Commission exempted three firms, Pronuptia, Yves Rocher, and Computerland, from the provisions of Article 85. Following this, a block exemption for franchise agreements was drafted by the Commission. These guidelines establish procedures for obtaining approvals and include examples of clauses that are forbidden. These guidelines were issued in the recognition that consumers, as well as franchisors and franchisees, can ultimately benefit from franchise arrangements. In order to simplify business for franchisors and franchisees and to avoid the necessity of "notifying" all agreements, the European Commission has developed a block exemption for retail distribution of goods and service franchises (these are franchise agreements where goods or services are supplied to end users).

Under this block exemption, the following restrictions in competition are allowed:

- sole and exclusive terms with regard to the franchise territory;
- an obligation that the franchisee desist from concluding franchise agreements with third parties outside its territory;
- an obligation that the franchisee exploit the franchise only from the contract premises;
- restraints on the franchisee engaging in sales outside his or her territory; and
- an obligation not to sell or use competing goods in the course of providing services, but this obligation may not extend to parts or accessories.

The following clauses have unconditional clearance and may be used without notification:

- confidentiality requirements during the course of the agreement and after termination;
- flow-back of information requirements;
- requirements that franchisees provide assistance in protecting trademarks;
- requirements that franchisees use know-how only in connection with the franchise, and not after termination;
- requirements that franchisees attend training courses provided by the franchisor;
- requirements that business methods prescribed by the franchisor be followed by the franchisee; and
- requirements that certain standards of cleanliness, presentation, and quality control set by the franchisor be followed by the franchisee.

The following is a list of provisions to be avoided because they will have the effect of negating the block exemptions (listed above) from applying.

1. Market-sharing agreements between undertakings that produce comparable goods or services.
2. Preventing or proscribing the franchisee from obtaining equivalent goods from other suppliers.
3. Preventing the franchisee from obtaining supplies from a designated third-party supplier unless the refusal is for the preservation of the trademark or maintaining the identity and reputation of the franchise.

4. Resale price maintenance.
5. "No challenge provision" with respect to the franchisor's intellectual property. A "no challenge provision" prohibits the franchisee from questioning or contesting the franchisor's patent, trademark, or copyright protection.
6. Prohibitions on the supply of users outside the territory (although the franchisee can be prohibited from actively seeking customers outside its territory).

JOINT VENTURE AGREEMENTS

Various Forms of Inter-Business Association

A **joint venture** is essentially an agreement reached between or among separate business entities for collaboration on a joint project or new entity, which creates an ongoing separate entity for the purpose of achieving the objectives of the joint venture. This must be differentiated from agreements that are merely contractual undertakings to work together on a common project. As the demands of international business become more complex, the range of business relationships developed by the continuous ingenuity and flexibility of entrepreneurs continues to increase. Terms to describe these business relationships, such as "strategic alliance," "business network," and "virtual corporation," have likewise developed. These terms to some extent defy exact definition because they are used by different commentators in different ways. Each business relationship is, by its nature, constantly changing in response to international business, whether the flexibility is dictated by the demands of different types of business, different parts of the world, or differing sizes and needs of individual businesses themselves.

Any discussion of joint venture relationships should include a consideration of other forms of "partnering" in which individual firms can retain the advantages of independence and entrepreneurial control while gaining access to resources possessed by other firms. These contractual arrangements include the following:

- *Cross-licensing*. This is an arrangement whereby firms agree to license some or all of their proprietary technologies to each other for use in each other's products, manufacturing process, or business.
- *Joint marketing, distribution, and sales agreements*. These are very common and are probably the form of alliance most vulnerable to attack on the basis of domestic anti-competition legislation.
- *Alliances or business networks*. These arrangements allow small and medium-sized enterprises to combine their resources and skills to build

critical mass to achieve competitive advantage in scale, scope, and speed. These organizations do not normally create a new corporate entity, although members sometimes purchase small amounts of equity in each other. Members usually remain independent and often compete with one another outside the alliance or network.

- *Consortiums.* These are arrangements in which an umbrella association takes on a part of the business of several "partners," and is usually limited to achieving the completion of one large project. A consortium may be simply a contractual arrangement or it may actually be a multiparty joint venture.

Remember that these forms of business relationships are constantly changing and that the line between one type of business relationship and another can become blurred. There are as many forms of strategic business cooperation as there are businesses and commercial reasons to co-operate, and the forms are limited only by the imagination and ingenuity of the partners. Various observers have predicted that, in business in the near future, managers will either be part of an alliance or competing with one. As one author has stated in a recent article on the types and purposes of technological joint ventures,

> [A]lliance building now is fundamental to the way US electronics companies conduct business ..... Some eight out of ten electronics companies now have alliances, and most CEOs are planning or negotiating new ones. The goal of these alliances is to deliver—not necessarily build—the highest quality products and bring them to market in the shortest time.[11]

Common reasons for entering into business alliances are:

- to expand market presence—one partner may have access to a market and the other(s) a product or service for that market;
- to share or develop technology to keep pace with global competition;
- to combine strong company attributes, such as expertise in marketing, export market development, research and development, strategic management, training, production, and financial expertise in acquiring venture capital; and
- to pool financial resources to take a project or venture into a new market.

Negotiation of a Joint Venture

What makes a joint venture successful? One experienced international trade consultant described his benchmarks for success as:

- open and frequent communication;
- a well-established hierarchy;

- a pre-determined dispute resolution mechanism;
- realistic expectations on both (all) sides;
- complementary strengths and weaknesses of partners;
- able management of the alliance; and
- non-competition between the partners.[12]

A joint venture agreement is not an arrangement to be entered into lightly or hastily. The importance of careful partner selection cannot be emphasized too strongly. Like marriage, a joint venture is easily entered into, but extrication from the resulting relationship can be painful and expensive. Careful and thorough planning and a willingness to anticipate and discuss potential problems should help the parties avoid some of the pitfalls awaiting the unwary and the impatient. Potential partners must make sure that, in their enthusiasm to see the enhanced business possibilities of an alliance, they fully understand the increased risks involved, and ensure that liability for the increased risk is clearly recognized and fairly spread between the parties.

Preliminary Documentation

At some stage in the negotiations, the parties may wish to exchange a memorandum of agreement or a letter of understanding. We will refer to this as a **memorandum of understanding** or MOU. An MOU may clarify the purpose of the negotiations and give comfort to the parties, but it is only an agreement to agree—not a binding contract. For example, an agreement by the parties to conduct a feasibility study may well be binding, but the common corollary that if specified results are obtained, a joint venture agreement will be signed, is not usually enforceable.

An MOU is often used to bar either company from entering into negotiations with other firms; to set a timetable for completing negotiations; and/or to provide a basis of comparison for the final legal agreement. Another important reason for an early MOU is the need to have a confidentiality agreement before essential information is released.

Types of Joint Ventures

The two major types of joint venture are the equity joint venture and the contractual joint venture.

The equity joint venture is one in which each party becomes a shareholder in a corporation formed specifically to conduct the joint venture business. The important characteristic of this form is that, once the joint venture corporation is formed, it has its own life and the relationship of the parties is governed not only by their joint venture agreement but by the corporation's articles of incorporation and bylaws and all law relating to corporations.

This must be borne in mind during negotiations and when giving instructions to legal advisers who may be incorporating a new entity, because it is easy to end up with two sets of inconsistent rules governing directors, meetings, and casting votes caused by inconsistencies between the joint venture agreement and the articles of the new corporation established for the joint venture.

The contractual or unincorporated joint venture is one in which each party retains its own corporate identity and the relationship between the joint venturers is defined entirely by the joint venture agreement they have entered into. This situation is more analogous to a partnership and it must be remembered that, like a partnership, there is no limited liability for the joint venturers and that each joint venture partner may risk being bound by the acts of the other joint venture partner.

Companies or partners who are anxious to be responsible for only a portion of the venture must beware of clauses providing for joint and several liability.

Drafting the Joint Venture Agreement

The joint venture agreement should define the form that the joint venture will take and set out the contributions of the parties, their participation in the profits and losses, the management structure of the joint venture, its termination, and the disposal of its assets after dissolution. The valuation of the contribution of the parties is often contentious, particularly when dealing with partners in planned economies. Some common issues between the joint venture partners include:

- *Control.* This is likely to be the predominant issue between the parties. Although the parties may envisage "shared control," this is a concept difficult to bring into successful practice. Mechanisms for exercising shared control must be carefully thought out and fully understood by both parties. The issue of control can arise at different levels of decision making. A distinction can be made between day-to-day operations, short-term policy decisions, and longer-term general policy. In a case where the law of a host country requires 51 percent local ownership, the risk presented by loss of control can be reduced by spreading the local investment among many investors.
- *Licensing and transfer of intellectual property rights.* Transfer of technology is often the major reason for a joint venture, and the clauses that relate to this should be carefully considered, just as carefully and completely as if the licensing agreement were between parties with an arm's-length relationship. Copyrights, trademarks, and patented and unpatented technology are among the most difficult assets to valuate.

How intellectual property is valued may have important tax implications, particularly for ventures with foreign partners.[13]

- *Capital requirements and distribution of earnings.* The parties should address the issue of additional direct equity contributions that may be required in the future. A limitation for future funding can be negotiated, together with a provision as to the consequences should either party fail to make its contribution. The parties should also make sure they have the same ideas about distribution of earnings. They may wish to include a minimum distribution policy or pre-determined distribution policy in the joint venture agreement. This advice is consistent with lessons learned by experienced joint venturers. Consider the advice of Investment Canada:

> The joint venture agreement should specify the level, mix (debt to equity ratio), sources (debt, equity, government incentives), timing, and circumstances for contribution of additional resources to the venture. The agreement should also specify what happens when one party fails to make a required contribution—for example, setting out penalties should either partner fail to meet its financial obligations. One way to deal with defaults is to tie share holdings or payouts to each partner's contribution. The defaulting party could also be required to reduce or forfeit its interest in the venture, or even to sell its share holding to its partner at a predetermined bargain price.[14]

- *Deadlock.* The parties should address the possibility of a deadlock situation in an "equal" joint venture situation. They may wish to provide for one person to have a casting vote in deadlock situations. It is possible that this position could be alternated between the parties or vested in a "neutral party." More drastic methods of dealing with deadlock are the buyout by one partner, the introduction of a new party, or the winding up of the joint venture.
- *Arbitration.* The parties may wish to specify arbitration in the case of a dispute rather than resort to the courts of either jurisdiction.

Antitrust and Competition Law Considerations

Because joint ventures are, by definition, collaborative activities between or among potential or actual competitors, they are likely to have significant competition law implications. The European Union in particular has been active in regulating various kinds of strategic alliances. The European Union has developed a number of regulations establishing which kinds of activities are acceptable and which are not. The United States has also acted to limit the effect of antitrust laws on businesses seeking to associate for the purposes of competing in the global environment. Canadian businesses are less affected by anti-competition considerations because the history of prosecutions under the Canadian *Competition Act* indicates a much less invasive approach than that of competition watchdogs in the United States or Europe. Businesses contemplating sizable strategic alliances in either the European Union or the United States should ensure that their plans are reviewed by counsel knowledgeable in competition law before the arrangement is allowed to proceed too far into firm commitments. This advice is now also applicable to emerging larger economies, which are now developing antitrust measures more comparable to those of the European Union and the United States. China, for example, is presently preparing its anti-monopoly law, which gives officials new powers to review private sector mergers, acquisitions, and other commercial agreements and assess these agreements for their potential to affect competition in China.

FOREIGN DIRECT INVESTMENT

What Is Foreign Direct Investment?

Although there is no universally agreed upon definition we will proceed on the basis that **foreign direct investment** is the establishment of a direct presence of a firm in a foreign country by a start-up operation, a greenfield investment, a new project, a merger or an acquisition. International direct investment has grown rapidly in the last 10 years and Canada's stock of direct investment in other countries has grown by almost 400 percent since 1988.[15] Because direct investment and trade development are closely linked, the Canadian government encourages Canadian companies to make direct investments in foreign markets. The business reasons for making a direct investment in a country are similar to those for entering into a joint venture arrangement and include reducing distance to customers; gaining new marketing and distribution channels; and sourcing cost-efficient components, services, and technologies. In addition, a presence in other countries can provide better access to skills, knowledge, and research.

Risks Associated with Foreign Direct Investment

A foreign investor's greatest fear is the seizure of its assets by the government of the host country without compensation. Other major concerns are the fear of inadequate access to legal redress in cases of unfair treatment, lack of transparency of rules and regulations, restricted rights to remove earnings, and host government requirements for local sourcing and hiring. There have been a number of high-profile instances of foreign direct investment difficulties, among them the confiscation of US oil properties in the Middle East and the notorious Bre-X fiasco in the Philippines.

Multilateral and Bilateral Measures to Protect Foreign Investment

The Multilateral Agreement on Investment

Concern for the risks of foreign investors motivated the **Organisation for Economic Co-operation and Development (OECD)** to begin negotiations in 1991 to establish a **Multilateral Agreement on Investment (MAI)**. This was a major attempt at achieving a multilateral agreement on investment protection provisions. The initiative was driven by three factors: rapid growth in investment flows by the early 1990s; the trend toward unilateral liberalization of national restrictions on foreign investment in developed and developing states; and the patchwork of investment instruments at the international level. Progress in the Uruguay Round at the time was disappointing, and the OECD was seen as an appropriate forum of like-minded countries that could forge a workable agreement with adequate investor protection. The original conception was similar to the NAFTA Chapter 11 model and the original time frame for the negotiations was two years. Negotiations were overshadowed by ongoing disputes among the United States, Canada, and the European Union, and were further complicated by an aggressive campaign in 1997 by non-governmental organizations (NGOs), which used the Internet very effectively to coordinate and link people concerned about economic globalization. Further difficulties emerged with the Asian economic crisis in 1997. By October 1998, Australia, Canada, France, Great Britain, and the United States had all instituted some form of parliamentary review of the MAI—a reflection of the power of domestic lobbying against the initiative. Just before negotiations were set to resume in October 1998, France withdrew, setting in motion a domino effect that led to the announcement by the OECD in December 1998 that negotiations would cease. The MAI was as dead as the proverbial door nail.

The World Trade Organization

Although it is generally agreed that foreign investment is much more politically sensitive than foreign trade, the **World Trade Organization (WTO)** appeared to be the natural forum to provide foreign investment with appropriate protection. Although the first attempt to create multilateral treaty-based rules on foreign investment can be traced back to the Charter for an International Trade Organization (ITO) in 1948, there has never been a comprehensive multilateral agreement on foreign investment, comparable in any way to the system of trade liberalization in the WTO. The significant challenge facing negotiators is to create a balance between the interests of developed and developing countries, and also a balance between strong investment protection and host countries' legitimate regulatory authority.

The United States had attempted to include investment in the GATT Tokyo Round of negotiations (1973–1979), but this failed due to the opposition of developing countries. The resulting compromise was the Agreement on Trade-Related Investment Measures (TRIMS Agreement) and the **General Agreement on Trade in Services (GATS)**, which provide very little in terms of investor protection. Thus, the system that emerged in the 1990s was a patchwork of international rules on foreign investment.

With the failure of the MAI negotiations, the unsuccessful Seattle WTO Ministerial Conference in 1999, and ongoing public demonstrations against economic globalization, WTO members were in a difficult position with respect to international rules on investment. The result was the agreement at the Doha Ministerial Conference in late 2001, which did not include investment rules in the list of topics for immediate negotiations. The so-called Singapore issues of investment, competition policy, government procurement, and trade facilitations have been deferred until a decision is taken, by "explicit consensus on the modalities of negotiations." To date, no progress has been made on these negotiations, nor is any expected because the issue has been effectively shelved due to the opposition of many developing countries as well as the reservations of some developed countries that have witnessed some of the difficulties experienced under the NAFTA Chapter 11 provisions.

The History and Role of Bilateral Investment Treaties

Bilateral investment treaties (BITs) have proliferated around the world in the last several decades. With the principal purpose of protecting the investments of capital-exporting nations, these have been the model for the investor–state protection provisions in NAFTA and are the foundation of most negotiations on investor–state protection. To date, more than 2,000 of these treaties have been concluded, most between a capital-exporting or developed country and a capital-importing or less-developed country. The first BITs were developed in the early 1960s by the Europeans, followed in 1967 by the OECD with the Draft Convention on Alien Property, and the United States with its model BIT Treaty in the 1970s, last updated in 1994. During the 1990s, a new consensus emerged in the Americas and elsewhere with respect to rules governing foreign investment. Since then, more than 70 BITs have been signed between countries in the western hemisphere. BIT-based litigation has exploded as investors become increasingly aware of its availability and the relatively favourable chances of success for the foreign investor.

Mounting numbers of actual damage awards make it evident that BIT undertakings have consequences that were not contemplated at the time that these treaties were first developed. In the western hemisphere, BITs have served as a leveller and liberalizer of the cross-border business playing field and represent a significant shift from the longstanding Latin American aversion to international arbitration under the **Calvo doctrine**. Very few observers would argue with the need for some investor protection from the actions of arbitrary host governments. History has made us all too aware of the perils of the foreign investor in countries experiencing political turmoil, social upheaval, revolution, or periods of economic reform. This is particularly true where the foreign investment is in crucial areas of the host country's economy. Add to these general risk factors the specific risks of countries with poor records for transparency, efficiency, and stability in maintaining legal order and the rationale for investor–state protection provisions is obvious.

Generally, BITs are very similar in their substantive provisions, and include rules on scope and coverage, general standards of treatment, performance requirements, transfer of funds, expropriation, and dispute settlement.

SCOPE AND COVERAGE

These provisions typically contain rules on the definition of investment and investor, and the territorial and temporal scope of the agreement. There may also be provisions excluding certain economic activities reserved to the state.

GENERAL STANDARDS OF TREATMENT

These provisions mandate the expectation of fair and equitable treatment, usually with a reference to the principles of customary international law. It is here that we find the requirements for national treatment and most-favoured-nation (MFN) treatment. Some agreements, notably NAFTA and the Canada-Chile Free Trade Agreement, require that the investment and the investor be granted the better of national treatment and MFN treatment. Also, depending on whether the contracting states have ratified the Investment Disputes Between States and Nationals of Other States (ICSID) Convention, the tribunal may have authority to apply the national law of the host state.

PERFORMANCE REQUIREMENTS

The majority of BITs signed between developing countries in the Americas do not address performance requirements. Examples of performance requirements are as follows: majority of locals in joint ventures, establishment in specific location, employment of local labour, restriction on domestic sales, technology transfer requirements, and requirements for certain ratio of exports. This is in contrast to NAFTA, which prohibits specific performance requirements for both goods and services.

TRANSFER OF FUNDS

All BITs state that the host country must guarantee the free transfer of funds related to investments to investors of the other party.

EXPROPRIATION

Under customary international law, states are allowed to expropriate foreign investment as long as this is done on a non-discriminatory basis—that is, respecting the principles of national treatment and MFN treatment—for a public purpose, under due process of law, and with compensation.

DISPUTE SETTLEMENT

In traditional treaty practice, disputes between the contracting parties are settled under the general dispute settlement mechanism included in the treaty. Most BITs, however, include separate provisions for the settlement of investor–state disputes. At one time, the foreign investor was limited to bringing a claim against the host state in a domestic court or having its home state assume its claim against the host state. Thus BITs are remarkable for their extension of public international law to relationships between the state and private parties. Common practice in modern investment agreements is to provide the investor with the choice of referring the dispute to local courts, or to arbitration under the ICSID Convention or under the ICSID Additional Facility Rules, where either the host or home state of the foreign investor is not an ICSID contracting party. Most agreements also include an alternative form of arbitration, commonly under the UN Commission on International Trade Law (UNCITRAL) rules. In some cases, the International Chamber of Commerce is also available. Under most BITs there is no requirement that local remedies must be pursued or exhausted prior to international arbitration. Under the typical BIT, the investor simply submits the notice of claim to the appropriate authority of the responsible government, which then responds by putting into motion the constitution of the appropriate arbitral tribunal. Thus, the process is ad hoc, and the arbitrators are private agents, typically private lawyers or academics. Much has changed in the decade since the NAFTA was signed and the explosion of BIT signing activity. This area, once the preserve of diplomats and state governments, is now the purview of the transnational adjudicator. Nuances and ambiguities of these treaties unimagined by the negotiators are now being plumbed by talented arbitrators as well as by vocal members of the public.

One of the most common criticisms of the BITs by members of the general public is the fact that the right to sue is determined by the investor's status as an alien. Although this special status was created in recognition of the particular vulnerability of the foreign investor, and reflects the long-standing concern of international law for the rights of aliens, it does result in the foreign investor having access to a process and remedy not available to nationals. This is particularly hard to accept in the very countries where protection is most demanded by foreign investors—that is, countries with weak legal systems.

The Investor–State Provisions of NAFTA

The investor–state provisions of Chapter 11 of NAFTA have had a considerable influence on the development of the jurisprudence relating to international investor protection. These provisions have proved to be controversial and have spawned a somewhat polarized commentary in the popular press as well as in academic circles. This topic is explored in more detail in chapter 5 of this text.

Practical Considerations for the Firm Making a Direct Investment in a Foreign Market

The practical considerations in this situation do not differ markedly from the approach that should be taken to any major initiative where negotiations lead to long-term legal commitments for the firm; but because foreign direct investment usually involves a long-term commitment of very substantial expenditures, parties must be especially careful to "get it right." Firms that are preparing to make a direct investment in a foreign market should:

1. Establish the business case for the investment clearly and carefully having consulted widely with all constituents in their organization, with country experts on the foreign market, and with legal and financial advisers before any negotiating commitments are made.
2. Assemble the best possible team to manage the negotiations, and the ongoing governance of the process.
3. Anticipate problems and be prepared to negotiate protection for these and, if not successful, be prepared to walk away.
4. Have a clear picture of how the deal is likely to be structured and what agreements will be required and with what parties. This includes all necessary government and regulatory approvals.
5. Be careful to ensure that all propriety and confidential information is protected.

6. Ensure that all matters are anticipated and clearly spelled out in the contracts, including the less glamorous but important issues of governing law, termination and breach provisions, and provisions for arbitration to settle disputes.

NOTES

1 Danielle Goldfarb, "Outsourcing's Not the Danger, Protectionism Is," *Globe and Mail*, October 4, 2004, A13.

2 *Personal Information Protection and Electronic Documents Act*, SC 2000, c. 5.

3 *An act respecting the protection of personal information in the private sector*, RSQ c. P-39.1.

4 *Freedom of Information and Protection of Privacy Act*, RSA 2000, c. F-25.

5 *Freedom of Information and Protection of Privacy Act*, RSBC 1996, c. 165; *Personal Information Protection Act*, SBC 2003, c. 63.

6 RSC 1985, c. P-21.

7 *Freeman & Lockyer v. Buckhurst Park Properties (Mangal) Ltd. et al.*, [1964] 2 QB 480.

8 Directive 86/653/EEC.

9 Described by Toronto lawyer Elo Tulving-Blais in "The Devil You Know: Competition Laws and International Distribution Agreements" (August 1994), 3(8) *Warrington International Newsletter*.

10 *Investment Canada Act*, RSC 1985, c. 28 (1st Supp.).

11 Charles Compton, "Cooperation, Collaboration and Coalition: A Perspective on the Types and Purposes of Technology Joint Ventures" (1993), 61 *Antitrust Law Journal* 863.

12 Peter J. Dawes, "Seizing the Opportunities through Consortia and Other Flexible Business Networks." Address delivered to a conference on Canadian SMEs in Asia, sponsored by the Asia-Pacific Foundation, Toronto, March 7, 1995.

13 *Growing Together: Exploring the Joint Venture Option in Canada* (Ottawa: Investment Canada, External Affairs and International Trade Canada, and Industry, Science and Technology Canada, 1991), at 16.

14 Ibid.

15 Jayson Myers, "Investments in International Markets Create New Export Opportunities for Canadian Companies" (July/August 2002), *Canadian Manufacturers and Exporters Magazine*.

1. Describe the several major forms of establishing a greater presence in a foreign market. Describe the circumstances in which each form would be most appropriate.
2. What two major considerations must a firm bear in mind from the outset when negotiating an outsourcing agreement?
3. Describe the process of establishing an outsourcing arrangement.
4. Why is a distributor often not a true "agent"? What is the essential difference between an agency agreement and a distributorship? In what circumstances is each form more appropriate?
5. What are the three most common ways an agency is terminated?
6. In what important way does an agency agreement differ from an ordinary commercial contract (under the common law)?
7. Under the common law, what are the duties of a principal? An agent? What is the difference between the actual and apparent authority of an agent?
8. What additional factors are relevant in negotiating an agency agreement in the European Union? In other civil law countries?
9. Why is knowledge of intellectual property law and competition law important in a licensing situation? What are the major risks associated with licensing a foreign manufacturer to manufacture and sell in a foreign country?
10. Describe the difference between licensing and franchising. How did the authorities in Europe react to initial licensing arrangements made in that region? What is the situation today?
11. Describe the different forms of inter-business associations that fall short of being joint ventures and explain why these are not truly joint ventures in the legal sense.
12. What are some of the most common reasons for entering into an inter-business association or a joint venture?
13. What are the major types of joint venture and what is the advantage of each?
14. Describe the most common issues that must be settled before coming to an agreement to establish a joint venture.
15. What are the major risks associated with foreign direct investment? What multilateral or bilateral agreements are in place to protect foreign investors?

CLASS ACTIVITIES

1. Assign student teams to negotiate various forms of business entry on behalf of their "firms."
2. Invite students to provide current media stories that illustrate companies' experiences with various forms of foreign market entry.

FURTHER READING

Monitor trade and scholarly journals with up-to-date articles on various forms of market entry. There is a great deal of information written from a marketing perspective, but very little general legal writing in this area.

WEBSITES

Canadian Manufacturers and Exporters:
> www.cme-mec.ca

Industry Canada:
> http://strategis.ic.gc.ca

CHAPTER 11

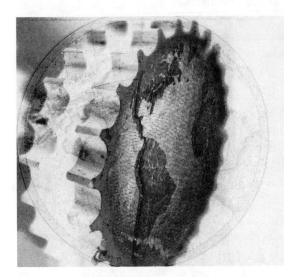

Settlement of International Business Disputes

INTRODUCTION

While no business person entering into a transaction, either domestic or international, likes to contemplate a dispute between the parties as the outcome of the "deal," experience tells us that this will happen in a certain percentage of cases. Settling a dispute in a domestic transaction can be time-consuming, expensive, and frustrating, but imagine how these factors can be compounded if the parties also need to agree on jurisdictional questions. If a dispute arises in an international transaction, there are, in addition to the matters in dispute, three potential issues:

- Which country's law will apply to the dispute?
- Which country's courts will hear the case?

LEARNING OBJECTIVES

After reading this chapter you will understand:

- that parties to an international contract should choose the law they wish to be applicable in the event of any contractual disputes between them, and that a plaintiff may generally sue in the country of its choice
- the importance of different countries' recognizing and enforcing judgments made by courts in other countries and the difference between a foreign judgment and a foreign arbitral award
- what sovereign immunity is
- the different forms of ADR and their respective advantages
- the leading international arbitration bodies—who they are and where they are—and the international agreements that provide for common rules for international arbitrations and enforcement of arbitral awards
- the relationship between arbitration and the courts

• Will the courts of one country recognize and enforce a judgment obtained in another country?

The parties to the contract have some control over the first two issues, and are less able to control the third. It is very important that the parties to a transaction address these issues when they are negotiating their contract. During negotiations, relations are usually amicable, optimism is in the air, and agreement on matters such as applicable law and jurisdiction can be achieved relatively easily. Once there is a dispute between the parties and relations have deteriorated, it is not so easy to agree as to which party's courts or law should prevail. Consider the typical situation described in box 11.1.

BOX 11.1   INTERNATIONAL CONSORTIUM TO CONSTRUCT HOTEL IN HANOI

Canexco Ltd., a Canadian engineering company located in Edmonton, is negotiating an arrangement with an Australian architect and an American steel supplier whereby the three companies will form a consortium to construct a new hotel in Hanoi, Vietnam. In the event of difficulties among the parties, which country's courts will have jurisdiction and what law will apply?

ACTIONS IN DOMESTIC COURTS: SUING AND BEING SUED

Choice of Law

The parties are free to specify in a choice of law clause that their contract will be governed by the law of a particular jurisdiction as long as their selection is made in good faith and is not for the purpose of avoiding the public policy of a country that has a connection to the contract. If a legal system is expressly chosen for the purpose of evading the provisions of the legal system with which the transaction is most closely connected, it is unlikely that such choice will be respected and enforced by a court. Parties must also bear in mind that a choice of law clause governs the law that applies to the *terms* in the contract; it does not affect the parties' subsisting obligation to obey the laws of any jurisdiction in which they carry on business or perform any activity. Canadians should note that they must always specify their provincial jurisdiction because a statement that the laws of Canada will apply is too vague. This advice applies where the choice of law is that of any federal country, such as the United States or Australia. International traders should condition themselves to check every transaction to make sure that the issue of potential disputes has been addressed and an appropriate provision on choice of law is included in the agreement. A recommended clause is:

> The conclusion, formalities, and performance of this contract will be governed by the laws of _____ (name of the province or country).

Proof of Foreign Law

Judges in the common law provinces of Canada and in most common law countries have no obligation to ascertain foreign law. In the event of litigation in which it is clear that the contract is to be governed by a foreign system of law, the law must be proved in our courts by an expert witness or some similar admissible evidence. Any fact or allegation that is to be relied on must first be raised in the pleadings in the case that precede any hearing at trial. A recent case that illustrates the application of this rule is the *Yordanes* case in box 11.2.

BOX 11.2   PLAINTIFF FAILS IN ATTEMPT TO PLEAD FOREIGN LAW IN ONTARIO COURT

Yordanes et al. v. The Bank of Nova Scotia et al.
(Ontario Superior Court of Justice, 2006)

In this case Yordanes, the plaintiff, brought an action under the *Class Proceedings Act* of Ontario seeking to represent a class consisting of the purchasers of corporate bonds issued by Scotiabank Quilmes S.A. (Quilmes), a commercial bank incorporated in Argentina. Quilmes was allegedly controlled by Scotia International Ltd., a Bahamian corporation that is a subsidiary of the Bank of Nova Scotia (BNS), a chartered bank with headquarters in Halifax, Nova Scotia. Quilmes defaulted in its payments under the bonds, became bankrupt, and was placed in liquidation. Yordanes sought a ruling from the Ontario court that BNS was jointly and severally liable with Quilmes to repay the debts under the bonds. Yordanes's claims against BNS were based on various claims made under Argentinean and Canadian law. The choice of law clause in the bond agreement stated that it was to be governed by English law. BNS brought an application in the Ontario court asking that the statement of claim (which was lengthy, over 100 pages) be "struck" under rule 21.01(1)(b) of the Ontario *Rules of Civil Procedure* on the grounds that it disclosed no reasonable cause of action and failed to comply with the rules of pleading.

The Court granted the application and ruled that the statement of claim should be struck in its entirety, with leave to deliver a fresh statement of claim that addressed the deficiencies.

The deficiencies noted by the Court included:

- inadequate, and sometimes inconsistent citations of foreign laws;
- excessive generality of descriptions of the contents of some foreign laws and a failure to describe the contents of others;
- failure to plead in the alternative where inconsistent allegations relating to the choice of governing laws were made; and
- references to the laws of multiple jurisdictions in connection with the same issue without identifying the appropriate jurisdiction.

The Court reiterated the legal principle that a court cannot take judicial notice of foreign law: it must be pleaded and proven as a matter of fact. The Court also stated that it did not discount the degree of difficulty involved in pleading foreign law to the extent required by the facts and the nature of the plaintiff's claims.

Thus, in a common law jurisdiction, if the party wishing to benefit from the foreign law fails to plead or bring such evidence, the law of the jurisdiction will be used. This is not normally the case in civil law jurisdictions, where judges and arbitrators are considered to have a duty to determine the foreign law that has been found to be applicable. In civil law countries the litigants are not responsible for bringing expert witnesses to give evidence of the foreign law.

The Proper Law of the Contract

If the parties have not made a choice of law, the proper law of the contract must be determined. A transaction may have several different aspects and it is possible that different law may be applicable to different aspects of the same transaction. The example in box 11.1 illustrates this type of situation. We could add to the complication of our example by noting that major financing for the project is being provided by Taiwanese interests. In the absence of choice of law clauses by the parties, different aspects of the transaction may be governed by different legal rules. Do the laws of Alberta apply? What about the law of the state of Queensland, the domicile of the architect? The American steel supplier will argue the applicability of the Uniform Commercial Code (UCC). It is unlikely that any party would want the law of Vietnam to apply because commercial law there is still in its infancy, just having emerged from a planned economy. In the absence of a choice of law clause, however, it could be the governing law. These kinds of situations can result in very expensive administration costs for the contract or, in the worst case, litigation.

If the parties have not made an express selection of the law they wish to apply, a court will have to determine what is the proper law of the contract. In Anglo-American law, this is the legal system with which the transaction has the closest and most real connection. To determine the proper legal system, the court looks at all the circumstances of the contract:

- the place the contract was made,
- the place the contract is performed,
- the place of business of the parties,
- the language, form, and terminology used in the contract, and
- the contract's connection with any preceding transaction.

Sometimes the parties have not made an express choice of law but they have made inferences by other clauses in their contract—for example, by designating a place of arbitration or stating that the courts of a certain country should have jurisdiction. In such cases, there is a strong inference in favour of the law of the arbitrator or place of arbitration or that of the court designated to hear the case.

European Convention on Contractual Law

The 1980 EC Convention on the Law Applicable to Contractual Obligations (Rome Convention) regulates cases between parties in EC (now EU) member states, and also cases of conflict between parties in member states and non-member states. This Convention states two basic principles: the first enshrines the right to choice of law, and the second provides that where the parties have not chosen, the law of the contract will be the law having *the closest connection with the contract*. Included in this concept is the *concept of characteristic performance*, which is not the law of the place where performance is carried out, but the law of the domicile of the performing party. Canadian business persons should be aware that Europeans may assume that the law of characteristic performance will apply. Consider, for example, a recent case, described in box 11.3.

BOX 11.3   PARTIES ASSUME DIFFERING LAWS

A Canadian construction firm was the mechanical and electrical contractor on a large project for an industrial installation in Alberta undertaken for the owner, a large American public company. The American company had contracted with a German firm to design the project and be responsible for delivering a "turn-key operation" to the owner. The German firm had, in turn, contracted with the Canadian construction firm, which had contracted with many local subcontractors. The parties did not, at the time of entering into these contracts, fully explore the question of choice of law, and the contract between the German firm and the Canadian construction firm did not provide for a choice of law, although it did provide for international arbitration in Switzerland. The parties each made different assumptions as to what law was applicable. The German firm assumed that

> the applicable law was that of Germany under the doctrine of characteristic performance. The Canadian firm assumed that the laws of Alberta applied, because that is where the contract was being performed. This uncertainty led to a number of disputes and high legal costs for all the parties.

Choice of Forum

The parties may also stipulate in advance where (in what jurisdiction's courts or forum) a case relating to their transaction will be heard. These clauses are honoured by most countries, subject to the following conditions:

- The choice of forum must not violate the public policy of a country having a genuine connection with the contract.
- The forum must not be seriously inconvenient for one or more of the parties or the court itself.

Choice-of-Forum Clauses

Choice-of-forum clauses may be "exclusive" or "non-exclusive." A non-exclusive clause is a statement by the parties that they submit to a particular court, but the clause does not specify that *all* disputes *must* be decided by that court. An example of a non-exclusive clause is:

> The parties submit to the jurisdiction of the courts in the Province of
> _____.

An example of an exclusive clause is:

> The parties agree that any and all disputes arising under the contract shall be determined exclusively by the courts of _____ (Province or Country), and agree to submit to the jurisdiction of _____ (same Province or Country).

If the parties have chosen to use an exclusive clause, they should each appoint an agent resident in the chosen jurisdiction for service of any relevant documents.

As a practical matter, choice of forum is not something usually contemplated by the parties to a contract. The usual way choice of forum occurs is, once the dispute has arisen, one party begins an action in the country (jurisdiction) of its choice. However, the court in which the action is initiated may not always agree to accept jurisdiction.

Who Can Sue and Be Sued in Canadian Courts?

Although the most practical rule to follow when deciding where to sue is to choose the jurisdiction in which the defendant's assets are located, a plaintiff cannot be sure that the jurisdiction it has chosen will hear the case if it has foreign elements. Foreign elements are matters such as foreign law or a preponderance of evidence in another country that is relevant to the issue in the case. Because the rules applied by the courts of different countries vary, it is impossible to outline them here. We can, however, briefly examine the rules in Ontario, which are based on English common law and are similar to those in the common law provinces of Canada, in England, and, to some extent, in the United States.

Ontario courts will assume jurisdiction if either of the following has occurred:

- the defendant was served while he/she/it was within Ontario; or
- the defendant was served outside of Ontario but there is "a connection to Ontario."

The Ontario *Rules of Civil Procedure* provide that "a connection to Ontario" exists where:

- the contract was made in Ontario;
- the contract provides that it is to be governed by or interpreted in accordance with the law of Ontario;
- the parties to the contract have agreed that the courts of Ontario are to have jurisdiction over legal proceedings in respect of the contract;
- the breach of contract has been committed in Ontario; and/or
- damage was sustained in Ontario as a result of a breach of contract wherever committed.

Where none of these connecting factors is present, the plaintiff must obtain the leave (or permission) of the court to start an action. This requires a preliminary motion before a **motions court** before the lawsuit can begin. This is a hearing before a judge to obtain decisions on matters relating to a lawsuit, which must be dealt with before or after a trial. It is also referred to in some jurisdictions as "chambers." Only after the action is started can the defendant be served with the documents giving details of the case. Box 11.4 describes a case in which an Ontario court declined jurisdiction on the grounds that the connection to Ontario was too weak.

BOX 11.4   PLAINTIFF FAILS TO SATISFY ONTARIO COURT OF REAL AND SUBSTANTIAL CONNECTION TO ONTARIO

Khan Resources Inc. et al. v. WM Mining Company, LLC et al. (Ontario Court of Appeal, 2006)

Mays was a resident of Colorado and his company WM Mining Co. was a Colorado corporation. The underlying assets at issue were three properties in Mongolia. Mays also owned a company in the British Virgin Islands,

Khan Resources Bermuda, of which the three assignor companies are wholly owned subsidiaries. Mays also incorporated a company, Khan Resources Inc., in Ontario in order to raise equity financing in Ontario for the development of the mining properties in Mongolia. Through a series of share exchange agreements and assignments, the properties in Mongolia were assigned to various Mays companies. It was alleged by the applicants that these assignments were unauthorized and of no force or effect. The applicants brought an action in Ontario for a declaration that the assignments were null and void and sought an injunction retraining the dealing with assigned assets. The motions judge stayed the application on the basis that there was *no real and substantial connection* between the relief claimed and the jurisdiction of the Ontario court.

The Ontario Court of Appeal confirmed the decision of the motions judge, that a stay of action should be ordered. It held that there are two major reasons why an Ontario court should not assert jurisdiction in this action:

1. The licences at issue in the case involve rights to land and the courts of most countries insist on the exclusive right to decide disputes over their own lands. Thus, ordinarily a judgment by a Canadian court on a disputed title of foreign land would be ineffective.
2. There is a rule in private international law that to be enforceable, the order of a foreign court must be for a fixed sum of money.

Because that is not what is asked for in this case, it is unlikely that a judgment of the Ontario court could be enforced in either Mongolia or the British Virgin Islands.

Thus, the connection to Ontario is very weak. Because the judgment requested is not likely to be enforceable in the jurisdiction where it needs to be effective, it is not appropriate for Ontario to assert jurisdiction.

Once a plaintiff has brought an action in its chosen jurisdiction (in our example, Ontario), the defendant may be able to object to the jurisdiction and have the action stayed or dismissed. The defendant's argument in these cases is usually one of the following:

- the case did not fall within the rules for service without leave; or
- if leave was granted, the leave of the court to serve outside the jurisdiction should not have been granted; or
- the court is not a convenient or appropriate forum for the hearing (**forum non conveniens**).

If the defendant is successful in any of these arguments, the court will **stay** or stop the action. This suspends the suit either temporarily or permanently.

If a stay is granted, the plaintiff must either give up the claim or sue in another jurisdiction.

Forum Non Conveniens

Under the doctrine of *forum non conveniens*, a court that has jurisdiction over a defendant under national law declines to exercise it and stays the action because it is not the appropriate venue for the action and considerations of justice require that the plaintiff litigate in another jurisdiction. This situation arises where a defendant served **ex juris** (outside the jurisdiction) brings an action asking for a stay of the action (for example, a French defendant served in France in connection with an action brought in Ontario). A good example of this type of situation is found in the *Nitsuko* case described in box 11.5.

BOX 11.5   BC COURT FINDS THAT BRITISH COLUMBIA IS A FORUM NON CONVENIENS FOR PLAINTIFF'S CASE

Canadian International Marketing Distributing Ltd. v. Nitsuko Ltd. et al. (BC Court of Appeal, 1990)

Canadian International Marketing, a Canadian company, started an action in British Columbia for breach of contract against Nitsuko, a Japanese company, alleging failure of Nitsuko to deliver goods FOB Japan. The contract provided that the law of Japan would govern the relationship. Nitsuko, the defendant, applied to the BC Supreme Court for a ruling that the BC court lacked jurisdiction or, alternatively, that it should decline jurisdiction. The chambers (motions) judge dismissed the application of Nitsuko on the ground that it had not established that the BC court was not a convenient forum. Nitsuko appealed and the case was heard by the BC Court of Appeal.

The appeal was allowed and an order was made stating that the BC courts had no jurisdiction.

On the facts, the only connection between this case and the province of British Columbia was that the plaintiff was a resident in British Columbia, and that was not enough. The defendants were not residents. They were residents of Japan. They neither carried on business in Canada nor had assets in Canada, nor had officers, employees, or agents in Canada. In short, they had no presence there. Furthermore, the alleged cause of action arose outside of Canada, on an alleged breach of contract to deliver goods FOB Japan. Moreover, the contract appeared to have incorporated the law of Japan to govern the contractual relationship. In those circumstances, the jurisdiction rested with the Japanese courts which, apparently, were open to the plaintiff.

Another good example of a *forum non conveniens* case is *Sterling Software*, described in box 11.6.

BOX 11.6   COURT STAYS ACTION BROUGHT IN ONTARIO COURT

Sterling Software International (Canada) Inc. v. Software Recording Corp. of America et al. (1993)

The plaintiff, Sterling Software, a wholly owned subsidiary of an American parent, entered into contracts with Software Recording Corporation (SRC) and Autotester, a Texas corporation, relating to the testing and licensing of computer software known as "Autotester." The contracts in dispute were negotiated and entered into in Texas and the governing law of the contracts was stated to be the law of the state of Texas. An action in Texas had been started before the plaintiff sued in Ontario. SRC and the other Ontario defendants moved for an order that the Ontario action be stayed, either permanently or pending the final resolution of the Texas action.

The application was granted. The Court offered that the Ontario action be stayed pending the outcome of the Texas action.

The core issue in both actions was the interpretation of a contract entered into in Texas and governed by Texas law: the two major Ontario defendants, SRC and Autotester, were both Texas corporations; the contracts that formed the nub of this dispute were negotiated and entered into in Texas; the governing law of the contract was the law of the state of Texas; the Texas action was commenced first; and the Canadian plaintiff was a wholly owned subsidiary of an American parent. In a commercial action of this nature that involves companies of international experience and background, it is not considered a major hardship on the Canadian plaintiff that some of the witnesses it will require to prove the causes of an action advanced in the Ontario action are situated in Ontario.

Another recent case in which an application for a stay of action was successful is the *Towne Meadow* case described in box 11.7. This case illustrates two important limitations on a foreign court's jurisdiction. The first limitation is that courts will not normally assert jurisdiction with respect to cases that involve real property in other countries and the second limitation is that foreign judgments are enforced only where the awards are monetary in character.

BOX 11.7   ONTARIO COURT MAKES DIFFICULT DECISION AS TO FORUM NON CONVENIENS

***Towne Meadow Development Corporation Inc. v. The Israel Discount Bank Ltd. et al.* (Ontario Court of Appeal, 2006)**

TD Bank in Ontario issued a letter of credit in favour of the Israel Discount Bank on the instructions of Towne Meadow Development Corporation. The credit was to secure general banking facilities. The letter of credit was later amended to secure credit facilities granted to Canada Ashdod. The TD Bank took the position that loans that it made to Kojfman, another Israeli company, were also covered by the letter of credit because the two companies were closely related and jointly carrying on the same construction business in Israel. Thus, the crucial question in the action was whether the letter of credit extended to the debts of Kojfman to the TD Bank. Towne brought an action in Ontario seeking to enjoin the Israel Discount Bank from drawing upon the letter of credit, and the Israel Discount Bank brought an application asking the Ontario court to stay the action because Ontario was not a convenient forum for the case.

The motions judge found that the letter of credit, which was to be governed by Ontario law, was not the major issue in the overall dispute and that Israel was the appropriate forum for the case. In reaching this decision, the judge noted that the substantial dispute rests in Israel and that the majority of the relevant witnesses, including key witnesses, reside in Israel; the bulk of the evidence is located in Israel; the factual matters in dispute arose in Israel; the Israel Discount Bank's principal home is in Israel; and it would not be to the disadvantage of the other parties if they were required to attend a trial in Israel. On this basis, the application for stay was granted and Israel was stated to be the more convenient forum. The decision was appealed.

In the Court of Appeal for Ontario, two judges concurred in the majority decision, and one judge dissented, indicating the difficulty of the issue.

The majority dismissed the appeal and confirmed the decision of the motions judge, stating that a decision of a motions judge as to the convenient forum for the resolution of a dispute is a discretionary one that is entitled to deference on appeal. In the absence of a demonstration that the motions judge erred in principle, the appeal must fail.

The dissenting judge's view was that the central issue in the action concerned the meaning of the letter of credit issued by the TD Bank and for that reason Ontario would be the more appropriate jurisdiction.

The examples above should not lead you to conclude that all applications for a stay of action on the ground of *forum non conveniens* are successful. Consider the somewhat typical case of *Upper Lakes Shipping* in box 11.8.

BOX 11.8   REQUEST FOR STAY OF ACTION FAILS

Upper Lakes Shipping Ltd. v. Foster Yeoman Ltd.
(Ontario Court (General Division), 1993)

The defendant, Foster Yeoman, a British company, entered into a contract with the plaintiff, Upper Lakes Shipping Ltd., a Canadian designer and supplier of ships, for the purchase of two ships, provided that the defendant could arrange satisfactory financing. The defendant eventually acquired the ships from another seller and the plaintiff sued the defendant in Ontario for breach of contract and breach of fiduciary duty. The defendant was served with the statement of claim in England pursuant to rule 17.02 of the Ontario *Rules of Civil Procedure*, which outlines situations where service may be made outside Ontario without leave. The defendant applied for an order from the Ontario court setting aside the service of the statement of claim or, alternatively, an order staying the action on the ground that Ontario was not the appropriate forum for the trial. The Ontario motions judge ruled that the plaintiff had established a "good arguable case" that the contract was made in Ontario thus bringing it within rule 17.02 and that the defendant had failed to satisfy the onus that England was the appropriate forum for the case. The defendant appealed this decision.

The appeal was dismissed and the Ontario action was permitted to proceed.

The Court concluded that this was a case in which service *ex juris* could be made without leave of the Court on the ground that the contract appeared to have been made in Ontario.

Other Methods Used by Defendants to Thwart a Plaintiff's Choice of Forum: The "Anti-Suit Injunction"

Much less common than an application for a stay of action is the situation in which a defendant in a foreign action brings an anti-suit injunction. This is an action in which the foreign defendant asks the court to enjoin or prevent plaintiffs resident in the court's jurisdiction from proceeding with their foreign action against the foreign defendant. For example, a French defendant who is being sued in France by an Ontario plaintiff may apply for an anti-suit injunction from the Ontario court.

This is the context for a case in which the Supreme Court of Canada recently examined the issue of a plaintiff's right to choose a forum. This was the issue in the *Amchem* case, set out in box 11.9. As the case shows, the existence of a more appropriate forum must be clearly established to displace the forum selected by the plaintiff.

BOX 11.9   SUPREME COURT OF CANADA DENIES ANTI-SUIT INJUNCTION

Amchem Products Inc. v. BC Workers Compensation Board **(Supreme Court of Canada, 1993)**

The issue before the Court in this case was an anti-suit injunction. In this case, 40 individual claimants, most of whom were residents of British Columbia, and the Workers' Compensation Board of British Columbia, which represented 154 additional claimants, commenced an action against defendant asbestos companies in the Texas District Court. The claimants alleged that the companies were engaged in **tortious** conduct in the United States, which caused injuries to the plaintiffs in British Columbia. (The word "tortious" is derived from the legal concept of tort, which is a wrong done to another legal person.) None of the defendants had any connection with British Columbia. The asbestos companies applied in the Supreme Court of British Columbia for anti-suit injunctions against the plaintiffs in order to prevent the continuation of the Texas actions. The injunctions were granted, and were upheld on appeal to the BC Court of Appeal, but were set aside by the Supreme Court of Canada (SCC). In making this decision, the SCC indicated that the application of the law in this area should not become too bound up with issues such as which party had begun the action, whether service *ex juris* had occurred, and which party has the **burden of proof**. (Burden of proof is the responsibility of one party to present evidence that raises an answerable case to which the other party must respond.) The SCC stated that a party whose case has a real and substantial connection with a forum has a legitimate claim to the advantages that forum provides.

Enforcement of Foreign Judgments

Enforcing a Foreign Judgment in Canada

Although the plaintiff may feel vindicated by a judgment in its favour in an international contract dispute, the real reason for the lawsuit is the recovery of damages. For this reason, the action should, whenever possible, be brought in a jurisdiction where the defendant has assets against which the judgments can be enforced. If judgment has been obtained in one jurisdiction and the defendant's assets are in another, the plaintiff must obtain recognition of the judgment in the second jurisdiction and attempt to enforce the judgment there.

In a case where the plaintiff has obtained a judgment in a foreign jurisdiction against a defendant in Canada, the plaintiff must then enforce its foreign judgment here. This will require a court proceeding in the Canadian province in which the judgment is to be enforced.

The law is developing rapidly in this area. Canadian courts are increasingly prepared to enforce judgments by US courts and by respected courts in other jurisdictions, provided the following conditions are met: there was proper subject matter jurisdiction over the Canadian parties; the judgment is not fraudulent or contrary to public policy or natural justice; and there is a real and substantial connection between the deciding court and the action. The law in this country has been substantially changed by the decision of the Supreme Court of Canada in *Morguard Investments Ltd. v. De Savoye*, a domestic family law case.[1] The question in this case was whether the judgment of an Alberta court could be enforced in British Columbia. The Supreme Court of Canada held unanimously in favour of enforceability, and the decision sets out in some detail the principles governing interjurisdictional enforcement of court orders. This has become a well-respected and frequently cited case and has since been relied on as a precedent in international cases for our courts to accept judgments made outside Canada. The following is an excerpt from the judgment in the *Morguard* case:

> Modern states, however, cannot live in splendid isolation and do give effect to judgments given in other countries in certain circumstances. Thus a judgment ... , such as a decree of divorce granted by the courts of one state to persons domiciled there, will be recognized by the courts of other states. In certain circumstances, as well, our courts will enforce personal judgments given in other states. Thus, we saw, our courts will enforce an action for breach of contract given by the courts of another country if the defendant was present there at the time of the action or has agreed to the foreign court's exercise of jurisdiction. This, it was thought, was in conformity with the requirements of comity, the informing principle of private international law, which has been stated to be the deference and respect due by other states to the actions of a state legitimately taken within its territory. Since the state where the judgment was given had power over the litigants, the judgments of its courts should be respected.

In the *Morguard* case the Supreme Court of Canada held that courts in one province in Canada should give "full faith and credit" to the judgments given by a court in another province, as long as the court had properly exercised jurisdiction in the action. As long as the court making the initial judgment had a "real and substantial connection" with the case, the judgment could be respected. Thus, provided that there is no manifest error or fraud on the face of the judgment and no natural justice or public policy problem, a Canadian court will recognize a foreign judgment. A recent example of Canadian judicial thinking in this area is the *Arrowmaster* case described in box 11.10.

BOX 11.10   US JUDGMENT ENFORCED IN CANADA

Arrowmaster Inc. v. Unique Forming Ltd. et al.
(Ontario Court (General Division), 1993)

The plaintiff, Arrowmaster, an Illinois corporation, had made a contract with the defendant, Unique Forming Ltd., an Ontario corporation, whereby Unique would purchase Arrowmaster's business. A dispute arose and Arrowmaster initiated a claim for breach of contract in the United States District Court, Central Division of Illinois. The defendant, Unique, **attorned** to the jurisdiction of a court. A full trial was held and judgment was delivered in favour of Arrowmaster in the amount of $93,210.20 plus interest, costs, and attorneys' fees. Although there was an appeal pending in Illinois, Arrowmaster brought an action in Ontario to enforce the Illinois judgment.

The Court was asked:

1. Whether the principles enunciated by the Supreme Court of Canada in the *Morguard* case apply in an international enforcement context.
2. Whether a stay of execution (or suspension of action) should be granted with respect to a foreign order because the judgment of the foreign court has been appealed from in a timely fashion and the results of that appeal are imminent.

The Court ruled:

1. The Illinois court order should be enforced because there is no triable issue (the issues had been fully tried in Illinois) and, therefore, the case is an appropriate one for summary judgment under the Ontario *Rules of Civil Procedure*.
2. A stay of execution is warranted until after the United States Appellate Court has rendered its decision.

The Court found that the foreign judgment was final and *res judicata* in the foreign jurisdiction. This occurs when the judgment of the foreign court is final in the sense that the court that made it no longer has the power to rescind or vary it; this test is not altered by reason that the judgment is under appeal. The Court also found that none of the grounds for impeachment of a foreign judgment was present. The judge enumerated five grounds for impeachment of a foreign judgment:

1. lack of jurisdiction over the subject matter or the parties;
2. lack of identity of the defendant—that is, the defendant was not a party to the foreign suit;
3. the judgment was procured by a fraud on the court;
4. there was a failure of natural justice; or
5. enforcement of the judgment would be contrary to public policy in Ontario.

Thus, a Canadian firm that has assets in Canada but is sued outside Canada should be careful before it assumes that such an action is no threat. If there is a chance that a Canadian court might find that a US or other foreign jurisdiction had a "real and substantial" connection to the matter, a Canadian defendant should not forgo the opportunity to defend the action on the merits in that foreign jurisdiction. Legal advice should always be sought in these circumstances before deciding whether or not to attorn to the foreign jurisdiction.

The *Arrowmaster* case indicates the five grounds available to a defendant seeking to persuade a court in Ontario (or other common law jurisdiction) not to recognize and enforce a judgment obtained outside the jurisdiction. One of those grounds is that the enforcement of the judgment would be contrary to the public policy of the enforcing jurisdiction. This argument was attempted in the two cases, described in boxes 11.11 and 11.12, the *Boardwalk* case and the *Shield* case.

BOX 11.11   IS GAMBLING AGAINST PUBLIC POLICY IN CANADA?

Boardwalk Regency Corp. v. Maalouf
(Ontario Court of Appeal, 1992)

Boardwalk, which operated a gambling casino in Atlantic City, New Jersey, lent money to Maalouf, who incurred a gambling debt at the casino. Maalouf failed to repay and dishonoured a cheque drawn on a Canadian bank representing the debt of $43,000. Boardwalk obtained a default judgment in New Jersey and brought an action in Ontario, on the grounds that the Ontario *Gaming Control Act* represented a public policy against gambling that precluded enforcement of the foreign judgment. Boardwalk appealed from the decision of the lower court.

The appeal was allowed. Judgment was awarded to the plaintiff in Canadian currency plus costs.

The Court held that the parties intended to be bound by the laws of New Jersey. The only connection to Ontario was that the cheques were drawn on an Ontario branch of a Canadian bank.

Although it is true that public policy can be a basis for denying recovery under a foreign judgment, the act that is alleged to be a breach of public policy must be one that breaches essential morality and offends more than the morality of some persons. The norm relied on must run throughout the fabric of society to the extent that the act impugned is not consonant with our system of justice and general moral outlook. The fact that there is limited licensing of gambling in Ontario prevents gambling from qualifying as being innately immoral.

BOX 11.12   CANADIAN COMPANIES FAIL TO AVOID US JUDGMENT ON GROUNDS OF BREACH OF NATURAL JUSTICE AND PUBLIC POLICY

United States of America v. The Shield Development Co. (Ontario Superior Court, 2005)

Shield, a Canadian company, had operated a copper-processing facility on a property in Utah, and the US government had removed hazardous substances from the site pursuant to the US *Comprehensive Environmental Response, Compensation, and Liability Act*. Shield alleged that it had not caused the environmental pollution, but that the pollution had been caused by an American corporation that had subleased the site and operated it from 1971 to 1974. The US government chose not to pursue the American corporation but sued the two Canadian corporations, the one that owned the property and Shield. A judgment was made by a Utah court for US $242,614.93 plus costs. The US government commenced an action in Ontario to enforce its Utah judgment. Shield resisted this action on two grounds:

1. there had been a breach of natural justice in that there had not been proper service on Shield of several court documents; and
2. the US decision to sue two Canadian companies and not the US corporation was contrary to public policy.

The motion for summary judgment was granted to the US government. The Ontario Superior Court found that the Utah judgment met the test in Canadian law for the recognition and enforcement of a foreign judgment and that neither of the two defences raised triable issues. In rejecting Shield's defences, the Court ruled that

1. the argument of breach of natural justice was unsustainable because the issue of service of documents was merely a procedural irregularity and Shield was aware of the legal proceedings and had retained counsel in Utah. Although two documents were sent to the wrong address, the notification of the hearing dates was sent to the correct address; and
2. the public policy defence was also unsustainable because Shield was not challenging the US law, but rather how that law had been applied. There was no evidence that the United States had improperly targeted Shield.

In the *Shield* case, the issue concerned an alleged breach of natural justice and a breach of public policy in the way the case had been prosecuted in the United States.

Another interesting case decided recently by a Canadian court involved allegations of bias and an absence of natural justice (see box 11.13).

BOX 11.13   ENFORCEMENT OF FOREIGN JUDGMENTS— ALLEGATIONS OF BIAS

Oakwell Engineering Ltd. v. Enernorth Industries Inc.
(Ontario Superior Court of Justice, 2005)

Oakwell Engineering Limited brought an application to enforce a judgment of the High Court of Singapore in Ontario. The defendant, Enernorth, opposed the recognition and enforcement of the judgment on the basis that the Singapore legal system does not conform to the Canadian concept of justice and that there are improper connections in Singapore among the judiciary, the executive, and business; that these connections suggested that there was a real risk that judges in Singapore were biased in this case; and that the Singapore legal system is not sufficiently independent for its judgments to be recognized by Canadian courts.

The facts behind the dispute were that the two companies entered into a settlement agreement to resolve various disputes between them. The settlement agreement provided that any disputes that arose in future under the agreement were to be governed by Singapore law and subject to the non-exclusive jurisdiction of the Singapore courts. Oakwell had brought an action against Enernorth in Singapore alleging that payments under the agreement had not been made. Enernorth defended that action and counterclaimed in the Singapore action.

The application for enforcement of the Singapore judgment was granted. The Court noted that the forum selection clause in the settlement agreement specified Singapore courts and both parties had attorned to the jurisdiction of Singapore. The defence of bias had not been raised at the trial. The Court stated that it was not clear that enforcement of a specific decision can be denied based on allegations that a whole system is biased, when there is no cogent evidence that there was bias in the specific case. The Court found that the respondent had failed to establish that Singapore's legal system did not meet the standards of the rule of law in Canada. There was no evidence that the respondent was denied natural justice.

Provision for Reciprocal Enforcement of Judgments

Within Canada, we have legislation that provides for reciprocal enforcement of judgments between the provinces. The only provision we have for reciprocal enforcement of judgments made outside Canada is with the United Kingdom with which we have the Convention Between Canada and the United Kingdom for the Reciprocal Recognition and Enforcement of Judgments in Civil and Commercial Matters. Most Canadian provinces have implemented this Convention, which provides a more convenient method of enforcing a judgment because it allows the plaintiff to apply for registration of a "foreign" judgment when it is from a court in the reciprocating jurisdiction. This avoids the necessity for an application to the court for the enforcement of the foreign judgment, although notice of the application to register the judgment must still be made to the defendant. Once a registration order is made, the foreign judgment becomes a judgment of the registering court and has the same force and effect as a judgment originating in that jurisdiction. The terms of such a judgment may not be varied by the registering jurisdiction.

There is no international system for the enforcement of awards obtained in domestic courts of other jurisdictions, and there is no international convention that provides for the reciprocal recognition or enforcement of foreign judicial decisions. Note that this is an important difference between a foreign judgment and a foreign arbitral award, which will be discussed further in the section on arbitration. Because courts are increasingly willing to recognize and enforce foreign judgments, a Canadian firm or individual that is sued in a well-recognized foreign jurisdiction should defend the case on its merits in that jurisdiction. Failure to do so will likely result in a default judgment, which may be enforced against the firm or individual in Canada.

Actions Involving Foreign States

If a contract is made directly with a foreign state, there is a possibility that in legal proceedings the foreign state will plead **sovereign immunity** in an attempt to escape its commercial obligations. Sovereign immunity is immunity from prosecution or suit claimed by a nation state. There are two theories of state immunity—**absolute immunity** and **restrictive immunity**. Under Anglo-American law, only absolute immunity is recognized. Absolute immunity applies where a country acts in exercise of its sovereign authority, that is, in connection with acts that are an integral part of functions of government. In cases where a state has been engaged in ordinary commercial activity, such as the sale and purchase of goods in a regular commercial transaction, the immunity is restricted and is not recognized.

Extraterritorial Effect of Foreign State Measures

As a rule, our courts reject the doctrine that foreign laws can be effective within another country as of right. Any claims made by foreign jurisdictions affecting our sovereignty will be rejected. Examples of laws that will not be enforced by our courts are:

- nationalization laws, where property is outside the territory of the nationalizing state; and
- foreign revenue laws, penal laws, and similar public laws of a foreign state.

Foreign Illegality

CIVIL ILLEGALITY

Our courts will not enforce a contract if performance is against the law of the country where the contract is to be performed.

CRIMINAL ILLEGALITY

If Canadians commit a criminal offence under the laws of another country, can they be convicted and punished in Canada? Generally speaking, no, because we do not normally enforce the criminal laws of another country, nor is an act committed abroad normally punishable in Canada unless such act falls under our *Criminal Code*, or is dealt with in special legislation. **Extradition** may be applied if the offence is an extraditable one and if Canada has an extradition treaty with the country in which the alleged crime was committed.

ALTERNATIVE DISPUTE RESOLUTION

Introduction

There has been a remarkable shift in recent years away from commercial litigation in the courts to alternative forms of dispute resolution. International litigation may frustrate the parties by taking years to resolve, costing a great deal of money, and destroying the commercial relationship. For this reason, dispute resolution that does not take place in the courts of any country is a popular option for the settlement of commercial disagreements. **Alternative dispute resolution (ADR)** provides the opportunity for the parties to determine what law will apply to their dispute, who will "judge" a dispute, and what forms of evidence will be permitted. The two most common methods of alternative dispute resolution available to the parties are mediation and conciliation, and arbitration.

- *Mediation and conciliation.* **Mediation** and **conciliation** are voluntary dispute resolution processes that make use of the "good offices" of a neutral third party but there is no promise of an outcome that is binding on the parties. Each process is similar in that it is an attempt to resolve a dispute on a consensual basis through the assistance of a third party. In conciliation, the third party meets with each disputing party separately and interprets and transmits each party's position to the other party, usually suggesting proposals for an acceptable resolution of the dispute. If in addition to these activities, the third party is also expected to provide a formal written report of the proceedings, the process is generally described as mediation. UNCITRAL has rules on conciliation.[2]

- *Arbitration.* **Arbitration** is a more formalized voluntary process whereby a neutral third party listens to the evidence and renders a decision that the parties have agreed in advance to honour.

Litigation, the process whereby the court settles a dispute, is traditionally more acceptable in the United States, Canada, and other common law countries than in many other countries. This acceptance is changing, however, because business relationships often include parties in countries that view a court case as a public acknowledgment of a breakdown between the parties. This has led both domestically and internationally to an increasing interest in methods of resolving disputes other than hard-fought "winner takes all" litigation. This trend is likely to continue, and as business persons become more familiar with the methods of alternative dispute resolution, it will become easier to include appropriate provisions in contracts and to use them when necessary. Most developed countries have identified a number of problems in connection with the administration of justice through the court system, the most common of which are high costs, delays, and unnecessary complexity.

In a few short years, Canada has moved from being distinctly behind in the development of ADR mechanisms to becoming a leader in providing the business community with an alternative to litigation.

Arbitration

Arbitration has emerged as the favoured form of ADR for international trade disputes. Some of the perceived advantages of arbitration over litigation are:

- its cost—arbitration may be cheaper than litigation;
- pre-trial discovery is more limited than it is in litigation, hence cheaper and less time consuming for the parties;
- arbitration is often faster than litigation;
- the rules governing admissibility of evidence are more flexible than those in litigation;
- an arbitral award is more easily enforced in foreign countries than is a judgment;
- an arbitration may be more private than litigation;
- arbitration proceedings are less adversarial than court proceedings and may be less destructive to the relationship of the parties; and
- there is limited right to appeal in arbitration (although this is a disadvantage for a party who is unsatisfied with the outcome).

Because arbitration has become the preferred method of settlement in international commercial disputes, it has become common practice to include an arbitration clause in most international commercial contracts.

Even when the parties fail to include such a clause, a dispute may be referred to arbitration by special submission or agreement.

The use of international commercial arbitration has been greatly assisted by the preparation and adoption of the following:

- international agreements that *provide common rules for arbitrations*:
  — 1976 UNCITRAL Arbitration Rules of Conciliation and Arbitration.
  — 1985 UNCITRAL Model Law on International Commercial Arbitration.

- an international agreement that *provides for the enforcement of arbitral awards*:
  — 1958 Convention on the Recognition and Enforcement of Foreign Arbitral Awards (the New York Convention).

International Arbitration Rules and Procedures

International arbitration rules and procedures have been devised because of the material differences between the various national laws of arbitration. In 1976, the United Nations Commission on International Trade Law (UNCITRAL) published the UNCITRAL Arbitration Rules and these rules were approved by the UN General Assembly. These rules are not a convention and do not have the force of law in any country but are intended to be adopted voluntarily by the parties of an international contract. Under these rules, the parties must specify the number of arbitrators, the place of arbitration, and the language of arbitration. These rules have gained wide acceptance and are incorporated by reference into the arbitration rules of many other international organizations. Business persons wishing to adopt the UNCITRAL rules may do so by specifying use of the rules in their arbitration clause.

In 1985, UNCITRAL established a task force to work on a modern uniform legislative framework for international commercial arbitrations. The result was the **UNCITRAL Model Law on International Commercial Arbitration**. It was designed to provide a comprehensive set of substantive rules to facilitate the resolution, by private arbitration, of civil disputes that are both international and commercial in character. Only after implementing legislation is passed by the appropriate national legislative bodies in each country does the framework have the force of law. In Canada, because of our federal system, arbitration legislation was required to be passed in each of the provinces and territories as well as by the federal government. Such legislation has been enacted by the federal government and by each of the 10 provinces and 3 territories. With the exception of Quebec, each of the provinces and territories has two arbitration statutes—one for domestic arbitrations and another for international arbitrations. In Quebec, the relevant provisions of the *Civil Code of Quebec* and the *Code of Civil Procedure* are interpreted in accordance with the transnational law providing for international commercial arbitration.

Leading Arbitral Institutions

There are many facilities for international commercial arbitration that have been established around the world. Each of these institutions has its own set of rules that conform to the UNCITRAL model rules, but each has its own character, language, and strengths, and each will appeal to businesses in different parts of the world or businesses from different economic sectors.

THE INTERNATIONAL CHAMBER OF COMMERCE

The ICC offers arbitration suitable for businesses in countries with sharply contrasting national systems of law. These arbitrations are administered by the Court of Arbitration headquartered in Paris, France.

THE AMERICAN ARBITRATION ASSOCIATION

The American Arbitration Association (AAA) was established to resolve disputes in fields as diverse as labour relations, insurance claims, election supervision, family disputes, criminal cases, and commercial matters, as well as disputes between Americans and foreign nationals. Arbitration under these rules is very common for contracts between parties in Canada and the United States. The AAA has also entered into agreements with institutions in Europe and Asia.[3]

THE LONDON COURT OF INTERNATIONAL ARBITRATION

The London Court of International Arbitration is another important international arbitration facility that is frequently used in international business. Established in the United Kingdom, this Court provides dispute resolution for parties, regardless of location or system of law, and operates under the "London rules."[4]

OTHER ARBITRAL INSTITUTIONS AROUND THE WORLD

Other acceptable sets of rules that international businesses will encounter are the Rules of Procedure of the Inter-American Commercial Arbitration Commission (common in South American contracts); the European Convention on International Commercial Arbitration (used primarily for arbitration between businesses located in Western Europe and the former socialist countries of Eastern Europe); the Foreign Economic and Trade Arbitration Commission (FETAC) in China; as well as the Stockholm Chamber of Commerce; the Netherlands Arbitration Institute; and the Arbitration Court of the Federal Chamber of Commerce in Vienna. Arbitration centres have been established in many important cities around the world, including Cairo, Kuala Lumpur, and Lagos. Many other countries have adopted the UNCITRAL rules and provide arbitral services.[5]

CANADIAN ARBITRAL INSTITUTIONS AND RULES

Canadians should be aware of the advantages of providing for arbitration in Canada. Canadians have a high degree of expertise in international arbitration. UNCITRAL, the ICC, and the AAA each have a direct or indirect presence in Canada through a local committee or through Canadian members on their panels of distinguished neutrals. In addition, we have well-respected arbitration centres in major cities in Canada. These include:

- ADR Chambers with offices in Toronto[6] and Ottawa.
- the British Columbia International Commercial Arbitration Centre.[7] This centre is especially well located for contracts involving parties from the Pacific Rim countries.
- the International Commercial Arbitration Centre in Quebec City, which is not only well placed linguistically but also attractive to international business because it represents both the common law and civil law traditions.

Enforcement of International Arbitration Decisions: The Importance of the New York Convention

Each of the provinces in Canada and the Parliament of Canada has implanted the 1958 New York **Convention on the Recognition and Enforcement of Foreign Arbitral Awards (the New York Convention)**. The New York Convention establishes rules for the recognition of an arbitration clause and requires the contract or arbitration agreement to be in writing, signed by the parties, or contained in the exchange of letters or telegrams. The parties must promise to submit to arbitration any differences that arise between them with respect to a commercial relationship. More than 70 states have acceded to the New York Convention, including such important trading partners as the United States, Mexico, the United Kingdom, France, and Japan. Some countries have acceded to this Convention with a reservation requiring reciprocity. Therefore, it is advisable for business persons to check on the status of countries with which they are dealing. Canada does not apply the reciprocity reservation and will enforce an award made in any member state. The UNCITRAL Model Law on International Commercial Arbitration provides for the recognition and enforcement of awards in Article 35, which states that "[a]n arbitral award, irrespective of the country in which it was made, shall be recognized as binding, and upon application in writing to the competent court, shall be enforced." Grounds upon which recognition or enforcement of an arbitral award may be denied are outlined in Article 36:

- a party to the arbitration agreement was under some incapacity, or the agreement is not valid under the law to which the parties were subject, or
- a party was not given proper notice of the appointment of an arbitrator or of the arbitral proceedings, or was otherwise unable to present its case, or
- the award deals with a dispute not contemplated and not within the terms of the submission to arbitration, or
- the composition of the arbitral tribunal or procedure was not in accordance with the agreement, or
- the award has not yet become binding on the parties or has been set aside or suspended, or
- the subject matter of the dispute is not capable of settlement by arbitration under the law of the state, or
- the award is in conflict with the public policy of the state.

An interesting example of a case in which public policy was presented as a reason that a foreign arbitral award should not be enforced is *Arcata Graphics Buffalo* (see box 11.14). Notice the similarity of the Court's approach to the previous cases (*Boardwalk* and *Shield*) that we considered in the context of *the enforcement of a foreign judgment*.

BOX 11.14   CANADIAN COURT ORDERS ENFORCEMENT OF US AWARD—ISSUE OF PUBLIC POLICY

Arcata Graphics Buffalo Ltd. v. Movie (Magazine) Corp.
(Ontario Court of Justice [General Division], 1993)

The plaintiff sought to enforce an award from an arbitrator in the United States against the defendant, which was located in Ontario. The arbitrator's award included a provision for interest at a rate higher than that allowed under Ontario legislation. The defendant argued that the award could not be enforced because the provision for interest at a rate higher than that allowed in Ontario was against public policy.

Was the American arbitration award unenforceable for reasons of public policy?

Eberle J of the Ontario Court of Justice held that in order to refuse enforcement of such an award, it must be contrary not merely to the law of the forum but to the essential fundamental morality of its community. He found that this was not the case with the provision for interest and ordered that the arbitration award be recognized and enforced.

Thus, this case that involved enforcement of an arbitrator's award applies substantially the same test as that used with respect to the enforcement of foreign judgments (as seen in the *Boardwalk* case).

The main benefit of Canadian adoption of the New York Convention and the UNCITRAL Model Law is that international arbitral awards are recognized and enforced almost automatically without the necessity of bringing an action on the award in a local court. Once an international commercial award is recognized by the court, it is enforceable in the same manner as a judgment or order of that court.

Types of Arbitration

There are two types of arbitration—ad hoc (for the purpose of a particular dispute) and institutional. In ad hoc arbitration the parties initiate and proceed with arbitration without the assistance of a permanent arbitral institution. This may present considerable problems because the arbitration provision must be thought through and drafted by the individual parties. If the place of arbitration is specified, however, domestic legislation in the place of arbitration may supply the parties with the necessary framework and rules for their arbitration. Institutional arbitration occurs when the parties have specified that arbitration will be conducted by a specified arbitral institution, according to its rules. Several of these institutions are listed above.

Wording of the Arbitration Clause or Agreement

The wording of the arbitration clause should be neither too restrictive nor too broad. For example, a well-worded arbitration clause will contain the words "all disputes arising in connection with the present contract." Specific reference should be made to the particular arbitral institution chosen, with a proviso that its rules "presently in force" or "in force at the time of the signing of this agreement" will apply. It may be desirable to specify the nationality of the arbitrator(s). It may also be necessary to stipulate an acceptable place of arbitration because this may determine the procedural law or rules applicable to the arbitration. Care should be taken to ensure that the location is in a country that is a party to the New York Convention and has adopted the UNCITRAL Model Law. The language of the arbitration should be stipulated and the law applicable to the substance of the dispute should be specified.

Do Courts Always Honour the Arbitration Clause?

Traditionally, the courts have rather zealously guarded their traditional jurisdiction over legal disputes. In the past there were cases decided by courts in a number of countries in which they were reluctant to apply the arbitration clause agreed to by the parties. In these cases, if one party sued and the other party asked for a stay of action on the grounds of the agreement to arbitrate, the courts would often find a reason to assert jurisdiction, usually on the grounds that the dispute concerned questions of law or that the dispute fell clearly within the jurisdiction of the court. The courts in Canada now fully accept international legal public policy in favour of allowing private arbitrators to resolve international business disputes. On the subject of arbitration agreement and substantive claim before court, the UNCITRAL Model Law on International Commercial Arbitration states in Article 8:

> A court before which an action is brought in a matter which is the subject of an arbitration agreement shall, if a party so requests, … refer the parties to arbitration unless it finds that the agreement is null and void, inoperative or incapable of being performed.

This change in the law was clearly expressed by Campbell J of the Ontario Supreme Court, High Court of Justice in *Boart Sweden AB v. NYA Stromnes*, a 1988 case:

> Public policy carries me to the consideration which I conclude is paramount having regard to the facts of this case, and that is the very strong public policy of this jurisdiction that where parties have agreed by contract that they will have the arbitrators decide their claims, instead of resorting to the Courts, the parties should be held to their contract … .
>
> It would also fail to give effect to the change in the law of international arbitration which, with the advent of Article 8 of the Model Law and the removal of the earlier wide ambit of discretion, gives the Courts a clear direction to defer to the arbitrators even more than under the previous law of international arbitration.

Article 8 was considered in another Ontario case, *Canada Packers v. Terra Nova*, in which its application was extended to both contractual and non-contractual matters arising out of a commercial legal relationship (see box 11.15).

BOX 11.15   COURT SUPPORTS ARBITRATION

Canada Packers Inc. et al. v. Terra Nova Tankers Inc. et al. (Ontario Court of Justice [General Division], 1992)

Canada Packers Inc. agreed with an agent of Terra Nova Tankers Inc. to charter the ship *Tove Cob* to carry vegetable oils from East Asian ports for discharge at Montreal and Toronto. The voyage charterparty (contract) included an arbitration clause that provided for any dispute to be settled by arbitration in New York State. Differences arose between the parties;

Terra Nova alleged various torts (not contract violations) had been committed against it and other defendants and started an action in Ontario courts. One of the parties to the lawsuit applied for a stay of the action on the grounds of the arbitration agreement, and the application was opposed on the ground that the claim was in tort, not contract.

The Court was asked: Does the fact that the claim is based in tort, not contract, exclude the application of the arbitration agreement?

The Court said that it did not and ordered that any dispute arising from the making, performance, or termination of the charterparty be referred to arbitration in New York in accordance with the provisions of the charterparty.

The mere fact that a claim sounds in tort does not exclude arbitration. The New York Convention and the UNCITRAL Model Law thus cover both contractual and non-contractual commercial relationships. They thus extend their scope to liability in tort so long as the relationship that creates liability is one that can fairly be described as "commercial."

A more recent example of the courts' deference to an arbitration agreement is the *Dalimpex* case summarized in box 11.16.

BOX 11.16   COURT DEFERS TO ARBITRATION AGREEMENT

Dalimpex Ltd. v. Janicki; Agros Trading Spolka v. Dalimpex Ltd.
(Ontario Court of Appeal, 2003)

This case is complex because it involved two connected actions being heard by the court and two legal issues: first, whether the Ontario court would accept jurisdiction in the action initiated by Dalimpex as plaintiff and, second, whether the Ontario court would recognize and enforce the arbitral award from Poland against Dalimpex. Dalimpex was a Canadian company that imported and distributed various goods, most of which were manufactured in Poland. Agros Trading was a large Polish food conglomerate and broker and was the major supplier to Dalimpex. In 1983, the two companies entered into an agency agreement that provided that Polish law applied to the agreement and any disputes would be settled by the College of Arbitrators at the Polish Chamber of Foreign Trade in Warsaw. In 1989, the Polish Chamber of Foreign Trade ceased to exist and a new body, the National Chamber of Commerce, was created to take over its function. As well, a new arbitral body, the Court of Arbitration, was established.

In 1998, Agros terminated the agency agreement. There was an allegation that Janicki, a long-term employee of Agros who became a senior executive with Dalimpex, had conspired with Agros and a third party to injure Dalimpex by appropriating Dalimpex's customers, confidential information, and business in Canada. Dalimpex brought an action against Janicki in Ontario claiming damages for breach of contract, breach of trust, breach of fiduciary duty, conspiracy, interference with economic relations, and inducing breach of contract. Agros countered with a proceeding in the Court of Arbitration in Poland. The Court of Arbitration found in Agros's favour and granted an award of US$440,236.56 to Agros. An application by Dalimpex before the Polish courts to set the award aside was dismissed. In 1998, Dalimpex also started an action in Ontario against Agros. An action was brought by Agros in the Ontario court to stay Dalimpex's action pending final resolution by arbitration of all disputes between Dalimpex and Agros.

The application for stay was granted: that is, the Court did not accept jurisdiction (legal issue one). The Court held that

> [i]t is not for the court on an application for a stay of proceedings to reach any final determination as to the scope of the arbitration agreement or whether a particular party to the legal proceedings is a party to the arbitration agreement, because those are matters within the jurisdiction of the arbitral tribunal. Only where it is clear that the dispute is outside the terms of the arbitration agreement, or that the party is not a party to the arbitration agreement, or that the application is out of time, should the court reach any final determination in respect of such matters on an application for a stay of proceedings. Where it is arguable that the dispute falls within the terms of the arbitration agreement ... then the stay should be granted and those matters left to be determined by the arbitral tribunal.

With respect to legal issue two, the Ontario court indicated that it would be prepared to enforce the Polish arbitration award, if it were final, but since the validity of the award was still a matter before the Polish courts, the application to recognize and enforce the arbitration award should be stayed.

Judicial Review of Arbitral Awards

One fundamental question remains to be dealt with if we are to assess the genuine effectiveness of an alternative system for dispute resolution—that is, are the courts prepared to accept the arbitrator's decision as final or will they find legal reasons for overturning the award, thus superimposing an appeal system on the arbitration process? Article 34 of the UNCITRAL Model Law on International Commercial Arbitration provides that recourse to a court against an arbitral award may be made only in accordance and upon proof that

- a party to the arbitration agreement was under some incapacity, or the agreement is not valid under the law to which the parties were subject, or
- a party was not given proper notice of the appointment of an arbitrator or of the arbitral proceedings or was otherwise unable to present its case, or
- the award deals with a dispute not contemplated and not within the terms of the submission to arbitration, or
- the composition of the arbitral tribunal or procedure was not in accordance with the agreement, or
- the subject matter of the dispute is not capable of settlement by arbitration under the law of the state, or
- the award is in conflict with the public policy of the state.

Note that the grounds for judicial review of arbitral awards are similar to the reasons why a foreign arbitral award may not be recognized. There are six grounds that would justify a judicial review of an arbitral award and they are identical to six of the seven grounds upon which recognition and enforcement of a foreign award can be denied. (See the discussion of "Enforcement of International Arbitration Decisions" earlier in this chapter.) The seventh ground for denial of recognition and enforcement—that is, "that the award has not yet become binding on the parties or has been set aside or suspended"—is excluded from the list of grounds for judicial review. The similarity of these grounds is not surprising when one considers that the policy behind each set of rules is to ensure fairness and transparency in the settlement of disputes by arbitration.

The attitude of Canadian courts to a request that the court review an award by an arbitrator is well illustrated by the *Quintette Coal* case described in box 11.17.

BOX 11.17   ARBITRATION REVIEW DENIED

Quintette Coal Limited v. Nippon Steel Corporation
(BC Supreme Court and BC Court of Appeal, 1991)

This case involved a lengthy arbitration in British Columbia over a long-term supply agreement between 10 Japanese purchasers and Quintette Coal Limited, a supplier of coal from northern British Columbia. The agreements provided for arbitration of all unresolved disputes between the parties in British Columbia according to British Columbia law. After a lengthy arbitration lasting 142 days, an award was made fixing the price to be paid to Quintette. Quintette, dissatisfied with the award, then sought to attack the award in the courts on the basis that it decided matters beyond the scope of the submission.

The Court was asked to decide whether this was a suitable case for the award to be reviewed by the courts.

The Court held that it was not. The trial court and the BC Court of Appeal found the award to be within the scope of the submission and not open to interference by the Court. In the words of Mr. Justice Gibbs,

> there is a world-wide trend toward restricting judicial control over international commercial arbitration awards. ... The concerns of international comity, respect for the capacities of foreign and transnational tribunals, and sensitivity to the need of the international commercial system for predictability in the resolution of disputes ... are as compelling in this jurisdiction as they are in the United States or elsewhere.

NOTES

1 *Morguard Investments Ltd. v. De Savoye*, Supreme Court of Canada, 1990.

2 See the UNCITRAL model conciliation clause, online at www.uncitral.org.

3 For further information on the AAA, see www.adr.org.

4 For further information on the London Court of International Arbitration, see www.lcia-arbitration.com.

5 For a list of countries and their facilities, see the Lex Mercatoria website: www.jus.uio.no/lm/arbitration/institution.rules.

6 For further information on ADR Chambers, see www.adrchambers.com.

7 For further information on the British Columbia International Commercial Arbitration Centre, see www.bcicac.com.

REVIEW QUESTIONS

1. What three potential issues may arise in connection with an international business dispute other than the particular issue between the parties?

2. Are the parties to an international contract completely free to specify what law will apply to their contract? What, if any, limitation is there?

3. What factors will a court consider if it is necessary for it to make a decision as to the proper law of the contract?

4. What is meant by "characteristic performance"? What is the source of this concept?

5. Are the parties to an international contract completely free to stipulate a choice of forum? What limitations are there on this choice?

6. Can a plaintiff always be sure that the jurisdiction it has chosen will hear the case, when there are foreign elements involved? What are the rules in your province or territory? What are the rules in Ontario? How do the two sets of rules compare?
7. What three arguments are available to a defendant who wishes to object to the jurisdiction of a court?
8. Describe circumstances in which an argument of *forum non conveniens* might be successful.
9. What is an "anti-suit" injunction? How might such a remedy arise?
10. What happens if a court grants a stay of action?
11. How has the philosophy of Canadian courts changed recently with respect to enforcement of a foreign arbitral award? Why? Explain which international agreements contribute to this situation.
12. Is there more certainty involved in the enforcement of a foreign judgment or in the enforcement of a foreign arbitral award? Why? Explain which international agreements contribute to this situation.
13. What is the significance of the 1976 UNCITRAL Arbitration Rules? The 1985 UNCITRAL Model Law? What are they and how are they used?
14. What is the New York Convention and what does it achieve? Is it in force in Canada? If yes, how do we apply it?
15. How does the issue of sovereign immunity arise? Does Canada always recognize this argument?
16. Provide some examples of sets of international arbitration rules that are well recognized and used. Identify which rules would be attractive to business persons in different parts of the world.
17. Outline some of the advantages of arbitration as a method of dispute settlement.
18. What is the attitude of the courts when one party to a contract wants to litigate a dispute but the contract provides for arbitration?
19. Why are the grounds upon which courts may refuse to recognize foreign arbitral awards and the grounds upon which courts will review arbitral awards so similar?

FURTHER READING

International Commercial Arbitration in the New Millennium Continuing Education Program. 2001. Toronto, Canadian Bar Association.

Barin, B. (1999). *Carswell's Handbook of International Dispute Resolution Rules.* Scarborough, ON: Carswell.

Haigh, D.R., Kunetzki, A.K., and Antony, C.M. "International Commercial Arbitration" (1995), *Alta. L Rev.* 137.

WEBSITES

Canadian Commercial Arbitration Centre:
   www.cacniq.org

Inter-American Arbitration Commission:
   www.sice.oas.org/dispute/comarb/iacac/rop_e.asp

Lex Mercatoria:

   UNCITRAL Model Law on International Commercial Arbitration:
   www.jus.uio.no/lm/un.arbitration.model.law.1985

   International Chamber of Commerce (Standard ICC Arbitration Clause):
   www.jus.uio.no/lm/icc.arbitration.rules.1998

   European Convention on International Commercial Arbitration:
   www.jus.uio.no/lm/europe.international.commercial.arbitration
   .convention.geneva.1961

United Nations Commission on International Trade Law:

   1958 Convention on the Recognition and Enforcement of Foreign
   Arbitral Awards (the New York Convention):
   www.uncitral.org/uncitral/en/uncitral_texts/arbitration/
   NYConvention.html

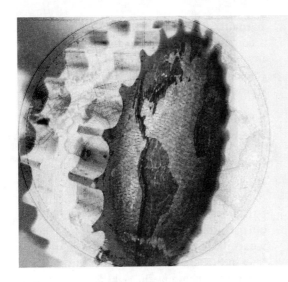

Glossary

absolute immunity
see sovereign immunity

advising bank
the bank in a documentary credit transaction (usually located in the exporter's country) that agrees to examine and forward the required documents presented by the exporter to the foreign bank that has issued the letter of credit on behalf of the importer

agency
relationship between one person who is a supplier of services or a manufacturer of goods (the principal) and another person who carries out a specific task on the principal's behalf, usually to sell the principal's product or service

agent
a person engaged by a principal to act on its behalf to arrange contracts between the principal and third parties

Agreement on Internal Trade
a Canadian agreement, in effect since 1995, that is intended to reduce barriers to the movement of persons, goods, services, and investments within Canada

Agreement on Trade-Related Aspects of International Property Rights (TRIPS Agreement)
a comprehensive multilateral agreement on the protection of intellectual property; it was agreed upon as a part of the Uruguay Round negotiations that created the WTO; it covers copyright, trademarks, geographical indication, industrial designs, patents, layout design of integrated circuits, and trade secrets

Agreement on Trade-Related Investment Measures (TRIMS Agreement)
one of the multilateral agreements on trade in goods; it prohibits trade-related investment measures, such as local content requirements, that are inconsistent with basic provisions of GATT 1994

Allies
countries that emerged as victors in World War II, including Great Britain, the United States, France, China, and Russia.

alternative dispute resolution (ADR)
methods of resolving disputes other than litigation in the courts; the most common examples are mediation, conciliation, and arbitration

American Customs Trade Partnership Against Terrorism (C-TPAT)
the US arm of the joint Canada–US program to facilitate the flow of legitimate goods and services across the Canada–US border.

anti-dumping (AD) duties
duties imposed by an importing country over and above the usual import duties when goods are being dumped into the importing country

appellate recourse
the ability to appeal decisions; an appellate tribunal or court is one that hears appeals of cases decided by a lower tribunal or court

arbitration
a method of resolving disputes outside the courts, in which the parties to a dispute refer it to a neutral third party called an "arbitrator" and agree to be bound by the decision (the award) of the arbitrator; in some cases, the case is referred to an arbitral tribunal

Area Control List (ACL)
list of countries to which a Canadian export of any good or technology requires an export permit

area treatment
treatment whereby beneficial NAFTA tariffs are available to goods deemed to originate in the NAFTA area

attorn
to acknowledge or submit to the jurisdiction of a court

bargain theory of contract
a common law contractual principle describing the situation where one party trades one thing to get another (related to the principle of consideration)

bilateral agreement
agreement between two countries

bilateral investment treaty (BIT)
an agreement between two countries establishing the terms and conditions for private investment by nationals and companies of one country in the other country; typically, a BIT grants investments made by an investor of one contracting state in the territory of the other a number of protections including the right to fair and equitable treatment, protection from expropriation without compensation, free transfer of capital and profits, and full protection and security

bill of lading
a document issued by a carrier, acknowledging that specified goods have been received on board as cargo for conveyance to a named place for delivery to the consignee, who is usually identified

binational panel
a panel of trade experts convened under the provisions of the CFTA or NAFTA to settle a dispute that has arisen under the provisions of chapter 19 or 20 of NAFTA

binding concessions rule
under GATT/WTO rules, the rule that once a country lowers a tariff, it becomes "bound" and the country is obligated not to increase the tariff above the negotiated bound level

block exemption
an exemption available for generic types of agreements, including specialization agreements, research and development agreements, vertical restraint agreements, technology-transfer agreements, and franchising agreements

Bolar provisions

provisions that some countries include in their patent laws permitting manufacturers of generic pharmaceuticals to use the technology of a patented pharmaceutical to perform work that would assist in the marketing or regulatory approval of the generic pharmaceuticals while the patent is in force, thus enabling the manufacturer to market and manufacture its goods as soon as the patent expires; limited versions of these provisions have been accepted by WTO panels as conforming to TRIPS

bound tariff

a tariff that a country has agreed not to increase or change

breach of condition

a common law concept referring to a breach of an important or material term of a contract

breach of warranty

a common law concept referring to a breach of a less important term of a contract

Bretton Woods Institutions

the IMF, the World Bank, and the GATT

burden of proof

the responsibility of one party to present evidence that raises an answerable case to which the other party must respond

Calvo doctrine

a foreign policy doctrine that requires a foreign investor, in the event of a dispute, to exhaust all local resources for recourse (that is, the local courts) before any diplomatic intervention can be made by the investor's home country; thus, jurisdiction in international investment disputes lies with the country in which the investment is located; the doctrine has been applied chiefly in Latin America

Canada Border Services Agency (CBSA)

the Canadian federal agency responsible for providing integrated border services

Canadian International Trade Tribunal (CITT)

the principal decision-making body for Canadian legislation affecting imports and exports

Canadian Partners in Protection (PIP)

the Canadian agency established to facilitate the flow of goods and services across the Canadian border

Canadian Wheat Board (CWB)

a Canadian Crown agency that buys the products of Canadian grain growers and resells the product to buyers around the world

capacity building

a term used among international development agencies such as the World Bank and the UNDP to describe the combination of people, institutions, and practices that enables countries to achieve their development goals

certificate of origin

a signed statement prepared by the exporter providing border services and government officials with information as to the place of origin, assembly, or manufacture of goods being exported, and usually also providing the HS classification number

Charter of Fundamental Rights of the European Union

charter that incorporates a sweeping range of civil, political, economic, and social rights and synthesizes the constitutional traditions and international obligations common to the EU member states; the rights described are divided into six categories: dignity, freedoms, equality, solidarity, citizens' rights, and justice, and go well beyond the rights enshrined in Canada and the United States

civil law

the code-based legal system, originating with the Justinian code of the Roman Empire, found in all of continental Europe, Central and South

America, parts of Asia, the Middle East, and African countries colonized by code-based countries

Climate Change Convention
see United Nations Framework Convention on Climate Change

Cold War
following World War II, the state of political tension and military rivalry between the United States and the Soviet Union and their respective allies

commercial invoice
the invoice issued by the exporter/seller in an international sales transaction describing the goods, the country of manufacture, and, if different, the country of export, as well as the destination, the importer/buyer, the price and currency, how the goods are packaged, and how much they weigh

Commission for Environmental Cooperation (CEC)
the tri-national organization to promote effective environmental enforcement; created by Canada, Mexico, and the United States under the North American Agreement on Environmental Cooperation, a NAFTA side agreement

common law
the Anglo-American legal system, based on precedent, or "judge-made" law, found in Canada, the United States, the United Kingdom, Australia, New Zealand, Ireland, Singapore, and other countries colonized by common law countries

competent investigating authorities
the domestic body in each of the NAFTA member countries that has the responsibility of making decisions as to whether anti-dumping or countervailing duties should be imposed; in Canada it is the deputy minister of National Revenue for Canadian Customs and Excise, in the United States it is the International Trade

Administration of the US Department of Commerce or the US International Trade Commission (ITC), and in Mexico it is the designated authority within the Secretariat of Trade and Industrial Development (SCFI)

conciliation
a method of settling a dispute out of court in which the parties choose a neutral third party who encourages dialogue and proposes a solution to resolve the dispute; differs from arbitration in that the proposed solution is usually not binding on the parties

confirming bank
the bank in a documentary credit transaction (usually located in the exporter's country) that undertakes a direct obligation to pay upon the proper presentation of documents under the letter of credit and is then entitled to reimbursement from the foreign bank that has issued the letter of credit on behalf of the importer

conflict of laws
where individuals or corporations from different jurisdictions have a dispute and it is not clear what law applies to the transaction

consideration
the common-law contractual principle that requires that to be enforceable a contract must by characterized by an exchange of value moving from each party to the other

contingency action
suspension of the benefits of tariff-free treatment, imposed on another country as a result of a perceived violation of the rules under an international trade agreement

contingency protection
measures taken by governments to counteract injury to domestic producers seen to arise from imports, often when such injury is determined to be caused by practices such as dumping or subsidization

contract of utmost good faith

a contract in which the parties have a higher standard of duty toward each other, requiring them to reveal all relevant information and always to put the interests of the other party before their own

Convention on the International Sale of Goods (CISG)

a convention that provides for a uniform law of sales in international sale of goods transactions; it came into force in 1988 and has achieved widespread aacceptance in civil and common law countries

Convention on the Recognition and Enforcement of Foreign Arbitral Awards (the New York Convention)

an international agreement that provides for the enforcement of arbitral awards in international trade disputes

conventions

binding agreements among several countries usually sponsored by an international organization

corporate social responsibility

a concept that encompasses ideas such as corporate citizenship, corporate sustainability, corporate sustainable development, and corporate responsibility

corresponding bank

either advising or confirming, this is the bank that has agreed with the foreign bank issuing a letter of credit to examine the documents under a letter of credit presented by the exporter/seller, usually in its own country

Corruption of Foreign Public Officials Act

Canadian anti-bribery legislation passed in 1998 for the purpose of conforming to the OECD Anti-Bribery Convention

countervailing duties (CVD)

duties imposed by an importing country over and above the usual duties when the goods have been subsidized by the country in which they are produced

Customs Automated Data Exchange System (CADEX)

a proprietary message-formatting standard that allows importers and customs brokers to file a Canada Border Services Agency electronic form directly to the Canada Border Services Agency, or through a third-party service provider

Customs Co-operation Council (CCC)

international organization concerned with the technical aspects of customs law and administration

customs union

an agreement in which tariffs and trade barriers are eliminated among member countries and a common external tariff is adopted

Department of Commerce (DOC)

US department that is one of the principal decision makers (that is, competent investigating authority under NAFTA) in cases for determining whether import duties will be payable in light of allegations of dumping or subsidy

directive

document used in the EU to help achieve harmonization of law; a directive prescribes objectives for legislation, and is binding upon each member country, but leaves the form and method used to achieve the result to individual member countries

Dispute Settlement Body (DSB)

the General Council of the WTO (all WTO members) sitting in a different capacity—that is, to supervise the WTO dispute settlement system

distributorship

a form of market entry where the foreign distributor purchases goods on its own account from the foreign supplier for resale to customers in its own market

documentary credit
a method of payment in which a bank (the issuing bank) acting at the request and on the instructions of a customer (the applicant) or on its own behalf, agrees to make payment to, or to the order of, a third party (the beneficiary) or authorizes another bank to effect such payment against stipulated documents, provided that the terms and conditions of the documentary credit are complied with

domestic
relating to the business and government in an individual country

embargo
a prohibition of the import of goods originating in a specified country

emergency safeguard mechanism (ESM)
a safety valve in multilateral trade agreements that allows a country that is experiencing hardship arising from intensified international competition in its domestic market as a result of trade liberalization obligations to impose temporary trade restriction, usually a surcharge or a quota

ex juris
outside the jurisdiction

Export and Import Controls Bureau (EICB)
the Canadian agency that administers the *Export and Import Permits Act*

Export and Import Permits Act (EIPA)
Canadian legislation providing for export controls

Export Control List (ECL)
a list of goods that are subject to export controls

Export Development Canada (EDC)
a Canadian Crown corporation that provides trade finance services to support Canadian exporters and investors

expropriation
the taking of private property by government for government purposes

extradition
the surrender by one country, at the request of another country, of a fugitive who is either accused or convicted of a crime by the requesting country; in Canada, a court hearing must be held before an extradition order is granted

extraordinary challenge committee (ECC)
a body established under the CFTA and NAFTA composed of three members who are judges or retired judges to hear any extraordinary challenges brought under NAFTA

facilitation payments
payment made to a low-level official to obtain or speed up the performance of a routine or non-discretionary duty

Food and Agricultural Organization (FAO)
UN organization, founded in 1945, that leads international efforts to defeat hunger, serving both developed and developing countries; the FAO helps developing countries and countries in transition modernize and improve agriculture, forestry, and fisheries practices

force majeure
an event that either could not be anticipated or which, if anticipated, could not be overcome; a *force majeure* clause in a contract protects the parties from liability in the event of such an occurrence

foreign direct investment
a long-term investment by a foreign investor in an enterprise resident in an economy other than that in which the foreign investor is based

foreign intermediary
an individual or corporation resident in a foreign jurisdiction that conducts business on behalf of an individual or corporation that is resident elsewhere

foreign sales corporation (FSC)
shell companies established by US corporations in tax havens such as the Bahamas and the Cayman Islands through which export transactions are routed to obtain sizable tax breaks

forum non conveniens
an inconvenient or inappropriate forum for a hearing

four freedoms of the single market
created by the EU in the *Single European Act* of 1986, they are freedom of movement of goods, unrestricted movement of capital, unrestricted movement of services, and unrestricted movement of people

franchising
a system used by businesses to distribute or market their products or services in domestic and international markets; one company, the franchisor, grants another company, the franchisee, the right to sell its products or services in a specified location and to use the franchisor's trademark or product name, business systems, and expertise

Free and Secure Trade (FAST) program
a Canada–US bilateral paperless cargo release program for importers, carriers, and drivers to speed border clearance

Free Trade Area of the Americas (FTAA)
first proposed at the Miami Summit in 1994, this agreement remains an unfulfilled plan to establish the largest trading bloc in the world that would comprise 34 countries in North, Central, and South America, including Canada and the United States

free trade area
arrangement among two or more countries that agree to remove substantially all tariff and non-tariff barriers between them while maintaining the existing individual tariffs against other countries

Free Trade Commission
provided for under NAFTA, it is composed of an equal number of Cabinet-level representatives from each country and is the body charged with the responsibility to consult when there is a dispute between parties to NAFTA

General Agreement on Tariffs and Trade (GATT)
arose out of Bretton Woods meetings in 1944; a multilateral treaty that prescribes rules for international trade

General Agreement on Trade in Services (GATS)
agreement that sets out agreed and legally enforceable rules and disciplines negotiated under the auspices of the WTO to liberalize international trade in services

general average
a historic principle of equity in which all parties in a sea adventure (ship, cargo, and freight) proportionately share losses resulting from a voluntary and successful sacrifice of part of the ship or cargo to save the whole adventure from an impending peril, or extraordinary expenses necessarily incurred for the joint benefit of ship and cargo

general export permit (GEP)
a general authority for the export of specified goods to specified destinations

generalized system of preference (GSP)
the system that provides that GATT members may give preferential treatment to exports from developing countries

global civil society
the worldwide totality of voluntary civic and social organizations and institutions (as opposed to state or government organizations and institutions)

global commons
the environment outside the territory of individual countries such as the oceans and the atmosphere

global value chain
the worldwide dispersion of production

globalization
economic, social, technological, cultural, and political changes leading to increased interdependence, integration, and interaction among people, companies, and countries around the world

gratuitous promise
a common law principle referring to a promise that is not enforceable because it is not supported by consideration

harmonization of laws
the process of making law in different countries in a common market uniform in either form or results

Harmonized Commodity Description and Coding System (HS)
a multilateral system adopted by many countries to bring tariff rates and trade statistics into conformity with each other

holder in due course
the person holding a cheque or promissory note, received for value (he or she paid for it) in good faith and with no suspicion that it might be defective, claimed by another, overdue, or previously dishonoured (a bank had refused to pay since the account was overdrawn); such a holder is entitled to payment by the maker of the cheque or note

horizontal agreement
an agreement between competing firms in the same industry, which may result in reduced competition; examples are common pricing policies, common production quotas, and information sharing

Incoterms
developed by the International Chamber of Commerce in 1936, these are internationally accepted commercial terms defining the respective roles of the buyer and seller in the arrangement of transportation and other responsibilities; Incoterms clarify when the ownership of the merchandise takes place and are used in conjunction with international sales agreements

individual export permit
a permit for specified goods to be exported to a specific destination

injunction
a court order requiring a person or corporation to do or cease doing a specific action

insurable interest
a basic requirement for all types of insurance, an interest in a subject of insurance such that loss or damage to it would cause the insurer a financial loss; for purposes of life insurance, everyone is considered to have an insurable interest in their own lives as well as the lives of their spouses and dependants; for property and casualty insurance, the insurable interest must exist both at the time the insurance is purchased and at the time a loss occurs; for life insurance, the insurable interest only needs to exist at the time that the policy is purchased

insurance policy or certificate of insurance
a notice that allows either party to a contract to fix an additional period of time for the other to perform and thus covers a situation of failure of delivery or one in which unacceptable goods have been delivered

International Court of Justice (ICJ)
headquartered in The Hague, Netherlands, a court that hears chiefly public international disputes

International Monetary Fund (IMF)
organization established at Bretton Woods in 1944 to restore and promote international monetary and economic stability

International Trade Association (ITO)
association proposed in the Havana Charter in 1947, and intended to be the third Bretton Woods institution; it failed to be established when the United States did not ratify the Havana Charter

ISO 9000
standards set by the International Organization for Standardization that are the international benchmark for acceptable quality management requirements in business-to-business dealings

joint venture
a legal arrangement that may take the form of a short-term partnership or a new incorporated entity in which the persons (individuals, groups of individuals, companies, or corporations) jointly undertake a transaction for mutual profit

judicialization
the process of ensuring that disputes are settled by impartial judges applying existing and transparent rules or standards to the facts of a case

letter of credit (L/C)
see documentary credit

licence agreement
a contract in which the owner (licensor) of a right (usually intellectual property rights such as patents, trademarks, or trade secrets) permits another party (the licensee) to manufacture and/ or market the licensor's products in return for royalties, fees, or other forms of compensation

limitation period
the time within which a plaintiff must bring an action—generally established by provincial legislation in Canada

Maastricht Treaty
the agreement signed on February 7, 1992 in the Dutch city of Maastricht that gave impetus to further integration of the EU, particularly in the areas of economic union, political integration, social policy, and foreign policy

mediation
a method of settling a dispute out of court in which an neutral third party assists the parties in working toward a negotiated agreement, with the parties maintaining ultimate control of the decision to settle and determine the terms of the resolution

memorandum of understanding
a legal document describing a bilateral agreement between parties; expresses a convergence of will between the parties, indicating an intended common line of action, rather than a legal commitment; in domestic law it is simply a letter of intent and falls short of creating a contractual relationship; in international law, it represents less commitment and more flexibility than a treaty because the usual ratification rules do not apply, leaving countries freer to manage the domestic issues raised by international agreements

mitigation
an important principle of contract law, the requirement that the injured party must reduce loss or prevent damages if possible

most-favoured-nation (MFN) rule
the rule that a tariff negotiated between any two GATT countries should be available to all other member countries

motions court
referred to in some jursidictions as chambers, it is a session of a court where a single judge hears preliminary applications relating to a case; these are not trials and there are no witnesses

multilateral agreement
agreement among three or more countries

Multilateral Agreement on Investment (MAI)
initiated by the OECD in 1991, this agreement was an attempt to develop a multilateral agreement on foreign investment protection provisions

Nachfrist notice
a concept rooted in German, Austrian, and Swiss law, it is a rule in the CISG that applies in certain breach-of-contract situations and allows the innocent party to fix an additional period of time for the breaching party to perform its obligations under the contract

National Energy Board (NEB)
the Canadian regulatory agency responsible for monitoring the use of energy resources in Canada

national treatment rule
the rule that once goods, services, or investment are imported into a member country, they must be treated in the same way as domestic goods, services, and investment; thus internal taxes and health and safety standards must be uniform for foreign and domestic concerns

nominated bank
see corresponding bank

non-arm's-length transaction
a transaction in which the parties are not independent from each other; for example, related companies are not at arm's length and may arrange transfer pricing that is not a reflection of market forces

non-governmental organization (NGO)
an organization that is not established by a governmental entity or an intergovernmental agreement; may or may not be a non-profit entity

non-self-executing treaty
a treaty that imposes requirements upon the government of the signatory country but does not directly impose any requirements on the citizens or subnational governments in the country

North American Agreement on Environmental Cooperation (NAAEC)
the side agreement on environmental protection for the NAFTA region negotiated by Canada, the United States, and Mexico after NAFTA was signed but before it was ratified by the US Congress

North American Agreement on Labour Cooperation (NAALC)
the side agreement on labour protection for the NAFTA region negotiated by Canada, the United States, and Mexico after NAFTA was signed but before it was ratified by the US Congress

North American Commission for Labour Cooperation (CLC)
the commission established under the side agreement on labour protection for the NAFTA region

nullification or impairment
a complaint referring to the nullification or impairment of benefits a party could reasonably expect under a trade agreement; to establish this complaint under NAFTA, it is necessary to show that a measure otherwise consistent with NAFTA has resulted in the impairment of an expected NAFTA benefit and that this outcome was not anticipated at the time the agreement was negotiated

oligopolistic
a market in which only a few large entities compete

Organisation for Economic Co-operation and Development (OECD)
an intergovernmental organization comprising 30 countries that have a commitment to a market economy and a pluralistic democracy

outsourcing
the delegation of specific operations from internal production to an external entity, often done for the purpose of lowering firm costs, obtaining desirable competencies, or making more efficient use of worldwide labour, capital, technology and resources

parol evidence rule
common law rule that prevents parties from successfully bringing evidence before a court to contradict the terms in a written contract and prove that changes to the contract had been agreed upon before or at the time a written contract was signed

particular average
a method of loss allocation used in the event that a portion of cargo, hull, or freight is jettisoned at sea in order to save the remainder; the loss is borne entirely by the individual who owns the property that is damaged or sacrificed; the loss must be less than total and not subject to the provisions of general average

performance bond
a bond issued to one party of a contract as a guarantee against the failure of the other party to meet obligations specified in the contract; for example, a contractor may issue a bond to a client for whom a building is being constructed, so that in the event the contractor fails to construct the building as required in the contract, the client is guaranteed compensation for any monetary loss

precautionary principle
authorization for taking protective action before there is complete scientific proof of risk

prima facie
Latin for "first view," this term refers to the situation where evidence is presented that is sufficient to raise a presumption of fact or to establish the fact in question unless rebutted

private international law
the law applicable to private parties involved in international transactions

privity of contract
the concept that only those who are parties to the contract can enforce the rights and obligations it contains

process-related standards
standards that allow one country or organization to dictate or specify how manufacturing or harvesting will be undertaken in another country's territory

product-related standards
standards set by an importing country based on the particular properties of the goods themselves; the standards may thus apply equally to imported and domestic goods

protectionism
the economic policy of restraining trade between nations, through methods such as high tariffs on imported goods, restrictive quotas, and a variety of restrictive government regulations designed to discourage imports, including anti-subsidy and anti-dumping laws; protectionism is an attempt to protect domestic industries in a particular nation from foreign takeover or competition

public international law
the law regulating relations among nations

ratification
in international law, the process of individual countries confirming under their own domestic law the international obligations undertaken by their country in a treaty or convention

remand
the process by which a higher court or tribunal sends a case back to the original body to be dealt with again, usually within certain parameters set by the highest court or tribunal

res judicata

Latin for "the thing has been judged," term meaning that the issue before the court has already been decided by another court, between the same parties

reservation

a process used in treaties and international agreements whereby signatories to the agreement may exempt themselves from specific obligations under the treaty or agreement

restrictive immunity

see sovereign immunity

right of establishment

the right to establish a business in another country without establishing previous residency or citizenship in that country

rules of origin

the rules that govern the assignment of nationality to goods being imported

sanitary and phytosanitary (SPS) measures

an expression used in WTO and trade circles that refers to any measure, procedure, requirement, or regulation taken by a government to protect human, animal, or plant life or health from the risks arising from the spread of pests, diseases, disease-causing organisms, or from additives, toxins, or contaminants found in food, beverages, or feedstuffs

self-executing treaty

a treaty that becomes part of the domestic law without the introduction of further implementing legislation in the signatory country

sight draft

a draft that is payable on demand

Single European Act

the legislation adopted by the European Economic Community in 1986 that provided for the many directives leading to a single market

to be adopted by majority vote of the Council of Ministers rather than the previously required unanimous vote

sovereign immunity

also called "state immunity," this doctrine prevents the institution of a lawsuit against a government without its consent

sovereignty

the supreme and independent power and authority claimed by a nation state in its own territory

Special Import Measures Act (SIMA)

the Canadian federal legislation that sets out the Canadian rules and procedures for dumping, subsidies, and safeguards

standby letter of credit

a written undertaking given by a financial institution to the "beneficiary" to pay a specified amount of money in the event that the person with whom the beneficiary is contracting does not meet specific financial or performance obligations

stare decisis

the common law principle meaning to "stand by" a decision—that is, respect and apply a previous decision with similar facts; this is the principle that ensures that similar disputes have similar legal outcomes and that the law is predictable

state

in the international context, a sovereign country

state trading enterprise

although the definition of this term is the subject of much controversy among WTO Members, it clearly includes enterprises owned by the state, enterprises granted special privileges such as subsidies by the state, and enterprises granted monopoly or exclusive privileges and that in the exercise of these rights and privileges influence imports or exports by their buying and selling activities

stay
to stop the action of court

strict liability
from early tort law, the imposition of the burden of compensation on the person who had caused an injury, despite the absence of any blameworthy conduct on their part; also called liability without fault

supra-national
extending beyond or transcending established borders and separate nations

tariff
a duty or tax levied by government on goods entering a country

tariffication
the conversion of all agricultural quotas and import restrictions (trade barriers) to tariffs

technology transfer agreement
an expression favoured in developing countries to describe a licensing agreement, the subject of which is technology, loosely defined

three pillars
terminology adopted by the EU after the Maastrict Treaty that describes the distribution of responsibilities in the EU

tortious
derived from the legal concept of tort, a wrong done to another legal person

trade restrictive quantities (TRQs) system
a system imposed by a government that limits trade by restricting the quantities of a good that may be imported or exported; this system was implemented by Canada to replace quotas that became impermissible after the Uruguay Round agreements

transnational corporations (TNCs)
corporations that operate in more than one country

Transparency International (TI)
a global non-governmental organization with more than 90 locally established national chapters and chapters-in-formation; it fight corruption around the world by bringing together representatives from government, civil society, business, and the media to promote transparency in elections, in public administration, in procurement, and in business

treaty
binding agreement between two or more countries (states)

Treaty of Rome
the founding treaty establishing the European Economic Community (EEC), signed by France, Belgium, Germany, Italy, Luxembourg, and the Netherlands

Treaty on European Union (TEU)
also known as the Maastricht Treaty; entered into force in 1993; it was this treaty that changed the name of the European Economic Community to the European Union and created the European concept of the three pillars

TRIMS Agreement
see Agreement on Trade-Related Investment Measures

triple bottom-line reporting
reporting system that expands the traditional company reporting framework to take into account not just financial outcomes, but also environmental and social performance

TRIPS Agreement
see Agreement on Trade-Related Aspects of International Property Rights

UNCITRAL Model Law on International Commercial Arbitration
document that is designed to assist countries in reforming and modernizing their laws on arbitral procedure so as to take into account

the particular features and needs of international commercial arbitration; covers all stages of the arbitral process from the arbitration agreement, the composition and jurisdiction of the arbitral tribunal, and the extent of court intervention, through to the recognition and enforcement of the arbitral award

Uniform Commercial Code (UCC)
US code developed by private organizations in 1952 to harmonize the law of sales and other commercial transactions throughout the country; has been adopted in all 50 states within the US

Uniform Customs and Practice for Documentary Credits (UCP)
a set of guidelines published by the International Chamber of Commerce (ICC) in Paris, France, that is widely accepted and used in the international trade and financial community for determining the roles and responsibilities of all parties involved in letters of credit, including standby letters of credit

United Nations Commission on International Trade Law (UNCITRAL)
an agency that has as its principal objective the harmonization of trade law

United Nations Conference on Trade and Development (UNCTAD)
the UN's arm for promoting the integrated treatment of trade and development and the related issues of investment, finance, technology, enterprise development, and sustainable development

United Nations Educational, Scientific, and Cultural Organization (UNESCO)
organization that serves as a laboratory of ideas, a standard setter, and a clearinghouse for the dissemination of information and knowledge, as well as providing assistance with capacity building, in matters related to education, science, culture, communications, and ethical issues

United Nations Environmental Program (UNEP)
an organization whose mission is to provide leadership and encourage cooperation in caring for the environment by inspiring, informing, and enabling nations and peoples to improve their quality of life without compromising that of future generations

United Nations Framework Convention on Climate Change (UNFCCC)
an international environmental treaty negotiated at the UN Conference on Environment and Development (UNCED), informally known as the Earth Summit, held in Rio de Janeiro in 1992; the purpose of the treaty is to reduce emissions of greenhouse gases in order to combat global warming; however, it sets no mandatory limits on greenhouse gas emissions for individual nations

US International Trade Commission (USITC)
an independent federal agency that determines import injury to US industries in anti-dumping, countervailing duty, and global and China safeguard investigations; directs actions against unfair trade practices involving infringment of patent, trademark, and copyright law; performs economic analysis and conducts research on the global competitiveness of US industries; and maintains the US Harmonized Tariff Schedule

vertical agreements
agreements made between parties who are at different levels of the production process, such as a distribution agreement between a manufacturer and a retailer or agent

World Bank
organization established at Bretton Woods in 1944 to help countries reconstruct their economies after World War II

World Health Organization (WHO)
the UN specialized agency for health whose objective is the attainment by all peoples of the highest possible level of health

World Intellectual Property Organization (WIPO)
a specialized agency of the United Nations that is dedicated to developing a balanced and accessible international intellectual property (IP) system, which rewards creativity, stimulates innovation, and contributes to economic development while safeguarding the public interest

World Trade Organization (WTO)
international organization that provides for freeing trade and for preventing trade discrimination; establishes rules that enable member countries to expand trade by making voluntary trade concessions among themselves on a relatively transparent, multilateral basis, and discourages member countries from practising trade discrimination against other trading partners that are members

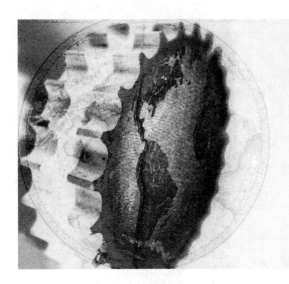

Index